The Fiscal Structure of the Russian Federation

EAST WEST INSTITUTE
New York Prague Moscow Kyiv Brussels Helsinki

The **EastWest Institute** is an international network of individuals working together in Central and Eastern Europe and Eurasia to:

- Defuse tensions that threaten stability and peace
- Strengthen democracy and the rule of law
- Build a middle class and develop free enterprise in emerging-market nations
- Create new forms of cooperation across borders.

An independent European-American non-profit organization founded in 1981, the EastWest Institute (EWI) has a core staff of 80 which is supplemented by a network of more than 3,000 specialists and officials in thirty nations—all dedicated to creating a safer and more open world, in the firm belief that this is possible through joint effort. Our offices—in New York, Prague, Moscow, Kyiv, Brussels and Helsinki—are funded by contributions from foundations, corporations, the public sector, and individuals on both sides of the Atlantic. The Institute is governed by a prestigious international Board of Directors.

For more information, please contact us at:

EastWest Institute
700 Broadway, Second Floor
New York, NY 10003
Tel (212) 824-4100, Fax (212) 824-4149
Website: http://www.iews.org
E-mail: iews@iews.org

THE FISCAL STRUCTURE OF THE RUSSIAN FEDERATION

Financial Flows Between the Center and the Regions

Alexei M. Lavrov and
Alexei G. Makushkin

With L.N. Bogdanov, A.G. Reus,
V.V. Klimanov, O.V. Kuznetsov,
A.L. Kolomnets, and V.A. Shuvalov

Foreword by Aleksandr G. Granberg

Translated by James E. Walker

EASTWEST INSTITUTE

M.E.Sharpe
Armonk, New York
London, England

This is a revised and updated version of the Russian edition, *Federal'nyi biudzhet i regiony. Opyt analiza finansovykh potokov*, published in Moscow by Dialog–MGU and

Library of Congress Cataloging-in-Publication Data

Federal'nyi biudzhet i regiony. English
The fiscal structure of the Russian Federation : financial flows between the center and the regions / by A.M. Lavrov, Alexei G. Makushkin, et al.
p. cm.
"By EastWest Institute".
Includes bibliographical references and index.
ISBN 0-7656-0713-1 (alk. paper)
1. Intergovernmental fiscal relations—Russia (Federation) 2. Finance, Public—Russia (Federation)—Statistics. I. Lavrov, A.M. II. Makushkin, Alexei G. III. EastWest Institute (New York, N.Y.) IV. Title.

HJ1211.52.Z7 F4413 2000
336.47—dc21 00-053159

Printed in the United States of America

The paper used in this publication meets the minimum requirements of American National Standard for Information Sciences Permanence of Paper for Printed Library Materials, ANSI Z 39.48-1984.

∞

BM (c) 10 9 8 7 6 5 4 3 2 1

CONTENTS

List of Tables

List of Figures

List of Maps

FOREWORD

A NEW MEASUREMENT IN ECONOMIC RELATIONS BETWEEN THE CENTER AND THE REGIONS

There is an urgent need, at this time, to fundamentally expand the capacities of Russian statistics so that the differences developing between regions can be taken into account and analyzed, identifying the leaders and stragglers, and suggesting well-founded political solutions in regard to equalizing the conditions for the regions' sustainable development. I am happy to say that the authors of the book that you are about to read are fully aware of how important this problem is and do not limit themselves to a narrow idea of regional differences determined by whether or not the regions receive financial aid from the Fund for Financial Support of Subjects of the Federation. This is a very gratifying sign that professional research is underway in our country on the actual relations between the Center and the regions, with eyes open to the objective difficulties one presently encounters in trying to obtain statistical information and fitting it into the framework of a general analytic forecasting model.

The book that you hold in your hands contains a rich lode of data on a very important part of this general problem: cumulative financial flows including not only direct financial aid from the Center, but also federal expenditures in the territories, and the movement of the extrabudgetary funds' revenues and expenditures. In principle, complete accounting of all financial flows (including horizontal ones between regions and an estimate of barter) encompassing public and private finances will make it possible in the future to obtain results corresponding to the balance of the gross regional product (GRP) produced and used. And though this is an objective for the future, judging from the results of the research presented in this book, we can say that an important step in this direction has already been taken.

I would like to draw attention to the fact that the results obtained by the authors of this book largely coincide with independent estimates made, for example, by experts at the Council for Study of Productive Forces (SOPS) and the Russian Statistical Agency in relation to donor and recipient regions.

In recent years, research has been conducted on regionalization of Russia's system of national accounts, which is aimed at creating a system of regional accounts that is methodologically compatible with the system of national accounts. Such a study could undoubtedly be helpful to specialists on the system of public finances attempting to answer questions involving the regions' tax base or the Center's participation in financial support of specific territories and creation of the necessary conditions for sustainable development in them.

One advantage of this procedure is that, in principle, it fully covers all channels through which economic resources move between regions, including those that are not taken into account by the usual tools of fiscal control. The procedure for determining GRP in Russia calls for additional accounting of the hidden, informal economy. This relates primarily to indices of the output and gross value added for individual industries, and to indices of consumption and capital formation. The total size of the corrections amounts to about one fourth of the gross domestic product (GDP). Unfortunately, the amounts of the corrections for individual regions are not set apart in official data, which limits the possibilities for using them, since it is known a priori that the relative share of the hidden (shadow) economy differs sharply in various regions.

Quite a bit of experience has already been accumulated in calculating GRP for subjects of the Russian Federation. The results of such calculations are published officially. Since 1994, the Russian Statistical Agency has so far calculated the GRP for 79 of the 89 subjects of the Federation. For understandable reasons, there are no data on Chechnya, and the data on the autonomous regions, with the exception of the Chukotka Autonomous Region, are included in the data for the corresponding territories and oblasts.

The calculations of GRP done by the authors of this book, as well as the results that they obtained, confirm the fundamentally important idea that there is a fairly large number of economically prosperous regions in Russia. Analysis of the expanded balance of financial flows yields a list of 26–27 subjects of the Federation; we estimate that there must be at least 22 such regions. (See Table F.1.)

Although all of the documents devoted to the Russian Federation's regional policy state the need to *equalize* the regions in their level of socioeconomic development and welfare, scientific analysis forces us to take a critical attitude toward the feasibility of their complete equalization with respect to an integral index such as *per capita GRP*. It is quite possible that this objective can be realized more quickly in the field of public finances, where we are talking more about supporting the current consumption of a given set of socially significant goods and services.

We had to specially investigate the question of *how many years* it would take for backward regions to reach the national average level of per capita GRP *with different economic growth rates*. The problem of determining the *growth rate of per capita GRP* in backward regions needed to achieve the national average level *in a certain number of years* was also posed. (See Table F.2.)

As we can see from Table F.2, it would take unrealistically high growth rates and a long time for the most backward regions to reach the national average level of per capita GRP. The "best" regions of this group (Adygeya and Kabardino-Balkaria) could scarcely achieve this goal in 15 years, and it would take at least 30 years for the most backward ones (Ingushetia and Dagestan). Aside from everything else, this means that the territorial structure of the Russian economy will change rather slowly, which, of course, requires a more long-term and complex government policy aimed at reducing the differences between regions. (See Table F.3.)

Table F.1

Distribution of GRP by Groups of Regions in Relation to the National Average Per Capita GRP

Groups of regions in relation to the national average per capita GRP	Number of regions in the group	Share of total GDP	Group average per capita GRP, % of average for Russia
More than 150% (leaders)	5	23.25	254.52
125–150% (developed)	4	7.65	138.05
100–125% (prosperous)	14	27.82	109.86
75–100% (less prosperous)	15	17.12	85.50
50–75% (underdeveloped)	30	22.32	61.27
Less than 50% (most backward)	11	1.85	35.09
Total	79	100	100

Table F.2

Annual Growth Rate of Per Capita GRP in the Most Backward Regions Needed to Reach the National Average Level (%)

Regions	in 30 years	in 20 years	in 15 years	in 10 years
Annual growth rate of national average per capita GRP = 3%				
Republic of Dagestan	8.374	11.165	14.028	19.997
Ingush Republic	7.712	10.149	12.640	17.794
Republic of Kalmykia	7.205	9.371	11.581	16.137
Republic of North Osetia	6.810	8.768	10.762	14.859
Republic of Tyva	6.708	8.612	10.550	14.530
Republic of Adygeya	6.168	7.788	9.434	12.800
Kabardino-Balkar Republic	6.147	7.757	9.391	12.734
Annual growth rate of national average per capita GRP = 5%				
Republic of Dagestan	10.478	13.324	16.242	22.307
Ingush Republic	9.804	12.288	14.827	20.081
Republic of Kalmykia	9.287	11.495	13.748	18.392
Republic of North Osetia	8.884	10.880	12.913	17.090
Republic of Tyva	8.780	10.721	12.696	16.754
Republic of Adygeya	8.230	9.881	11.559	14.990
Kabardino-Balkar Republic	8.209	9.849	11.515	14.923

It cannot be denied that, in many cases, comparison of subjects of the Federation with respect to per capita GRP demonstrates its *inadequacy* as a generalizing indicator of the regions' socioeconomic development. At least two negative points can be distinguished: (1) the gap between the cost estimate of GRP and its "physical" content as a certain mass of goods and services; (2) the disparity between GRP and the level of material welfare of

Table F.3

Number of Years Needed for the Most Backward Regions to Reach the National Average Level of Per Capita GRP

Regions	3%	4%	5%	6%	7%	8%	9%	10%
	Annual growth rate of national average per capita GRP = 3%							
Republic of Dagestan	—	158	80	54	41	33	27	24
Ingush Republic	—	139	70	47	36	29	24	21
Republic of Kalmykia	—	125	63	42	32	26	22	19
Republic of North Osetia	—	113	57	38	29	23	20	17
Republic of Tyva	—	110	56	37	28	23	19	17
Republic of Adygeya	—	95	48	32	24	20	17	14
Kabardino-Balkar Republic	—	94	47	32	24	20	16	14
	Annual growth rate of national average per capita GRP = 5%							
Republic of Dagestan	—	—	—	116	81	55	41	33
Ingush Republic	—	—	—	142	72	48	36	29
Republic of Kalmykia	—	—	—	127	64	43	33	26
Republic of North Osetia	—	—	—	115	58	39	30	34
Republic of Tyva	—	—	—	112	57	38	29	23
Republic of Adygeya	—	—	—	96	49	33	25	20
Kabardino-Balkar Republic	—	—	—	96	48	33	25	20

Table F.4

Distribution of Regional Final Consumption (RFC) by Groups of Regions in Relation to the National Average Per Capita in 1996

Groups of regions in relation to the national average per capita RFC	Number of regions in the group	Share of total RFC, %	Group average per capita RFC, % of average for Russia
More than 150% (leaders)	5	23.10	325.61
125–150% (developed)	3	4.62	139.96
100–125% (prosperous)	8	17.45	113.65
75–100% (less prosperous)	26	28.02	86.89
50–75% (poor)	33	26.29	65.64
Less than 50% (poorest)	4	0.52	26.61
Total	79	100	100

the regions' population, particularly for subjects of the Federation at the very top and bottom of the list with respect to the per capita value of this index.

For example, the leading position of northern regions is explained mainly by the high concentration there of enterprises that produce oil, gas, diamonds, gold, and nonferrous and rare metals, which provide the highest monetary return per worker. It does not follow from this, however, that all of these regions are prosperous in a broad socioeconomic sense. The natural climatic conditions are most severe there; the cost of living is highest; investment costs per unit of fixed assets in physical terms are highest, etc. In recent years, as a consequence of the drop in production and investment activity in a considerable part of the northern territories, unemployment has risen, and a rapid outflow of the population has begun. Thus, a top place with respect to per capita GRP (in actual prices) and an adverse social situation turn out to be compatible.

It is also known that a significant part of the financial resources of regions that have high GRP flows from them to other regions or abroad. On the other hand, regions that lag behind in per capita GRP, as a rule, receive various kinds of financial transfers, nominally from the Center, but actually from other subjects of the Federation.

The main direction for improving the system of regional socioeconomic indicators on the basis of the system of national accounts is to calculate, in physical terms, the various ways in which GRP is used.

In regard to the system of regional accounts and GRP, the most important aspect of the answer to the question of donor and recipient regions is *to calculate regional final consumption*. The Russian Statistical Agency has calculated actual final consumption for individual regions since 1995. Although the data given in Table F.4 are for 1996 only and are somewhat outdated, the grouping of subjects of the Federation according to per capita regional final consumption also seems typical of the present. In 1996, the range of variation among 79 regions was 22.3 times (between Moscow and Ingushetia), and the coefficient of variation was 44.9%. In relation to the national average per capita regional final consumption, the regions are divided into six groups: (1) "leading" regions (more

Table F.5

Distribution of Regions of the Russian Federation with Respect to the Ratio of the Sum of Regional Final Consumption and Investments in Fixed Capital to GRP in 1996

More than 100%	11 regions
From 90 to 100%	21 regions
From 82.5 to 90%	16 regions
From 75 to 82.5%	10 regions
From 65 to 76%	15 regions
Less than 65%	6 regions

than 150% of the average); (2) "developed" (125–150%); (3) "prosperous" (100–125%); (4) "less prosperous" (75–100%); (5) "poor" (50–75%); and (6) the "poorest" regions (less than 50% of the average).

The group of unquestionable leaders includes five regions: Moscow (355.0% of the average), the Chukotka Autonomous Region (205.7%), Magadan Oblast (185.0%), Yakutia (182.7%), and Kamchatka Oblast (172.6%). There are four regions in the "most backward" group: Altai (about 50% of the average), Kalmykia (40.6%), Dagestan (23.7%), and Ingushetia (15.9% of the average).

Although the number of prosperous regions with respect to this index is somewhat less than what is given by calculation of per capita GRP (16 as opposed to 23), we can also note the difference between this figure and the traditional list of prosperous regions, which includes 9–10 subjects of the Federation.

Without a doubt, *indices of regional final consumption should be corrected for the purchasing power of household incomes*, which depends on regional characteristics of consumer prices and charges for goods and services, or on the purchasing power of the ruble in a given region. Such a study has already been done, and it produced interesting results.

Within the framework of the expanded idea of donor and recipient regions, *comparisons of the GRP produced and used* in each subject of the Federation have key significance. At present, the official statistics do not give data on gross capital formation in the regions. Fairly reliable data are available only on the main part of gross capital formation: investments in fixed capital, which amount to three quarters of the amount of gross capital formation for Russia as a whole. The data on other elements of gross capital formation ("acquisition cost minus capital retirement" and "changes in inventories") are much less reliable. Therefore, instead of "GRP used," we think that it is better to compare regions according to the sum of their regional final consumption and investments in fixed capital.

The average ratio of the sum of regional final consumption and investments in fixed capital to GRP for all regions is 82.5%. It is higher than average in 48 regions and less than average in 31. The distribution of subjects of the Federation with respect to this index is given in Table F.5.

With high probability, this distribution makes it possible to separate donor regions, which give back part of the GRP that they produce, and recipient regions, which receive part of the GRP that they use through the system of redistributions between regions.

If we assume that the interval between 75% and 90% is a zone of indeterminacy for identifying donors and recipients (unaccounted elements of gross capital formation and errors may play a significant role in this interval), then there are 21 regions among the reliable donors, and the list of reliable recipients includes 32 regions. So the zone of indeterminacy covers 26 regions. The group of donor regions distinguished according to this rule includes most of the regions that do not receive transfers from the Fund for Financial Support of Subjects of the Federation and are considered "donors" according to that characteristic. These are Bashkortostan and Tatarstan, Krasnoyarsk Territory, and Samara, Sverdlovsk, and Tyumen Oblasts. The group of recipient regions (those that have a ratio of the sum of regional final consumption and investments in fixed capital to GRP of more than 90%) includes regions that are usually classified as backward and depressed (republics of the North Caucasus and southern Siberia, a number of oblasts in central Russia, and some others).

In the future, we need to refine the data on regions in which the population spends a significant part of their income in other regions. The stages of the subsequent analysis should be: (1) estimation of the regional final consumption by nonresidents of the regional economy; (2) correction of data on investments, taking into account regional differences in the cost of investment objects; (3) inclusion of other elements of gross capital formation in the calculations.

It seems to me that consolidating the efforts of all researchers on the problem of economic relations between the Center and the regions can produce very important results in regard to the development of our ideas about the actual differentiation of regions, about rich and poor territories, and about leading regions and last-place regions. And what is most important, it would finally make it possible to base federal regional policy on a firm foundation of reliable data and protect the government from ill-considered political decisions.

Aleksandr Grigorievich Granberg
Academician of the Russian Academy of Sciences,
Chairman of the Council for Study of Productive Forces of the Ministry of the Economy of the Russian Federation and the Russian Academy of Sciences

PREFACE

In the time that has passed since the Russian Federation announced its sovereignty, regional studies cannot complain of any lack of attention from either researchers or politicians. However, few other disciplines can be found where the former have taken so many different approaches and the latter have interpreted the scientific conclusions in so many different ways. After all these years, the hunger for reliable and complete statistical information about the regions' interrelation with each other and with the federal authorities is still a basic problem. This book, which is based on a major scientific investigation conducted as part of the "Fiscal Transparency" program organized by the Moscow office of the EastWest Institute, makes a significant contribution to solving this problem.

Our book is intended to help those who would like to base their views on knowledge of real budget statistics characterizing the interrelation of the federal center and the regions, rather than political and scientific biases, which are no more convincing for being so often repeated. The objection may be raised, perhaps, that in recent years the public has already seen studies that were also based on statistical analysis. Indeed, this is so. The main publications of this sort, which have come out, in particular, thanks to the efforts of the International Bank for Reconstruction and Development and the International Monetary Fund, will be mentioned below. However, none of these studies had access to such an extensive data base as the authors of this book analyzed in the course of their research, the key points of which are generalized here. It is no exaggeration to say that this book is the most complete investigation of budget statistics reflecting the interrelations of the Center and the regions during the period from 1996 through 1998. Such a publication was bound to appear sooner or later, if only due to the enormous demand for such information. In our case, the group of researchers made use of certain objective circumstances that had developed by the end of 1999. The beginning of the Moscow office of the EastWest Institute's Economic Program coincided almost exactly with the completion of an important stage of budget reform in Russia: the establishment of a new role for the Federal Treasury, which is now responsible for administering the federal budget. It is quite natural that new problems required new ways of collecting and analyzing budget information, and it would be a mistake to let such an historic moment slip by.

In order to properly appreciate the full diversity and thoroughness of the material presented in this book, it is necessary to think about the development of budget federalism in Russia during the period before this study came out, as well as now, when the changes that have come to fruition in the country's political system dictate new approaches and set new strategic goals for the Russian federal state.

The formation of the Russian Federation as a sovereign state gave a powerful impetus to the development of true federalist relations, creating conditions in which the regions could be transformed into truly effective participants in the life of Russian society. The fact that they have been real political actors, with ambitions, but devoid of any practical experience of independent survival, is indicated by all of the "childhood illnesses" that the Federation of Russian regions has come down with in the past few years. At first, federalism was understood in the spirit of opposition to the former unitary model of the state, which encouraged the regions' aspirations to maximum freedom of action by transferring to them rights and resources that had traditionally been at the disposal of the central authorities. In 1992–1993, many key positions in the federal government were held by people who saw the essence of what was happening in the country as maximum "decentralization." But, at the same time, this concept was advanced under the influence of a new ideology and for political motives based on the emerging regional elites, and also the urgent need to survive on their own in a severe crisis situation. It can be said that the federal budget at that time could do nothing constructive to withstand the decentralizing trends. This was aggravated by the total collapse of the country's budget system.

The new rules of independent financial behavior that were gradually established in most of the economically strong regions, on the one hand, and the exhaustion of federal funds, on the other, led many subjects of the Federation to attempt to rectify their economic situation by borrowing as much money as possible in the open market. This was also due to the acute shortage of liquidity, which was a result of the widespread growth of barter and other nonmonetary forms of economic relations. Nonpayments, surrogate currency circulation, and barter made the operation of the government's tax system an exceptionally acute problem. In conditions when nonmonetary settlements amounted to more than 50% of the gross domestic product, it was simply impossible to correctly appraise the tax potential of various levels of the budget sphere without making a correction for the actual collectability of tax payments in the form of "cash" money. The prospect of trading the regions' indebtedness for blocks of stock that they hold became a lure for all of the major investment companies present in the Russian financial market prior to 1998.

By the beginning of 1998, the vigorous activity in this direction that had unfolded at the end of 1995 came to an end after the participants realized their total failure in using direct loans to create a stably operating mechanism for replenishing regional finances. For a long time, this cooled the ardor of the most active proponents of rapid transition to the regions' full financial independence. This approach not only reflected "adolescent" self-confidence, but primarily the desire to compensate for the sluggishness of the federal budgetary mechanism and the complexity of the tax system, while making financial resources more manageable at the same time. But the underlying cause of the failure was the elementary economic incompetence of regional leaders. They decided to go into debt at precisely the time when the central authorities made them responsible for keeping up the expensive social sphere, which did not bring in any income. Therefore, it was simply impossible to pay back the large loans spent on social needs. Regional public finances very quickly fell into a deep hole.

It is now perfectly clear how seriously the struggle for authority and financial resources affected the loss of manageability of public finances. The Center and the regions fully felt the consequences of subordinating budget policy to the job of supporting the level of consumption, to the detriment of economic development. Together with the established practice of suing various levels of the system for failing to fulfill their obligations, the budget system's imbalance produced a flood of claims and counterclaims, which overwhelmed the possibilities for expeditious management of public finances that had been opened up by dividing authority and the tax base between the Center and the territories. In its present form, this system is more and more bogged down in inefficient conflict-resolution procedures.

The concept of reforms in the budget sphere built on an orderly division of responsibility, starting with the spending obligations of the federal part of the budget system, was finally adopted in the middle of 1998. The first results of this, primarily the decisive expansion of the Federal Treasury's functions, produced a significant effect in the form of considerably more stable execution of the expenditure part of the budget, which encompassed many channels that were previously not included in the unified system for execution of the federal budget. This gave a number of economists in federal financial agencies the right to claim that in the foreseeable future such desirable transparency of the financial system and even higher priority for development in comparison with funding of current expenditures will depend on giving the Center a much greater role in the system of budgetary federalism.

All of these events characterizing various stages in the interrelations between federal authorities and the regions created a wide choice of political scenarios, including reform of the Russian Federation's constitutional arrangement, as well as a new Budget Code, which for now cannot fundamentally and consistently divide the spheres of authority of the Center and the regions in the system of public finances. The choice of specific versions is significantly hindered by the incompleteness of available statistical data on the balance of financial flows between the Center and the territories, by the actions of corporate and regional lobbyists, and also by the lack of clear principles of the government's regional policy and mechanisms for implementing them.

At present, we can only make out the general outlines of the relations that will, in the future, create the foundation for effective interaction of the central authorities with the subjects of the Federation in the field of public finances. That is why the "Fiscal Transparency" program is primarily focused on evaluating the movement of financial flows between the Center and the regions as objectively as possible and does not emphasize political aspects of the distribution of finances. In our opinion, questions of this sort should be addressed in the next stage of the study.

Our institute is justly proud of its role in helping to make possible this significant research, which has not only provided the court of public opinion with important data illustrating previously known patterns, but has also changed ideas about a number of key elements in the model of budget federalism in Russia.

What have we accomplished? The real scale of movement of funds between the Center and the subjects of the Federation was established on the basis of the latest statistical data. Problems of including information on a regional cross section of direct expenditures from the federal budget and the distribution of money from extrabudgetary funds in the overall balance of financial flows were solved. What is important here is not only that the statistics on this spending are considerably more complete, but also the indirect influence that the aggregate balance of financial flows has on the political position of the leaders of subjects of the Federation in determining the amount of aid to be granted to them from federal funds.

The departure from the old model, which, up until 1998, had divided the country into donor and recipient regions depending on whether or not they received aid from the Federal Fund for Financial Support of Subjects of the Federation, and adoption of the concept of *complete accounting* of financial flows stemming from a region's tax base and all of the channels of redistribution of budgetary resources between a territory and the federal budget set the stage for a qualitatively new idea about the regions' financial independence. Collection and analysis of such information, including correction for the monetary component in payment of taxes (in contrast to nonmonetary setoffs), opened up new approaches to a number of well-known hypotheses and claims, such as: (1) a revised idea of the actual differences in levels of tax collection in individual regions of Russia, (2) more precisely determined proportions of the division of taxes between the Federation and the territories, (3) an assessment of liquidity for most of the territories, (4) an index of how fully a region's tax potential is being used, and finally, (5) a substantiated breakdown of tax receipts in subjects of the Federation.

Analysis of the statistical data debunked a number of myths that had sprung up in recent years in Russian regional studies. The research showed that in 1996–1998 the amount of taxes collected and credited to the federal budget in 50 regions of Russia exceeded the amount of financial aid turned over to them. In other words, 50 subjects of the Federation were donors to the federal budget to one degree or another. More than 80% of the country's entire population lives in these regions, while only 10% lives in regions that are consistent recipients. Of course, on the strength of the balance principle of evaluating donors and recipients, consideration of direct expenditures from the federal budget in various regions reduces the number of consistent donor territories. But even with a correction for this factor, the list of them includes no fewer than 26 regions, in which more than 40% of the entire population of Russia lives. Another 14 regions have periodically made it into the group of donors in recent years, and this makes almost two thirds of the country's population.

The difference between these figures and the conventional idea that there are only 9–12 donor regions is striking. From this dry statistic, it is only one step further to serious conclusions about the real base of economic stability in Russia and the role of tens of new regional leaders of those subjects of the Federation that make up the true core of this stability. Dispensing with this figure, we are justified in revising the concept of certain regions as the locomotives of development in the Russian economy, and also the concept of enlarging the regions, on which certain politicians have succeeded in building a whole ideology for themselves. But probably the most interesting thing for the central authorities should be, what role is to be played in the government's overall regional strategy by the almost 30 subjects of the Federation that have been a zone of economic stability for a number of years? This question is not at all academic, if one considers that many of these territories are not under the guardianship of the powerful political lobby in the federal Center, which, for example, Moscow can brag about, and therefore they are deprived of the ability to present a common front in the face of the federal Center and the other regions. In our opinion, to put this factor into operation in regional development strategy would mean a change in the basic spirit of Russian regional policy, which is now concentrated on how to extract money from the superrich and placate the forever disgruntled poor. However, it turns out that a different question should be asked in the Center: how to stimulate economic activity and preserve political stability at the local level.

Unfortunately, it has to be said that, while remaining supporters of the concept of manageability within the framework of the expanded balance of financial flows between the Center and the regions, in the course of their research the authors could not completely fill in the blank spot in the data in regard to the extrabudgetary funds' resources. What is distressing is not simply the unfinished methodological work, but mainly the sheer size of this blank spot, which is comparable with half of the expenditure part of the annual federal budget.

However, we can now feel comfortable in saying that we have done everything possible to ground the political and scientific issues awaiting resolution in the field of budgetary federalism in comprehensive and reliable empirical data. This book is the outcome of the first stage of the "Fiscal Transparency" program, and we hope that others will follow. We would like to believe that the facts presented here will provide a good foundation for a broad range of specialists and politicians to think about problems of the federal budget's interaction with the regions, so that they can draw conclusions about the how things stand now and what needs to be done to reform Russia's fiscal structure.

A.G. Makushkin, candidate of economic sciences
Leader of the "Fiscal Transparency" Program
Moscow Center of the EastWest Institute

INTRODUCTION

In a federative state, the budget is a key factor integrating the country and smoothing out disproportions between regions. In order to create budgetary federalism and conduct an effective regional policy, the budget must be territorially "transparent." In Russia, the criteria, mechanisms, and results of redistributing budgetary resources among the regions have not yet been made sufficiently clear. This destabilizes political and fiscal relations between the Center and the subjects of the Federation, leading to such extreme negative manifestations as tax separatism. The need to develop and analyze a territorial profile of the federal budget has been repeatedly emphasized by various researchers and in official documents (such as the Concept for Reforming Interbudgetary Relations in the Russian Federation in 1999–2001, and the medium-range Program of Economic Reforms). However, no real steps have yet been taken to solve this problem.

The goal of the research conducted in the first stage of the "Fiscal Transparency" Program was to collect and analyze data that most fully characterize the distribution of the federal budget's revenues and expenditures over the territory of Russia. On the basis of the results, proposals will be formulated for optimizing financial flows and relations between the Center and the regions.

The research is distinguished by an untraditional approach to analysis of financial relations between the Center and the regions. As a rule, this problem is narrowly studied. The analysis is limited to examining how revenues and expenditures are delineated between the Center and the regions, and how funds are redistributed among the federal, regional, and local budgets. The most important studies in this field are: "Russia and the Challenge of Fiscal Federalism," ed. by C. Wallich (Moscow, World Bank, 1993); "Fiscal Management in Russia. A World Bank Country Study," ed. by P. Le Houerou (World Bank, 1997); V. Lexin and A. Schvetsov, "Government and the Regions: Theory and Practice of the State Regulation of Regional Development" (Moscow, 1997); H. Martinez and J. Boex, "Fiscal Decentralization in Russia: Trends, Problems, Recommendations" (Georgia State University, 1998); "Subnational Budgeting in Russia: Preempting a Potential Crisis" (World Bank Technical Paper, 1998); and O. Betin, "Budget Federalism in Russia: Issues and Perspectives" (Moscow, 1999).

However, financial relations between the Center and the regions can be interpreted more broadly to include questions of the territorial distribution of revenues and, especially, expenditures from federal extrabudgetary funds, as well as the federal budget. No one has examined these problems yet, mainly due to the lack of adequate information.

In 1998, the establishment of the Federal Treasury system with its territorial agencies made it possible, for the first time, to get a fairly complete territorial profile of the federal budget. Together with the data that was already available from the Ministry of Taxes and Duties on receipts to the federal budget from the territory of each subject of the Federation, from the Ministry of Finance of the Russian Federation on the amount of financial aid given to subjects of the Federation, from the Ministry of the Economy of the Russian Federation and the Russian Statistical Agency on the regional distribution of capital investments funded from the federal budget, and also data on revenues and expenditures from federal extrabudgetary funds in individual subjects of the Federation, this information provided the basis for the research that was conducted—the first in a series of absolutely necessary studies in this field.

The objectives of the research were:

- to compile the most complete possible balance of financial flows between the federal Center and each region 1996–1998
- to reveal interrelations between the distribution of financial aids to the budgets of subjects of the Federation and the distribution of direct federal expenditures of a socioeconomic nature
- to reveal interrelations and contradictions between the redistribution of budgetary and extrabudgetary financial resources
- to develop indices of the extent to which the economy and population of various regions are supported (subsidized) from the budgets of all levels, and evaluate their effect on the regions' development.

The research was conducted with the knowledge that most of the problems under consideration can only be stated, not solved. The point of the study was to relieve scientists and regional analysts of the most laborious part of studying any new problem: the collection and primary processing of initial data, assessment of them, and identifying the most promising directions of analysis.

This book covers the basic results of the research. It is organized as follows. Chapter 1 looks at the sources of statistical information and also gives a brief glossary of concepts used in the text. Chapter 2 is devoted to the balance of financial flows between the Center and subjects of the Federation (in particular, it gives diagrams of financial flows and the financial balance, and a division of regions into donors and recipients). The next five chapters analyze individual components of the balance of financial flows. Chapter 3 considers the regions' tax potential; Chapter 4, financial aid to regional budgets from the federal budget; Chapter 5, direct expenditures from the federal budget in the regions; Chapter 6, federal investments and investment policy; and Chapter 7, territorial aspects of the extrabudgetary funds' activity. The concluding Chapter 8, substantially revised for this edition, is devoted to the geography of public finances. It contains an analysis of the total amount of subsidies provided to individual regions, differences between regions and the role of the budgetary sphere in their economy, and federal economic policy in relation to the regions. The appendices give the basic statistical parameters that were used in the research for all subjects of the Russian Federation.

The following people took part in conducting the research and writing the book:

A.G. Makushkin, candidate of economic sciences (project coordinator)
A.M. Lavrov, candidate of geographical sciences (concept of the project, overall leadership, technical editing)
L.N. Bogdanov, candidate of economic sciences (Chapters 1, 5, and 6)
A.G. Reus, candidate of economic sciences (Chapters 4 and 7)
V.V. Klimanov, candidate of geographical sciences (Chapters 6 and 8)
O.V. Kuznetsov, candidate of economic sciences (Chapters 1, 2, 3, 4, 7, and 8)
A.L. Kolomnets (preparation of data for Chapters 3 and 7)
V.A. Shuvalov, candidate of geographical sciences (maps).

The judgments and conclusions presented in the book reflect the authors' personal opinions and should not be taken as the point of view of any government agency or institution, or of the EastWest Institute.

CHAPTER 1

General Information

1.1 STATEMENT OF THE PROBLEM

We will begin to acquaint the reader with the results of our study of territorial problems of public finances with an introductory chapter of an explanatory nature. This subject is so new and undeveloped that a number of comments need to be made on general questions. The chapter begins by describing the sources of statistical information used in the research. They are fairly numerous, and each one has its own specific features.

Then we will look at how the creation of the Federal Treasury changed the sphere of public finances, how its territorial structure was set up, and its network of agencies in the regions. The system for funding federal expenditures that was in effect before the Federal Treasury began to operate is described.

The last section is a brief glossary of the concepts found in subsequent chapters. It will help the reader to understand a number of the terms used in the research that are not yet part of the common vocabulary.

1.2 SOURCES OF STATISTICAL INFORMATION

1.2.1 Ministry of Taxes and Duties and Ministry of Finance of the Russian Federation

The greater part of the statistical data from the Ministry of Taxes and Duties of the Russian Federation used in the research is information about tax and nontax revenue to the federal and territorial budgets. The information from this ministry forms the foundation for analysis of the tax potential of subjects of the Federation. It was also used in compiling the balance of financial flows between the regions.

Data from the Ministry of Taxes and Duties of Russia for 1996–1998 were used in the research. The ministry's very expeditious collection and processing of data enabled us to use final, rather than preliminary data for 1998. As was already mentioned in the introduction, the research was conducted in February through July of 1999, and far from all federal ministries and departments had final statistical information for 1998 by that time.

A great deal of statistical data from the Ministry of Finance of the Russian Federation was also used in the research. This data can be divided into the following four groups:

- on the execution of regional budgets, including the scale of financial aid from the federal budget
- on direct expenditures from the federal budget in the regions
- on loans from the International and European Banks for Reconstruction and Development
- on the execution of the federal budget.

The statistical data from the Ministry of Finance used in the research is also fairly up-to-date. However, the final summary information for the reporting year on the execution of budgets only comes out at the end of the first half or beginning of the second half of the following year. By the time that the Ministry of Finance's final data for 1998 came out, the research was already nearly finished. Therefore, it was based on preliminary data for 1998, which may differ slightly from the final totals. The situation was similar for data that came directly through the Federal Treasury.

1.2.2 Sources of data on extrabudgetary funds

There has been no prior practical experience in analyzing territorial aspects of the activity of extrabudgetary funds in Russia. So the statistical information needed is lacking, and as a result, the chapters concerning extrabudgetary funds were written on the basis of the most diverse statistical sources.

The assessment of the significance of extrabudgetary funds in comparison with the budgets of all levels for Russia as a whole was based on data from the State Committee of the Russian Federation on Statistics (at the end of 1999 it was renamed the Russian Statistical Agency).

The distribution of revenues and expenditures for extrabudgetary funds in individual regions was analyzed on the basis of data made available by:

- the extrabudgetary funds' central divisions
- the extrabudgetary funds' territorial divisions
- the Ministry of Taxes And Duties of Russia
- the Ministry of Economic Affairs of Russia.

The first group of data encompasses all of the regions, but it does not provide sufficiently complete information for analysis. In particular, these data do not reflect the distribution of revenues between the extrabudgetary funds' regional and central divisions. At the time when the research was done, data on execution of the budgets of the territorial mandatory medical insurance funds for individual subjects of the Russian Federation were available only for the first nine months of 1998. The data for the whole year were calculated on the assumption that the figures for the first nine months amounted to three fourths of the totals for the whole year.

Data obtained from the regions enable us to look at a large number of parameters reflecting financial flows within the framework of extrabudgetary funds, however they are not available for all subjects of the Federation and may not be accurate enough. Thus, for a number of regions they do not agree with the Ministry of Taxes And Duties' data reflecting the distribution of tax receipts between the Federal and territorial road funds.

Out of all of the subjects of the Federation, there were complete, reliable data on all five extrabudgetary funds for 53 of them,[1] and incomplete data for 15 regions.[2]

In connection with this, centralized data were used in the research whenever possible; and only in their absence were data obtained from the regions used.

The data included in the research also include information from a preliminary version of the predicted financial balance for subjects of the Russian Federation in 2000, which was prepared by the Ministry of Economic Affairs of Russia. The forecast was interesting in that it gives separate data on the revenues and expenditures of territorial divisions of the social extrabudgetary funds.

1.2.3 The Russian Statistical Agency

Along with the data on extrabudgetary funds mentioned above, the Russian Statistical Agency is a source of information on federal investments in the regions and various socioeconomic indices. The latter include data on the population of subjects of the Russian Federation and its breakdown by categories (portion of those employed in various industries, number of students, etc.), regional values of the subsistence level, gross regional product, industrial and agricultural output, and the level of provision with social infrastructure.

One of the main problems with using the Russian Statistical Agency's information on the regions is that it is not sufficiently current. Even by the end of the first half of 1999 we did not have all of the data for the previous year. For 1998 we had information only on the industrial output and the subsistence level, and the population on January 1, 1999. Thus, most of the information used in the research, including that on the distribution of federal investments in the regions, is unfortunately limited to 1997.

---

[1] Karelia; Komi; Arkhangelsk and Vologda Oblasts; St. Petersburg; Leningrad, Novgorod, Pskov, Bryansk, Vladimir, Ivanovo, Kostroma, Moscow, Smolensk, and Yaroslavl Oblasts; Marii El; Belgorod, Voronezh, Kursk, Lipetsk, Tambov, Astrakhan, Volgograd, Penza, Samara, Saratov, and Ulyanovsk Oblasts; Adygeya; Dagestan; Kabardino-Balkaria; Krasnodar Territory; Udmurtia; Orenburg, Perm, Sverdlovsk, and Chelyabinsk Oblasts; Altai; Altai Territory; Kemerovo, Novosibirsk, Omsk, Tomsk, and Tyumen Oblasts; the Yamal-Nenets Autonomous Region; Irkutsk and Chita Oblasts; the Ust-Orda Buryat Autonomous Region; Yakutia; the Jewish Autonomous Oblast; Khabarovsk Territory; and Amur, Kamchatka, and Kaliningrad Oblasts.

[2] Murmansk, Smolensk, Tula, Kirov, Rostov, and Kurgan Oblasts; Mordovia; Chuvashia; Ingushetia; Buryatia; Khakasia; Stavropol, Krasnoyarsk, and the Maritime Territories; and the Aga Buryat Autonomous Region.

1.3 TERRITORIAL ASPECTS OF THE FEDERAL TREASURY'S ACTIVITY

1.3.1 Funding of federal expenditures before the Federal Treasury system was established

In the first years of market reforms, when the Federal Treasury was not yet responsible for administering the federal budget, federal expenditures were funded through the budget accounts of the ministries and departments responsible for disbursing the money, which were opened in institutions of the Central Bank of the Russian Federation or in commercial banks. From there, the money was transferred to the accounts of institutions and organizations under their jurisdiction, and also to the accounts of contractors who supplied goods, performed work, and provided services for federal needs. In addition, money was transferred to the accounts of second- and third-level disbursers, which funded their own activity out of this money and also paid institutions, organizations, and contractors under their jurisdiction (Figure 1.1).

Since the ministries and departments are located in Moscow, where their bank accounts were opened, information about the subsequent movement of money to the personal accounts of recipients of budgetary funds in regional commercial banks was not available for collection and study.

Moreover, this way of funding expenditures had the following shortcomings:

- it did not allow expeditious collection of information on revenues received by the federal budget and expenditures paid out, and consequently it deprived the federal authorities of the possibility of actually controlling their finances
- it lengthened the route that the money took to get to its ultimate recipients, which caused delays in carrying out socially significant expenditures and increased indebtedness
- it led to an unjustified increase in the balance of budgetary funds left in accounts
- it did not allow monitoring of the growth of the recipients' creditor indebtedness
- it created possibilities for use of federal budget money for purposes other than intended.

The creation and development of the Federal Treasury's system provided the prerequisites for eliminating these shortcomings, and for tracking and then planning the territorial profile of federal expenditures.

1.3.2 Territorial structure of the Federal Treasury

The Federal Treasury was created as part of the Ministry of Finance. It was established and developed on the basis of the decree of the President of the Russian Federation of December 8, 1992, No. 1556, "On the Federal Treasury," and resolutions of the Government of the Russian Federation of August 27, 1993, No. 864, "On The Federal Treasury of the Russian Federation" (which approved the rules and regulations for the Federal Treasury), and of August 28, 1997, No. 1082, "On Steps to Accelerate the Transition to the Treasury System of Executing the Federal Budget," and subsequent regulatory acts.

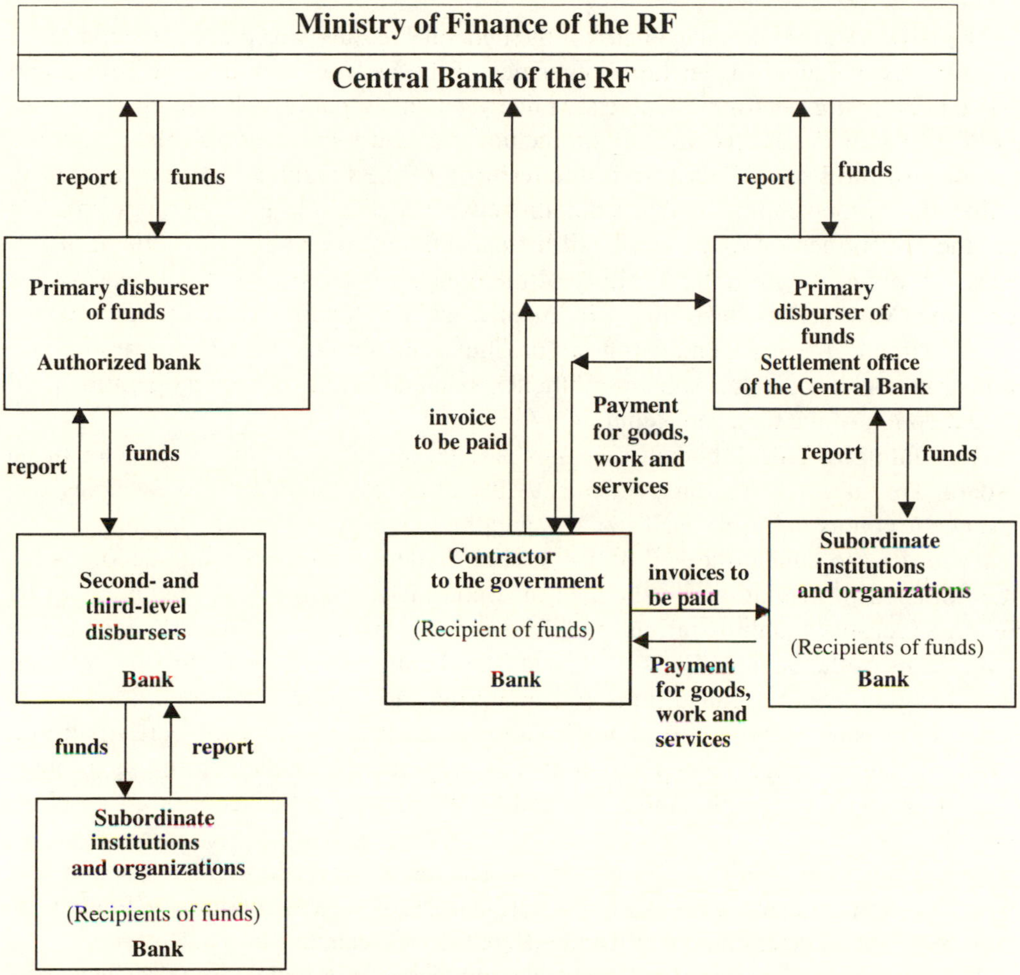

Figure 1.1. **Diagram of execution of the federal budget before the Federal Treasury system was established.**

The Federal Treasury consists of the Central Administration of the Federal Treasury, which is a department of the Ministry of Finance's central staff, its subordinate Federal Treasury Administrations for individual subjects of the Federation, and territorial agencies of the Federal Treasury in cities and districts. The latter are legal entities and are under the control of the heads of the Federal Treasury Administrations and the Central Administration of the Federal Treasury.

As the Federal Treasury system developed, federal budget revenues and funds in its accounts were increasingly centralized. The portion of recipients of budgetary funds who have personal accounts in agencies of the Federal Treasury also grew. It became possible to track the movement of budgetary funds from the Federal Treasury's accounts all the way to personal accounts opened by the ultimate recipient in regional administrations and territorial agencies.

The network of territorial agencies of the Federal Treasury was practically completed in 1998. As of January 1, territorial agencies of the Federal Treasury had been established in 88 regions of Russia. There are none yet in the Republic of Tatarstan. However, the Ministry of Finance is working on including a clause about establishing territorial agencies of the Federal Treasury in the territory of the republic in a draft agreement delineating responsibilities and jurisdiction between agencies of the federal government and the government of Tatarstan. Until the execution of the budget for federal institutions and organizations in the territory of the republic is converted to the treasury system, since May 1, 1998, the Ministry of Finance has been funding them through accounts of the Federal Treasury Administration for Chuvashia. Of the 88 Federal Treasury Administrations for individual subjects of the Russian Federation, 87 are in operation (with the exception of the Chechen Republic).

Accounting of federal budget revenues is done by 2,222 territorial agencies of the Federal Treasury in 85 regions, which is 99.2% of the total number. Tax agencies keep revenue accounts in Bashkiria, Tatarstan, and the Evenk Autonomous Region.

According to data at the end of 1998, 3,224 federal budget revenue accounts had been opened in institutions of the Central Bank of Russia for 1,347 agencies of the Federal Treasury (administrations and divisions); 1,758 accounts for 806 agencies, in institutions of the Savings Bank of Russia (Sberbank); and 125 accounts for 60 agencies, in other credit organizations (not counting the Central Administration of the Federal Treasury's revenue accounts). Commercial banks' share of participation in servicing federal budget revenue accounts (not counting Sberbank institutions) dropped 6 points since May 1, 1998, and at the end of 1998 it was 2.4% according to preliminary data.

As of January 1, 1999, 2,226 territorial agencies of the Federal Treasury had been given the right to carry out accounting transactions for federal budgetary funds in 87 subjects of the Federation (except for the Republic of Tatarstan).

According to preliminary data, 2,688 accounts for federal budgetary funds have been opened in institutions of the Central Bank of Russia for 1,348 agencies of the Federal Treasury; 1,628 accounts for 851 agencies, in Sberbank institutions; and 132 accounts for 80 agencies, in other credit institutions (not counting the Central Administration of the Federal Treasury's revenue accounts). Commercial banks' share of participation in servicing accounts for federal budgetary funds (not counting Sberbank institutions) dropped 4.2 points since May 1, 1998, and at the end of 1998 it was 3.0% according to preliminary data.

Of the almost 49,300 recipients of budgetary funds (not counting recipients in Tatarstan and Chechnya, or the Ministry of Defense), more than 48,100 have been switched over to funding through personal accounts in agencies of the Federal Treasury, which is more than 91% of the total number (Figure 1.2).

Thanks to the development of the Federal Treasury system, for the first time in the modern history of Russia it is possible to obtain information on execution of the federal budget for practically all sections of the budget classification (including direct expenditures) in a regional profile.

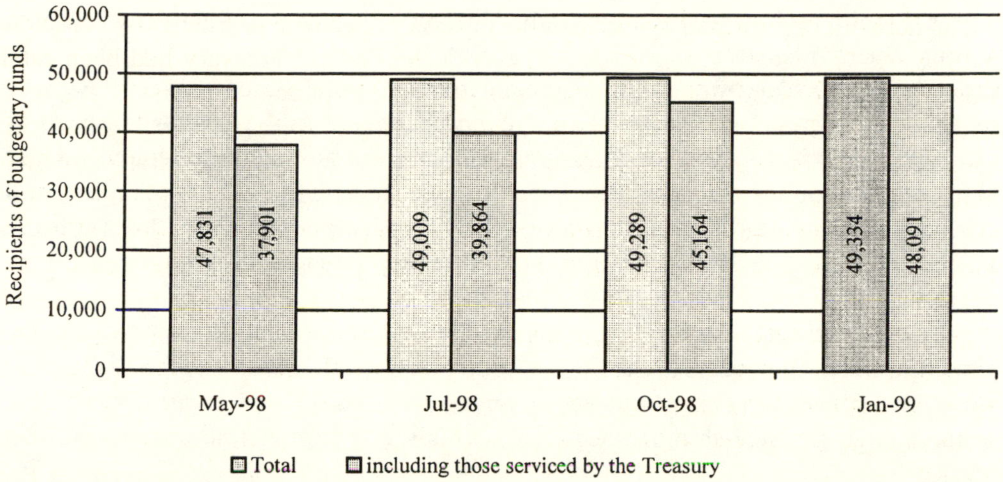

Figure 1.2. **Number of recipients of budgetary funds switched over to servicing through the Federal Treasury system.**

1.4 BRIEF GLOSSARY

Subject of the Russian Federation, region: used as synonyms.

Extraterritorial revenues (revenues not connected to a particular territory): revenues received from outside of Russia, or revenues that by their nature cannot be attributed to a particular territory (revenues from international activity, customs duties, etc.).

Extraterritorial expenditures (expenditures not connected to a particular territory): expenditures made outside of Russia, or expenditures that by their nature cannot be attributed to a particular territory (expenditures on international activity, servicing of the national debt, etc.).

Financial aid: the amount of money turned over from the federal budget to a regional budget (it includes transfers, subsidies, grants, mutual settlements, and the remainder of budget loans not repaid at the end of the year).

Transfers: financial aid to regions provided from the Federal Fund for Financial Support of Subjects of the Federation.

The Federation's direct expenditures: expenditures from the federal budget made in a region.

Balance with respect to financial aid: the difference between the revenues collected in a region and credited to the federal budget and the financial aid from the federal budget to the regional budget. **Donor regions:** regions where this difference is positive. **Recipient regions:** regions where it is negative.

Balance taking into account direct expenditures from the federal budget: the difference between the revenues collected in a region and credited to the federal budget and the total amount of financial aid and direct expenditures from the federal budget in the region. **Donor regions:** regions where this difference is positive. **Recipient regions:** regions where it is negative.

Balance taking into account extrabudgetary funds: the difference between revenues collected in a region and credited to the federal budget or to the central divisions of extrabudgetary funds and the total amount of financial aid from the federal budget to the regional budget, direct expenditures from the federal budget in the region, and financial aid from the central divisions of extrabudgetary funds. **Donor regions:** regions where this difference is positive. **Recipient regions:** regions where it is negative.

A region's consolidated budget: the amount of revenues collected in a region and expenditures from the budgets of all levels (federal, regional, local) made in the region.

Production expenditures: expenditures on funding of industry, power generation, construction, agriculture, fishing, transportation, roads, communication, and information services.

A region's "expanded" budget: the amount of revenues and expenditures from the region's consolidated budget and extrabudgetary funds.

Social expenditures: expenditures on education, culture and art, mass media, public health and physical fitness, and social policy.

Extrabudgetary funds: the Pension Fund of the Russian Federation, the Social Insurance Fund of the Russian Federation, the State Employment Fund of the Russian Federation, mandatory medical insurance funds (the Federal Mandatory Medical Insurance Fund and territorial mandatory medical insurance funds of subjects of the Russian Federation), road funds (the Federal Road Fund and territorial road funds of subjects of the Russian Federation).

Social extrabudgetary funds: the Pension Fund of the Russian Federation, the Social Insurance Fund of the Russian Federation, the State Employment Fund of the Russian Federation, the Federal Mandatory Medical Insurance Fund, and territorial mandatory medical insurance funds of subjects of the Russian Federation.

Index adjusted for the subsistence level: an index divided by the regional value of the subsistence level.

CHAPTER 2

Balance of Financial Flows Between the Center and the Regions

2.1 STATEMENT OF THE PROBLEM

For a fairly long time now, one of the subjects most often discussed in regard to budgetary interrelations between the Center and the regions has been the problem of "donors and recipients." In the overwhelming majority of cases, regions that do not receive transfers from the Federal Fund for Financial Support of the Regions are called donors. It is believed that approximately ten such regions "feed" the whole country. There is also the idea that expenditures from the federal budget that are not transferred to the budgets of subjects of the Federation in the form of financial aid have no relation to the regions.

This is a narrow and essentially false view of things. First of all, it makes no allowance for the fact that funds are distributed among the regions not only in the form of financial aid, but also in the form of direct expenditures (and in much larger amounts, at that). Payment of wages to federal workers, funding of federal programs, and the like, are always done in specific subjects of the Federation. Federal budgetary expenditures of this sort are at least as important for the regions' development as funds along the line of financial aid. A complete idea of the financial flows between the Center and the regions also cannot be formed without consideration of the territorial profile of the revenues and expenditures of extrabudgetary funds.

Putting together a balance of all known financial flows between the Center and the regions (we are talking about a balance as the ratio of federal budgetary expenditures and revenues coming from the regions) makes it possible to distinguish the real donors and recipients. This kind of analysis will hardly have any direct economic consequences. Regional economic policy is only part of the government's regulation of the economy, therefore it is unlikely that a territorial approach to drawing up the federal budget will become a primary factor. However, the political consequences of compiling a financial balance and publicizing it are obvious. The myth about ten donor regions and their special status will disappear; the tension in relations between regions will lessen; and the inadvisability of introducing a single-channel tax model will become obvious. Much more attention will be given to revealing and solving the real problems of interbudgetary relations, which will ultimately have a positive economic effect.

This chapter describes the procedure for compiling a balance of financial flows between the Center and the regions. It looks at the financial flows and evaluates how well their individual components are taken into account in calculations of the financial balance. Results are also given from calculations carried out in the course of investigating various types of the balance of financial flows between the Center and the regions. Each successive balance includes additional data in a cumulative total. At first, only budgetary revenues and financial aid to regional budgets were considered in the balance. Direct expenditures from the federal budget in a region were subsequently added to the balance. Then the revenues and expenditures of federal extrabudgetary funds were included on both sides of the balance.

2.2 PROCEDURE FOR COMPILING THE BALANCE

2.2.1 Financial flows between the Center and the regions

The financial balance consists of two flows going in opposite directions: revenues coming in to the federal level from the territory of subjects of the Federation, and expenditures made from the Center in the regions (Figure 2.1).

In this case, the Center, or the federal level, means the federal budget and federal extrabudgetary funds (the Federal Road Fund of the Russian Federation, the Pension Fund of the Russian Federation, the Social Insurance Fund of the Russian Federation, the Federal Mandatory Medical Insurance Fund, and the State Employment Fund of the Russian Federation).

The mechanisms by which financial flows are formed within the framework of extrabudgetary funds are fairly simple. Each extrabudgetary fund has its own revenue sources. For the social funds, these are deductions of a certain percentage from the payroll fund; and for the Federal Road Fund of the Russian Federation, road taxes (on the sale of fuels and lubricants, on highway use, and some others). A large part of the deductions to extrabudgetary funds collected in the regions goes to their territorial divisions. Payments from enterprises and individuals transferred to the Center are partly spent on centralized operations and partly for providing financial aid to the regions. Additional assistance to the territorial divisions of extrabudgetary funds comes from the federal budget.

It is much harder to establish the financial flows connected with the federal budget. The greater part of the revenues received by the federal budget is controlled by the Ministry of Taxes and Duties of Russia. All taxes pass through this ministry, with the exception of taxes on foreign trade and foreign economic activity, and also the revenues of targeted budgetary funds and part of the nontax revenues. The tax revenues controlled by the Ministry of Taxes and Duties make up the overwhelming part of all tax receipts (approximately four fifths in 1998, and more than 90% in 1997). The portion of nontax revenues passing through this ministry is much lower (approximately three fourths in 1998, and a little less than half in 1997).

Collection of taxes on foreign trade and foreign economic activity, most of which is customs duties, is controlled by the State Customs Committee of the Russian Federa-

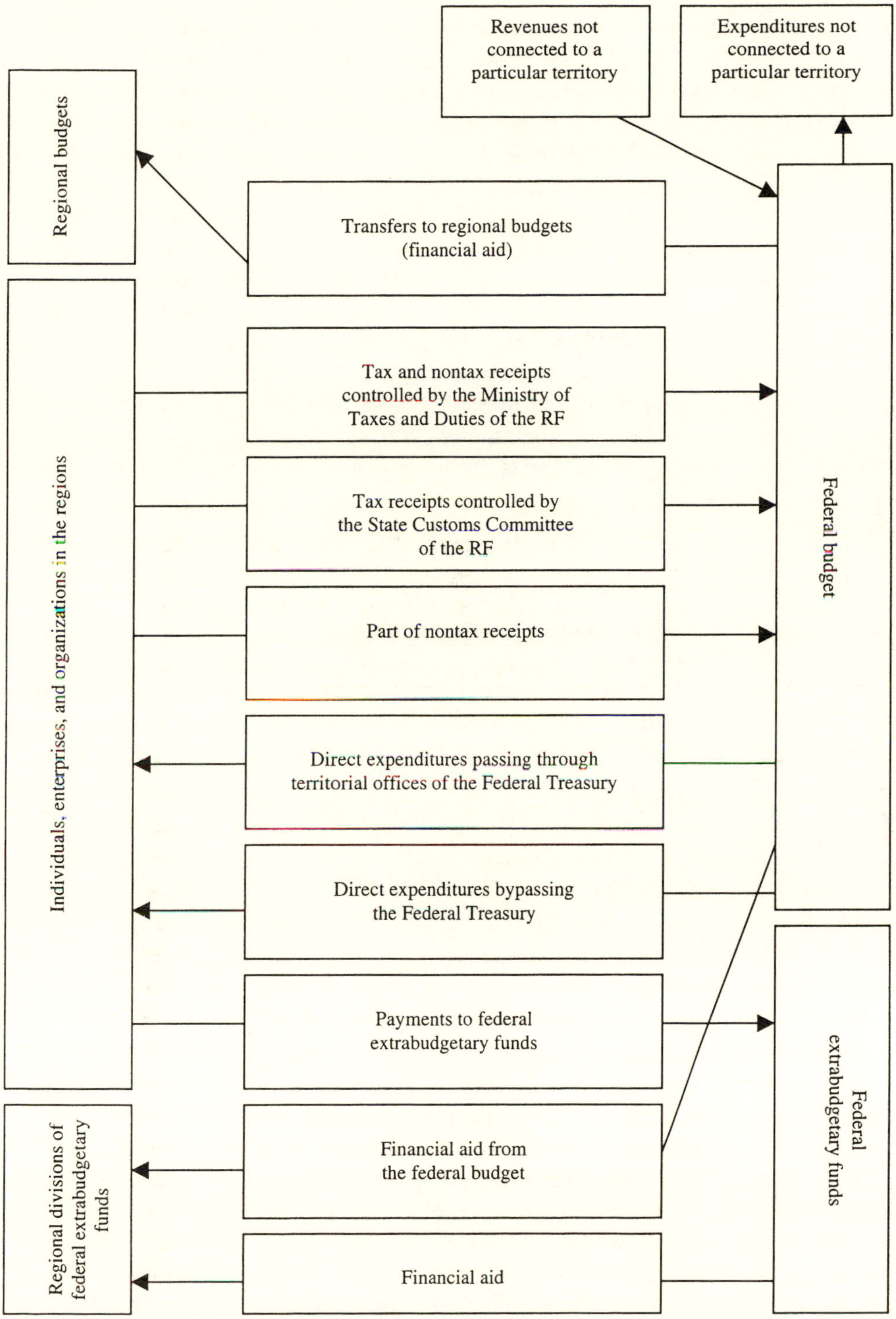

Figure 2.1. **Organizational structure of flows between the Center and the regions.**

tion. It is practically impossible to connect them to individual territories, since the places where export products are produced (or import products are consumed) and the places where export and import duties, respectively, are paid do not coincide. In principle, it is possible to distribute export and import duties among the regions in proportion to the recorded volume of exports or imports, but significant distortions are inevitable in this case (Sidebar 2.1).

So, export and import duties will not be considered in the following analysis. Their territorial structure and the place of Russian regions in general in the international division of labor and Russia's foreign trade can be the subject of special research.

Nontax revenues that do not pass through the Ministry of Taxes and Duties are credited directly to the federal budget from their source. One part of this group of nontax revenues does have a territorial connection (i.e., it is formed in the regions), while another part is of an extraterritorial nature and is formed outside of the regions (outside of the country). The latter includes, for example, interest on state credits provided by the Russian Federation to the governments of foreign countries. All in all, nontax revenues of an extraterritorial nature make up a relatively small share of federal budgetary revenues, but, unfortunately, it does not seem possible to evaluate them accurately.

There is also a group of extraterritorial expenditures in federal budgetary expenditures. In contrast to extraterritorial revenues, they are much more significant and make up almost half of all expenditures. They include expenditures on international activity, on servicing the national debt, and, partially, defense expenditures. Expenditures on replenishing national stockpiles and government reserves can also be placed in this group.

In one way or another, all of the remaining expenditures are distributed among the regions. One part of these expenditures is made up of transfers to regional budgets (financial aid to regional budgets); another is direct expenditures from the federal budget in the regions (funding of federal operations and institutions in the regions, and also various federal programs).

Technically, direct expenditures from the federal budget are made in two ways: through the Federal Treasury system and directly to recipients of budgetary funds through ministries and departments (see Chapter 1).

Sidebar 2.1 ***Distribution of exports and imports by regions***

Comparison of the regions' share in exports and imports with their role in turning out the gross product or their share of the population (see table) confirms the impossibility of connecting export and import duties to individual territories. The clearest example of how the statistics do not adequately reflect the actual situation is provided by the data for Moscow. It is perfectly obvious that approximately 6% of the country's population cannot account for almost two fifths of all imports. The relationship of the regions' shares of exports and the gross regional product is also unrealistic.

Sidebar 2.1 (continued)

Regions' Shares of Exports, Imports, Population, and Gross Regional Product in 1997

	Regions' share of, %					Regions' share of, %			
Region	**exports**	**imports**	**population**	**GRP**	**Region**	**exports**	**imports**	**population**	**GRP**
Republic of Karelia	0.57	0.29	0.53	0.44	Republic of Adygeya	0.00	0.04	0.31	0.11
Komi Republic	0.97	0.33	0.79	1.18	Republic of Dagestan	0.10	0.26	1.43	0.40
Arkhangelsk Oblast	0.86	0.33	1.02	0.83	Republic of Ingushetia	0.10	1.90	0.21	0.04
Vologda Oblast	1.82	0.39	0.92	0.90	Kabardino-Balkar Republic	0.02	0.12	0.54	0.24
Murmansk Oblast	1.57	1.04	0.70	0.82	Karachaevo-Cherkess Republic	0.01	0.06	0.30	0.12
St. Petersburg	2.13	8.27	3.25	3.28	Republic of North Osetia	0.13	0.17	0.45	0.15
Leningrad Oblast	1.82	0.77	1.15	0.84	Krasnodar Territory	0.46	1.22	3.47	2.12
Novgorod Oblast	0.40	0.28	0.51	0.33	Stavropol Territory	0.31	0.46	1.84	1.11
Pskov Oblast	0.08	0.25	0.56	0.30	Rostov Oblast	0.69	1.53	3.01	1.52
Bryansk Oblast	0.10	0.29	1.00	0.53	Republic of Bashkortostan	2.02	0.61	2.81	2.79
Vladimir Oblast	0.35	0.38	1.12	0.66	Udmurt Republic	0.78	0.38	1.12	0.96
Ivanovo Oblast	0.08	0.39	0.85	0.38	Kurgan Oblast	0.20	0.16	0.76	0.39
Kaluga Oblast	0.15	0.34	0.75	0.47	Orenburg Oblast	1.21	0.98	1.53	1.32
Kostroma Oblast	0.07	0.07	0.55	0.38	Perm Oblast	2.05	1.05	2.04	2.23
Moscow	29.34	38.40	5.91	13.84	Sverdlovsk Oblast	3.51	2.05	3.19	3.20
Moscow Oblast	2.32	4.66	4.49	4.21	Chelyabinsk Oblast	2.45	1.72	2.52	2.23
Orlov Oblast	0.06	0.25	0.62	0.38	Altai Republic	0.02	0.08	0.14	0.06
Ryazan Oblast	0.25	0.25	0.89	0.62	Altai Territory	0.23	0.37	1.83	0.95
Smolensk Oblast	0.30	0.17	0.79	0.52	Kemerovo Oblast	2.92	1.13	2.07	2.11
Tver Oblast	0.17	0.22	1.12	0.70	Novosibirsk Oblast	0.39	0.98	1.88	1.69

Sidebar 2.1 (continued)

Regions' Shares of Exports, Imports, Population, and Gross Regional Product in 1997

	Regions' share of, %					Regions' share of, %			
Region	exports	imports	population	GRP	Region	exports	imports	population	GRP
Tula Oblast	0.76	0.48	1.22	0.72	Omsk Oblast	0.98	0.72	1.49	1.46
Yaroslavl Oblast	0.51	0.38	0.98	0.91	Tomsk Oblast	1.14	0.53	0.73	0.92
Marii El Republic	0.03	0.11	0.52	0.27	Tyumen Oblast	13.46	4.36	2.20	9.05
Republic of Mordovia	0.02	0.08	0.65	0.40	Republic of Buryatia	0.15	0.59	0.72	0.50
Chuvash Republic	0.10	0.21	0.93	0.50	Tyva Republic	0.00	0.02	0.21	0.08
Kirov Oblast	0.33	0.11	1.10	0.75	Republic of Khakasia	0.51	0.34	0.40	0.35
Nizhegorod Oblast	1.25	1.25	2.53	2.29	Krasnoyarsk Territory	4.32	1.58	2.11	2.83
Belgorod Oblast	0.73	0.85	1.02	0.79	Irkutsk Oblast	2.83	1.34	1.90	2.43
Voronezh Oblast	0.26	0.36	1.70	1.11	Chita Oblast	0.15	0.16	0.87	0.55
Kursk Oblast	0.20	0.39	0.91	0.67	Republic of Sakha (Yakutia)	0.25	0.54	0.69	1.30
Lipetsk Oblast	1.58	0.51	0.85	0.68	Chukotka Auton. Region	0.00	0.05	0.06	0.10
Tambov Oblast	0.05	0.16	0.88	0.41	Maritime Territory	0.77	1.57	1.52	1.32
Republic of Kalmykia	0.16	0.31	0.22	0.08	Khabarovsk Territory	0.58	0.59	1.06	1.36
Republic of Tatarstan	2.35	1.33	2.58	2.90	Amur Oblast	0.06	0.18	0.70	0.68
Astrakhan Oblast	0.20	0.26	0.70	0.49	Kamchatka Oblast	0.40	0.53	0.27	0.35
Volgograd Oblast	0.81	0.67	1.85	1.41	Magadan Oblast	0.02	0.28	0.17	0.28
Penza Oblast	0.06	0.20	1.06	0.56	Sakhalin Oblast	0.42	0.66	0.42	0.58
Samara Oblast	2.51	2.43	2.27	3.14	Kaliningrad Oblast	0.41	2.54	0.65	0.37
Saratov Oblast	0.48	0.48	1.86	1.37					
Ulyanovsk Oblast	0.14	0.23	1.02	0.72					

2.2.2 Reflection of financial flows in the balance

If we start from the organizational structure of financial flows between the Center and the regions, it is perfectly obvious that extraterritorial revenues and expenditures should not be considered in compiling the financial balance, and that revenues and expenditures that do have a territorial connection should be included.

Unfortunately, in conducting this research it was not possible to take into account all of the revenues and expenditures coming from the regions and going out to them. Components of the financial flow that were not taken into account include:

- taxes controlled by the State Customs Committee of the Russian Federation
- nontax revenues not controlled by the Ministry of Taxes and Duties of the Russian Federation
- most expenditures on national defense
- direct expenditures from the federal budget going directly to recipients of budgetary funds, bypassing the Federal Treasury system.

Even though part of the financial flows was not taken into account, the research presented here did consider all presently known components of the financial balance. The balances that were calculated are the most complete summary of financial flows that anyone has ever compiled or analyzed. In contrast to all previous research, this study considers direct expenditures from the federal budget in the regions, and the territorial profile of the revenues and expenditures of federal extrabudgetary funds.

Figure 2.2 shows a diagram of how the balance of financial flows is compiled, with the undistributed part of the federal budget's revenues and expenditures set apart. The quantitative ratio of the individual revenue and expenditure items that are and are not taken into account in compiling the financial balance is presented in Table 2.1. Among other things, the data in this table indicate the growing role of the Federal Treasury. In 1998, more than 60% of all expenditures was funded through the treasury system, not counting financial aid to regional budgets. If the latter is taken into account, as well as extraterritorial expenditures, we can talk about a high degree of accuracy of the balances of financial flows that were compiled.

As we can see from Table 2.1, since 1996 the portion of the federal budget's expenditure items taken into account in the balance of financial flows has increased, and by 1998 it had reached approximately two fifths of all expenditures. If we consider that extraterritorial expenditures account for approximately half of all expenditures (defense expenditures made up 15%; servicing of the national debt, almost 30%; and international activity, 5%), then only 10% of all of the federal budget's expenditures is actually not taken into account.

We must also note that this research studied the financial flows between the Center and the regions that have actually been established. Budget loans to regional budgets were taken into account in compiling the balance, while tax arrears and the federal budget's indebtedness (for example, on funding of federal target programs) were not.

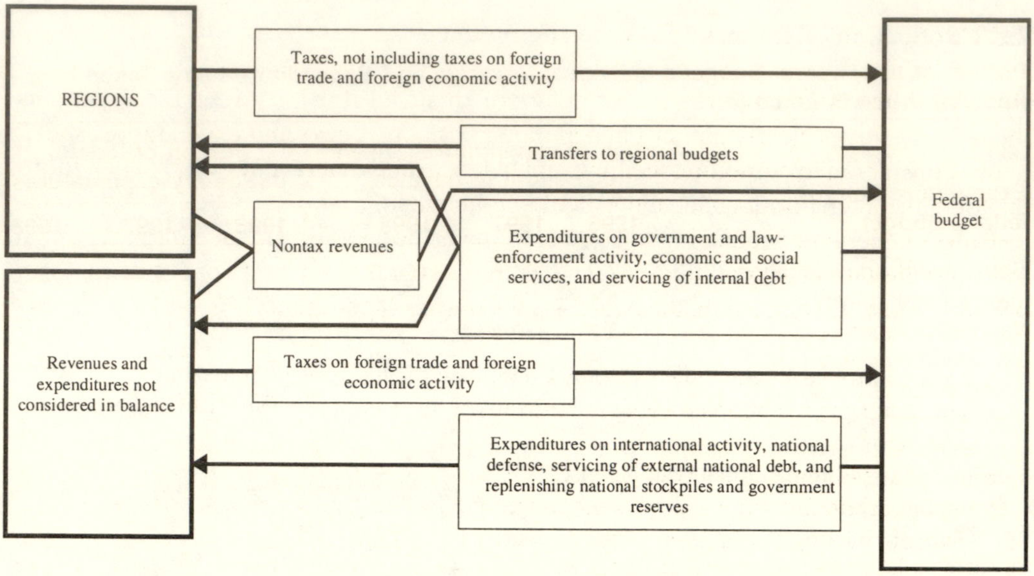

Figure 2.2. **Diagram of compiling the balance of financial flows between the federal budget and the regions.**

So the balance of financial flows reflected only the taxes that were collected (rather than accrued) and the federal budget's expenditures that were actually funded.

In the statistics on execution of the budgets of subjects of the Federation, budget loans from the federal budget to regional budgets are considered as one of the sources for covering the deficit. Actually, the remainder of budget loans not paid off at the end of the year is one of the mechanisms by which financial aid is provided to the regions, and therefore it was considered in precisely this capacity in compiling the financial balance (i.e., it was included in the amount of funds transferred to regional budgets).

The balance of financial flows for individual regions can be characterized by two indices:

- the percent ratio of revenues collected in the region and credited to the federal budget and federal budgetary expenditures in the region (hereinafter, the percentage of funds returned to the region)
- the difference between the revenues collected in the region and credited to the federal budget and federal budgetary expenditures in the region figured per capita (hereinafter, the balance per capita).

The former index enables us to evaluate the degree to which individual regions acted as donors or recipients, while the latter one characterizes how much the regions depend on transfers from the federal budget (or, vice versa, how much the federal budget depends on transfers from the regions).

Table 2.1

Portion of the Federal Budget's Individual Revenue and Expenditure Items Taken into Account in the Balance (%)

Expenditure item of federal budget	Portion of expenditures taken into account in balance			Portion of federal budgetary expenditures		
	1996	1997	1998	1996	1997	1998
Government administration	67.2	64.5	≈100.0	1.2	2.0	2.5
International activity	0.1	0.7	22.0	6.1	1.7	5.0
National defense	0.7	0.2	0.0	14.7	16.1	14.7
Law-enforcement activity and security	23.3	42.8	6.0	6.6	8.8	8.0
Basic research and support for scientific and technical progress	30.4	38.3	≈100.0	1.5	1.9	1.3
Industry, power generation, and construction	42.8	27.5	≈100.0	6.0	5.4	2.9
Agriculture and fishing	20.5	14.1	99.9	2.0	2.5	2.4
Environmental protection and natural resource management	94.6	88.3	≈100.0	0.5	0.5	0.5
Transportation, roads, communications, and information systems	49.9	16.8	≈100.0	0.2	0.8	0.3
Prevention and relief of emergencies and natural disasters	53.7	60.6	72.8	0.9	1.3	1.6
Total for government services to the national economy	41.9	30.4	98.5	9.5	10.6	7.7
Education	84.7	91.8	≈100.0	2.6	2.9	3.4
Culture and art	25.3	59.1	≈100.0	0.2	0.2	0.3
Mass media	1.8	16.7	≈100.0	0.2	0.3	0.3
Public health and fitness	62.2	54.1	≈100.0	1.0	1.8	1.5
Social policy	6.2	8.9	47.6	3.1	4.6	9.4
Total for social services	42.8	43.2	71.0	7.2	9.8	14.8
Servicing of the national debt	0.0	0.0	0.0	29.2	23.8	27.6
Other direct expenditures	17.0	11.5	60.5	18.6	17.8	8.0
Financial aid to regional budgets	100.0	100.0	100.0	13.9	15.7	10.3
Total	27.1	31.0	39.5	100.0	100.0	100.0

2.3. THE BALANCE AND CHANGES—1996–1998[1]

2.3.1 Structure of the balance in 1996–1998

The absolute values of the components of financial flows between the federal budget and the regions as a whole in 1996–1998 are presented in Table 2.2. According to the data

[1] In this section, we are talking about the financial balance that we were able to compile from the available data.

Table 2.2

Structure of the Balance of Financial Flows in 1996–1998

	billion undenominated rubles		million rubles
Components of the balance	**1996**	**1997**	**1998**
Federal budgetary revenues	206,824	249,131	191,898
including:			
tax revenues	205,927	229,418	176,125
nontax revenues	898	19,713	15,773
Federal budgetary expenditures	117,534	153,509	248,793
including:			
transfers to regional budgets	60,281	77,663	39,716
of this amount, grants	*26,818*	*36,181*	*29,668*
funding of federal operations and institutions in the regions through the Federal Treasury	57,253	75,847	209,078

cited, the portion of direct expenditures in the federal budgetary expenditures increased, and the portion of transfers to regional budgets decreased accordingly. These changes were primarily due to the increased role of the Federal Treasury.

The ratio of financial aid and direct expenditures in 1998, which was 1:4, can be considered close to the actual one. Analysis showed that the ratio of transfers to regional budgets and the Federation's direct expenditures in the regions differs noticeably for individual regions (Table 2.3 and Figure 2.3).

The main reason for the differences between regions in the structure of federal budgetary expenditures consists in how much the regional budgets depend on the Federation's financial aid (Figure 2.4). The coefficient of correlation between the portion of transfers to regional budgets in total federal budgetary expenditures in the regions and the portion of financial aid in the revenues of regional budgets in 1998 was 0.84.

Based on this, we can assume that direct expenditures from the federal budget are distributed more evenly among the regions than is financial aid to regional budgets.

2.3.2 Balance with respect to financial aid

In this section, we will look at the financial balance in which only financial aid to regional budgets is taken into account in federal budgetary expenditures. The need to consider this balance separately is dictated by the fact that transfers to regional budgets are the most obvious channel for redistribution of budgetary revenues. Moreover, the distribution of these transfers is most often the subject of discussions; it has to be authorized in laws on the federal budget, and then they are fully taken into account by statistics.

According to the balance of financial flows that was compiled, in 1996–1998 there were 50 regions that were donors to the federal budget for all three years (the amount of

Table 2.3

Classification of Regions by Ratio of Transfers to Regional Budgets and Direct Expenditures from the Federal Budget in 1998

Portion of transfers to regional budgets in sum of transfers and direct expenditures from the federal budget	Regions	Population
Less than 20%	Moscow, St. Petersburg, Chelyabinsk and Perm Oblasts, Krasnoyarsk Territory, Komi Republic, Lipetsk, Novosibirsk, and Samara Oblasts	39.8 million people, or 27.0%
20–35%	Tula, Moscow, Bryansk, Sverdlovsk, Irkutsk, Orenburg, Nizhegorod, Postov, Tomsk, Leningrad, Arkhangelsk, Vologda, Belgorod, Volgograd, and Omsk Oblasts	40.3 million people, or 27.4%
35–50%	Kursk, Saratov, Ryazan, Kemerovo, and Orlov Oblasts, Republic of Khakasia, Krasnodar Territory, Chuvash Republic, Yaroslavl, Penza, and Sakhalin Oblasts, Republic of Sakha (Yakutia), Ulyanovsk, Tver, and Voronezh Oblasts, Republic of Karelia, Khabarovsk Territory, Marii El Republic, Chita Oblast, Khanty-Mansi Autonomous Region, Tyumen and Kurgan Oblasts, Taimyr Autonomous Region	34.7 million people, or 23.6%
50–65%	Smolensk Oblast, Karachaevo-Cherkess Republic, Maritime Territory, Tambov and Ivanovo Oblasts, Republic of Mordovia, Nenets Autonomous Region, Kaluga Oblast, Republic of North Osetia, Altai Republic, Stavropol Territory, Kirov, Astrakhan, and Magadan Oblasts, Republic of Kalmykia, Kamchatka and Vladimir Oblasts, Republic of Buryatia, Pskov Oblast, Udmurt Republic, Chukotka Autonomous Region, Kostroma Oblast	21.6 million people, or 14.7%
More than 65%	Altai Territory, Jewish Autonomous Oblast, Murmansk and Amur Oblasts, Komi-Permyak Autonomous Region, Republic of Tyva, Novgorod Oblast, Koryak Autonomous Region, Republic of Adygeya, Republic of Dagestan, Aga Buryat and Ust-Orda Autonomous Regions	10.0 million people, or 6.8%

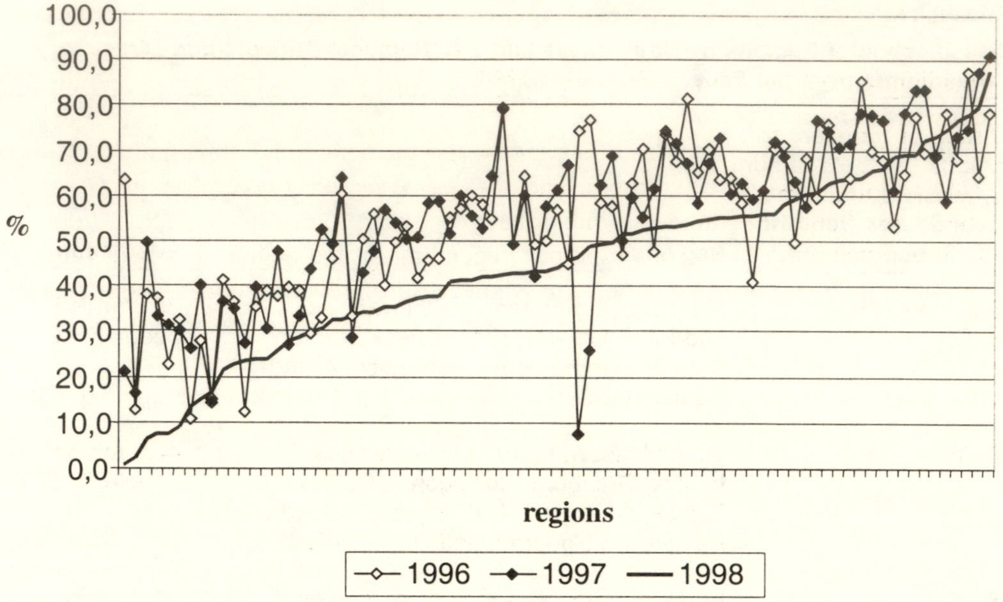

Figure 2.3. **Portion of transfers to regional budgets in total federal budgetary expenditures in the regions in 1996–1998.**

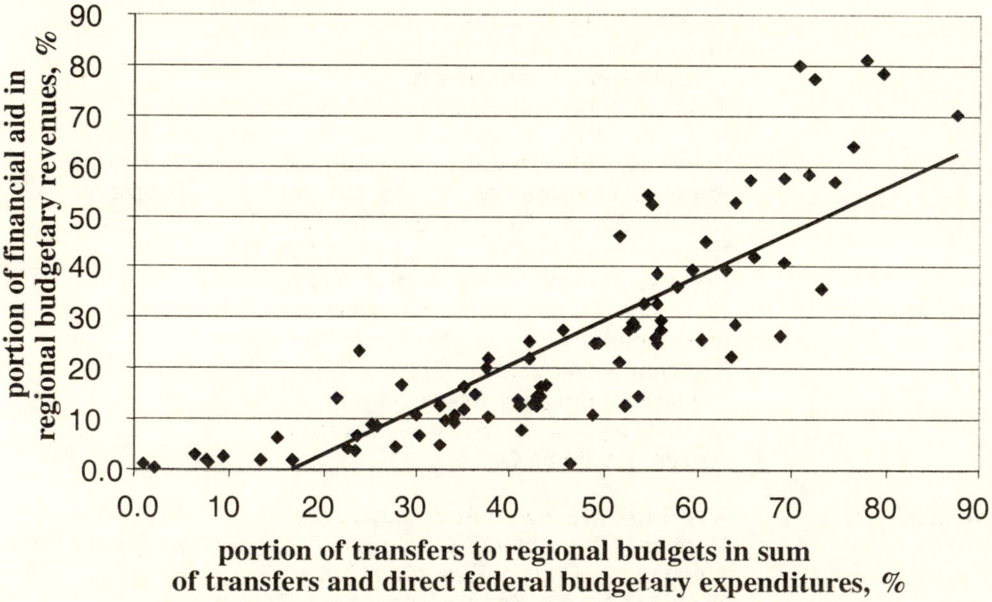

Figure 2.4. **Relationship of structure of federal budgetary expenditures in the regions and regional budgets' dependence on financial aid in 1998.**

taxes collected in their territory and credited to the federal budget exceeded the amount of financial aid turned over to them) and 24 recipient regions (consistent donors and recipients). Another 14 regions were donors in some years and recipients in others ("inconsistent" regions).

In 1998, the donors included 62 regions; and the recipients, 26 (Figure 2.5; *see also* Map 1 in the back of this volume). The division of regions into consistent donors, consistent recipients, and donors in individual years is presented in Table 2.4.

The distribution of regions by types depending on the degree to which funds were returned to them corresponds, on the whole, to the prevailing ideas about financially "strong" and "weak" regions. The percentage of funds returned depends to a significant extent on the portion of financial aid in the revenues of regional budgets. The regions that gave the greatest portion of collected taxes to the federal budget include Moscow and St. Petersburg, oil- and gas-producing autonomous regions, and major economically developed regions. Among the recipients are the republics of the North Caucasus and Southern Siberia, and most of the autonomous regions.

A number of subjects of the Federation depend enormously on the federal budget. For instance, the amount of financial aid to the Republic of Tyva is 18 times more than the amount of taxes collected in its territory. Aid was 14 times greater than taxes for the Ust-Orda Buryat Autonomous Region, 12 times greater for the Republic of Dagestan and the Koryak Autonomous Region, 10 times for the Chukotka Autonomous Region, 6.5 times for the Kabardino-Balkar Republic, and 5 times greater for the Jewish Autonomous Oblast.

The fact that approximately one third of the regions are recipients when the balance of financial flows is compiled solely on the basis of transfers from the federal budget to the regional budgets means that even if all of the taxes collected in these regions were to stay in their budgets they would still need additional financial aid from the federal budget. Thus, establishing differentiated rates for crediting taxes to the regional budgets (which is frequently proposed as one way of reforming the system of interbudgetary relations in Russia) cannot fully solve the problem of providing financial aid to regions from the federal budget.

Research showed that the percentage of funds returned to the regions in 1996–1998 was fairly stable (Figure 2.6). The coefficient of correlation between the indices for 1997 and 1998 was 0.82, and between the indices for 1996 and 1998 it was 0.56.

To a significant extent, the differences between regions in specific indices of the amount of financial aid (Table 2.5 and Map 2) correspond to the differences in percentage of funds returned. However, this correspondence is not complete (the coefficients of correlation in 1996–1998 vary from 0.41 to 0.56).

2.3.3 Balance taking into account the Federation's direct expenditures

In this section, we will look at the balance of financial flows on the basis of all available data on federal budgetary expenditures in the regions.

Table 2.4

Donor Regions and Recipient Regions in 1996–1998 (Balance with Respect to Financial Aid)

Consistent donors	Donors in individual years (indicated in parentheses)	Consistent recipients
Population 118.6 million people, or 80.6%	*Population 12.3 million people, or 8.4%*	*Population 15.4 million people, or 10.5%*
Komi Republic. Vologda Oblast, St. Petersburg, Leningrad, Bryansk, Vladimir, and Kaluga Oblasts, Moscow, Moscow, Ryazan, Smolensk, Tver, Tula, and Yaroslavl Oblasts, Chuvash Republic, Kirov, Nizhegorod, Belgorod, Voronezh, Kursk, Lipetsk, and Tambov Oblasts, Republic of Tatarstan, Volgograd, Penza, Samara, Saratov, and Ulyanovsk Oblasts, Krasnodar and Stavropol Territories, Rostov Oblast, Republic of Bashkortostan, Udmurt Republic, Orenburg, Perm, Sverdlovsk, Chelyabinsk, Kemerovo, Novosibirsk, Omsk, Tomsk, and Tyumen Oblasts, Khanty-Mansi and Yamal-Nenets Autonomous Regions, Republic of Khakasia, Krasnoyarsk Territory, Irkutsk Oblast, Khabarovsk Territory, Sakhalin and Kaliningrad Oblast	Republic of Karelia (1998), Arkhangelsk Oblast (1196, 1998), Nenets Autonomous Region (1996, 1998), Ivanovo (1998) and Orlov Oblasts (1996, 1998), Marii El Republic (1998), Kalmykia (1997, 1998), Astrakhan (1997, 1998) and Kurgan Oblasts (1996), Altai Republic (1998), Chita Oblast (1996, 1998), Aga Burya Autonomous Region (1998), Republic of Sakha (Yakutia) (1998), Maritime Territory (1996)	Murmansk, Novgorod, Pskov, and Kostroma Oblasts, Republics of Mordovia, Adygeya, Dagestan, and Ingushetia, Kabardino-Balkar and Karachaevo-Cherkess Republics, Republic of North Osetia, Komi-Permyak Autonomous Region, Altai Territory, Republics of Buryatia and Tyva, Taimyr, Evenk, Ust-Orda, and Buryat Autonomous Regions, Jewish Autonomous Oblast, Chukotka Autonomous Region, Amur and Kamchatka Oblasts, Koryak Autonomous region, Magadan Oblast

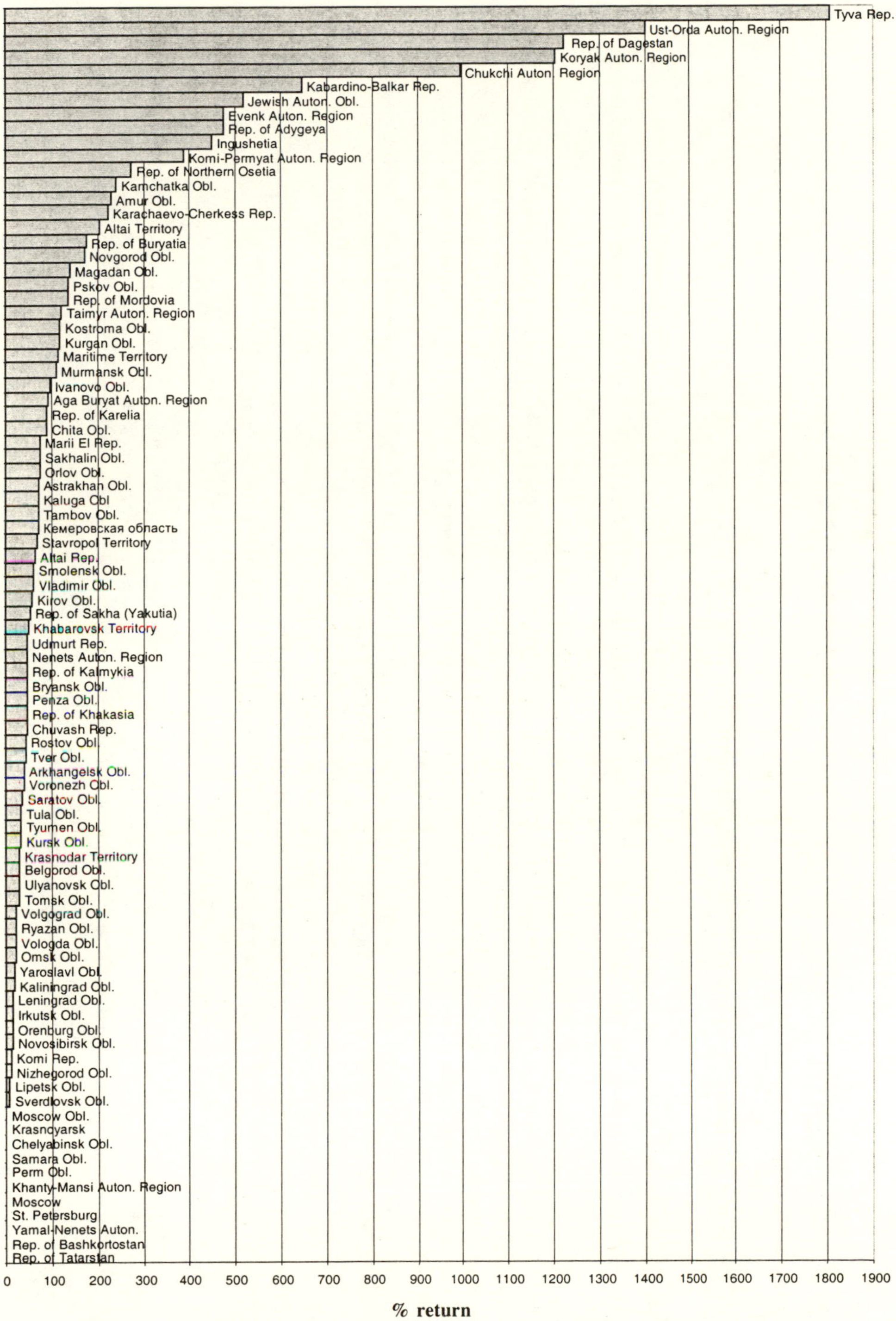
Tyva Rep.
Ust-Orda Auton. Region
Rep. of Dagestan
Koryak Auton. Region
Chukchi Auton. Region
Kabardino-Balkar Rep.
Jewish Auton. Obl.
Evenk Auton. Region
Rep. of Adygeya
Ingushetia
Komi-Permyat Auton. Region
Rep. of Northern Osetia
Kamchatka Obl.
Amur Obl.
Karachaevo-Cherkess Rep.
Altai Territory
Rep. of Buryatia
Novgorod Obl.
Magadan Obl.
Pskov Obl.
Rep. of Mordovia
Taimyr Auton. Region
Kostroma Obl.
Kurgan Obl.
Maritime Territory
Murmansk Obl.
Ivanovo Obl.
Aga Buryat Auton. Region
Rep. of Karelia
Chita Obl.
Marii El Rep.
Sakhalin Obl.
Orlov Obl.
Astrakhan Obl.
Kaluga Obl
Tambov Obl.
Кемеровская область
Stavropol Territory
Altai Rep.
Smolensk Obl.
Vladimir Obl.
Kirov Obl.
Rep. of Sakha (Yakutia)
Khabarovsk Territory
Udmurt Rep.
Nenets Auton. Region
Rep. of Kalmykia
Bryansk Obl.
Penza Obl.
Rep. of Khakasia
Chuvash Rep.
Rostov Obl.
Tver Obl.
Arkhangelsk Obl.
Voronezh Obl.
Saratov Obl.
Tula Obl.
Tyumen Obl.
Kursk Obl.
Krasnodar Territory
Belgorod Obl.
Ulyanovsk Obl.
Tomsk Obl.
Volgograd Obl.
Ryazan Obl.
Vologda Obl.
Omsk Obl.
Yaroslavl Obl.
Kaliningrad Obl.
Leningrad Obl.
Irkutsk Obl.
Orenburg Obl.
Novosibirsk Obl.
Komi Rep.
Nizhegorod Obl.
Lipetsk Obl.
Sverdlovsk Obl.
Moscow Obl.
Krasnoyarsk
Chelyabinsk Obl.
Samara Obl.
Perm Obl.
Khanty-Mansi Auton. Region
Moscow
St. Petersburg
Yamal-Nenets Auton.
Rep. of Bashkortostan
Rep. of Tatarstan
0
100
200
300
400
500
600
700
800
900
1000
1100
1200
1300
1400
1500
1600
1700
1800
1900
% return

Figure 2.5. **Distribution of regions according to the percentage of funds returned in 1998 (balance with respect to financial aid).**

Table 2.5

Classification of Regions by Balance (with Respect to Financial Aid) Per Capita in 1998

Balance per capita	Regions	Population
Contributing more than 1,000 rubles/person	Yamal-Nenets Autonomous Region, Moscow, Khanty-Mansi Autonomous Region, Moscow Oblast, St. Petersburg, Samara Oblast, *Nenets Autonomous Region*, Sverdlovsk Oblast	29.8 million people, or 20.3%
Contributing from 500 to 1,000 rubles/person	Nizhegorod Oblast, Komi Republic, Perm Oblast, *Republic of Kalmykia*, Yaroslavl and Leningrad Oblasts, Krasnodar Territory, Irkutsk, Novosibirsk, Tyumen, Ryazan, Tomsk, Omsk, Orenburg, and Chelyabinsk Oblasts, Udmurt Republic, Kaliningrad and Volgograd Oblasts, *Altai Republic*	36.8 million people, or 25.0%
Contributing from 250 to 500 rubles/person	*Republic of Sakha (Yakutia)*, Khabarovsk Territory, Ulyanovsk Oblast, Republic of Bashkortostan, Krasnodar Territory, Lipetsk, Kursk, Belgorod, Vologda, Tula, and Saratov Oblasts, Republic of Tatarstan, Voronezh, *Arkhangelsk*, Tver, Sakhalin, Rostov, Vladimir, Bryansk, and Kirov Oblasts, Republic of Khakasia	42.8 million people, or 29.1%
Contributing from 0 to 250 rubles/person	Kemerovo and Penza Oblasts, Chuvash Republic, Kaluga and Smolensk Oblasts, Stavropol Territory, *Astrakhan, Orlov*, and Tambov Oblasts, *Marii El Republic, Aga Buryat Autonomous Region, Chita Oblast, Republic of Karelia, Ivanovo Oblast*	18.2 million people, or 12.3%
Receiving from 0 to 500 rubles/person	*Kurgan Oblast, Maritime Territory*, Kostroma and Murmansk Oblasts, Republic of Mordovia, Pskov Oblast, Taimyr Autonomous Region, Karachaevo-Cherkess Republic, Republic of Buryatia, Altai Territory, Novgorod, Magadan, and Amur Oblasts	13.1 million people, or 8.9%
Receiving more than 500 rubles/person	Republic of North Osetia, Komi-Permyak Autonomous Region, Jewish Autonomous Oblast, Republic of Dagestan, Adygeya, Kamchatka Oblast, Kabardino-Balkar and Ingush Republics, Ust-Orda Buryat Autonomous Region, Republic of Tyva, Evenk, Koryak, and Chukotka Autonomous Region	5.6 million people, or 3.8%

Note: Regions that were donors and recipients in different years are shown in italics.

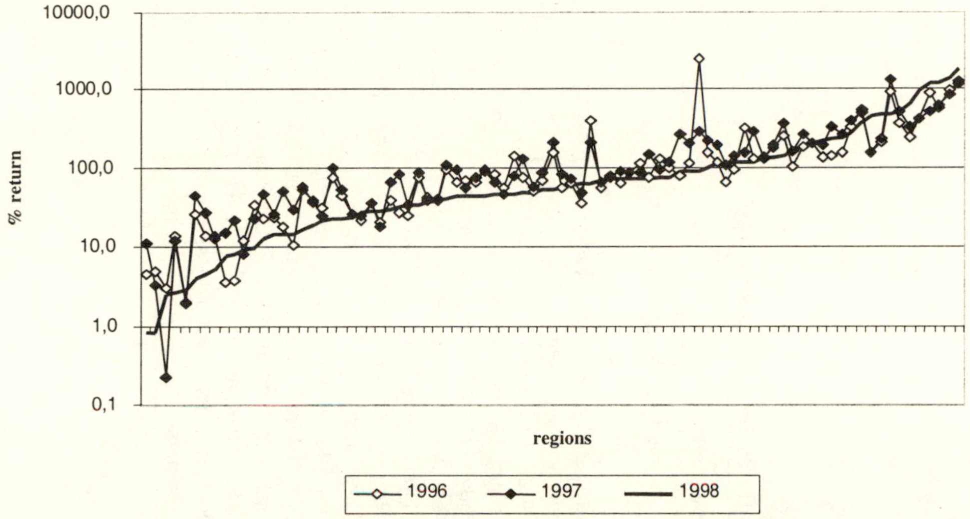

Figure 2.6. **Percentage of funds returned to the regions in 1996–1998 (balance with respect to financial aid).** *Note:* To make the graph easier to read, a logarithmic scale is used on the y-axis. The graph does not include the Republics of Bashkortostan and Tatarstan, or the Yamal-Nenets Autonomous Region, where the return was equal to zero.

For 1998, we were able to get information on direct expenditures from the federal budget for all subjects of the Federation. For the preceding years, unfortunately, the data were incomplete. For 1996, there are no data for Tatarstan, Kabardino-Balkaria, Ingushetia, Bashkiria, Kaliningrad Oblast, and the Yamal-Nenets and Evenk Autonomous Regions. For 1997, data are lacking for Ingushetia, Bashkiria, and the Evenk Autonomous Region. True, the missing data did not particularly affect the final result. The Republic of Tatarstan, Kaliningrad Oblast, and the Yamal-Nenets Autonomous Region were obvious donors in 1997–1998. Bashkiria was on the list of donors in 1998. The rest of the regions were recipients, even when the Federation's direct expenditures are taken into account (Table 2.6).

The distribution of regions by percentage of funds returned is shown in Figure 2.7 and on Map 3.

Naturally, when direct expenditures from the federal budget are taken into account the number of donor regions drops noticeably. In 1996–1998, only 26 regions were consistent donors, and 48 subjects of the federation were consistent recipients. So the remaining 14 regions can be classified as inconsistent (donors and recipients in different years). In 1998, there were 35 donor regions.[2]

[2] Thus, when the balance is compiled with respect to financial aid only, approximately one third of the regions are recipients, but if direct expenditures from the federal budget are taken into account, on the other hand, approximately one third of the regions are donors.

Table 2.6

Donor and Recipient Regions in 1996–1998 (Balance Taking into Account the Federation's Direct Expenditures)

Consistent donors	Donors in individual years	Consistent recipients
Population of 72.8 million people, or 49.5%	*Population of 25.8 million people, or 17.5%*	*Population of 47.7 million people, or 32.5%*
St. Petersburg, Leningrad Oblast, Moscow, Moscow, Yaroslavl, Nizhegorod, Belgorod, Voronezh, and Lipetsk Oblasts, Republic of Tatarstan, Volgograd, Samara, and Ulyanovsk Oblasts, Republic of Bashkortostan, Udmurt Republic, Orenburg, Perm, Sverdlovsk, Chelyabinsk, Omsk, Tomsk, and Tyumen Oblasts, Khanty-Mansi and Yamal-Nenets Autonomous Regions, Krasnoyarsk Territory, Kaliningrad Oblast	Komi Republic (1997), Nenets Autonomous Region (1996, 1998), Vologda (1998), Vladimir (1996, 1998), Ryazan (1996, 1998), Smolensk (1996, 1997), Kirov (1996), and Kursk Oblasts (1996, 1998), Republic of Kalmykia (1998), Saratov Oblast (1996, 1997), Krasnodar (1996, 1998) and Stavropol Territories (1996), Novosibirsk (1996, 1998), Irkutsk Oblast (1996, 1998)	Republic of Karelia, Arkhangelsk, Murmansk, Novgorod, Pskov, Bryansk, Ivanovo, Kaluga, Kostroma, Orlov, Tver, and Tula Oblasts, Marii El Republic, Republic of Mordovia, Chuvash Republic, Tambov, Astrakhan, and Penza Oblasts, Republics of Adygeya and Dagestan, Ingush, Kabardino-Balkar, and Karachaevo-Cherkess Republics, Republic of North Osetia, Rostov and Kurgan Oblasts, Komi-Permyak Autonomous Region, Altai Republic, Altai Territory, Kemerovo Oblast, Republics of Buryatia, Tyva, and Khakasia, Taimyr, Evenk and Ust-Orda Buryat Autonomous Regions, Chita Oblast, Aga Buryat Autonomous Region, Republic of Sakha (Yakutia), Jewish Autonomous Oblast, Chukotka Autonomous Region, Maritime and Khabarovsk Territories, Amur and Kamchatka Oblasts, Koryak Autonomous Region, Magadan and Sakhalin Oblasts

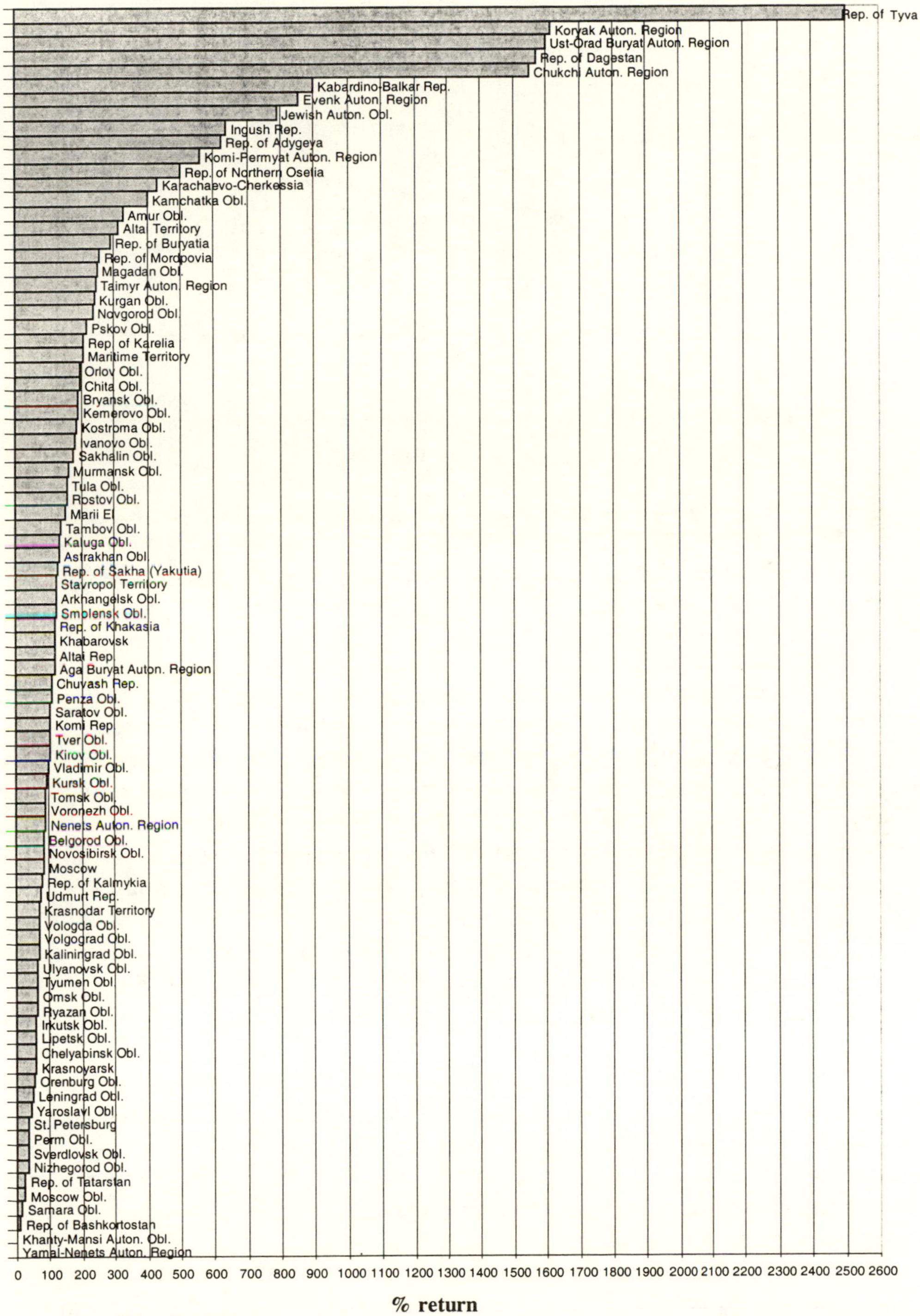
Rep. of Tyva
Koryak Auton. Region
Ust-Orad Buryat Auton. Region
Rep. of Dagestan
Chukchi Auton. Region
Kabardino-Balkar Rep.
Evenk Auton. Region
Jewish Auton. Obl.
Ingush Rep.
Rep. of Adygeya
Komi-Permyat Auton. Region
Rep. of Northern Osetia
Karachaevo-Cherkessia
Kamchatka Obl.
Amur Obl.
Altai Territory
Rep. of Buryatia
Rep. of Mordpovia
Magadan Obl.
Taimyr Auton. Region
Kurgan Obl.
Novgorod Obl.
Pskov Obl.
Rep. of Karelia
Maritime Territory
Orlov Obl.
Chita Obl.
Bryansk Obl.
Kemerovo Obl.
Kostroma Obl.
Ivanovo Obl.
Sakhalin Obl.
Murmansk Obl.
Tula Obl.
Rostov Obl.
Marii El
Tambov Obl.
Kaluga Obl.
Astrakhan Obl.
Rep. of Sakha (Yakutia)
Stavropol Territory
Arkhangelsk Obl.
Smolensk Obl.
Rep. of Khakasia
Khabarovsk
Altai Rep.
Aga Buryat Auton. Region
Chuvash Rep.
Penza Obl.
Saratov Obl.
Komi Rep.
Tver Obl.
Kirov Obl.
Vladimir Obl.
Kursk Obl.
Tomsk Obl.
Voronezh Obl.
Nenets Auton. Region
Belgorod Obl.
Novosibirsk Obl.
Moscow
Rep. of Kalmykia
Udmurt Rep.
Krasnodar Territory
Vologda Obl.
Volgograd Obl.
Kaliningrad Obl.
Ulyanovsk Obl.
Tyumen Obl.
Omsk Obl.
Ryazan Obl.
Irkutsk Obl.
Lipetsk Obl.
Chelyabinsk Obl.
Krasnoyarsk
Orenburg Obl.
Leningrad Obl.
Yaroslavl Obl.
St. Petersburg
Perm Obl.
Sverdlovsk Obl.
Nizhegorod Obl.
Rep. of Tatarstan
Moscow Obl.
Samara Obl.
Rep. of Bashkortostan
Khanty-Mansi Auton. Obl.
Yamal-Nenets Auton. Region
0 100 200 300 400 500 600 700 800 900 1000 1100 1200 1300 1400 1500 1600 1700 1800 1900 2000 2100 2200 2300 2400 2500 2600
% return

Figure 2.7. **Distribution of regions by percentage of funds returned in 1998 (balance taking into account direct expenditures from the federal budget).**

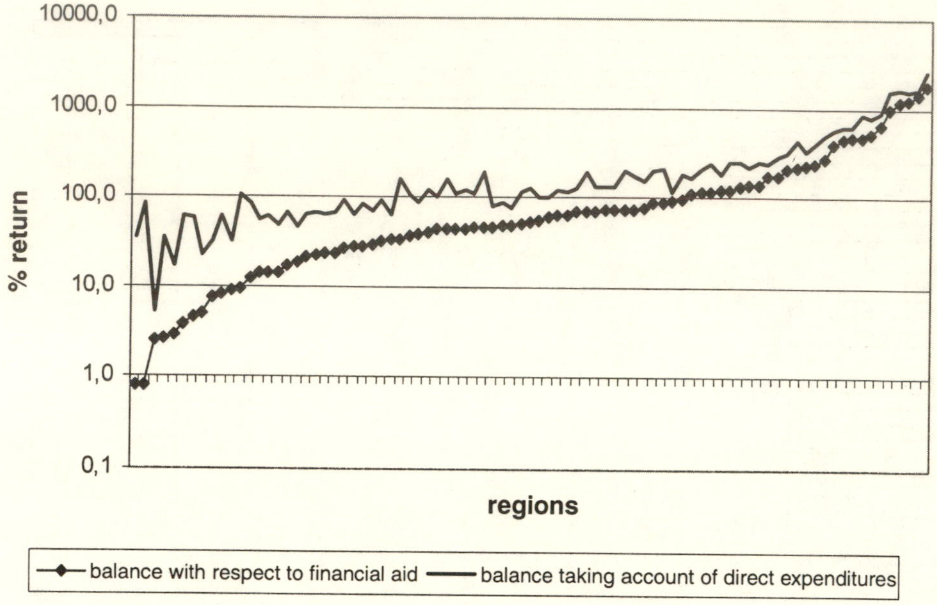

Figure 2.8. **Correlation of percentage of return according to balance with respect to financial aid only and taking into account the Federation's direct expenditures in 1998.**

When we switch from a balance that only takes into account transfers to the regional budgets to one that includes direct expenditures from the federal budget, 12 regions move from the category of consistent donors to consistent recipients. They are Bryansk, Kaluga, Tver, Tula, Tambov, Penza, Rostov, Kemerovo, and Sakhalin Oblasts, Khabarovsk Territory, Khakasia, and Chuvashia. The rest of the regions from the consistent donor group changed to the inconsistent type, and those from the group of inconsistent donors changed to consistent recipients. The Nenets Autonomous Region and Kalmykia were inconsistent in both cases.

To a significant extent, the classification of regions according to the percentage of funds returned taking into account direct expenditures from the federal budget coincides with the classification by percentage of funds returned on the basis of financial aid only (Figure 2.8).

In 1998, less than 20% of the funds collected in taxes was returned to four regions: the Yamal-Nenets (3.7%) and Khanty-Mansi (5.3%) Autonomous Regions, Bashkiria (8.7%), and Samara Oblastast (17.1%). The Republic of Tyva received 25 times more money than taxes credited to the federal budget from its territory. The Koryak, Ust-Orda Buryat, and Chukotka Autonomous Regions, and also Dagestan, had a 16-fold excess of funds returned over taxes collected.

The situation with Moscow deserves a special comment. While the return of funds to this region in 1996 was only 7.8% in 1996 and 15.9% in 1997, in 1998 it rose to 83.2%. This puts the capital of the Federation far from first place on the list of donor regions. Moscow has the largest role in forming the federal budget's tax revenues, and organiza-

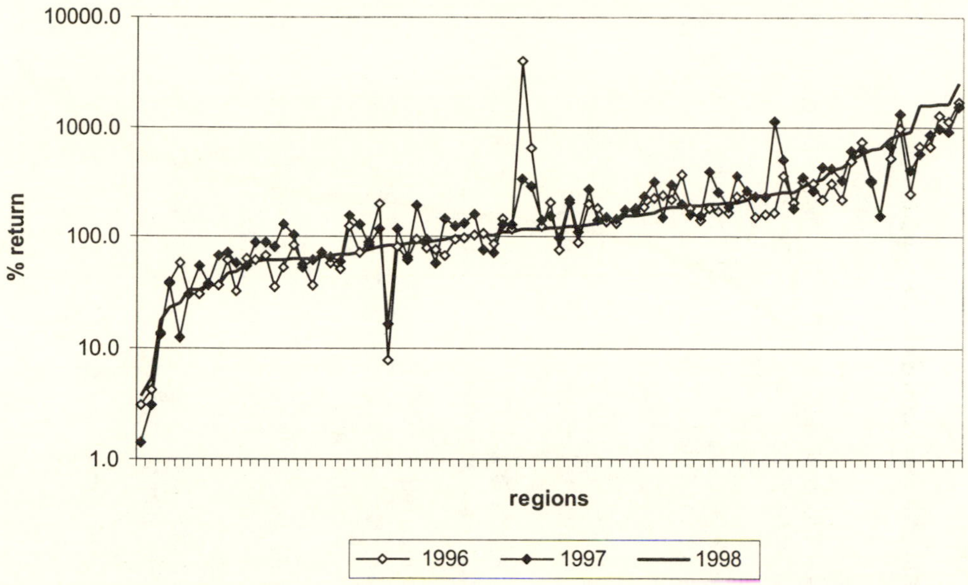

Figure 2.9. **Percentage of funds returned to the regions in 1996–1998 (balance taking into account the Federation's direct expenditures).** *Note:* To make the graph easier to read, a logarithmic scale is used on the y-axis. The graph does not include the Republic of Bashkortostan, where the % return in 1997 was equal to zero.

tions located in Moscow receive a considerable part of the funds from these revenues. The overwhelming majority of federal bureaucrats work in Moscow, and many federal facilities are located there (scientific research institutes, higher educational institutions, libraries, etc.).

The differences between regions in the percentage of funds returned are approximately as consistent as the differences between regions in the percentage of funds returned according to the balance that only takes into account financial aid to regional budgets (Figure 2.9).

Table 2.7 and Map 4 show the classification of regions according to the balance per capita in 1998.

As in the case of the balance with respect to financial aid, to a significant extent the distribution of regions by types corresponds to the distribution according to the percentage of funds returned, though there are certain discrepancies.

2.3.4 Balance taking into account extrabudgetary funds

Unfortunately, there was not enough data to compile a complete balance of financial flows between the Center and the regions taking into account extrabudgetary funds. The results of calculations for the 67 regions for which data were available on collection of

Table 2.7

Classification of Regions by Balance (Taking into Account the Federation's Direct Expenditures) Per Capita in 1998

Balance per capita	Regions	Population
Contributing more than 500 rubles/person	Yamal-Nenets and Khanty-Mansi Autonomous Regions, Moscow, and Samara Oblasts, Moscow, St. Petersburg, Sverdlovsk Nizhegorod, Perm, Yaroslavl, and Leningrad Oblasts	39.4 million people, or 26.8%
Contributing from 250 to 500 rubles/person	Republic of Bashkortostan, Tyumen Oblast, Krasnoyarsk Territory, *Irkutsk Oblast, Republic of Kalmykia, Ryazan*, Orenburg, and Omsk Oblasts, Republic of Tatarstan, Udmurt Republic, *Nenets Autonomous Region*	22.6 million people, or 15.4%
Contributing from 0 to 250 rubles/person	Ulyanovsk, Chelyabinsk, Kaliningrad, Volgograd, and Lipetsk Oblasts, *Krasnodar Territory, Vologda, Novosibirsk*, Belgorod, Tomsk, Voronezh, *Kursk*, and *Vladimir* Oblasts	27.2 million people, or 18.5%
Receiving from 0 to 250 rubles/person	*Kirov*, Tver, and *Saratov* Oblasts, Chuvash Republic, Penza Oblast, *Komi Republic,* Republic of Khakasia, *Smolensk Oblast, Stavropol Territory*, Arkhangelsk and Tambov Oblasts, Aga Buryat Autonomous Region, Astrakhan Oblast, Khabarovsk Territory, Marii El and Altai Republics	20.8 million people, or 14.2%
Receiving from 250 to 500 rubles/person	Kaluga and Rostov Oblast, Republic of Sakha (Yakutia), Ivanovo, Tula, Kurgan, and Chita Oblasts, Republic of Karelia, Pskov, Bryansk, and Kostroma Oblasts	15.7 million people, or 10.7%
Receiving from 500 to 1,000 rubles/person	Orlov Oblast, Republic of Mordovia, Murmansk and Novgorod Oblasts, Altai and Maritime Territories, Kemerovo Oblast, Republic of Buryatia, Karachaevo-Cherkess Republic, Amur and Sakhalin Oblasts	14.6 million people, or 10.0%
Receiving more than 1,000 rubles/person	Komi-Permyak Autonomous Region, Republics of Dagestan and North Osetia, Ust-Orda Buryat Autonomous Region, Republic of Adygeya, Jewish Autonomous Oblast, Taimyr Autonomous Region, Kabardino-Balkar and Ingush Republics, Magadan Oblast, Republic of Tyva, Kamchatka Oblast, Koryak, Evenk, and Chukotka Autonomous Region	5.9 million people, or 4.0%

Note: Regions that were donors and recipients in different years are shown in italics.

revenues for extrabudgetary funds and the structure of revenues received by the extrabudgetary funds' territorial divisions are given below (Tables 2.8 and 2.9, Figures 2.10 and 2.11).

Of course, it is impossible to draw unequivocal conclusions on donors and recipients among subjects of the Federation based on data for approximately half of the regions. Nevertheless, we can say that consideration of financial flows within the framework of extrabudgetary funds does change the characteristics of the balance for individual regions to a certain degree. For instance, the Komi Republic and Vladimir Oblast change from inconsistent to consistent donors, while, on the other hand, Ulyanovsk Oblast moves from the category of consistent donors to inconsistent ones. The Republic of Chuvashia changes to an inconsistent recipient; and Krasnodar and Stavropol Territories, from inconsistent to consistent recipients.

2.4 BASIC CONCLUSIONS AND PROPOSALS

The analysis of the balance of financial flows between the Center and the regions that was conducted gives us a picture of the financial situation in subjects of the Federation that is fundamentally new in comparison with existing ideas. It is most commonly claimed (in the mass media, as well as in scientific circles) that there are only about ten donor regions in Russia. The criterion for classifying a region as a donor is that it does not receive a transfer from the Federal Fund for Financial Support of Subjects of the Federation.

Sidebar 2.2 ***Political aspects***

Political scientists fairly often try to consider a region's financial situation as a factor influencing the electorate's political behavior. To confirm or refute this hypothesis, we can compare the data obtained from calculating the balance of financial flows with the results of votes in the second round of the 1996 presidential election. Subjects of the Federation where the percentage of votes that went to the leader of the Communist Party Gennadii Zyuganov was above the national average are classified as regions with a "communist" orientation, while those where the percentage of votes that went to Boris Yeltsin was above the national average are classified as regions with a "democratic" orientation. If we compare this classification with the division of regions into donors and recipients according to the balance taking into account direct expenditures from the federal budget (see table), it turns out that there are practically no interrelations between these characteristics, though there are more "communist" regions among recipients and "democratic" ones among donors.

Sidebar 2.2 (continued)

The Population's Political Preferences in Donor and Recipient Regions

Orientation	Consistent donors	Donors in individual years	Consistent recipients
"Democratic" regions	St. Petersburg, Republic of Tatarstan, Krasnoyarsk Territory, Kaliningrad, Leningrad, Moscow, Perm, Sverdlovsk, Tomsk, Tyumen, Chelyabinsk, and Yaroslavl Oblasts, Khanty-Mansi and Yamal-Nenets Autonomous Region	Moscow, Republic of Kalmykia, Komi, Vologda and Irkutsk Oblasts, Nenets Autonomous Region	Ingush Republic, Kabardino-Balkar Republic, Republics of Karelia, Sakha (Yakutia), and Tyva, Maritime and Khabarovsk Territories, Arkhangelsk, Ivanovo, Kamchatka, Magadan, Murmansk, Novgorod, and Sakhalin Oblasts, Taimyr, Komi-Permyak, Koryak, Chukotka, and Evenk Autonomous Regions
"Communist" regions	Republic of Bashkortostan, Udmurt Republic, Belgorod, Volgograd, Voronezh, Lipetsk, Nizhegorod, Omsk, Orenburg, Samara, and Ulyanovsk Oblasts	Krasnodar and Stavropol Territories, Vladimir, Kirov, Kursk, Novosibirsk, Ryazan, Saratov, and Smolensk Oblasts	Republic of Adygeya, Altai Republic, Republics of Buryatia and Dagestan, Karachaevo-Cherkess and Marii El Republics, Republics of Mordovia, North Osetia, and Khakasia, Chuvash Republic, Altai Territory, Amur, Astrakhan, Bryansk, Kaluga, Kemerovo, Kostroma, Kurgan, Orlov, Penza, Pskov, Rostov, Tambov, Tver, Tula, and Chita Oblasts, Jewish Autonomous Oblast, Aga Buryat and Ust-Orda Buryat Autonomous Regions

Table 2.8

Donor and Recipient Regions in 1996–1998 (Balance Taking into Account Extrabudgetary Funds)

Consistent donors	Donors in individual years (indicated in parentheses)	Consistent recipients
Population 51.5 million people, or 35.0%	*Population 17.5 million people, or 11.9%*	*Population 47.9 million people, or 32.6%*
Komi Republic, St. Petersburg, Leningrad, Vladimir, Moscow, Yaroslavl, Belgorod, Voronezh, Lipetsk, Volgograd, and Samara Oblasts, Udmurt Republic, Orenburg, Perm, Sverdlovsk, Chelyabinsk, Omsk, and Tyumen Oblasts, Yamal-Nenets Autonomous Region, Krasnoyarsk Territory, Kaliningrad Oblast	Vologda (1998) and Smolensk Oblasts (1996), Chuvash Republic (1998), Kirov (1996), Kursk (1996, 1998), Saratov (1996, 1997), Ulyanovsk (1996), Novosibirsk (1996, 1998), Tomsk (1996, 1997), and Irkutsk Oblasts (1996, 1998)	Republic of Karelia, Arkhangelsk, Murmansk, Novgorod, Pskov, Bryansk, Ivanovo, Kostroma, and Tula Oblasts, Marii El Republic, Republic of Mordovia, Tambov, Astrakhan, and Penza Oblasts, Republics of Adygeya and Dagestan, Ingush and Kabardino-Balkar Republics, Krasnodar and Stavropol Territories, Rostov and Kurgan Oblasts, Altai Republic, Altai Territory, Kemerovo Oblast, Republics of Buryatia and Khakasia, Ust-Orda Buryat Autonomous Region, Chita Oblast, Aga Buryat Autonomous Region, Republic of Sakha (Yakutia), Jewish Autonomous Oblast, Maritime and Khabarovsk Territories, Amur and Kamchatka Oblasts

Table 2.9

Classification of Regions by Balance (Taking into Account Extrabudgetary Funds) Per Capita in 1998

Balance per capita	Regions	Population
Contributing more than 500 rubles/person	Yamal-Nenets Autonomous Region, Moscow Oblast, St. Petersburg, Samara, Sverdlovsk, Yaroslavl, Tyumen, Leningrad, and Perm Oblasts	27.1 million people, or 18.4%
Contributing from 250 to 500 rubles/person	Omsk, Kaliningrad, Orenburg, and *Irkutsk Oblasts*, Krasnoyarsk Territory, Volgograd, *Vologda*, and Chelyabinsk Oblasts, Udmurt Republic, Voronezh Oblast	22.8 million people, or 15.5%
Contributing from 0 to 250 rubles/person	Lipetsk and Belgorod Oblasts, Komi Republic, Vladimir and *Kursk Oblasts*, *Chuvash Republic, Novosibirsk Oblast*	11.0 million people, or 7.5%
Receiving from 0 to 250 rubles/person	*Saratov, Kirov*, and Penza Oblasts, Republic of Khakasia, *Ulyanovsk*, Arkhangelsk, *Tomsk*, and *Smolensk Oblasts*, Republic of Sakha (Yakutia), Rostov Oblast, Aga Buryat Autonomous Region, Astrakhan Oblast, Khabarovsk Territory, Marii El Republic	20.5 million people, or 13.9%
Receiving from 250 to 500 rubles/person	Krasnodar Territory, Chita Oblast, *Altai Republic*, Ivanovo, Tula, and Kostroma Oblast, Republic of Karelia	11.1 million people, or 7.5%
Receiving more than 500 rubles/person	Stavropol Territory, Murmansk and Novgorod Oblasts, Maritime Territory, Kemerovo Oblast, Altai Territory, Republics of Mordovia and Buryatia, Tambov, Kurgan, Amur, and Pskov Oblasts, Republic of Dagestan, Bryansk Oblast, Jewish Autonomous Oblast, Kabardino-Balkar and Ingush Republics, Republic. of Adygeya, Ust-Orda Buryat Autonomous Region, Kamchatka Oblast	24.4 million people, or 16.6%

Note: Regions that were donors and recipients in different years are shown in italics.

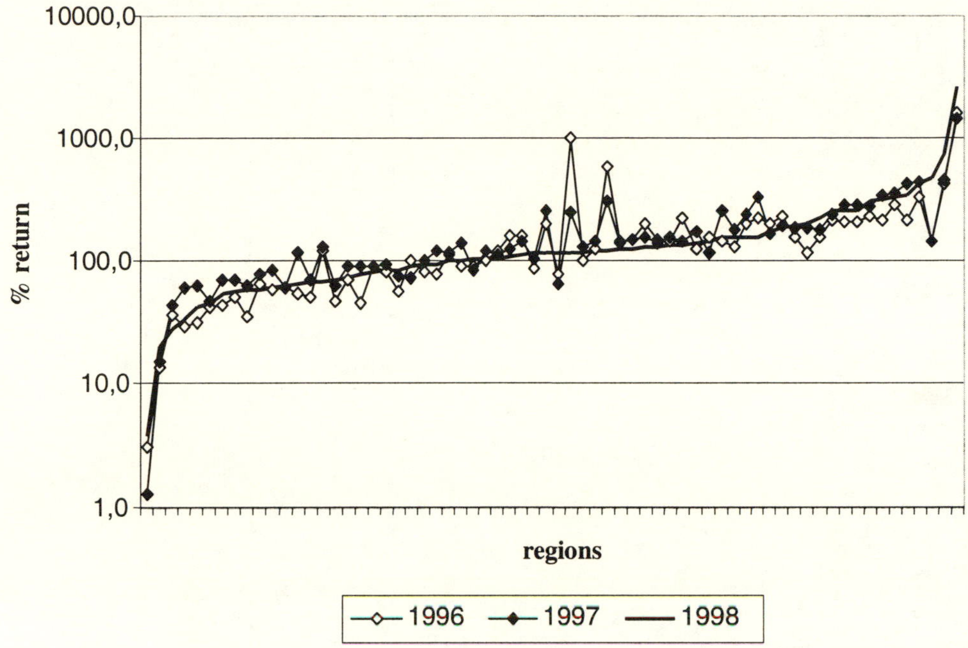

Figure 2.10. **Percentage of funds returned to the regions in 1996–1998 (balance taking into account extrabudgetary funds).** *Note:* To make the graph easier to read, a logarithmic scale is used on the y-axis.

As our research showed, the actual situation is not nearly so simple. First of all, transfers are not the only kind of financial aid that regional budgets receive; there are also subsidies, funds from mutual settlements, and budget loans. Secondly, the greater part of federal budgetary expenditures is connected to particular territories, i.e., these expenditures are made in specific regions. Direct expenditures from the federal budget are no less important for the regions' socioeconomic development than financial aid proper. Thirdly, along with budgetary funds, money from extrabudgetary funds is also redistributed among regional budgets. And finally, it is important to consider not only the amount of money that a region receives, but also the amount of revenues credited to the federal budget and to central divisions of the extrabudgetary funds from its territory, since the proportions of distribution of expenditures, as well as revenues, between levels of the budget system may change with time on the strength of legislative changes, or as a result of increased transparency of budgetary relations.

Due to the insufficiency of data on extrabudgetary funds, the main balance of financial flows considered in the research is the difference between revenues collected in a region and credited to the federal budget and the amount of financial aid to the regional budget from the federal budget plus direct expenditures from the federal budget in the region (the balance taking into account direct expenditures from the federal budget). On the basis of the results that were obtained, we can draw the conclusion that there are

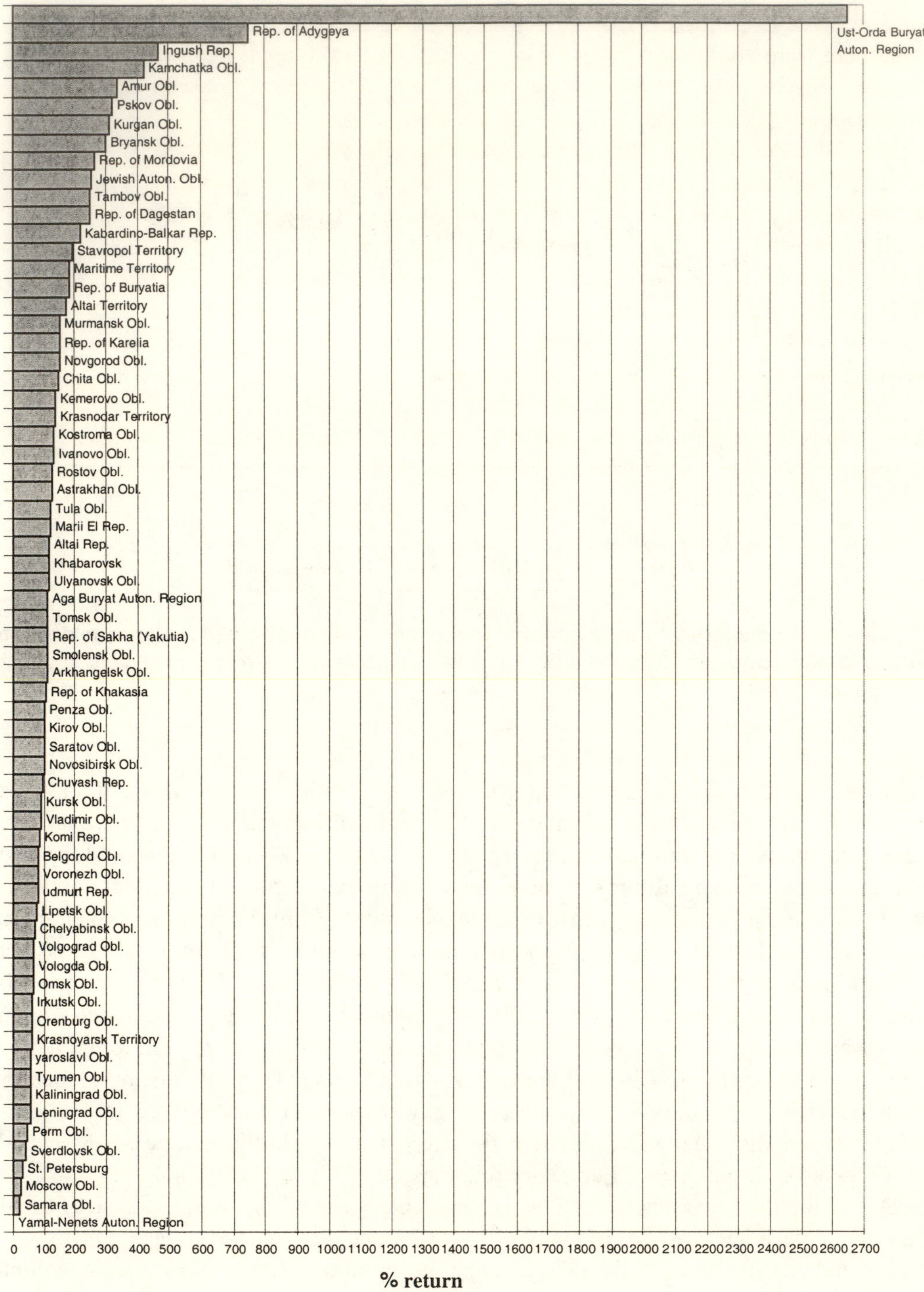

Figure 2.11. **Distribution of regions by percentage of funds returned in 1998 (balance taking into account extrabudgetary funds).**

many more relatively prosperous regions in Russia than is customarily believed. In 1996–1998, there were 26 donor regions from which the federal budget received more than it spent in their territory. Another 14 subjects of the Federation were inconsistent donors (donors in individual years).

Thus, far from just 10, there are approximately 30 relatively prosperous and stable regions. It is precisely these 30 subjects of the Federation that should be considered as the most promising from the point of view of the possibilities of economic growth and attracting investments. They are the ones that can be of the greatest interest for potential creditors and investors. Regions that are recipients, but not on a very large scale, are somewhat less reliable and attractive, but also deserving of special attention.

It is important to compile balances of financial flows in order to understand the real interrelations between the Center and the regions. So this kind of information must be widely disseminated among the people who are interested in it. Steps should also be taken to improve the system for collecting statistical data, particularly by the federal extrabudgetary funds. Further development of the Federal Treasury will be of some help in this regard.

CHAPTER 3

Territorial Structure of Tax Potential

3.1 STATEMENT OF THE PROBLEM

The amounts of taxes collected in individual subjects of the Federation, how they are divided between the federal and regional budgets, and how fully the regions' tax potential is being used are the most important factors determining the characteristics of the balance of financial flows for each region.

As we already said in Chapter 2, the revenues received by the budgets at all levels and the extrabudgetary funds are formed from tax and nontax receipts controlled by the Ministry of Taxes and Duties of Russia, taxes on foreign trade and foreign economic activity controlled by the State Customs Committee of Russia, and payments to the social extrabudgetary funds. This chapter is devoted to analysis of the territorial structure of tax payments passing through the Ministry of Taxes and Duties, since the taxes controlled by the State Customs Committee cannot be broken down by regions.

The chapter begins with a description of the procedure for analyzing the tax potential, including the distribution of taxes between the federal and regional budgets. Then it gives the characteristics of the tax collection that took place in the regions in 1996–1998. The differences between regions, how taxes are divided between the federation and the territories, the collectability and liquidity of tax receipts, the degree to which the regions' tax potential is being realized, and the structure of tax receipts are all analyzed.

3.2 PROCEDURE FOR ANALYZING TAX POTENTIAL

The basic law governing the principles of the Russian tax system throughout the 1990's was the federal law "On the principles of the tax system in the Russian Federation." It was adopted in 1991, has been repeatedly amended, and is still in effect today. However, in the future the main role in the tax sphere should be played by the Tax Code of the Russian Federation. So far, only the first part of it has gone into effect.

According to the current laws, there are federal, regional, and local taxes in Russia (Table 3.1). This division primarily reflects the delineation of legislative authority in the tax sphere. Actually, part of the federal and regional taxes, and also the local land tax, is divided in certain proportions between the budgets of all three hierarchical levels (Table 3.2).

Table 3.1

Division of Taxes into Federal, Regional, and Local According to the Tax Code of the Russian Federation

Federal taxes	Regional taxes	Local taxes
Value-added tax	Property tax for organizations	Land tax
Excise taxes on individual types of goods (services) and individual types of mineral raw material	Real-estate tax*	Property tax for individuals
Profit (income) tax for organizations	Road tax	Advertising tax
Capital income tax	Transportation tax	Inheritance or gift tax
Income tax for individuals	Sales tax	
Payments to government social extrabudgetary funds	Gaming tax	Local license fees
Stamp tax	Regional license fees	
Customs duties and customs fees		
Tax on use of mineral resources		
Mineral-resource replacement tax		
Tax on extra income from production of hydrocarbons		
Fee for the right to use wildlife and aquatic biological resources		
Forest tax		
Water tax		
Environmental tax		
Federal license fees		

* When the real-estate tax is put into effect, the property tax for organizations, the property tax for individuals, and the land tax are discontinued in the territory of that subject of the Federation.

At present, there is a "closed" list of federal, regional, and local taxes. This means that regional and local authorities do not have the right to institute taxes or fees that are not specified by the Tax Code of the Russian Federation. At the same time, the territories have been given fairly broad legislative powers in the tax sphere. So, the authorities of subjects of the Federation and local self-government can make independent decisions about introducing regional and local taxes in their territory and can set tax rates and tax incentives (within the limits established by the Tax Code of the Russian Federation), and also the procedure and deadlines for paying taxes, and how they are reported.

Thus, regional and local authorities do not have the right to raise the tax burden in a region above the limit established by federal law, but they can create the most favorable tax conditions for their population, as well as for enterprises and organizations, by setting lower tax rates, making various tax incentives available, and not introducing all of the regional and local taxes that federal legislation allows. In the 1990's, there was a period when regional and local authorities did have the right to introduce their own taxes. However, this experience was mostly negative (sidebar 3.1).

Table 3.2

Division of Taxes between the Federal and Consolidated Regional Budgets

Tax	Years	Federal budget	Consolidated regional budgets
Profit tax	1994–QI 1999	At the rate of 13%	At a rate no higher than 22%; for banks, credit institutions, insurance organizations, exchanges, brokerage houses, and other enterprises, on profit received from intermediary organizations and transactions at a rate no higher than 30%
	since QI 1999	At the rate of 11%	At rates of 19% and 27%, respectively
Value-added tax (with the exception of VAT on imported goods, and also precious metals and gems turned over to the State Precious-Metals and Gems Fund and sold from it)	1994–QI 1999	75%	25%
	since QI 1999	85%	15%
Income tax	1994, 1997–1999	0%	100%
	1995–1996	10%	90%
Excise taxes on drinking alcohol, vodka, and liquor	1994–1999	50%	50%
All other excise taxes (with the exception of excise taxes on imported goods, oil, gas, coal, gasoline, and automobiles)	1994–1999	0%	100%
Tax on purchase of foreign currency	1997	100%	0%
	1998–1999	60%	40%
Land tax	1994–1995	20%	20% to the regional budgets proper and 60% to local budgets
	1996–1999	30%	20% to the regional budgets proper and 50% to local budgets
Special tax paid by enterprises, institutions, and organizations for financial support of the most important industries in the Russian Federation to ensure their stable operation	1994	80%	20%
	1995–1996	67%	33%
Payments for use of natural resources	1994–1999	Individual standards for different types of payments	

Sidebar 3.1 ***The experience of Russian regions' tax "freedom"***

The decree of the President of the Russian Federation No. 2268, signed on December 22, 1993, "On formation of the republican budget of the Russian Federation and interrelations with the budgets of subjects of the Russian Federation in 1994," (which had the status of federal law at that time), gave regional and local authorities the right to introduce taxes beyond the limits of the list established by the federal law "On the principles of the tax system of the Russian Federation." As a result, the number of taxes in effect in Russia began to rise rapidly. By some estimates, their number had reached 200 by 1996.

Tax "freedom" led to a deterioration of the tax climate. Most local taxes were "annoying" and did not even justify the expense of collecting them. Highly specific tax systems based on "duplication" of federal taxes were created in some regions.

Here is an excerpt from the law of Belgorod Oblast dated January 31, 1995, "On the operation of oblast and local taxes and fees in the territory of the oblast in 1995":

"Article 1.

As of January 1, 1995, the following oblast taxes and fees shall be in effect in the oblast's territory:

- tax for the needs of educational institutions in the amount of 1% of enterprises' and organizations' payroll fund (except for enterprises and organizations financed from the budget)
- tax on the sale in the oblast's territory of individual food products produced in countries of the near and far abroad, in the following amounts:

Food product	**Fee in % of supplier's selling price**
Sausage and sausage goods	15
Vodka, alcohol	20
Sugar	20
Poultry	30

- tax in the amount of 10% of banks' gross profit, to be taken into account in figuring the federal profit tax
- tax on excess aggregate income received by individuals, in the following amount:

Amount of income	**Tax in % of income**
From 20 to 40 times the minimum wage	10
From 40 to 60 times	15
From 60 to 80 times	20
From 80 to 100 times	30
From 100 times or more	40

- tax on the sale of gasoline in the amount of 20 rubles per liter
- tax on the sale of electric power in the amount of 3 rubles per 1 kW×hr
- tax in the amount of 3% of commercial markup added to the free selling price of vodka, drinking alcohol, liquor, cognac, champagne, and wine
- tax on the sale of livestock outside the oblast in the amount of 10% of the value of the livestock sold (not including VAT or special tax), whether raised by the seller or purchased, to be stipulated in the delivery contract
- oblast license and registration fees."

In conditions of tax "freedom," various "targeted" taxes and fees appeared in a number of regions, which were intended to subsidize a particular industry (mostly agriculture). The most alarming thing was the widespread introduction of taxes and duties on bringing goods into or out of the region, in violation of Article 74 of the Constitution of the Russian Federation, which prohibits any restriction on the movement of goods, services, or financial assets within the country.

For the most part, taxes and duties of this sort were imposed on alcoholic products brought into the region (with the "shadow" market in such products flourishing, the federal government looked the other way and did not prevent regional authorities from doing this). However, there were examples of even more egregious regional "customs duties." A 10% tax on sales of all excisable goods brought into the republic was introduced in Mordovia in 1996, and duties on bringing in chicken legs were established in Orlov and Sverdlovsk Oblasts.

On August 18, 1996, Boris Yeltsin signed decree No. 1214 "On recognizing as null and void paragraph 7 of the decree of the President of the Russian Federation of December 22, 1993, No. 2268, 'On formation of the republican budget of the Russian Federation and interrelations with the budgets of subjects of the Russian Federation in 1994'," which proposed that as of January 1, 1997, regional and local authorities repeal taxes and duties not specified by federal law. This step was very poorly received by the subjects of the Federation. The Komi Republic, Altai Territory, and Vladimir, Volgograd, and Irkutsk Oblasts tried to dispute in the Constitutional Court of the Russian Federation the right of federal authorities to limit the list of regional and local taxes. However, the court upheld the constitutionality of the relevant rule of the federal law "On the principles of the tax system in the Russian Federation," which gives the President this right.

Nevertheless, taxes not specified by this federal law or by the Tax Code of the Russian Federation are still in effect in places. In order to overcome the existing situation, the government of the Russian Federation must take a stricter position in relation to regional "tax-making."

The balance of financial flows between the Center and the regions is determined by the amount of taxes collected in the regions and how they are divided between the federal and regional budgets. However, to understand the reasons for disproportions between regions in these indices and to get a full idea of the territorial structure of tax potential a number of other parameters must also be taken into account. These include the collectability and liquidity of tax payments, differences in the tax burden, and the structure of tax receipts.

The collectability of tax payments is one indication of how fully a region's tax potential is being used. It can be characterized by the fulfillment of the plan for collecting tax receipts, as well as the percent increase in tax arrears in relation to accrued taxes.

The portion of various kinds of nonmonetary forms of budget execution (setoffs, promissory notes, etc.) characterizes the liquidity of tax payments. It is not directly reflected in the financial balance, but it primarily affects the prospects of an increase or decrease in the collectability of taxes. A higher portion of "noncash" receipts also creates additional problems for regional budgets in the process of funding expenditures, which may indirectly affect how much financial aid is provided from the federal budget.

The prospects of change in the collectability of taxes are also affected by the structure of tax receipts in a region: the more diversified it is with respect to different types of taxes, as well as different industries, the more stable the tax payments will be.

Evaluation of the tax burden is important from two points of view. First of all, it characterizes the objectivity of the prevailing balance of financial flows (how fully the regions' tax potential is used determines the degree to which regional budgets depend on assistance from the federal budget). Secondly, it determines the possibility of increasing the collection of tax payments in the future (the more fully the tax potential is being used, the less likely it is that the collectability of taxes will rise).

3.3 THE REGIONS' TAX POTENTIAL IN 1996–1998

3.3.1 Differences between regions in per capita tax revenues

Differences between regions in the amounts of tax revenues per capita are determined by a number of factors. The first one is the significant difference in the level of prices between subjects of the Federation. This factor has a considerable effect on the regional structure of the federal budget's tax revenues. However, theoretically it should not affect the balance indices. In regions where revenues are higher due to higher prices, expenditures from the federal budget, as well as the regional budget, are also higher. Therefore, we used the amount of per capita tax receipts adjusted for regional values of the subsistence level as the main index in this research. At present, the subsistence level is the most widely accepted indicator for taking into account differences in regional price levels.

The research showed that the differences between regions in per capita tax revenues are enormous, even when adjusted for the subsistence minimum (Figure 3.1 and Map 5).

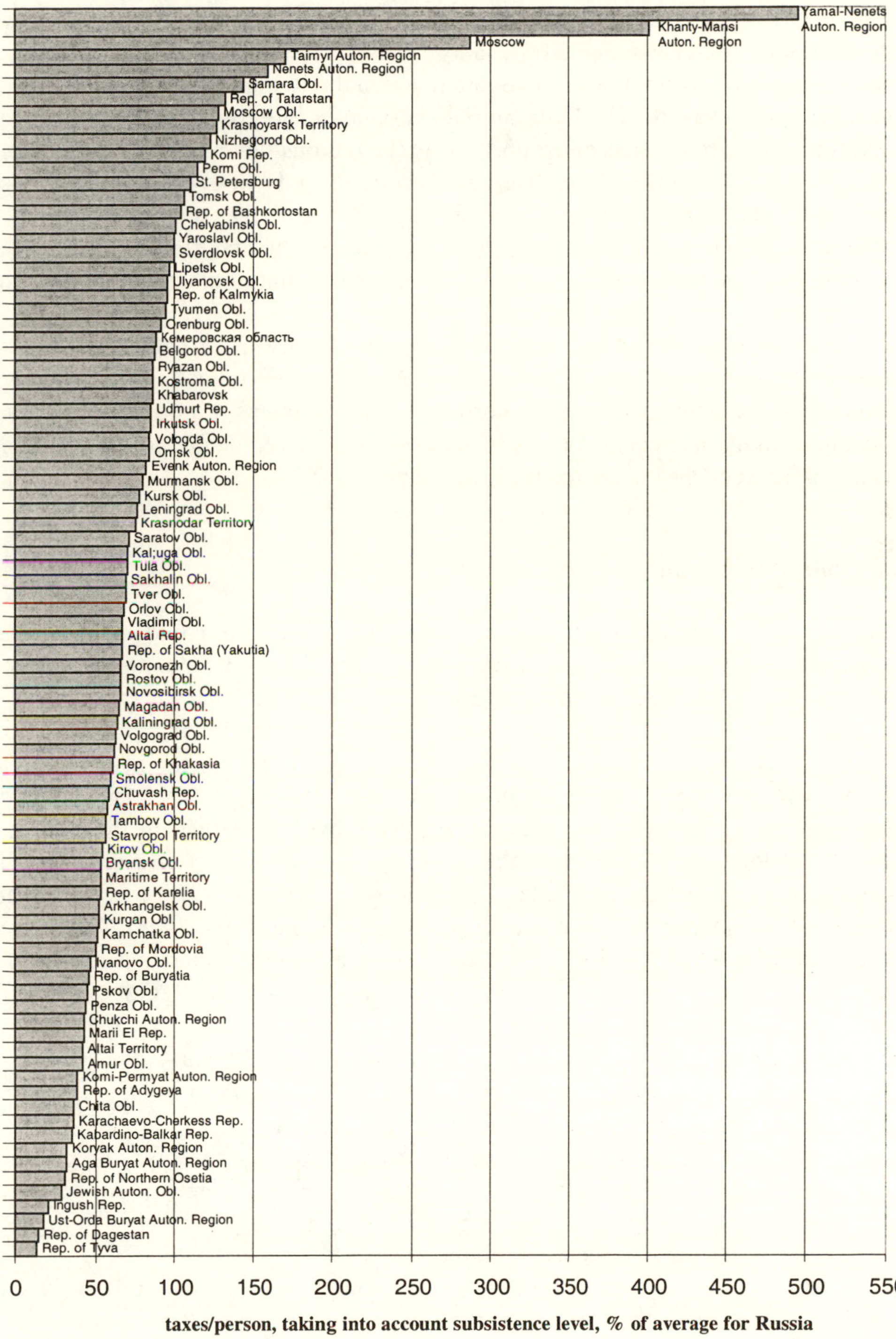
Yamal-Nenets Auton. Region
Khanty-Mansi Auton. Region
Moscow
Taimyr Auton. Region
Nenets Auton. Region
Samara Obl.
Rep. of Tatarstan
Moscow Obl.
Krasnoyarsk Territory
Nizhegorod Obl.
Komi Rep.
Perm Obl.
St. Petersburg
Tomsk Obl.
Rep. of Bashkortostan
Chelyabinsk Obl.
Yaroslavl Obl.
Sverdlovsk Obl.
Lipetsk Obl.
Ulyanovsk Obl.
Rep. of Kalmykia
Tyumen Obl.
Orenburg Obl.
Кемеровская область
Belgorod Obl.
Ryazan Obl.
Kostroma Obl.
Khabarovsk
Udmurt Rep.
Irkutsk Obl.
Vologda Obl.
Omsk Obl.
Evenk Auton. Region
Murmansk Obl.
Kursk Obl.
Leningrad Obl.
Krasnodar Territory
Saratov Obl.
Kal;uga Obl.
Tula Obl.
Sakhalin Obl.
Tver Obl.
Orlov Obl.
Vladimir Obl.
Altai Rep.
Rep. of Sakha (Yakutia)
Voronezh Obl.
Rostov Obl.
Novosibirsk Obl.
Magadan Obl.
Kaliningrad Obl.
Volgograd Obl.
Novgorod Obl.
Rep. of Khakasia
Smolensk Obl.
Chuvash Rep.
Astrakhan Obl.
Tambov Obl.
Stavropol Territory
Kirov Obl.
Bryansk Obl.
Maritime Territory
Rep. of Karelia
Arkhangelsk Obl.
Kurgan Obl.
Kamchatka Obl.
Rep. of Mordovia
Ivanovo Obl.
Rep. of Buryatia
Pskov Obl.
Penza Obl.
Chukchi Auton. Region
Marii El Rep.
Altai Territory
Amur Obl.
Komi-Permyat Auton. Region
Rep. of Adygeya
Chita Obl.
Karachaevo-Cherkess Rep.
Kabardino-Balkar Rep.
Koryak Auton. Region
Aga Buryat Auton. Region
Rep. of Northern Osetia
Jewish Auton. Obl.
Ingush Rep.
Ust-Orda Buryat Auton. Region
Rep. of Dagestan
Rep. of Tyva
0 50 100 150 200 250 300 350 400 450 500 550
taxes/person, taking into account subsistence level, % of average for Russia

Figure 3.1. **Distribution of regions by amount of tax receipts per capita, adjusted for the subsistence level in 1998.**

This index reaches its maximum values in the Yamal-Nenets Autonomous Region (495.5% of the national average), the Khanty-Mansi Autonomous Region (400.7%), and Moscow (288.0%). Its minimum values are noted in the Republics of Tyva (13.9%) and Dagestan (14.6%), and the Ust-Orda Buryat Autonomous Region (17.7%). The primary reason for such differences is disproportions in the regions' level of economic development. Large regions with a highly diversified economy and a high level of development of the service sphere are in the most favorable position, as well as regions that specialize in production of natural resources. The most adverse situation takes place in subjects of the Federation with a low level of industrial development and a higher than normal share of agriculture.

Another factor determining differences between regions in per capita tax revenues, especially those going to the regional budgets, is differences in tax laws.

It must also be noted that the disproportions between regions in amounts of per capita tax receipts, taking into account the subsistence level, are very stable (the coefficient of correlation between the values for 1997 and 1998 is 0.97).

3.3.2 Collectability and liquidity

Indices of the fulfillment of the plan for tax collection to the federal budget are available for analyzing the collectability of tax receipts. For Russia as a whole, the target for tax collection was 91% fulfilled in 1997 and 117% in 1998. Such an increase in the collectability of taxes was undoubtedly due to the surge of inflation in the second half of 1998, which was not taken into account in the tax target. The collectability of taxes also rose in most regions. In many of them, underfulfillment of the target turned to overfulfillment (in the Altai Republic, it was 61% over the target; in the rest of the regions it did not exceed 50%). Nevertheless, the plan for tax collection was not fulfilled in 39 subjects of the Federation (Table 3.3). On the other hand, in 1997 it was overfulfilled in seven of them (Moscow, Kalmykia, Dagestan, Tyva, Samara and Perm Oblasts, and the Aga Buryat Autonomous Region). Actual tax collection amounted to just 42% of the target that was set in Tatarstan, 44% in the Koryak Autonomous Region, and 52% is Bashkiria.

For the most part, the differences between regions in fulfillment of the plan for tax collection to the federal budget can be considered stable. The differences in the percent increase in tax arrears in relation to accrued taxes (the sum of tax arrears and taxes actually collected), on the other hand, are not characterized by stability. The instability of this index is illustrated in Figure 3.2. In individual regions, there was either a reduction or an increase in tax arrears in the years that were analyzed. In our view, it makes no sense to classify the regions according to this index.

The portion of "cash" money in the regional budgets' revenues is a relatively stable index. Since the values of this index for 1998 had not come out by the time the research was conducted, Table 3.4 classifies the regions according to averaged data from 1996 through the first nine months of 1998.

Table 3.3

Classification of Regions by Degree of Fulfillment of the Target for Tax Collection to the Federal Budget

Fulfillment of target	Regions	Population
Overfulfilled by more than 25%	Altai Republic, Evenk and Komi-Permyat Autonomous Region, Moscow, Vladimir, and Ryazan Oblasts, Krasnodar Territory, Stavropol Territory, Irkutsk and Rostov Oblasts, St. Petersburg, Republic of North Osetia, Magadan and Chita Oblasts	31.5 million people, or 21.4%
Overfulfilled by 10–25%	Murmansk and Vologda Oblast, Republic of Khakasia, Novosibirsk Oblast, Republic of Buryatia, Udmurt Republic, Astrakhan Oblast, Khabarovsk Territory, Arkhangelsk and Novgorod Oblasts, Republic of Mordovia, Belgorod, Tula, Voronezh, Leningrad, and Sverdlovsk Oblasts, Altai Territory, Kursk Oblast, Kaliningrad Oblast, Nenets Autonomous Region, Republic of Karelia, Ingush Republic	32.3 million people, or 21.9%
Overfulfilled by less than 10%	Kirov, Kaluga, Yaroslavl, Tver, Ivanovo, Volgograd, Ulyanovsk, Amur, Saratov, and Sakhalin Oblasts, Maritime Territory, Tambov and Kemerovo Oblast	22.1 million people, or 15.0%
Underfulfilled by less than 10%	Moscow, Chuvash Republic, Krasnoyarsk Territory, Jewish Autonomous Oblast, Smolensk, Orlov, Kamchatka, and Bryansk Oblasts, Karachaevo-Cherkess Republic, Kostroma Oblast, Aga Buryat Autonomous Region, Nizhegorod, Pskov, and Penza Oblasts	24.5 million people, or 16.6%
Underfulfilled by 10–20%	Orenburg and Perm Oblasts, Republics of Dagestan and Adygeya, Marii El Republic, Lipetsk, Chelyabinsk, and Omsk Oblasts, Taimyr and Yamal-Nenets Autonomous Region, Republic of Sakha (Yakutia), Tyumen Oblast, Kabardino-Balkar Republic, Kurgan Oblast	20.3 million people, or 13.8%
Underfulfilled by more than 20%	Republic of Kalmykia, Ust-Orda Buryat Autonomous Region, Samara Oblast, Republic of Tyva, Tomsk Oblast, Komi Republic, Khanty-Mansi and Chukotka Autonomous Region, Republic of Bashkortostan, Koryak Autonomous Region, Republic of Tatarstan	15.7 million people, or 10.7%

The differences between regions in these indices of collectability and liquidity are mostly of a random nature and, in our view, are hard to explain (particularly in regard to tax arrears). Both highly developed and poorly developed regions are distinguished by high or low collectability and liquidity. The research also did not establish any relationship between the indices of collectability and liquidity themselves.

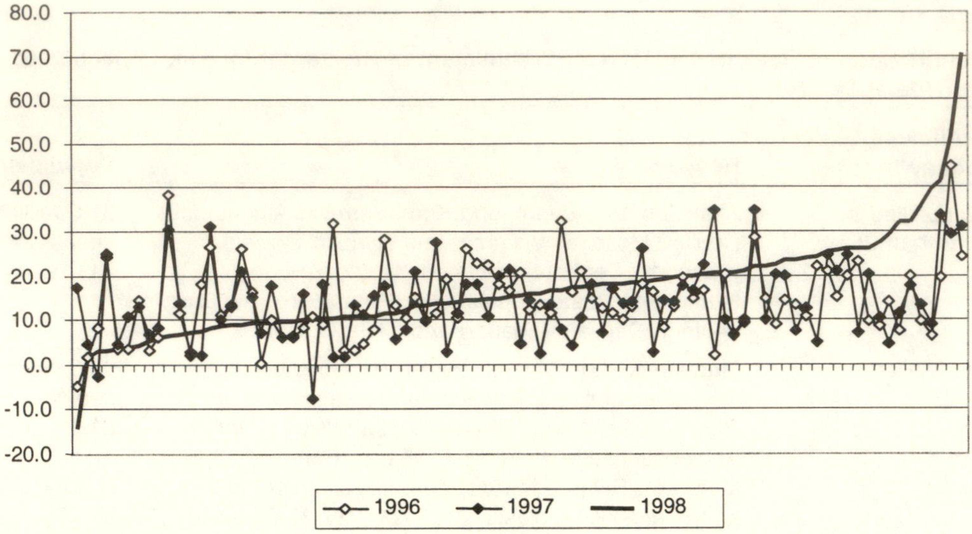

Figure 3.2. **Percent increase in tax arrears in relation to accrued taxes in 1996–1998 (not including the Taimyr Autonomous Region).**

3.3.3 Tax burden

How fully a region's tax potential is being used has enormous significance for assessing the prospects for change in the region's financial situation. However, such an assessment does present a certain difficulty, primarily due to the lack of an adequate index characterizing the taxable base. Theoretically, it could be properly represented by the gross regional product (GRP). The portion of tax receipts in the gross product is a generally accepted index reflecting differences between territories (countries, regions) in the tax burden.

However, a number of problems are encountered in trying to use the index of gross regional product (especially in Russia). First of all, the tax burden in relation to the gross regional product depends on how it is structured. Secondly, the data on this index are not sufficiently up to date at present (at the time when the research was conducted, data were available only through 1997). And thirdly, there are doubts about the reliability of this index's calculation.

A classification of regions according to the ratio of tax receipts to gross regional product in 1997 is presented in Table 3.5 and on Map 6. While average value of this index for Russia was 25.7%, its maximum values took place in Tyumen Oblast (including the autonomous regions), where it was 34.8%; Moscow, 39.9%; and Kalmykia, 52.7%. In the latter case, and also in Ingushetia, this is connected with the existence of so-called offshore zones in the territory of these republics.

There are both objective and subjective reasons for the differences between regions in the tax burden in relation to the gross regional product. Among the former, we can mention the structure of the gross regional product (Figure 3.3), while the latter include the tax

Table 3.4

Classification of Regions According to Percentage of "Cash" Money in Taxes Averaged for 1996 through the First Nine Months of 1998

Portion of "cash" money in taxes	Regions	Population
More than 70%	Moscow, Ingush Republic, St. Petersburg, Koryak Autonomous Region, Moscow Oblast, Nenets and Taimyr Autonomous Regions, Kaliningrad Oblast, Krasnodar Territory, Tula Oblast, Aga Buryat Autonomous Region, Lipetsk Oblast	29.5 million people, or 20.1%
60–70%	Novgorod and Kaluga Oblasts, Altai Republic, Astrakhan and Samara Oblasts, Karachaevo-Cherkess Republic, Stavropol Territory, Volgograd Oblast	12.2 million people, or 8.3%
50–60%	Orlov Oblast, Republics of Tyva, Adygeya, and North Osetia, Belgorod and Smolensk Oblasts, Republic of Karelia, Pskov, Nizhegorod, and Leningrad Oblasts, Republic of Bashkortostan, Bryansk, Murmansk, Irkutsk, Sakhalin, and Rostov Oblasts, Republic of Kalmykia, Maritime and Khabarovsk Territories, Tver, Tomsk, Perm, and Ryazan Oblasts, Komi-Permyat Autonomous Region	37.3 million people, or 25.3%
40–50%	Tyumen, Penza, Kamchatka, Vladimir, and Yaroslavl Oblasts, Ust-Orda Buryat Autonomous Region, Voronezh, Vologda, Saratov, Novosibirsk, Kirov, and Sverdlovsk Oblasts, Republic of Tatarstan, Jewish Autonomous Oblast, Tambov and Orenburg Oblasts, Republic of Dagestan, Krasnoyarsk Territory, Chelyabinsk, Amur, and Magadan Oblasts, Republic of Mordovia, Udmurt Republic, Khanty-Mansi Autonomous Region	43.5 million people, or 29.6%
Less than 40%	Ivanovo, Chita, and Kostroma Oblasts, Republic of Sakha (Yakutia), Kabardino-Balkar Republic, Omsk Oblast, Marii El and Komi Republics, Kursk, Kemerovo, Arkhangelsk, Ulyanovsk, and Kurgan Oblasts, Republic of Buryatia, Altai Territory, Republic of Khakasia, Chuvash Republic, Chukotka, Yamal-Nenets, and Evenk Autonomous Regions	23.7 million people, or 16.2%

policy followed by regional and local authorities. In the final analysis, the amount of the tax burden in each specific region is determined by a whole set of quite diverse factors.

Instead of the gross regional product, a number of other indices can be used to evaluate the tax burden in a region (industrial output, profit, wages). These indices are more precise than the gross regional product. They do give more arbitrary evaluations of how fully the tax potential is being used, but this does not interfere with using them for comparison with the tax burden in relation to the gross regional product.

Table 3.5

Classification of Regions According to Ratio of Tax Receipts to Gross Regional Product

Ratio of tax receipts to GRP	Regions	Population
10–15%	Republic of Dagestan, Amur Oblast, Republic of Tyva, Irkutsk Oblast	6.2 million people, or 4.2%
17–17.5%	Republic of Buryatia, Kabardino-Balkar Republic, Stavropol Territory, Chita Oblast, Republic of Karelia, Marii El Republic, Pskov, Kursk, Voronezh, and Smolensk Oblasts, Khabarovsk Territory	14.7 million people, or 10.0%
17.5–20%	Altai Territory, Republic of Khakasia, Kurgan, Belgorod, Kamchatka, Kirov, and Vologda Oblasts, Krasnodar Territory, Karachaevo-Cherkess Republic, Arkhangelsk, Astrakhan, Magadan, and Bryansk Oblasts, Republic of Mordovia, Volgograd, Tver, Tambov, Ivanovo, and Orlov Oblasts, Republic of North Osetia, Penza, Rostov, Ulyanovsk, Saratov, and Novgorod Oblasts, Republic of Bashkortostan, Novosibirsk Oblast	46.1 million people, or 31.3%
20–22.5%	Tula Oblast, Republic of Sakha (Yakutia), Lipetsk and Orenburg Oblast, Maritime Territory, Omsk, Kaluga, Murmansk, and Vladimir Oblasts, Krasnoyarsk Territory, Kostroma and Ryazan Oblasts, Altai Republic, Kemerovo and Chelyabinsk Oblast	26.5 million people, or 18.0%
22.5–25%	Yaroslavl Oblast, Chuvash Republic, Kaliningrad and Sakhalin Oblasts, Republic of Adygeya, Udmurt Republic, Leningrad and Sverdlovsk Oblasts, Komi Republic, Perm Oblast	16.9 million people, or 11.5%
More than 25%	Republic of Tatarstan, Nizhegorod Oblast, Ingush Republic, Moscow Oblast, St. Petersburg, Samara and Tomsk Oblasts, Chukotka Autonomous Region, Tyumen Oblast, Moscow, Republic of Kalmykia	35.7 million people, or 24.3%

Note: There are no regions in the interval of 15–17%.

The ratio of tax receipts to the accrued payroll fund was calculated as such an index in this research (Table 3.6). Its average value for Russia was 96.2%. The maximum values took place in Moscow (206.5%), the Khanty-Mansi (173.3%) and Yamal-Nenets Autonomous Regions (143.1%), and Kalmykia (136.5%); the minimum was in the Republic of Tyva (28.8%).

The calculations showed that there is a fairly close relationship between the ratios of tax receipts to the payroll fund and tax receipts to the gross regional product. The coefficient of correlation between them was 0.80 (Figure 3.4).

The research showed that the tax burden in relation to the payroll fund, as it is in relation to the gross regional product, is higher than the national average in the most

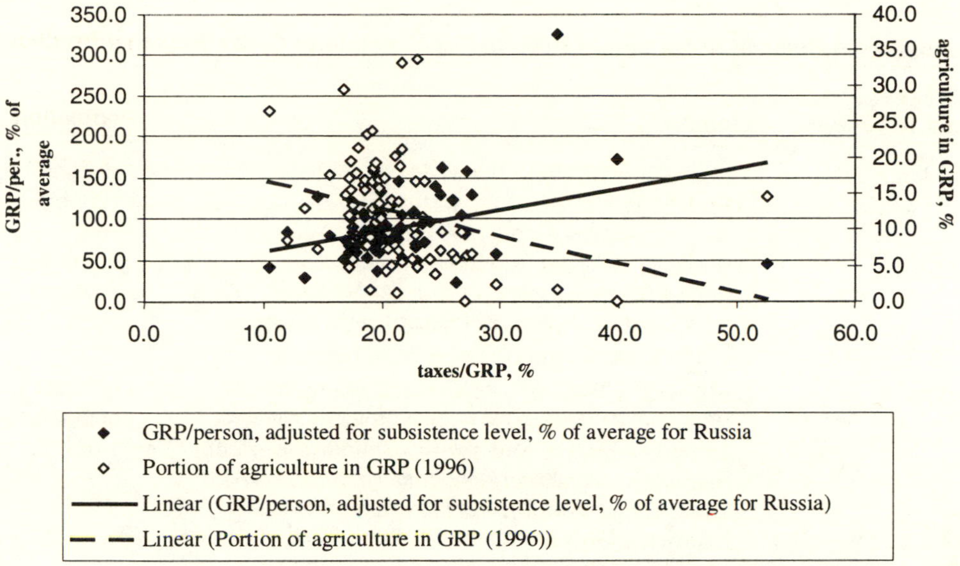

Figure 3.3. **Relationship of tax burden in 1997 to per capita GRP and portion of agriculture in GRP**

economically developed regions. This is also confirmed by calculating the coefficient of correlation. Between tax receipts per capita, taking into account the subsistence minimum, and the tax burden in relation to the gross regional product it is equal to 0.62; and between the tax receipts and the tax burden in relation to the payroll fund, 0.75. The values of the coefficients of correlation between the indices of the tax burden and the per capita values of the gross regional product and the accrued payroll fund are 0.4 and 0.9, respectively.

3.3.4. Structure of tax receipts

Examining the structure of tax receipts (Figure 3.5) is exceptionally important from the point of view of assessing the prospects for change in the amounts of tax collection in the future. The more diversified the structure of tax receipts is in a region (with respect to different types of taxes, as well as different industries), the more likely it is that tax receipts will be stable in the future.

The structure of tax receipts with respect to different types of taxes differs noticeably in various regions of the country. So, the average portion of the value-added tax for Russia as a whole is 27.7%. Its maximum portion is 45.3% in Ingushetia, and the minimum is 11.0% in the Koryak Autonomous Region. The maximum and minimum portions of the profit tax are 56.3% (Kalmykia) and 3.0% (the Nenets Autonomous Region), with an average of 20.2%. The figures for the income tax are 36.6% (Tyva) and 8.1%

Table 3.6

Classification of Regions by Ratio of Tax Receipts to Payroll Fund in 1997

Ratio of tax receipts to payroll fund	Regions	Population
Less than 50%	Republic of Tyva, Ust-Orda Buryat Autonomous Region, Kamchatka Oblast, Koryak Autonomous Region, Jewish Autonomous Oblast, Amur Oblast, Republic of Dagestan, Evenk Autonomous Region, Chita Oblast, Republic of Karelia, Magadan Oblast, Republic of Buryatia, Komi-Permyat Autonomous Region	7.6 million people, or 5.2%
50–65%	Arkhangelsk and Irkutsk Oblasts, Altai Territory, Republic of Sakha (Yakutia), Kurgan Oblast, Chukotka Autonomous Region, Murmansk Oblast, Republic of Khakasia, Maritime Territory, Ivanovo Oblast, Republic of North Osetia, Vologda and Tula Oblasts, Khabarovsk Territory, Pskov Oblast, Marii El Republic, Sakhalin Oblast, Tambov Oblast, Altai Republic, Rostov and Novgorod Oblasts	28.2 million people, or 19.2%
65–75%	Vladimir and Kirov Oblasts, Krasnoyarsk Territory, Republic of Adygeya, Kabardino-Balkar Republic, Penza and Kemerovo Oblasts, Karachaevo-Cherkess Republic, Kaluga, and Smolensk Oblasts, Krasnodar Territory, Taimyr Autonomous Region, Voronezh, Belgorod, Orlov, Kursk, Astrakhan, Kaliningrad, Tver, Ulyanovsk, Lipetsk, and Bryansk Oblasts, Aga Buryat Autonomous Region, Volgograd Oblast, Stavropol Territory	39.4 million people, or 26.8%
75–95%	Republic of Mordovia, Novosibirsk, Chelyabinsk, and Leningrad Oblasts, Chuvash Republic, Omsk and Orenburg Oblasts, St. Petersburg, Kostroma Oblast, Republic of Bashkortostan, Udmurt Republic, Saratov, Ryazan, Yaroslavl, and Perm Oblasts	40.2 million people, or 27.3%
More than 95%	Tyumen and Nizhegorod Oblasts, Republic of Tatarstan, Nenets Autonomous Region, Tomsk Oblast, Ingush Republic, Moscow and Samara Oblasts, Republic of Kalmykia, Yamal-Nenets and Khanty-Mansi Autonomous Regions, Moscow	730.9 million people, or 21.0%

(Aga Buryat Autonomous Region), respectively, with an average of 14.7%. For excise taxes, 28.8% (Moscow Oblast) and zero (Komi-Permyat Autonomous Region), with an average of 12.6%. And for the property tax for enterprises, 26.2% (Taimyr Autonomous Region) and 1.4% (Kalmykia), with an average of 9.4%. In individual regions, other taxes are becoming quite important. For instance, in the Nenets Autonomous Region the portion of payments for use of mineral resources is 28.8% (with an average portion of

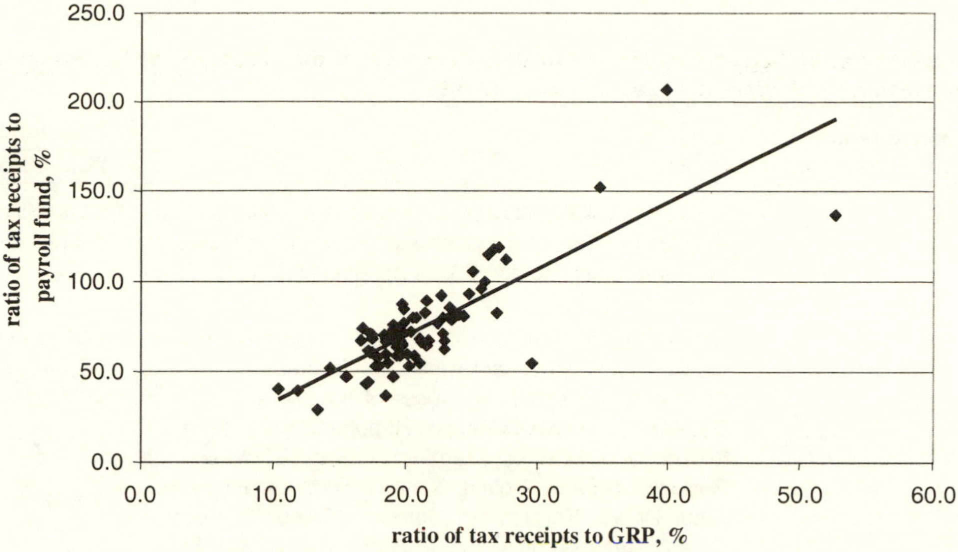

Figure 3.4. **Tax burden in relation to GRP and payroll fund in 1997.**

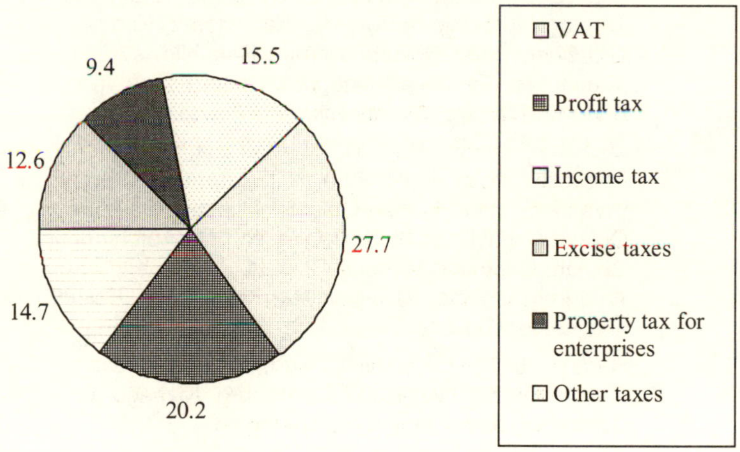

Figure 3.5. **Structure of tax receipts in Russia in 1998.**

3% for Russia); in the Ust-Orda Buryat Autonomous Region, the portion of the land tax reaches 8.7% (average 2.3%); and in Kurgan Oblast, targeted taxes for supporting the police amount to 8.4% (average 0.2%).

Table 3.7 presents a classification of regions by degree of diversification of the structure of tax receipts with respect to different types of taxes (the variance index was calculated on the basis of 25 separate taxes or groups of taxes). As in the case of collectability and liquidity, the differences between regions in this index are hard to explain, in our

Table 3.7

Classification of Regions by Degree of Diversification of the Structure of Tax Receipts with Respect to Different Types of Taxes in 1998

Variance (with respect to taxes)	Regions	Population
40–50	Omsk Oblast, Khanty-Mansi Autonomous Region, Republic of Tatarstan, Lipetsk and Orenburg Oblasts, Komi Republic, Belgorod Oblast, Republic of Sakha (Yakutia)	14.4 million people, or 9.8%
50–55	Novgorod, Tyumen, and Leningrad Oblasts, Altai Territory, Kurgan Oblast, Ust-Orda Buryat Autonomous Region, Republics of Karelia and Dagestan, Astrakhan Oblast, Republic of Mordovia, Krasnoyarsk Territory, Magadan Oblast, Chuvash Republic, Saratov Oblast, Kabardino-Balkar Republic, Amur Oblast, Karachaevo-Cherkess Republic, Perm Oblast, Republic of Adygeya, Arkhangelsk Oblast	26.8 million people, or 18.3%
55–60	Kemerovo and Sakhalin Oblasts, Republic of Bashkortostan, Tomsk, Smolensk, and Tambov Oblasts, Stavropol Territory, Komi-Permyat, Taimyr, and Yamal-Nenets Autonomous Regions, Krasnodar Territory, Republic of Buryatia, Kaliningrad, Kirov, and Chelyabinsk Oblasts, Udmurt Republic, Khabarovsk Territory, Volgograd, Chita, Pskov, Tula, Bryansk, Ivanovo, Sverdlovsk, and Penza Oblasts	45.6 million people, or 31.0%
60–70	Maritime Territory, Republic of Khakasia, Marii El Republic, Irkutsk, Tver, Ryazan, Kostroma, Kursk, Ulyanovsk, and Moscow Oblasts, Moscow, Samara Oblast, Republic of North Osetia, Nenets Autonomous Region, Orlov and Vladimir Oblasts, Jewish Autonomous Oblast, Novosibirsk, Kamchatka, Rostov, and Kaluga Oblasts	43.3 million people, or 29.5%
70–80	Republic of Tyva, Yaroslavl, Murmansk, Vologda, and Voronezh Oblasts, St. Petersburg, Nizhegorod Oblast, Chukotka Autonomous Region	15.1 million people, or 10.3%
More than 80	Evenk and Koryak Autonomous Region, Altai and Ingush Republics, Aga Buryat Autonomous Region, Republic of Kalmykia	9.6 million people, or 0.7%

Note: the higher the variance, the less diversified the structure of tax receipts is.

view. We should just note that a higher than normal portion of individual taxes in the total amount of them is characteristic primarily of economically poorly developed regions with slight diversification of the economy.

Like the structure with respect to different types of taxes, the differences between regions in the industry structure of tax receipts (Table 3.8) are connected, to a certain

Table 3.8

Industry Structure of Tax Receipts in 1998 (%)

Indices	Average for Russia	Maximum	Regions with maximum value
Industry	41.0	77.3	Yamal-Nenets Autonomous Region
		74.7	Khanty-Mansi Autonomous Region
including:			
power generation	5.7	32.2	Magadan Oblast
fuel industry	11.7	75.5	Yamal-Nenets Autonomous Region
		70.7	Khanty-Mansi Autonomous Region
ferrous and nonferrous metallurgy	3.6	41.2	Republic of Sakha (Yakutia)
chemical and petrochemical industry	1.5	15.2	Tomsk Oblast
machine building and metalworking	6.4	29.4	Samara Oblast
forest, woodworking, and paper and pulp	1.1	17.7	Republic of Karelia
construction materials	1.2	8.9	Karachaevo-Cherkess Republic
light industry	0.6	12.4	Ivanovo Oblast
food industry	7.5	34.0	Kabardino-Balkar Republic
Agriculture	1.2	21.8	Ust-Orda Buryat Autonomous Region
Transportation	14.6	25.1	Moscow
including:			
railroads	3.6	18.0	Yaroslavl Oblast
pipelines	7.9	21.3	Moscow
Communications	3.2	7.4	Republic of North Osetia
Construction	6.6	32.6	Republic of Ingushetia
Trade and food service	9.1	79.3	Aga Buryat Autonomous Region
		60.0	Altai Republic
Supply and sales of material and equipment	1.9	13.3	Republic of Kalmykia
Real-estate transactions	2.8	11.4	Moscow
Housing and utilities	2.8	16.9	Kostroma Oblast
Finance, credit, insurance, and pension coverage	4.1	19.7	Republic of Kalmykia
including banking	3.7	18.5	Republic of Kalmykia

Table 3.9

Classification of Regions by Degree of Diversification of the Industry Structure of Tax Receipts in 1998

Variance	Regions	Population
Less than 15	Evenk Autonomous Region, Republic of Tyva, Maritime and Khabarovsk Territories, Kaliningrad, Novgorod, and Rostov Oblasts, Stavropol Territory, Arkhangelsk, Volgograd, Saratov, and Pskov Oblasts, Khabarovsk Territory, St. Petersburg, Jewish Autonomous Oblast, Perm Oblast, Komi-Permyat Autonomous Region, Novosibirsk and Voronezh Oblasts	38.8 million people, or 26.4%
15–20	Ivanovo Oblast, Republic of Karelia, Kamchatka and Chita Oblast, Marii El Republic, Kursk Oblast, Karachaevo-Cherkess Republic, Vladimir and Kaluga Oblasts, Ust-Orda Buryat Autonomous Region, Sakhalin Oblast, Republic of Dagestan, Belgorod Oblast, Republic of Tatarstan, Amur, Kurgan, Smolensk, Murmansk, and Kostroma Oblast, Moscow	38.8 million people, or 26.4%
20–25	Orlov Oblast, Republic of Karelia, Kamchatka and Chita Oblasts, Marii El Republic, Kursk Oblast, Karachaevo-Cherkess Republic, Vladimir and Kaluga Oblasts, Ust-Orda Buryat Autonomous Region, Sakhalin Oblast, Republic of Dagestan, Belgorod Oblast, Republic of Tatarstan, Amur, Kurgan, Smolensk, Murmansk, and Kostroma Oblasts, Moscow	23.9 million people, or 16.3%
25–30	Leningrad, Kemerovo, and Nizhegorod Oblasts, Republic of Khakasia, Lipetsk and Ryazan Oblasts, Republic of Bashkortostan, Tambov, Tomsk, and Penza Oblasts	30.4 million people, or 20.6%
30–40	Chuvash and Udmurt Republics, Tyumen Oblast, Republic of North Osetia, Astrakhan Oblast, Republics of Adygeya and Mordovia, Samara and Ulyanovsk Oblasts, Komi Republic, Krasnoyarsk Territory	19.6 million people, or 13.3%
40–50	Vologda, Moscow, and Magadan Oblasts, Kabardino-Balkar Republic, Republic of Kalmykia, Orenburg Oblast, Koryak Autonomous Region, Omsk Oblast	16.4 million people, or 11.2%
More than 50	Republic of Sakha (Yakutia), Taimyr Autonomous Region, Ingush Republic, Nenets Autonomous Region, Altai Republic, Khanty-Mansi, Yamal-Nenets, and Aga Buryat Autonomous Regions	3.5 million people, or 2.4%

extent, with the level of the regions' industrial development. The greatest contribution of a particular industry to tax receipts, primarily individual industries in the service sphere, is characteristic, as a rule, of the least economically developed regions. Another important factor determining a higher than normal contribution of one industry or another to tax receipts is the regions' specialization (for example, the specialization of the Yamal-Nenets and Khanty-Mansi Autonomous Regions in the fuel industry; or of Karelia in the forest, woodworking and paper and pulp industry).

Like the variance with respect to different types of taxes, the variance of the industry structure of tax receipts (Table 3.9) was calculated on the basis of 25 separate items in the course of the research.

3.3.5 Distribution of tax receipts between the Center and the regions

Throughout the period of 1996–1998, the federal budget's share of tax receipts gradually declined. In 1996, it was 43.6%; in 1997, 41.0%; and in 1998, 37.1%. The regional budgets' share rose accordingly. There are quite significant differences between regions in the portion of taxes collected in their territory that was credited to the federal budget (Table 3.10 and Map 7).

The largest portion of taxes is credited to the federal budget in the Aga Buryat Autonomous Region (79.8%), Altai Republic (66.5%), Kalmykia (63.8%), Moscow (57.7%), Ingushetia (50.4%), and Moscow Oblast (47.6%). In the rest of the regions, it does not exceed 40%. There are many reasons for such disproportions. There are differences in the structure of tax receipts (different taxes are divided between the federal and regional budgets in different proportions), special rules for regional taxes (Ingushetia, Kalmykia, Altai), and special agreements on the division of taxes (Tatarstan and Bashkiria).

3.3.6 Territorial structure of federal budget receipts

The significant differences between Russian regions in the size of their population, as well as their level of economic development, lead to a situation in which the greater part of the federal budget's tax revenues are formed by receipts from a small number of regions (Table 3.11). In 1997–1998, tax collection became even more concentrated in a few regions.

During 1996–1998, the role of individual regions in forming federal budget revenues did not change, for the most part. The regional structure of the federal budget's receipts is shown in Figure 3.6.

For all three years, Moscow has contributed the largest portion of the federal budget's taxes, with its share gradually increasing. Moscow Oblast's share also rose steadily. On the other hand, the share of the Khanty-Mansi Autonomous Region, which had held second place in contributions to the federal budget up until 1998 (9.6% in 1996 and 8.9% in 1997), dropped noticeably. Nine subjects of the Federation were consistently among the ten regions that contributed the greater part of taxes to the federal budget in 1996–1998. In 1998, Krasnodar Territory joined this group for the first time; in 1996–1997 it had been in fourteenth place. Prior to that, Irkutsk (in 1996) and Tatarstan (in 1997) had been included in the top ten.

Table 3.10

Classification of Regions by the Federal Budget's Share of Taxes Collected in Their Territory in 1998

Federal budget's share of tax receipts	Regions	Population
10–20%	Koryak and Taimyr Autonomous Regions, Republic of Tatarstan, Chukotka Autonomous Region, Republic of Tyva, Ust-Orda Buryat Autonomous Region, Republic of Karelia, Vologda Oblast, Jewish Autonomous Oblast, Kabardino-Balkar Republic, Republic of Khakasia	12.2 million people, or 8.3%
20–25%	Chelyabinsk Kurgan, Kamchatka, Lipetsk, and Amur Oblasts, Evenk Autonomous Region, Republic of Sakha (Yakutia), Krasnoyarsk Territory, Kostroma Oblast, Republic of Dagestan, Altai Territory, Novgorod and Murmansk Oblasts, Komi Republic, Magadan Oblast, Republic of Mordovia	12.2 million people, or 8.3%
25–30%	Chuvash Republic, Tomsk Oblast, Komi-Permyat Autonomous Region, Karachaevo-Cherkess Republic, Chita and Arkhangelsk Oblasts, Republic of Adygeya, Belgorod and Kemerovo Oblasts, Yamal-Nenets Autonomous Region, Tyumen, Sakhalin, and Tver Oblasts, Maritime Territory, Perm Oblast, Khabarovsk Oblast, Orlov and Smolensk Oblasts, Marii El Republic, Republic of Buryatia, Pskov, Ivanovo, Saratov, and Orenburg Oblasts	21.1 million people, or 14.4%
30–35%	Nenets Autonomous Region, Rostov, Penza, Tula, Kirov, Sverdlovsk, Irkutsk, Kaliningrad, Astrakhan, and Ulyanovsk Oblasts, Republic of North Osetia, Kursk Oblast, Stavropol Territory, Khanty-Mansi Autonomous Region, Nizhegorod, Novosibirsk, Volgograd Oblasts	32.2 million people, or 21.9%
35–50%	Voronezh Oblast, Krasnodar Territory, Vladimir, Bryansk, Yaroslavl, Leningrad, Kaluga, and Samara Oblast, St. Petersburg, Ryazan Oblast, Udmurt Republic, Moscow Oblast	39.0 million people, or 26.4%
More than 50%	Ingush Republic, Moscow, Republic of Kalmykia, Altai Republic, Aga Buryat Autonomous Region	9.5 million people, or 6.5%

The reasons for the differences between regions in their role in forming the federal budget's tax revenues are perfectly obvious. The higher a region's share in the sum of gross regional products is, the higher its share in tax receipts to the federal budget will be (the coefficient of correlation between these indices was 0.95). We should note that Moscow's share in tax receipts (30.9%) is much higher than its share in gross regional product (13.8%).

Table 3.11

Characteristics of the Concentration of the Federal Budget's Tax Receipts in 1996–1998

Indices	1996	1997	1998
Portion of federal budget's taxes collected in Moscow, %	26.0	30.9	36.1
Share of first 5 regions in federal budget's taxes, %	47.3	52.7	55.1
Share of first 10 regions in federal budget's taxes, %	59.6	64.3	65.4
Number of regions contributing 50% of all tax receipts to the federal budget	6	5	4
Number of regions with share of more than 1% in federal budget's taxes	26	19	17

The problem of tax separatism is particularly significant in Russia. Regional authorities periodically announce their intention to stop transferring taxes to the federal budget. This issue came up most acutely during the crisis of 1998. However, Russia's tax and budget systems are set up in such a way that it is almost impossible to carry out separatist threats.

Federal taxes are credited to the Federal Treasury, and only after that are they divided in the proportions determined by law among the budgets of different levels. The sole exception to this system is Tatarstan, where, as we already said in Chapter 1, territorial agencies of the Federal Treasury have not yet been created. Agencies of the Federal Treasury have been established in Bashkiria and Yakutia, which, like Tatarstan, almost did not transfer taxes to the federal budget in 1991–1993, and therefore it is unlikely that the situation of the early 1990's will be repeated. In Tatarstan, as before, taxes are split

Sidebar 3.2 ***Special tax arrangements***

Since 1994, a clear trend can be seen toward "legalization" of individual tax and budget interrelations of various subjects of the Federation with the Center by particular legal acts. At present, the main form of "legal" asymmetry in budget arrangements is treaties delineating jurisdiction and authority between government agencies of the Russian Federation and subjects of the Federation, and intergovernmental agreements on budget and tax issues signed as part of them.

The first agreements to be signed actually legalized the special budget status of Tatarstan, Bashkiria, and Yakutia, which they had instituted de facto back in 1991–1992. At present, a lower portion of taxes is transferred to the federal budget from the territory of these republics than from other regions. Payments go to the federal budget mostly through excise taxes, and partly through the value-added tax (see table).

Sidebar 3.2 (continued)

Portion of Taxes Actually Transferred to the Federal Budget in 1992–1998 from Individual Republics and for Russia as a Whole, % of Total Amount of Taxes Collected

Subject of the Federation	Type of tax receipts	1992	1993	1994	1995	1996	1997	1998
Republic of Tatarstan	Total	0.1	0	16.6	22.7	19.0	24.6	11.1
	Profit tax	0	0	27.0	34.5	27.6	26.4	23.6
	VAT	0	0	32.7	41.1	37.9	37.9	22.4
	Excise taxes	0	0	0	0	0	0	0
Republic of Bashkortostan	Total	0.1	0	12.5	26.2	27.0	27.0	17.8
	Profit tax	0	0	18.3	32.1	32.5	32.5	19.9
	VAT	0	0	23.8	43.6	59.7	59.7	51.2
	Excise taxes	0	0	0	0	0	0	0
Republic of Sakha (Yakutia)	Total	1.2	0.2	0	0.5	28.3	28.3	22.1
	Profit tax	0	0	0	0	36.0	36.0	40.0
	VAT	0	0	0	0	68.9	68.9	50.9
	Excise taxes	0	0	0	0	35.5	35.5	47.2
Average for Russia	Total	51.7	37.1	30.2	40.9	43.7	43.7	37.1
	Profit tax	41.2	62.5	34.7	36.0	36.0	36.0	37.5
	VAT	74.1	62.4	59.5	66.4	68.4	68.4	62.7
	Excise taxes	47.5	50.4	60.0	73.0	84.4	84.4	74.8

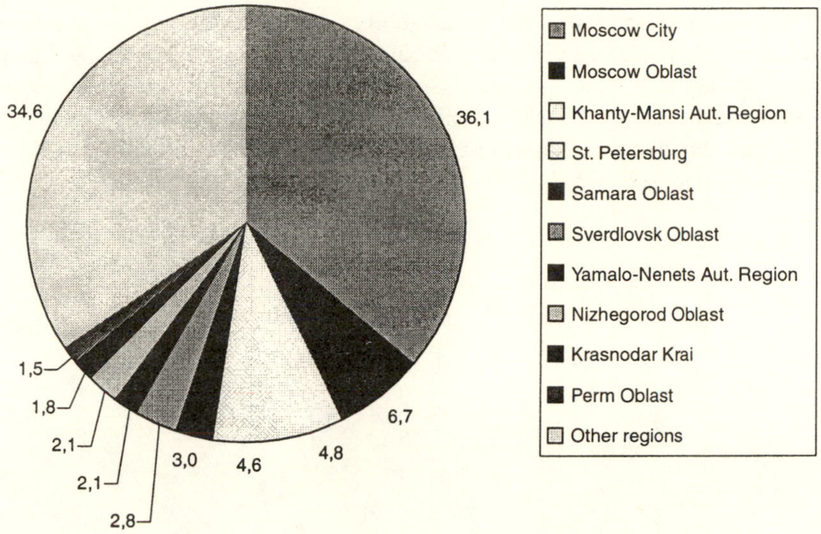

Figure 3.6. **Regional structure of the federal budget's tax receipts.**

up by republican authorities, who could theoretically block the transfer of taxes to the federal budget with no particular problem.

In all the rest of the regions, in order to stop the transfer of taxes to the federal budget the head of the territorial administration of the Federal Treasury and the head of the Central Bank's settlement office (which handles the treasury's accounts) would have to violate federal law. So far, that has happened only once, during the August crisis of 1998. Then the People's Assembly of Kalmykia adopted a resolution as a result of which 236 billion rubles was illegally transferred to the republic's budget. As a response, the Central Bank shut down the National Bank of Kalmykia, and the Ministry of Finance of Russia stopped providing financial aid to the republic and funding federal programs in its territory. As a result, the People's Assembly revoked its resolution, but the money taken illegally was not returned to the federal budget.

3.4 CONCLUSIONS AND SUGGESTIONS

- The differences in tax potential between Russian regions are enormous, and in individual regions the tax potential is many times higher or lower than the national average. The considerable differences between regions in per capita tax revenues only confirm the thesis that the use of differentiated rates of regional deductions from federal taxes, much less a single channel for the distribution of taxes, is not an adequate means of regulating the level of budgetary support.
- The reasons for the differences between regions in per capita tax revenues are primarily objective: the scale of disproportions between subjects of the Federation in their level of economic development is extremely large. At the same time, there are also a number of

subjective factors determining the collectability of taxes in the regions. These include differences in regional tax laws, the efforts of regional authorities to increase the portion of “cash” money and reduce tax arrears, etc. Unfortunately, it is not presently possible to quantitatively evaluate the relationship of objective and subjective factors in a region. Developing a procedure for assessing the tax burden in a region will have to be the subject of separate research.

CHAPTER 4

Financial Aid to Subjects of the Federation from the Federal Budget

4.1 STATEMENT OF THE PROBLEM

Provision of financial aid from the federal budget to the regions, or rather to the regional budgets, is the most obvious and therefore the most widely discussed channel for redistributing funds between the Center and the regions. First of all, this part of the financial flows is fully reflected in statistical data (reports on execution of the regional budgets). Secondly, in contrast to the Federation's direct expenditures, the distribution of the greater part of financial aid among the subjects of the Federation is approved in laws on the federal budget and is a subject of open discussions.

In the course of such discussions, the opinion is frequently expressed that financial aid to the regions is too large and an effort should be made to reduce it. However, such statements are incorrect, in our view. In comparison with other countries, the amount of money redistributed through interbudgetary relations is a relatively small part of the gross domestic product and federal budget expenditures, or of regional budget revenues (Table 4.1). In connection with this, the problem of fair and efficient redistribution of the rather limited funds among the subjects of the Federation becomes especially important.

This chapter looks at the current mechanisms for financial aid to the regions in Russia, their evolution throughout the 1990's, and also the actual situation with distribution of funds among the regions in 1996–1998 and the equalizing effect of financial aid from the federal budget.

4.2 FORMS OF PROVIDING FINANCIAL AID TO THE REGIONS

4.2.1 Mechanisms for providing financial aid

The current system of interbudgetary relations corresponding to a federative arrangement of the Russian state began to be set up in 1991. Two stages can be distinguished during this period of providing financial aid to the regions: before and after the second quarter of 1994. These stages differ fundamentally in the mechanisms for providing funds to the regions.

Table 4.1

Financial Aid to Budgets at the Subnational Level in Russia and Some Other Countries

Country	Year	Direct financial aid from the central budget to subnational budgets: in % of GDP	in % of central government's expenditures: including social funds	in % of central government's expenditures: to budgets proper	in % of subnational budgets' revenues
Russia	1992	1.64*	no data	8.0	11.8
	1993	3.57*	no data	18.3	20.1
	1994	3.61*	11.6	16.6	19.9
	1995	1.79	6.9	10.6	12.4
	1996	2.06	8.1	13.1	14.3
	1997	1.87	no data	12.2	12.0
	1998	1.48	no data	10.3	11.1
Federative states					
Developed countries					
USA	1994	2.95	12.2	18.1	20.3
Canada	1995	4.01	15.9	17.8	15.2
Australia	1995	6.48	13.8	23.8	34.7
Germany	1995	1.47	3.5	7.3	8.4
Austria	1995	2.86	7.1	12.0	20.4
Switzerland	1995	4.17	14.4	no data	18.6
Developing countries					
Brazil	1993	2.39	6.4	no data	17.2
Mexico	1994	1.42	8.9	no data	27.0
India	1994	4.78	23.4	no data	39.4
Malaysia	1995	0.68	3.0	no data	12.9
South Africa	1994	10.64	31.4	no data	68.8
Unitary states					
Developed countries					
France	1995	3.05	6.3	12.1	30.6
Great Britain	1994	8.33	19.7	23.3	71.0
Italy	1995	7.61	15.8	22.5	57.8
Spain	1994	4.94	11.9	22.9	43.2
Sweden	1995	4.78	9.8	13.2	20.2
Japan	1995	5.43	21.6	37.8	36.8
Postsocialist countries					
Poland	1995	2.50	5.8	no data	29.4
Czech Republic	1995	2.78	7.0	no data	16.4
Bulgaria	1995	3.32	8.0	no data	42.8
Rumania	1994	1.54	4.8	no data	41.8

Prior to 1994, there were two main methods of budget regulation: setting differentiated rates for regional deductions from federal taxes, and subsidies. Rate differentiation amounted to setting different percentages for regional deductions from national taxes for different regions. The mechanisms for providing financial aid were not based on any formalized criteria and were worked out between federal and regional authorities, which made them subjective to a considerable extent.

Since 1994, the same rates of regional deductions from federal taxes have applied to all regions (they are given in Chapter 3, Table 3.2). Transfers have become another important mechanism for providing financial aid to the regions: subsidies from the Federal Fund for Financial Support of Subjects of the Russian Federation (or the Fund for Financial Support of the Regions), which was established as part of the federal budget. Transfers have become the first and only mechanism for providing financial aid to the regions that uses special calculations to determine how the money is distributed. The sources from which the Fund is formed and the regions' shares in it are approved in the laws on the federal budget, which are passed each year. As a result, transfers are the most objective channel for allocating money to the budgets of subjects of the Federation.

Along with transfers, a number of other mechanisms for providing financial aid to the regions have been preserved. These are mutual settlements, subsidies and grants to Moscow for performing the functions of the capital of the Federation (prior to 1999), subsidies, and budget loans. However, the very existence of such channels for providing aid raises certain doubts. Thus, it is debatable, in our view, whether or not additional money needs to be allocated to Moscow, whose functioning as the federal capital not only leads to additional expenditures, but also to additional revenues.

The amount of the grants to Moscow was approved in the law on the federal budget. The distribution of the rest of the money among the regions is not specified in the law, and the total amount is only partially approved. For example, individual lines in the law approve allocations for supplying northern regions and subsidies for the power industry in the Far East. The budget statistics give no details as to how they are cleared, so it does not seem possible to judge the objectivity or efficiency of their territorial distribution. In the statistics, budget loans are classified in general as a source of financing for regional budget deficits, although the unrepaid remainder of them is actually one of the mechanisms for providing financial aid to the regions.

4.2.2 Fund for Financial Support of the Regions

The procedure for calculating the transfers due to the regions from the Fund for Financial Support of the Regions (FFSR) has undergone significant changes since it was first established (Table 4.2). In particular, the number of taxes from which the Fund is formed has been considerably expanded. Now it includes not only the value-added tax, but the greater part of other taxes going to the federal budget. This has made the Fund's income more stable and predictable. Moreover, the division of regions into needy and especially needy has been abandoned, and the grouping of regions is now done differently.

The basic purpose of transforming the procedure for calculating transfers was to make the distribution of money among the regions more objective. One of the main shortcomings of the calculation procedure was the use of regional budgets' actual expenditures in

Table 4.2

Evolution of the Procedure for Calculating Distribution of Money from the Fund for Financial Support of the Regions in 1994–1999

Components of calculation procedure	1994	1995	1996	1997	1998	1999
Taxes from which the Fund is formed	22% of VAT going to the federal budget	27% of VAT going to the federal budget	15% of tax revenues, with the exception of import customs duties		14% of tax revenues, with the exception of customs payments and the revenues of targeted budgetary funds	14% of tax payments, with the exception of those controlled by the State Customs Committee
Constituents of the Fund	needy regions and especially needy regions (with no indication of the proportion)	56.04% of the money goes to needy regions, 43.96% to especially needy regions	65.79% of the money goes to needy regions, 34.21% to especially needy ones		no division	
Revenue basis	reported data for 1993		reported data for 1994 in conditions of 1996	reported data for 1995 in conditions of 1997	reported data for 1996 in conditions of 1998	reported data for 1997 in conditions of 1999
Expenditure basis			reported data for 1991 reduced to 1994 and converted to conditions of 1996	reported data for 1991 reduced to 1995 and converted to conditions of 1997	reported data for 1991 reduced to 1996 and converted to conditions of 1998	
Grouping of regions	division into economic areas for calculating adjustment factor (ratio of average per capita budget expenditures of regions included in the economic area to the average per capita revenue of all regions of the Russian Federation)			3 groups, depending on distance from central regions of the country, length of the heating season, and limitation of time for delivering goods		the same 3 groups + economic areas + mountainous regions of the North Caucasus
Criteria for determining the amount of transfers	(1) reduction of region's per capita budget revenue to the average for the budgets of all regions (taking the adjustment factor into account)—needy regions; (2) reduction of revenues to current expenditures—especially needy regions			(1) reduction of region's per capita budget revenue to the average for the budgets of all regions in the group; (2) reduction of revenues to current expenditures		reduction of per capita budget revenue to adjusted average per capita revenues

the base year as the underlying index. Since differences between regions in actual expenditures are of a subjective nature, the distribution of transfers was also subjective.

The most significant changes in the procedure for calculating transfers were introduced in 1999. Their principles were established in the "Concept for reforming interbudgetary relations in the Russian Federation in 1999–2001," which was approved by resolution of the Government of the Russian Federation No. 862 of July 30, 1998.

The novelty of the procedure consists primarily in abandoning the orientation toward covering the so-called "calculated excess of expenditures over revenues." Many regions are critical of the new procedure precisely because they still have a "calculated deficit" even after receiving the transfers. But this is the fundamental position of the Ministry of Finance of Russia, abandonment of which would make all of the other improvements in the budget-equalization procedure meaningless. Even partial compensation of the "calculated deficit" at the expense of federal aid would provide distorted incentives for budget policy. Regions that raise the collectability of taxes and cut wasteful spending, such as subsidies to housing and utilities, would lose out in transfers, and vice versa. Such a system becomes absolutely unworkable.

The new procedure is built on a more objective assessment of the regions' budget needs. It is not known today how justified regional budgets' particular expenditures are. There are no budget standards ready to be applied. In these conditions, the only realistic possibility of making the distribution of transfers more objective is to group regions with similar conditions of funding budget expenditures. This gets us out of a situation where the level of budgetary support in two neighboring regions that receive transfers could differ by 1.5 times.

Sidebar 4.1 ***Formula for calculating transfers from the Fund for Financial Support of the Regions***

Transfers are calculated so as to raise the internal revenues of subjects of the Federation adjusted for (divided by) the index of budgetary expenditures (IBE) to the same level, which is determined by the total amount of the Fund for Financial Support of the Regions:

$$T_i = (R_0 - R_{adj}) \times \text{IBE}_i \times P_i,$$

where T_i — calculated amount of a transfer to a given subject of the Federation (provided that $T_i > 0$);

R_0 — equalization level of adjusted per capita budget revenues (level of revenue equalization);

R_{adj} — adjusted internal per capita budget revenues of that subject of the Federation;

IBE_i — index of budgetary expenditures for that subject of the Federation;

P_i — population of that subject of the Federation.

According to the "Concept for reforming interbudgetary relations in the Russian Federation in 1999–2001," instead of actual expenditures, indices of budgetary expenditures must be used in calculating the transfers. These indices are calculated for regions or groups of regions according to a single procedure (formula) on the basis of objective parameters that make it possible to reduce the regions' specific budget expenditures to comparable levels (the subsistence level, the level of budgetary support, the ratio of calculated revenues and expenditures, etc.). After the Government of the Russian Federation approves a set of budget standards for evaluating the spending authority of the regions' budgets with respect to the basic branches of budgetary funding, calculation of the indices of budgetary expenditures will be based on integrated consideration of the budget standards.

Since this set of standards had not yet been developed by the end of 1998, the indices of budgetary expenditures for 1999 were calculated on the basis of the specific (per capita) expenditures from the budgets of subjects of the Federation in 1997. The disadvantages of using actual expenditures were partially offset by using average specific expenditures for groups of regions, rather than individual ones.

Due to the present lack of a pattern to follow when regionalizing the country for budget purposes, the grouping of regions was based on dividing the subjects of the Federation into economic areas, plus the three groups of regions that were used for calculating transfers in 1997–1998, and also the "mountainous" regions of the North Caucasus (Table 4.3). It is perfectly obvious that such a grouping is subjective and debatable to a significant extent.

As was already pointed out, the "Concept for reforming interbudgetary relations in the Russian Federation in 1999–2001" also changed the principle for determining the regions' share in the Fund for Financial Support of the Regions. While prior to 1999 the subjects of the Federation received an equal percentage of the difference between calculated revenues and expenditures (taking into account the adjustment factors), since 1999 the calculated transfers must equalize the adjusted per capita tax revenues for all subsidized regions.

For 1999, the transfers were calculated as follows. First the region with the least adjusted per capita revenue of all of the subjects of the Federation and the next region after it in the value of this index were determined. Then the amount of money that the former region's budget needed in order to bring its adjusted per capita budget revenue up to the level of the latter one was calculated. This amount was multiplied by the index of budgetary expenditures and by the region's population. The derived amount was subtracted from the projected amount of the Fund for Financial Support of the Regions. This procedure was repeated for a number of subjects of the Federation increasing by one in each step until the transfers to be distributed exceeded the amount of the Fund. The level of adjusted per capita budget revenues up to which equalization was carried out was adjusted so as to make the sum of the calculated transfers equal to the projected amount of the Fund for Financial Support of the Regions. As a result, the adjusted per capita budget revenues of subjects of the Federation (divided by the indices of budgetary expenditures) were raised to the maximum possible level given the assigned amount of

Table 4.3

Grouping of Regions for Calculating Indices of Budgetary Expenditures and Transfers from the Fund for Financial Support of the Regions in 1999

Region	Group	IBE	Subjects of the Federation
Northwest	3	1.39	St. Petersburg, Vologda, Novgorod, Pskov, and Kaliningrad Oblasts
	2	2.00	Arkhangelsk and Murmansk Oblasts, Republic of Karelia, Komi Republic
	1	5.32	Nenets Autonomous Region
Center	3	1.26	Bryansk, Vladimir, Ivanovo, Kaluga, Kostroma, Moscow, Orlov, Ryazan, Smolensk, Tver, Tula, Yaroslavl, Belgorod, Voronezh, Kursk, Lipetsk, and Tambov Oblasts
Volga	3	1.26	Nizhegorod and Kirov Oblasts, Marii El Republic, Republic of Mordovia, Chuvash Republic, Astrakhan, Volgograd, Penza, Samara, Saratov, and Ulyanovsk Oblasts, Republics of Kalmykia and Tatarstan
Northern Caucasus	3a)	1.00	Krasnodar and Stavropol Territories, Rostov Oblast
	3b)	1.59	Republics of Adygeya and Dagestan, Kabardino-Balkar and Karachaevo-Cherkess Republics, Republics of North Osetia and Ingushetia
Ural	3	1.40	Kurgan, Orenburg, Perm, Sverdlovsk, and Chelyabinsk Oblasts, Republic of Bashkortostan, Udmurt Republic
	2	1.55	Komi-Permyak Autonomous Region
Siberia	3	1.50	Altai Territory, Omsk and Novosibirsk Oblasts
	2	1.99	Kemerovo, Tomsk, and Tyumen Oblasts, Altai Republic, Krasnoyarsk Territory, Irkutsk and Chita Oblasts, Republics of Buryatia, Tyva, and Khakasia, Ust-Orda Buryat and Aga Buryat Autonomous Regions
	1	8.22	Khanty-Mansi, Yamal-Nenets, Taimyr, and Evenk Autonomous Regions
Far East	2	2.12	Maritime and Khabarovsk Territories, Amur Oblast, Jewish Autonomous Oblast
	1a)	3.90	Kamchatka and Sakhalin Oblasts, Republic of Sakha (Yakutia)
	1b)	6.56	Magadan Oblast, Koryak and Chukotka Autonomous Regions
Moscow	3	2.54	Moscow

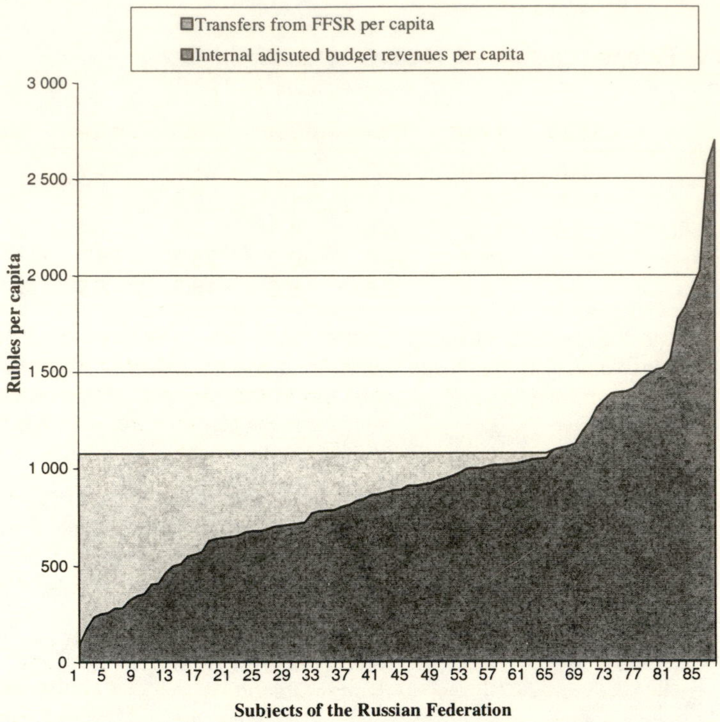

Figure 4.1. **Equalization of budgetary support for subjects of the Russian Federation in accordance with the procedure for calculating transfers for 1999.**

the Fund. For subsidized regions, it was the same, but no higher than for regions that did not receive transfers (Figure 4.1).

Of course, the new formula for calculating transfers did not solve all of the problems. First of all, so far the changes only concern one aspect of budget equalization: spending needs. As before, the regions' revenues were evaluated on the basis of actual receipts in the "base" or "reporting" year, which undermines incentives to increase the collectability of taxes. This raises the question of switching from the established level of budget revenues to evaluation of the territories' tax potential.

Second, a pattern of regionalization that is directly oriented toward the problems of budget equalization needs to be developed. The existing groupings of subjects of the Federation, including the one by economic areas, do not entirely fit these problems. This is primarily true of regions with large internal diversity (the North Caucasus, the Far East) or "transition" zones (Kirov Oblast). It is precisely this aspect of the new formula for calculating transfers that has provoked the sharpest debates.

Third, the calculations according to the new procedure failed to fully maintain the "purity" of the principles incorporated in it. In contrast to past years, when the budget for 1999 was being considered, it was possible to avoid individual agreements. But by decision of the tripartite working group, the calculated shares in the Fund were adjusted

Table 4.4

Components of Financial Aid to the Regions in 1993–1998 (%)

Portion of financial aid	1993	1994	1995	1996	1997	1998	1998 (not including loans)
Transfers	0.0	9.6	49.8	44.8	46.7	74.7	70.4
Subsidies	14.9	0.0	1.7	1.7	2.9	5.3	5.0
Grants	5.8	11.2	6.8	4.4	3.1	1.4	1.3
Mutual settlements	77.9	76.7	39.0	40.5	28.7	24.7	23.2
Budget loans*	1.4	2.4	2.6	8.6	18.5	6.1	—

* In accordance with the existing statistics, budget loans are considered as a source of funding for the budget deficit. Since budget loans that are not covered at the end of the year are actually a mechanism for providing financial aid to the regions, in this research they are considered as precisely that.

according to a single procedure for all of the regions tying them to the level for 1998 (in the range of ±35%). This political compromise "facilitated" the transition to the new proportions of distribution of financial aid. However, as a result, not only were the equalization criteria violated, but the number of unsatisfied regions also rose sharply. The distribution of transfers was criticized both by those whose share decreased in comparison with 1998, and by those who suffered in relation to the calculated transfer.

For 2000, the Ministry of Finance of Russia plans to keep the formula described above for calculating transfers from the Fund of Financial Support of the Regions, but significant improvements in it are planned. In particular, it may be possible to switch from using actual budget revenues in the calculations to the regions' tax potential, and to measure inflation factors more objectively.

4.3 FINANCIAL AID IN 1996–1998

4.3.1 Components of financial aid to the regions

The components of financial aid to the regions for Russia as a whole is presented in Table 4.4. The data cited in this table indicate that such aid has been distributed on a more objective basis over the course of recent years, In particular, 1998 stands out, when the share of transfers rose sharply and, on the other hand, the share of subsidies to Moscow and mutual settlements declined.

The situation with budget loans turned out completely differently in 1998. For the first time, the regions repaid more money in loans than they received. The opposite was true in only 16 regions (they received more than they repaid). These were, the Altai and Komi Republics, the Republics of Mordovia and Udmurtia, Krasnodar Territory, Volgograd, Vologda, Kamchatka, Kemerovo, Lipetsk, Moscow, Nizhegorod, Novosibirsk, Samara, and Sverdlovsk Oblasts, and the Komi-Permyak Autonomous Region.

The research showed that there are large differences in the components of financial aid to individual regions. Transfers made up 100% of the amount of aid in only four regions: Karelia, Marii El, the Jewish Autonomous Oblast, and the Nenets Autonomous Region. In Tatarstan and the Khanty-Mansi Autonomous Region, mutual settlements accounted for 100% of financial aid. In Moscow, grants made up 99.9%, and 0.1% was mutual settlements. The maximum portion of budget loans in financial aid was at the level of 97.2% in Lipetsk Oblast. The portion of them was more than half in Krasnoyarsk Territory (78.5%) and Komi (57.7%).

In 1998, 19 regions received subsidies.[1] The portion of them was highest in Murmansk Oblast (74.3%). In the rest of the regions, subsidies amounted to no more than one fourth of the total amount of financial aid.

Unformalized sources of providing financial aid play a comparatively large role in regions that do not receive transfers. In other respects, the differences between regions are of a rather random nature and may be, to a certain extent, evidence of the lack of objectivity in interrelations between the Center and the regions (Table 4.5).

4.3.2. Distribution of financial aid among the regions

While the list of regions from which the greater part of tax revenues goes to the federal budget remained stable, to a significant extent, in 1996–1998, we can talk about stability in relation to the regions that received the most financial aid from the federal budget only with a certain amount of qualification.

Only four regions (Altai, Krasnodar, and Maritime Territories, and Kemerovo Oblast) were included in the top ten recipients of financial aid in all three of these years. Moscow received the largest amount of money from the federal budget in 1996 (4.4%), Yakutia in 1997 (4.5%), and Dagestan in 1998 (5.1%). Along with the growth of the first region's share in the total amount of financial aid, the increasing concentration of financial aid in 1996–1998 is also indicated by the change in the portion of money provided to the ten largest recipients of funds from the federal budget (24.3% in 1996, 24.8% in 1997, and 32.1% in 1998). In addition to those already mentioned, in different years the top ten recipients also included Kabardino-Balkaria, Stavropol and Khabarovsk Territories, and Amur, Moscow, Murmansk, and Rostov Oblasts.

On the whole, the shares of individual regions in the Fund for Financial Support of the Regions (approved and actual) were stable in 1996–1998, as were their shares in financial aid. The coefficients of correlation between the indices in different years were no less than 0.7 (Figures 4.2–4.4). However, these shares could change for individual regions and did so very significantly. For instance, we can note that nine regions were recipients of transfers in only one or two years out of the three that were analyzed.

[1] Arkhangelsk, Murmansk, Moscow, Tver, Kirov, Astrakhan, and Saratov Oblasts, Dagestan, Krasnodar Territory, Orenburg, Perm, Sverdlovsk, and Chelyabinsk Oblasts, Altai, Krasnoyarsk, and Maritime Territories, Chita, Amur, and Kamchatka Oblasts.

Table 4.5

Classification of Regions by Portion of Financial Aid in Regional Budget Revenues and Portion of Transfers in Financial Aid in 1998

Portion of financial aid in revenues	Portion of transfers in financial aid		
	less than 60%	60–80%	more than 80%
Less than 10%	Komi Republic, Leningrad Oblast, Moscow, Moscow, Yaroslavl, Belgorod, and Lipetsk Oblasts, Republic of Tatarstan, Samara Oblast, Republic of Bashkortostan, Sverdlovsk Oblast, Khanty-Mansi and Yamal-Nenets Autonomous Regions, Krasnoyarsk Territory, Kaliningrad Oblast	St. Petersburg, Nizhegorod Orenburg, Perm, and Irkutsk Oblasts	Vologda, Chelyabinsk, Novosibirsk, and Omsk Oblasts
10–30%	Murmansk, Vladimir, and Volgograd Oblasts, Udmurt Republic, Khabarovsk Territory	Ryazan, Smolensk, Tver, and Tula Oblasts, Republic of Mordovia, Kirov, Voronezh, and Tambov Oblasts, Stavropol Territory, Rostov and Kemerovo Oblasts, Republic of Khakasia, Sakhalin Oblast	Republic of Karelia, Arkhangelsk Oblast, Nenets Autonomous Region, Bryansk, Ivanovo, Kostroma, and Orlov Oblasts, Marii El and Chuvash Republics, Kursk, Astrakhan, Penza, Saratov, and Ulyanovsk Oblasts, Krasnodar Territory, Kurgan, Tomsk, and Tyumen Oblasts, Taimyr Autonomous Region, Chita Oblast, Republic of Sakha (Yakutia), Magadan Oblast
More than 30%	Novgorod and Kaluga Oblasts, Komi-Permyak Autonomous Region, Altai Republic, Kamchatka Oblast	Pskov Oblast, Republics of Kalmykia, Adygeya, and Dagestan, Ingush and Kabardino-Balkar Republics, Republics of Buryatia and Tyva, Evenk and Chukotka Autonomous Regions, Maritime Territory, Amur Oblast	Karachaevo-Cherkess Republic, Republic of North Osetia, Altai Territory, Ust-Orda Buryat and Aga Buryat Autonomous Regions, Jewish Autonomous Oblast, Koryak Autonomous Region

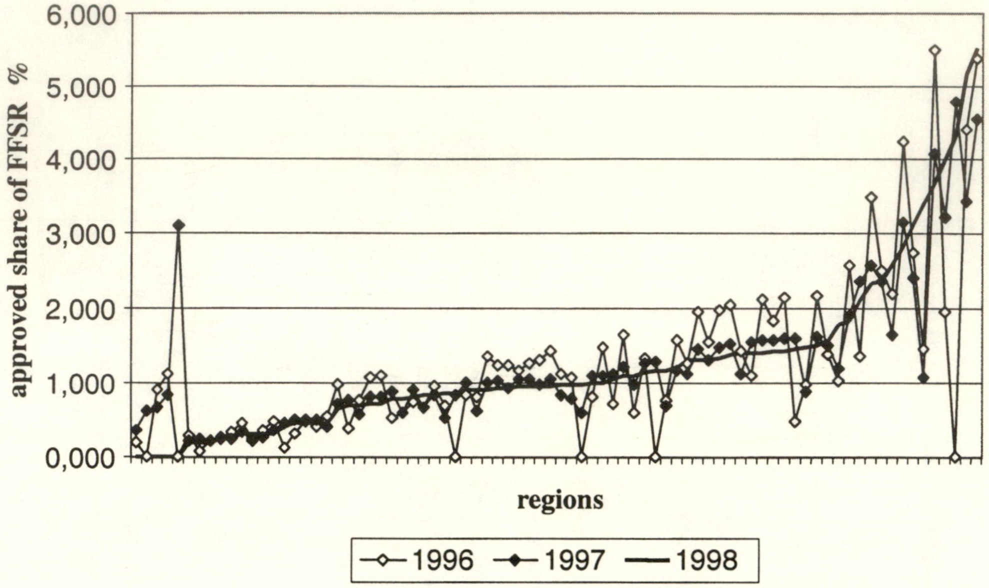

Figure 4.2. **Regions' approved shares of the Fund for Financial Support of the Regions in 1996–1998.**

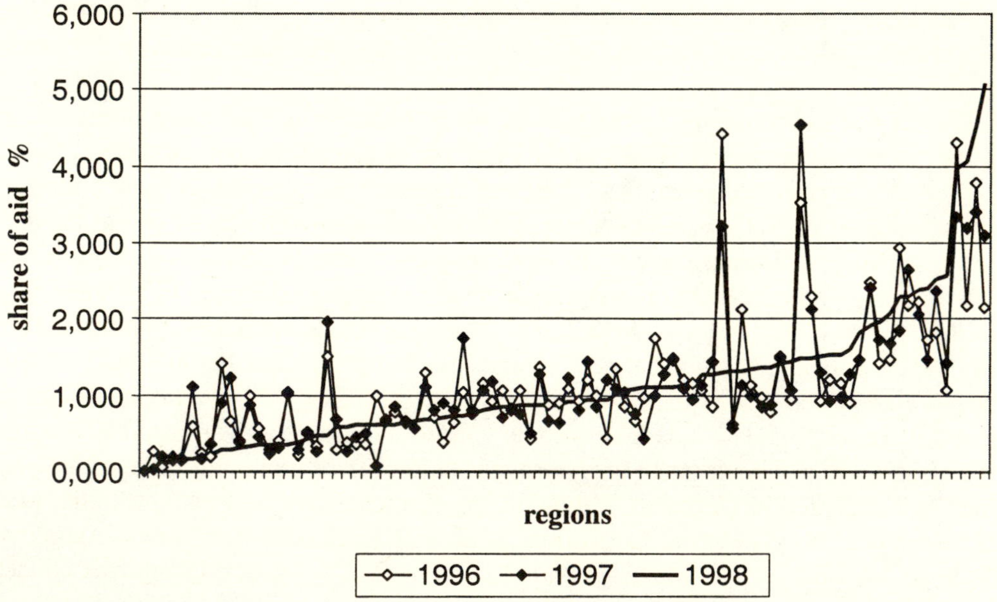

Figure 4.3. **Regions' shares of financial aid from the federal budget in 1996–1998.**

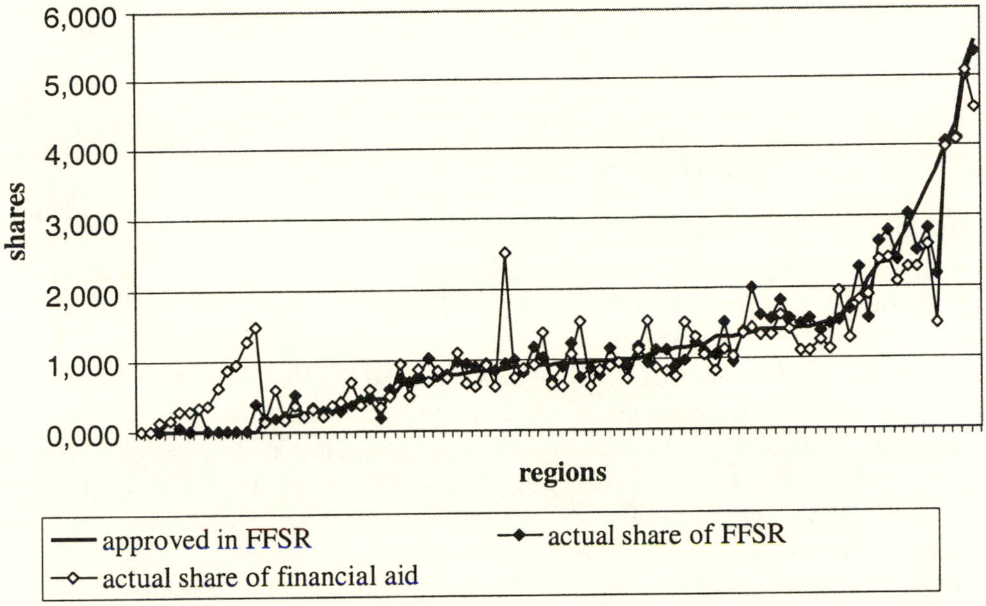

Figure 4.4. **Relationship of regions' shares of the Fund for Financial Support of the Regions (approved and actual) and financial aid in 1998.**

The Komi Republic, St. Petersburg, and Tatarstan received transfers in 1996–1997 and not in 1998. Moscow and Perm Oblasts did not receive transfers only in 1997, and Murmansk, Irkutsk, and Kamchatka Oblasts, and the Maritime Territory did not receive them in 1996.

One of the shortcomings of the way in which transfers are provided is that the regions' actual and approved shares of the Fund for Financial Support of the Regions do not match. Of course, the regions' shares of financial aid also do not match their approved shares. As for the relationship of actual and approved shares of the Fund for Financial Support of the Regions, in most subjects of the Federation it changes from year to year. The actual shares were lower than the approved shares in all three years only in Yakutia, while they were higher in Adygeya, Komi, Khakasia, Stavropol Territory, and Astrakhan, Kurgan, Magadan, Penza, Sakhalin, and Tomsk Oblasts. If we compare the approved shares of the Fund for Financial Support of the Regions with the actual shares of financial aid, there are many more such regions. For instance, the share of financial aid was lower than the approved share of the Fund in all three of the years that were analyzed in Dagestan, Kalmykia, the Karachaevo-Cherkessia, Karelia, Marii El, Mordovia, North Osetia, Chuvashia, Altai and Krasnodar Territories, Astrakhan, Bryansk, Ivanovo, Kursk, Magadan, Orenburg, Penza, Tomsk, and Ulyanovsk Oblasts, the Jewish Autonomous Oblast, and the Nenets, Taimyr, and Chukotka Autonomous Regions. The shares were higher than what was approved in Altai, Komi, Udmurtia, Moscow, Krasnoyarsk Territory, Belgorod, Volgograd, Vologda, Kamchatka, Lipetsk, Murmansk, Perm, Samara, Sverdlovsk, Tver, and Yaroslavl Oblasts, and the Khanty-

Mansi and Yamal-Nenets Autonomous Regions. The reasons for such discrepancies are most likely of a subjective nature.

4.3.3 The regions' dependence on financial aid

For Russia as a whole, the portion of financial aid from the federal budget in regional budget revenues decreased in 1996–1998, and the change was particularly noticeable in 1998 (18.0% in 1996, 17.6% in 1997, and 11.1% in 1998).

The differences between regions in the portion of financial aid in their revenues are enormous (Figure 4.5 and Map 8). While Bashkiria and the Yamal-Nenets Autonomous Region did not receive any money at all from the federal budget in 1998, the portion of financial aid in the budget revenues of Ingushetia and Dagestan was about 80%.

The differences between regions in the portion of financial aid in their revenues remained stable to a significant extent (Figure 4.6). The coefficients of correlation between the indices in different years were above 0.9.

As we already pointed out, the distribution of financial aid between the regions is partly explained by subjective factors, but it is determined to a significant extent by differences between regions in the amount of taxes collected per capita, taking into account the subsistence level (Figure 4.7). The coefficient of correlation between the indices shown on the graph was 0.52.

To a significant extent, the distribution of regions by the portion of financial aid in their revenues (Figure 4.5) corresponds to the distribution of regions by per capita tax revenues (see Chapter 3). Large regions with a diversified economy and a high level of development of the service sphere and regions that specialize in production of individual types of natural resources are the least dependent on the federal budget. On the other hand, regions with poorly developed industry and a high portion of depressed industries (machine building, textile industry) are the most dependent.

4.4 ASSESSMENT OF THE EQUALIZING EFFECT OF FINANCIAL AID

Provision of current financial aid from the federal budget is primarily aimed at reducing differences in the regions' ability to fund the necessary expenditures. As we already said, at present there is no procedure for assessing the regions' objective spending needs. This not only makes it hard to increase the objectivity of the distribution of transfers among the regions, but also to assess the equalizing effect of financial aid.

The degree of equalization of the regions' budgetary support can be evaluated according to the change in indices of the budget deficit calculated as the difference between revenues and expenditures in percent of expenditures, or budget revenues per capita adjusted for the subsistence minimum. Each of these indices has its own advantages and disadvantages. Calculations of the budget deficit include expenditures, which are determined not only by objective factors, but also by subjective ones. The index of per capita

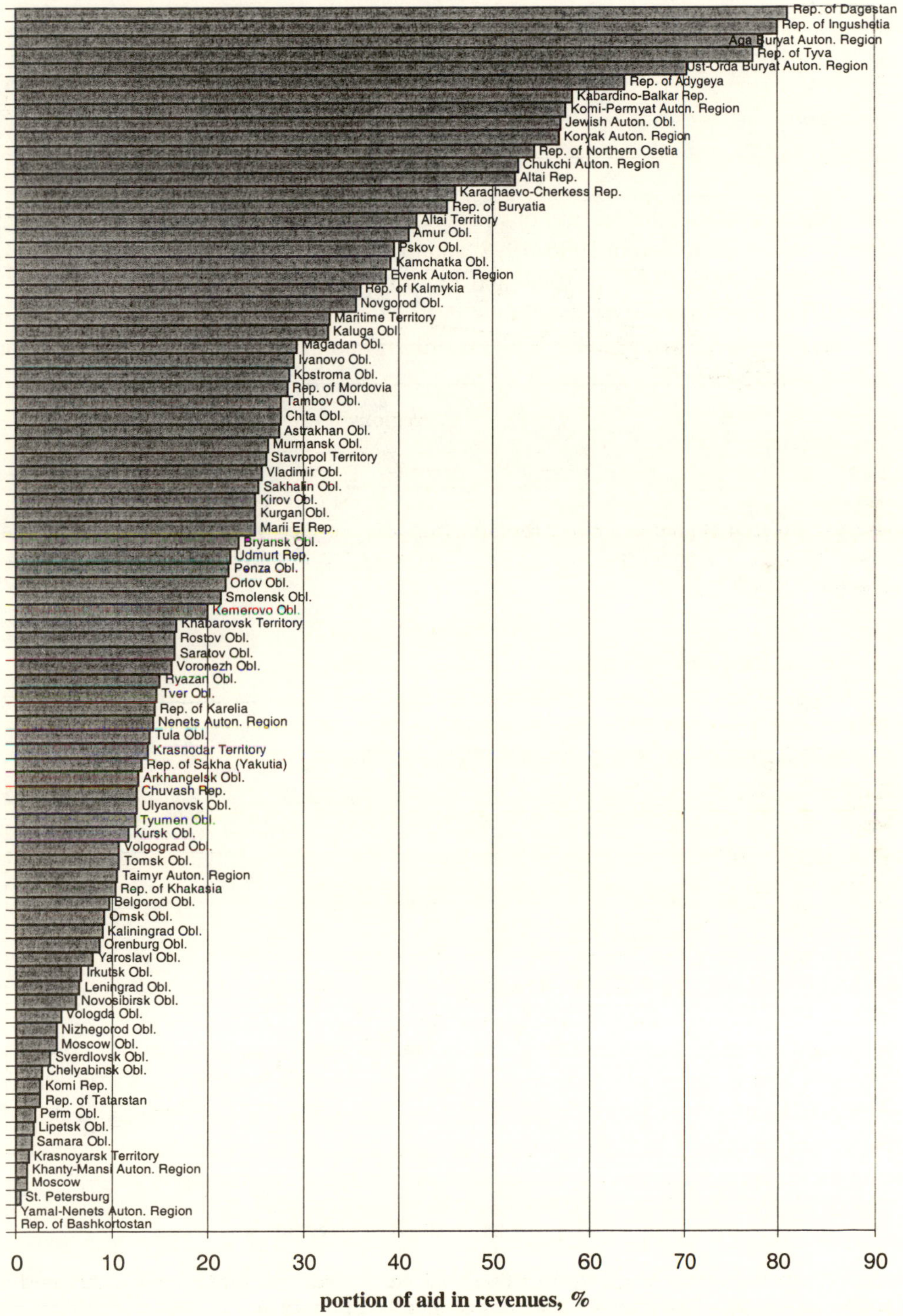
Rep. of Dagestan
Rep. of Ingushetia
Aga Buryat Auton. Region
Rep. of Tyva
Ust-Orda Buryat Auton. Region
Rep. of Adygeya
Kabardino-Balkar Rep.
Komi-Permyat Auton. Region
Jewish Auton. Obl.
Koryak Auton. Region
Rep. of Northern Osetia
Chukchi Auton. Region
Altai Rep.
Karachaevo-Cherkess Rep.
Rep. of Buryatia
Altai Territory
Amur Obl.
Pskov Obl.
Kamchatka Obl.
Evenk Auton. Region
Rep. of Kalmykia
Novgorod Obl.
Maritime Territory
Kaluga Obl.
Magadan Obl.
Ivanovo Obl.
Kostroma Obl.
Rep. of Mordovia
Tambov Obl.
Chita Obl.
Astrakhan Obl.
Murmansk Obl.
Stavropol Territory
Vladimir Obl.
Sakhalin Obl.
Kirov Obl.
Kurgan Obl.
Marii El Rep.
Bryansk Obl.
Udmurt Rep.
Penza Obl.
Orlov Obl.
Smolensk Obl.
Kemerovo Obl.
Khabarovsk Territory
Rostov Obl.
Saratov Obl.
Voronezh Obl.
Ryazan Obl.
Tver Obl.
Rep. of Karelia
Nenets Auton. Region
Tula Obl.
Krasnodar Territory
Rep. of Sakha (Yakutia)
Arkhangelsk Obl.
Chuvash Rep.
Ulyanovsk Obl.
Tyumen Obl.
Kursk Obl.
Volgograd Obl.
Tomsk Obl.
Taimyr Auton. Region
Rep. of Khakasia
Belgorod Obl.
Omsk Obl.
Kaliningrad Obl.
Orenburg Obl.
Yaroslavl Obl.
Irkutsk Obl.
Leningrad Obl.
Novosibirsk Obl.
Vologda Obl.
Nizhegorod Obl.
Moscow Obl.
Sverdlovsk Obl.
Chelyabinsk Obl.
Komi Rep.
Rep. of Tatarstan
Perm Obl.
Lipetsk Obl.
Samara Obl.
Krasnoyarsk Territory
Khanty-Mansi Auton. Region
Moscow
St. Petersburg
Yamal-Nenets Auton. Region
Rep. of Bashkortostan
0
10
20
30
40
50
60
70
80
90
portion of aid in revenues, %

Figure 4.5. **Distribution of regions by portion of financial aid in regional budget revenues in 1998.**

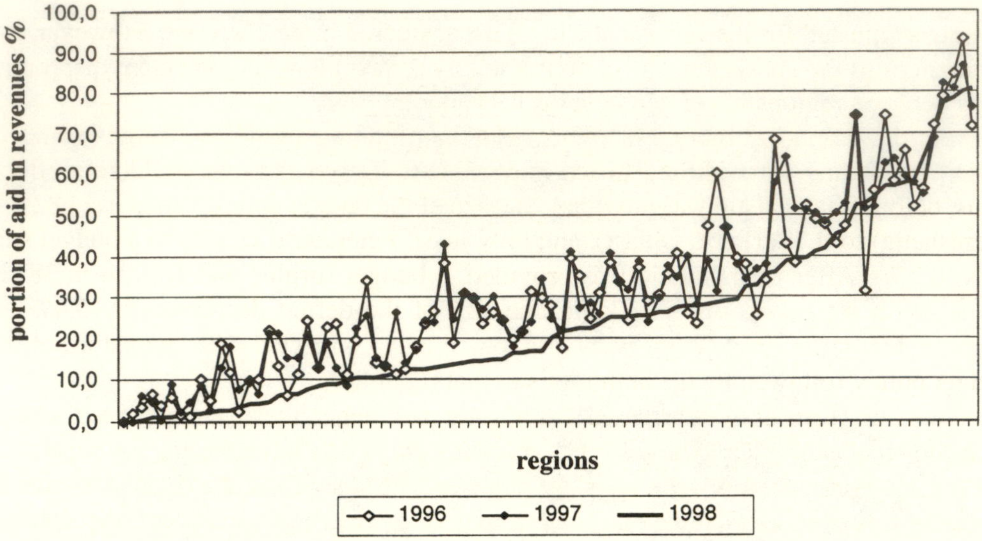

Figure 4.6. **Portion of financial aid in regional budget revenues in 1996–1998.** *Note:* To make it easier to read, the graph does not show Moscow, or the Khanty-Mansi and Yamal-Nenets Autonomous Regions.

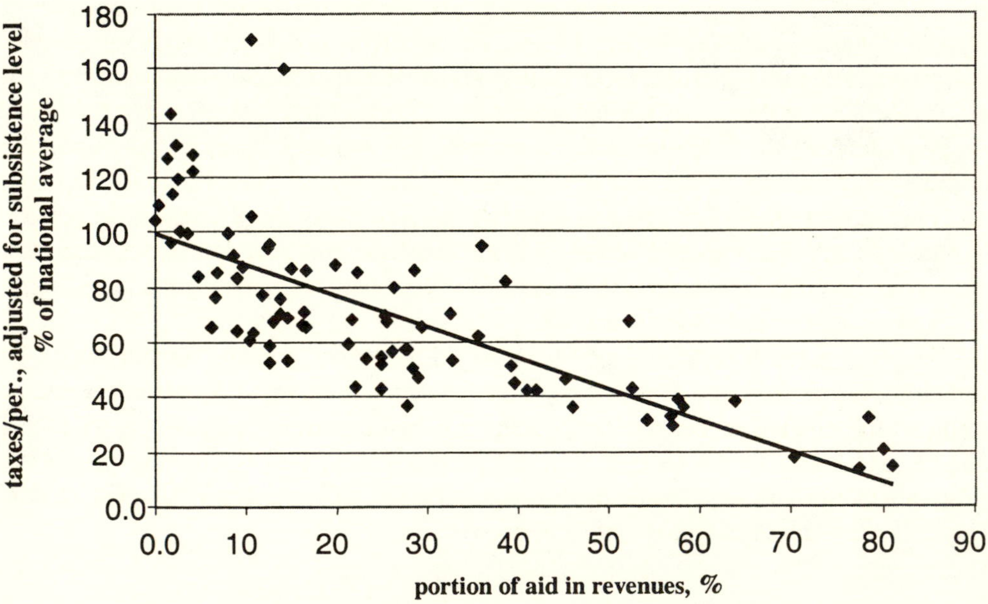

Figure 4.7. **Relationship of portion of financial aid in regional budget revenues and tax receipts per capita, adjusted for the subsistence level, in 1998.**

revenues adjusted for the subsistence level is considered more objective. However, the differences in the subsistence level do not nearly reflect all of the objective disproportions between regions in per capita budget revenues.

From the graph in Figure 4.8, we can see that, judging from the change in budget deficit, providing financial aid to the regions does have a definite equalizing effect. Thus, before financial aid was provided, the size of the budget deficit varies from 82.3% (Ingushetia) to 0.7% (Perm Oblast), and only in St. Petersburg was there a budget surplus (0.7%). After financial aid was provided, a budget surplus was formed in 38 regions. With the exception of Yakutia, the size of the deficit decreased to 13.4%. In Yakutia, the deficit was 40.3%, which is most likely connected with the nature of the budget policy followed by the authorities in that republic.

At the same time, it must be noted that it is not the financially strong regions (the ones with the smallest deficits with internal revenues only) that have the largest surpluses, but, on the contrary, the weak ones. In our view, no unequivocal explanation can be given for this situation. On the one hand, it may be evidence of excessive redistribution of budgetary funds, or on the other, that the differences in budgetary expenditures between regions are not objective.

Evaluating the equalizing effect according to the change in per capita revenues adjusted for the subsistence level (Figure 4.9) gives different results from evaluation according to the budget deficit. To make it easier to read, the graph in Figure 4.9 was constructed without data on the seven regions in which specific revenues, taking into account the subsistence level, were at least 1.5 times higher than the national average (Moscow, Tatarstan, and the Nenets, Evenk, Taimyr, Khanty-Mansi, and Yamal-Nenets Autonomous Regions). For the rest of the regions, the differences with respect to this index almost do not decrease. While the extreme values of internal revenues per capita, taking into account the subsistence level, were 11.0% and 548.3% of the national average, the extreme values of the sum of all revenues were 43.9% and 475.3% (Map 10).

In contrast to indices of the budget deficit, there is a fairly close correlation between different indices of per capita revenues. So, the coefficient of correlation between internal revenues and total revenues is 0.99, and if we disregard the seven financially "strongest" regions mentioned above it is 0.72.

Although as a result of providing financial aid the "rich" regions remain "rich," for the most part; and the "poor" ones, "poor," when the equalizing effect is evaluated according to the change in per capita revenues the same pattern is traced as when it is evaluated according to the budget deficit. In many cases, less financially prosperous regions are better off as a result of the redistribution of revenues (the most striking example is the Chukotka Autonomous Region).

4.5 CONCLUSIONS AND SUGGESTIONS

As the research showed, the main problem with providing financial aid to the regions is still its subjectivity. Even now, spending authority, which should be the basis for all

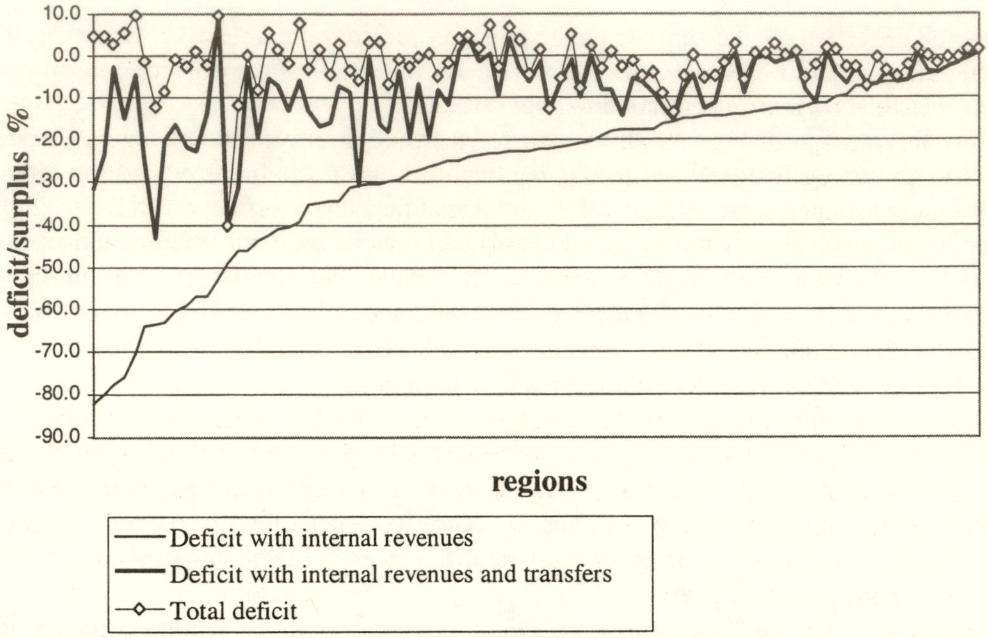

Figure 4.8. **Regions' budget deficit before and after provision of financial aid to the regions in 1998.**

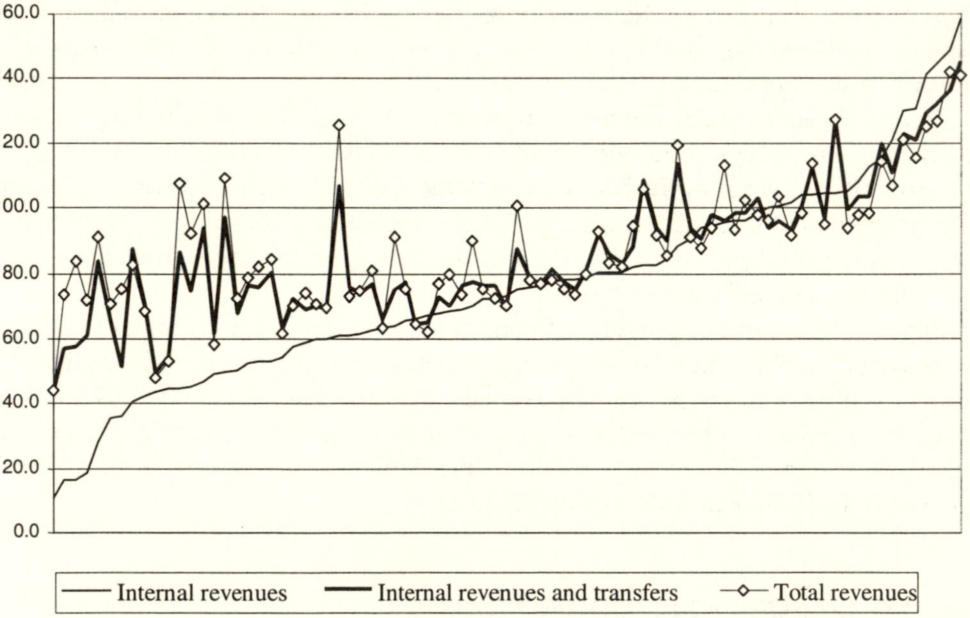

Figure 4.9. **Regions' budget revenues per capita, adjusted for the subsistence level, before and after provision of financial aid in 1998.**

budget interrelations, has not been clearly delineated between levels of the budget system. No procedure has been developed for assessing the regions' objective spending needs and, what is no less important, how fully their tax potential is being used. Among other unsolved problems, we can mention the preservation of a fairly high portion of unformalized mechanisms for providing financial aid to the regions, and the lack of sufficient incentives for them to cut wasteful spending and increase revenues.

One of the biggest shortcomings of providing financial aid to the regions is the lack of a noticeable equalizing effect. As a result, after money is allocated to the regions from the federal budget, enormous differences remain in the level of budget revenues per capita (even taking into account the subsistence level).

Ways of solving a number of the problems indicated above are set forth in the "Concept for reforming interbudgetary relations in the Russian Federation in 1999–2001," which was adopted in 1998. All that needs to be done is to implement it soon.

CHAPTER 5

Direct Expenditures from the Federal Budget in the Regions

5.1 STATEMENT OF THE PROBLEM

Federal budgetary funds connected to a specific region go directly to the region, being transferred to the personal accounts of recipients of budgetary funds or through an intermediary using the mechanism of interbudgetary relations (including financial aid).

However, in the laws on the federal budget adopted by the Federal Assembly in 1996–1998, as well as in the reports on budget execution, information on the territorial distribution of budgetary expenditures has traditionally been limited almost exclusively to the category "Financial aid to the regions" (section 21). But financial aid accounts for no more than 24% of all of the federal budget's territorial expenditures.

At the same time, the distribution among subjects of the Federation of such an important component of territorial expenditures as *direct expenditures*, which make up about four fifths of all of the federal budget's territorial expenditures, has never been planned or analyzed. Programs included in the federal budget that are to be implemented in specific regions contain only very scanty and incomplete information on the territorial distribution of a small part of direct expenditures (*program expenditures*).

The greater part of direct expenditures from the federal budget goes to *departmental* (nonprogram) *expenditures*. They are not included in programs and are spent locally. However, the drafts of the federal budget and attachments to it that were submitted by the Government of the Russian Federation to the Federal Assembly for its consideration in 1996–1998 contain practically no information on the territorial distribution of this type of expenditures. The only exceptions were budget appropriations for the support of regional mass media and maintenance of particularly valuable objects of cultural heritage located in the regions.

Thus, a situation has developed in Russia in which federal authorities do not have a reliable idea about the regional distribution of direct territorial expenditures from the federal budget. This deprives them of the possibility of using this most powerful tool of financial impact on the regions. This situation can be partly explained by the fact that the necessary prerequisites for real control of federal expenditures (primarily conversion of the federal budget to execution by the treasury) were not finally set up until 1998 (see section 5.3 for more details).

For the first time in the practice of Russian economic research, this chapter analyzes the distribution of direct (program and departmental) expenditures from the federal budget among subjects of the Federation. Problems of insufficient compatibility of the indices of federal expenditures in 1996–1998, the reasons for which are described in Chapter 1, forced us to limit the analysis of their geographic distribution to 1998. In our view, the results of the research that was done can be used as a basis for developing proposals for improving regional policy and interbudgetary relations in the Russian Federation.

5.2 PROCEDURE FOR ANALYZING THE DISTRIBUTION OF DIRECT EXPENDITURES FROM THE FEDERAL BUDGET AMONG THE REGIONS

When analyzing direct territorial expenditures from the federal budget, not only the *volumes of financial flows* are important, but also the *forms* (methods) *of funding*.

Direct expenditures from the federal budget in subjects of the Federation were funded in three main ways in 1998:

- with money from federal budget revenues (using *monetary resources*)
- with money from federal budget receipts in the territory of a region (*nonmonetary resources*)
- without money (using different forms of *setoff* between the federal budget and recipients of budgetary funds in the territory of a given region).

The forms of funding characterize the level of the Center's interaction with the regions and determine how quickly money goes into the accounts of the regional authorities and how liquid the funding is. Funding out of federal budget receipts in the territory of a subject of the Federation is the most predictable for regional authorities. The use of setoff schemes reduces the portion of "cash" money in regional budgets, which has a negative effect on the social situation in the region.

Analysis of the absolute values of federal expenditures in individual territories is not very informative, in view of the enormous differences between the subjects of the Federation in the size of their territory and population, as well as in their economic and financial potential. Therefore, in studying the geography of direct territorial expenditures the greatest attention was paid to relative indices, primarily per capita.

So, summary indices of federal expenditures in individual territories, and also the characteristics of expenditures on social needs, were also adjusted in relation to an index that takes into account, to a certain extent, territorial differences in prices and the purchasing power of the ruble (the subsistence level was used for this purpose; see Chapter 1).

The subjects of the Federation were classified on the basis of comparison of relative indices of federal expenditures in individual territories with the national average, and types of regions with a similar nature of federal budgetary expenditures were identified.

In their most general form, indices of the efficiency (results) of federal budgetary expenditures in the territories were obtained by comparing the amount of expenditures in different categories of the budget and the results achieved in the corresponding industries. For example, the gross regional product in industry and agriculture was compared with federal budgetary expenditures supporting various industries and the countryside.

5.3 FORMS OF FUNDING OF FEDERAL BUDGETARY EXPENDITURES

5.3.1 Method of funding federal budgetary expenditures in the regions

Funding of direct expenditures from the federal budget, including expenditures on implementing government programs and other activities taken through the system of accounts of agencies of the Federal Treasury, began on the basis of the order of the Ministry of Finance of the Russian Federation No. 111 of February 17, 1995, "On the procedure for transferring funds for spending and activities of the Federal budget." In accordance with the order, when federal budgetary expenditures are funded, along with the payment orders for transferring funds, offices of the Federal Treasury in subjects of the Federation receive registers for funding of regional disbursers and recipients of funds coming out of federal budget receipts in that territory.

The method of treasury execution of the federal budget was later improved by trying to reduce financial flows moving in opposite directions. So, since February 1, 1996, 12 regional offices of the Federal Treasury have had the right to transfer money for funding of expenditures and activities specified in the federal budget, within the limit of federal budget receipts in the region, according to the registers provided by the Central Administration of the Federal Treasury.

For these offices of the Federal Treasury, payment orders began to be sent with registers attached for funding out of receipts in the territory of that subject of the Federation (so-called clearing registers). In this funding procedure, monetary registers are sent to offices of the Federal Treasury in subjects of the Federation only when the amount of revenues received in the territory turns out to be insufficient. By 1998, funding by clearing registers encompassed 81 regions.

In the first years of the Federal Treasury's operation, the specific nature of tax receipts and other federal budget revenues led to a situation in which the registers for funding of various budgetary organizations were received unevenly, with the greater part of the funding coming toward the end of the month. In order to make the funding process more uniform, in March 1996 the territories were permitted to make advance payments for a number of expenditures and activities (wages with accruals, stipends, welfare benefits, other social compensatory payments, and also expenditures on nutrition and food support, and acquiring medicines and dressings in public-health agencies). Permission was given to fund these expenditures up to a limit of 50% of the previous month's funding.

Figure 5.1 shows how the federal budget was executed in 1998.

Federal budget spending was executed within the limits of the funds actually present in budget accounts. The main stages of execution were approval and funding of expenditures.

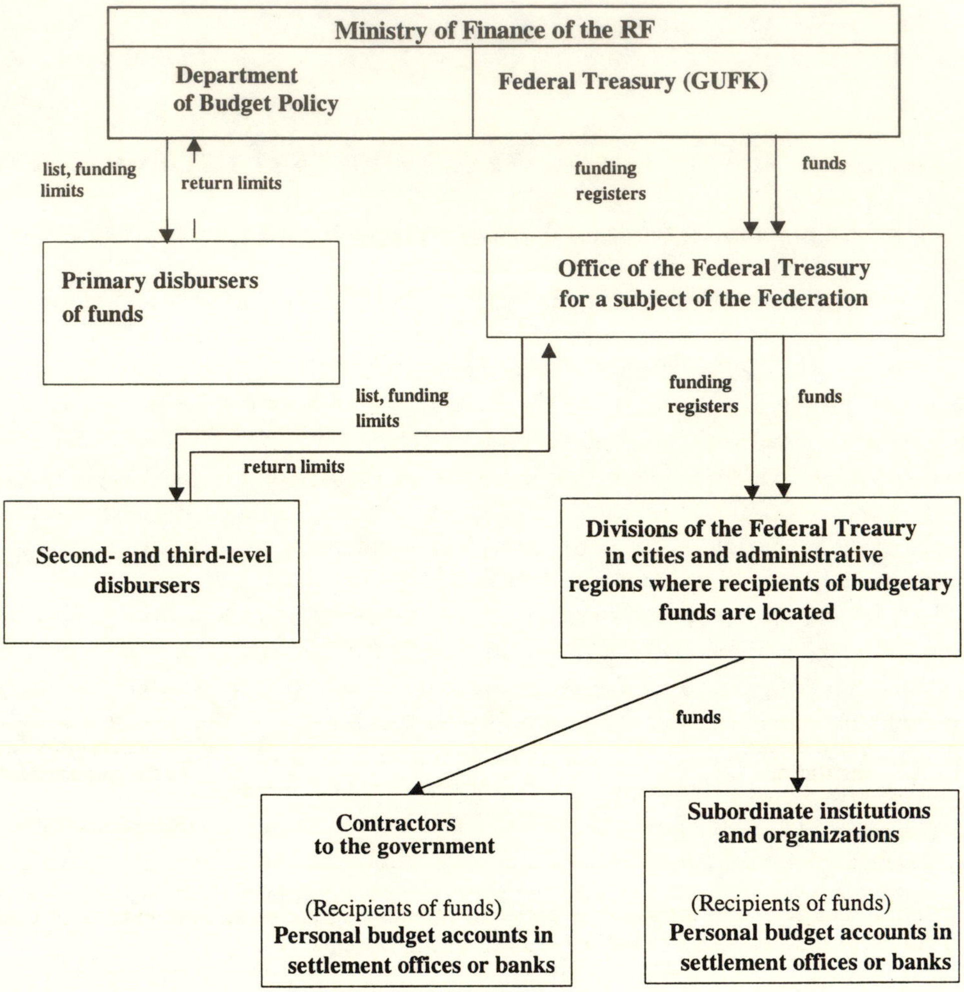

Figure 5.1 **Diagram of treasury execution of the federal budget.**

Approval of expenditures included:

- compilation and authorization of a budget list and budgetary appropriations, and getting them to the (primary) disbursers and recipients of federal budgetary funds
- precise verification of the disbursers' and recipients' estimated income and expenditures
- authorization of notifications of the limits of budgetary obligations and getting them to the (primary) disbursers and recipients of federal budgetary funds
- confirmation and reconciliation of the execution of federal budgetary obligations.

Funding of expenditures included disbursal of budgetary funds by transferring them from the Central Administration of the Federal Treasury with payment orders and by handing over registers for funding out of federal budget revenues.

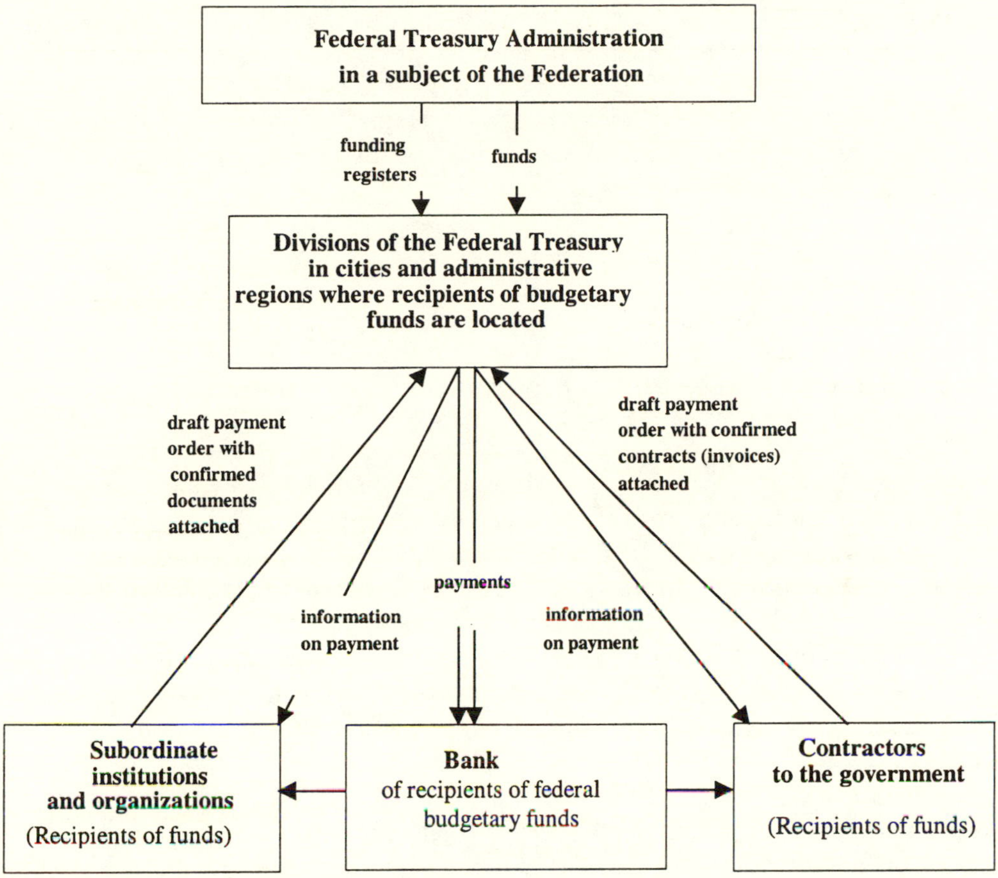

Figure 5.2. **Diagram of interrelations between treasury agencies and recipients of budgetary funds in the process of cash execution of the budget.**

The interrelations between the treasury's territorial agencies and the recipients of budgetary funds in the process of cash spending from the federal budget are presented in Figure 5.2.

Immediately after receiving the "Registers for transfer of funds" and summary payment orders by e-mail from the Central Administration of the Federal Treasury, the Federal Treasury Administrations in individual subjects of the Federation began to draw up the paperwork for the disbursers and recipients of budgetary funds in one of the following versions:

- in the case of funding with the use of monetary registers, the funds were transferred by payment order at the same time as the funding limits were reported in registers for specific disbursers or recipients of federal budgetary funds
- in the case of funding with the use of clearing registers out of federal budget revenues received in the territory of a subject of the Federation, the Federal Treasury Administra-

tion transferred the funds from account 100, "Federal budget revenues," with the symbol 95, to account 120, "Expenditures from the federal budget," with the symbol 99.

The funding paperwork included recording the registers in a special logbook, checking to see that they correspond to the summary payment order, and authorizing individual allocations. This process consisted of:

- written notification of the disbursers of funds about the appropriated funding limits
- receiving from the disbursers of funds instructions for the distribution of funds to individual subordinate institutions and organizations (and also a profile of their functional and economic classification)
- preparing registers and orders for the divisions of the Federal Treasury that directly serve the recipients of federal budgetary funds.

When the funding registers are processed, they are decreased by the amounts previously provided in advance for protected current expenditure items (mostly for wages with accruals and stipends). The funds on monetary registers are transferred only after they are received from the Ministry of Finance of Russia in the account of the Federal Treasury Administration in a subject of the Federation.

For agencies of the Federal Treasury, which existed in practically all cities, administrative regions, and city districts by 1998, funds were also transferred by payment orders to account 120, "Federal budgetary funds," on the basis of the summary orders that were prepared. Upon receiving a register and funds in its account, a division of the Federal Treasury prepared an extract from the list and an order for crediting federal budgetary funds to the personal accounts of the disbursers and recipients of those funds.

To fund their own activity, and to pay for goods, work, and services, the recipients of budgetary funds provided territorial agencies of the Federal Treasury with draft payment orders, with confirming documents attached (contracts, invoices, etc.). Expenses are paid from personal treasury accounts by agencies of the Federal Treasury after checking the disburser's documents to see that they correspond to the items in the estimate, and also contracts with suppliers for delivering products (work, services).

The transition to treasury execution of the federal budget, which was mostly completed in 1998, gave representative and executive authorities in the Center, as well as in subjects of the Federation, new opportunities to analyze and plan the territorial profile of budgetary expenditures. Now this information can be taken into account in forming interbudgetary relations.

5.3.2 Differences between regions in forms of funding direct expenditures from the federal budget

The forms in which direct expenditures from the federal budget are funded are a significant element in analyzing financial relations between the Center and the regions. Financially strong regions are interested in increasing the portion of clearing registers. This gives them the opportunity to influence federal expenditures in their territory (the priority of funding recipients of budgetary funds, etc.) and keep more funds for regional needs. For example, that was the reason for the demand put forth during discussion of the draft budget for 1999 that 50% of tax revenues "over and above the planned target" go to funding of federal programs in the region. Financially weak regions are interested in receiving funds from outside the region (including planned transfers), since the revenues collected in the region do not even cover their minimum needs.

In 1998, funding of direct expenditures out of *federal budget revenues* (on clearing registers) amounted to 14.8 billion rubles, or 13.7% of all direct expenditures from the federal budget. The regional profile of funding out of revenues is presented in Table 5.1.

By 1998, 81 Federal Treasury Administrations already had the right to transfer money for funding of expenditures out of federal budget revenues received in their region. Throughout the year there were conflicts between federal executive authorities and the regions in connection with failure to observe the procedure for transferring federal budget revenues. In the course of the most dramatic of these conflicts, on August 27, 1998, the Federal Treasury Administration for Kalmykia was deprived of the right to transfer federal budget revenues for funding of expenditures in the republic. It had grossly violated the joint letter of the Ministry of Finance and the Central Bank of Russia dated June 30, 1995, "On the procedure for compiling a statement of the amount of federal budget revenues to be transferred for funding of expenditures from the federal budget in the territory of a subject of the Russian Federation."

As expected, funding out of revenues accounted for the greatest portion of direct expenditures from the territorial budget in economically developed regions, which are donors, for the most part (see Chapter 2 for the list of donors). According to the calculations that were done, the coefficient of correlation between the portion of funding out of revenues and "being a donor" is equal to 0.46.

The group of subjects of the Federation with a low portion of funding through clearing registers mostly includes economically underdeveloped territories that are highly dependent on federal aid. Regions with a special relationship with the Federation are an exception (Moscow, Tatarstan, Bashkiria).

In 1998, funding in the form of *nonmonetary settlements* amounted to 10.1 billion rubles, or 9.4% of all direct expenditures from the federal budget. The regional profile of funding through nonmonetary settlements is presented in Table 5.2. Nonmonetary settlements reduce the actual portion of "cash" money in regional budgets, and therefore regions with a high portion of nonmonetary settlements with the federal budget are in the position of losers.

Funding of federal expenditures out of revenues makes up an insignificant part of federal expenditures. However, it does have a tendency to grow. This form is disadvantageous to the federal budget, since it gives the regions opportunities to understate federal revenues. International financial organizations, led by the International Monetary Fund, actively oppose the use of this form of funding (as they do all forms of nonmonetary settlements). However, the tenacity and extent of nonmonetary settlements demonstrate the considerable political capabilities of regional elites.

Table 5.1

Portion of Funding out of Federal Budget Revenues in All Direct Expenditures from the Federal Budget in Individual Regions

Portion of expenditures %	Regions	Population 1,000	Population %
0–4	*Republics of Bashkortostan, Dagestan, North Osetia, Tatarstan, and Ingushetia, Kaliningrad Oblast, Taimyr (Dolgan-Nenets) and Evenk Autonomous Regions*, Republic of Tyva, Kabardino-Balkar Republic, Chukotka Autonomous Region, Moscow, Maritime Territory, Jewish Autonomous Oblast, Kamchatka, Sakhalin, and Chita Oblasts, Republic of Buryatia	28,810	19.7
4–10	Komi-Permyat and Nenets Autonomous Regions, Republic of Karelia, Komi Republic, Kostroma Oblast, Khabarovsk Territory, Amur Oblast, Koryak Autonomous Region, Magadan and Kurgan Oblasts, Republic of Adygeya, Karachaevo-Cherkess Republic, Republic of Khakasia, Ust-Orda Buryat Autonomous Region, Tomsk Oblast, Republic of Mordovia	31,636	21.6
10–30	Orenburg and Kaluga Oblasts, Yamal-Nenets Autonomous Region, Novosibirsk Oblast, Republic of Sakha (Yakutia), Altai Territory, Pskov, Tula, Rostov, Arkhangelsk, and Saratov Oblasts, Altai Republic, Bryansk and Kemerovo Oblasts, Aga Buryat Autonomous Region, Penza and Tambov Oblasts, Marii El Republic, Ivanovo, Kirov, and Orlov Oblasts, Krasnoyarsk and Stavropol Territories, Voronezh, and Tver Oblasts, Republic of Kalmykia, Udmurt Republic	49,034	33.5
30–50	Novgorod Oblast, Krasnodar Territory, Tyumen, Chelyabinsk, Murmansk, Ryazan, Astrakhan, and Kursk Oblasts, Chuvash Republic, Belgorod, Sverdlovsk, Omsk, Perm, Irkutsk, Smolensk, Vologda, Volgograd, Moscow, and Ulyanovsk Oblasts	34,606	23.7
More than 50	Leningrad, Yaroslavl, Lipetsk, and Vladimir Oblasts, Khanty-Mansi Autonomous Region, Samara and Nizhegorod Oblasts, St. Petersburg	2,221	1.5

Note: Regions in which funding out of federal budget revenues did not occur in 1998 are shown in italics.

Table 5.2

Portion of Nonmonetary Settlements of Subjects of the Federation with the Federal Budget as a Percentage of Federal Budgetary Expenditures in the Region

Portion of expenditures %	Regions	Population 1,000	Population %
0–1.5	Novgorod Oblast, Republic of Karelia, Amur and Moscow Oblasts, Aga Buryat Autonomous Region, Republics of Bashkortostan and Ingushetia, Magadan Oblast, Nenets, Taimyr (Dolgan-Nenets), Ust-Orda Buryat, Khanty-Mansi, Chukotka, and Yamal-Nenets Autonomous Regions, Altai Republic, Republic of Sakha (Yakutia), Tula, Sakhalin, and Kaliningrad Oblasts, Evenk Autonomous Region, St. Petersburg, Republic of Kalmykia, Kursk, Lipetsk, Murmansk, Yaroslavl, and Kaluga Oblasts, Stavropol Territory, Chita Oblast, Krasnodar Territory, Arkhangelsk and Kamchatka Oblasts, Komi-Permyat Autonomous Region, Ivanovo Oblast	60,446	41.3
1.5–5	Republic of Khakasia, Jewish Autonomous Oblast, Ryazan, Sverdlovsk, Voronezh, Perm, and Kemerovo Oblasts, Udmurt Republic, Leningrad Oblast, Khabarovsk Territory, Kirov and Volgograd Oblasts, Komi Republic, Samara, Tyumen, and Astrakhan Oblasts, Republic of Dagestan, Novosibirsk, Rostov, and Nizhegorod Oblasts, Republic of North Osetia, Smolensk Oblast, Republic of Adygeya, Bryansk and Pskov Oblasts	45,691	31.2
5–10	Maritime Territory, Kostroma, Tomsk, Vologda, Tver, and Ulyanovsk Oblasts, Koryak Autonomous Region, Altai Territory, Irkutsk, Belgorod, Penza, and Tambov Oblasts, Republic of Tatarstan, Vladimir and Orlov Oblasts, Kabardino-Balkar Republic, Republic of Buryatia, Krasnoyarsk Territory	37,133	25.4
10–20	Omsk and Chelyabinsk Oblasts, Republic of Tyva, Karachaevo-Cherkess Republic, Kurgan Oblast, Moscow, Marii El Republic	1,082	0.7
More than 20	Saratov Oblast, Chuvash Republic, Orenburg Oblast, Republic of Mordovia	1,955	1.3

Table 5.3

Distribution of Direct Federal Expenditures among Different Groups of Regions in 1998 (%)

Groups of regions	Share of direct expenditures	Share of population	Share of GRP (1997)
By economic areas	**100.0**	**100.0**	**100.0**
Northern	2.9	4.0	4.6
Northwestern	3.7	5.5	5.0
Central	56.7	20.3	20.5
including:			
Moscow and Moscow Oblast	50.8	10.4	13.9
not including Moscow and Moscow Oblast	5.9	9.9	6.7
Volga-Vyatka	2.2	5.7	4.2
Central Chernozem	2.3	5.4	3.7
Lower Volga	4.2	11.5	11.0
Northern Caucasus	6.4	11.6	6.1
Ural	4.9	13.9	14.2
Western Siberian	7.4	10.3	16.8
Eastern Siberian	4.0	6.2	7.0
Far East	5.0	5.0	6.5
Kaliningrad Oblast	0.3	0.6	0.4
Regions by level of development (specific GRP adjusted for the subsistence level)	**100**	**100**	**100**
Developed	4.5	7.4	3.7
Upper middle	15.1	26.2	18.1
Middle	15.0	24.5	21.2
Lower middle	12.3	22.4	23.9
Underdeveloped	53.1	19.4	33.1
By balance of financial flows	**100**	**100**	**100**
Consistent donors*	67.3	49.8	60.5
including:			
Moscow	48.7	5.9	10.9
not including Moscow	18.6	43.9	49.6
Inconsistent donors	9.6	17.6	14.6
Consistent recipients	23.1	32.6	24.9
By status	**100**	**100**	**100**
Oblasts	33.9	61.7	56.4
Territories	6.5	11.8	10.2
Republics	6.8	14.8	13.0
Autonomous regions	1.4	2.5	6.2
including:			
Khanty-Mansi and Yamal-Nenets	0.4	1.3	5.1
not including Khanty-Mansi and Yamal-Nenets	1.1	1.2	1.1
Moscow, St. Petersburg	51.5	9.1	14.2

* According to the balance of financial flows taking into account the Federation's direct expenditures (see Chapter 2).

5.4 DISTRIBUTION OF DIRECT EXPENDITURES FROM THE FEDERAL BUDGET AMONG THE REGIONS IN 1998

5.4.1 Differences between regions in specific expenditures from the federal budget

Analysis showed that territorial direct expenditures from the federal budget were unevenly distributed among the regions in 1998 (Table 5.3). This results in sharp differences between regions in specific federal expenditures. For instance, with an average per capita level of expenditures for the whole Federation equal to 735 rubles, the per capita expenditures in individual regions varied from 43 rubles in Bashkiria to 6074 rubles in Moscow.

In analyzing the level of expenditures, first of all, our attention is drawn to the relatively small number of people living in territories with the minimum and maximum values. The group with the minimum expenditures includes six regions; with the maximum, four. The group with the middle level of specific expenditures included 71 regions. However, even within this set, the extreme values differ by almost four times.

In 1998, the minimum level of per capita expenditures was noted in a highly heterogeneous group of regions. The Khanty-Mansi Autonomous Region, Bashkiria, Tatarstan, and Samara and (with a certain qualification) Vologda Oblasts, which are all part of this group, are classified as generally accepted donors to the federal budget. Besides that, the low level of federal expenditures in Bashkiria and Tatarstan is explained by their specific relations with the federal financial system, which are dictated by bilateral treaties. In our view, there is no reasonable explanation for the abnormally low level of federal expenditures in the Ust-Orda Buryat Autonomous Region.

The group of regions with the highest level of specific direct expenditures from the federal budget is just as heterogeneous. Along with Moscow, which is traditionally recognized as a donor, it includes underdeveloped northern autonomous regions.

The information received from the Federal Treasury Administration for Moscow on indices of direct expenditures from the federal budget in 1998 includes data on expenditures by a number of federal ministries and departments (the court system, in particular) that were not divided up by regions. On the strength of peculiarities of the way in which the information was presented in 1998, it did not seem possible in our research to correct the data on Moscow so as to completely eliminate the information on expenditures that were not divided up by territories.

In order to even out, as much as possible, the effect of geographic and natural climatic factors on the amount of budgetary expenditures and reduce the data on different regions to a more comparable form, in the course of the research the index of direct expenditures was adjusted for the subsistence level (see Chapter 1, and Tables 5.4 and 5.5).

Adjustment for the cost of living, so that the index of budgetary expenditures better reflects the purchasing power of budget appropriations, makes the composition of the groupings with the extreme levels of expenditures even more heterogeneous (Map 11).

Table 5.4

Specific Direct Expenditures from the Federal Budget in 1998 (Adjusted for the Subsistence Level)

Share of expenditures, %	Regions	Population	
		1,000	%
Less than 300	*Sverdlovsk* and Tyumen Oblasts, Aga Buryat, Ust-Orda Buryat, *Khanty-Mansi*, and Yamal-Nenets Autonomous Regions, Vologda, Kirov, and *Samara* Oblasts, *Republics of Bashkortostan and Tatarstan*	8,361	5.7
300–450	Saratov, Smolensk, Tambov, Ulyanovsk, Chelyabinsk, Chita, and Yaroslavl Oblasts, Republic of Adygeya, Jewish Autonomous Oblast, Republic of Khakasia, Voronezh, Nizhegorod, Ivanovo, *Irkutsk*, Kaliningrad, Tver, Kostroma, Kurgan, Leningrad, *Lipetsk, Moscow,* Murmansk, Novgorod, Omsk, Orenburg, Penza, *Perm*, and Pskov Oblasts, Republics of Buryatia, Dagestan, and Karelia, Marii El Republic, Republic of Tyva, Udmurt and Chuvash Republics, Republic of Sakha (Yakutia), Altai, Krasnodar, Maritime, and Stavropol Territories, Amur, Arkhangelsk, Astrakhan, Vladimir, and Volgograd Oblasts	70,481	48.2
450–550	Ryazan Oblast, Komi-Permyat Autonomous Region, Kamchatka Oblast, Republic of Mordovia, *Krasnoyarsk* and Khabarovsk Territories, Belgorod Oblast	64,429	44.0
550–800	Sakhalin and Tomsk Oblasts, *St. Petersburg*, Altai Republic, Karachaevo-Cherkess Republic, Koryak Autonomous Region, Kaluga, Kursk, Magadan, Novosibirsk, and Rostov Oblasts, Kabardino-Balkar Republic, Republic of Kalmykia, Komi Republic, Republic of Ingushetia	1,082	0.7
More than 800	Tula Oblast, *Moscow*, Nenets, Taimyr (Dolgan-Nenets), Chukotka, and Evenk Autonomous Regions, Kemerovo and Orlov Oblasts, Republic of North Osetia, Bryansk Oblast	1,955	1.3

Note: Regions that did not receive transfers in 1998 are shown in italics.

The grouping of subjects of the Federation with the minimum level of expenditures included both donors (Sverdlovsk Oblast and the Yamal-Nenets Autonomous Region) and typical depressed regions (the Aga Buryat Autonomous Region and Kirov Oblast).

The group of regions with the highest level of expenditures was expanded by two Arctic regions (the Nenets and Taimyr Autonomous Regions), and also two problem regions (Kemerovo Oblast, with programs supporting the coal industry, and North Osetia, which has ethnic social problems). It also included the three oblasts most affected by the consequences of the Chernobyl catastrophe (Orlov, Bryansk, and Tula).

Table 5.5
Specific Direct Expenditures from the Federal Budget by Groups of Regions of Russia in 1998 (%)

Groups of regions	Specific direct expenditures in relation to the national average: nominal	Specific direct expenditures in relation to the national average: actual (adjusted for the subsistence level)	Ratio of direct expenditures to GRP (1996)
By economic areas	**100**	**100**	**100**
Northern	73	64	63
Northwestern	68	59	75
Central	280	223	276
including:			
Moscow and Moscow Oblast	489	363	366
not including Moscow and Moscow Oblast	60	172	210
Volga-Vyatka	38	47	52
Central Chernozem	43	60	62
Lower Volga	36	44	38
Northern Caucasus	55	74	105
Ural	35	41	35
Western Siberian	72	71	44
Eastern Siberian	65	64	58
Far East	100	69	77
Kaliningrad Oblast	42	49	70
Regions by level of development (specific GRP adjusted for the subsistence level)	**100**	**100**	**100**
Developed	60	64	122
Upper middle	57	62	83
Middle	61	65	71
Lower middle	55	61	52
Underdeveloped	273	207	160
By balance of financial flows	**100**	**100**	**100**
Consistent donors*	135	112	111
including:			
Moscow	826	600	448
not including Moscow	43	47	38
Inconsistent donors	55	61	66
Consistent recipients	71	76	92
By status	**100**	**100**	**100**
Oblasts	55	62	60
Territories	55	60	63
Republics	46	49	52
Autonomous regions	57	44	23
including:			
Khanty-Mansi and Yamal-Nenets	30	20	7
not including Khanty-Mansi and Yamal-Nenets	85	70	95
Moscow, St. Petersburg	563	412	362

Table 5.6

Specific Expenditures Adjusted for the Subsistence Level, Rubles

Region		Region	
Bryansk Oblast	998.7	Orlov Oblast	940.3
Vladimir Oblast	317.4	Ryazan Oblast	541.9
Ivanovo Oblast	383.3	Smolensk Oblast	364.2
Tver Oblast	405.8	Tula Oblast	967.4
Kaluga Oblast	580.4	Yaroslavl Oblast	332.7
Kostroma Oblast	441.5	*Moscow*	*4,840.5*
Moscow Oblast	368.4		

Table 5.7

Coefficients of Variation in the Per Capita Index of Expenditures on Different Functions of Government, Adjusted for the Subsistence Level (%)

Function	Coefficient of variation
Government administration	65.8
Science	222.5
Ministry of Emergency Situations of Russia	254.2
Production	104.0
Social sphere	55.4

Our attention is drawn to the level of federal budgetary expenditures in Moscow, which is in a special position as a subject of the Federation. It is anomalous, in our view, even taking into account its status as the capital. This is particularly obvious in comparison with neighboring regions in the Central economic area (Table 5.6).

Information about the level of federal budgetary expenditures in Moscow (even taking into account the adjustments stipulated above) forces us to take a more cautious attitude toward the generally accepted thesis that Moscow is unquestionably one of the regions that are donors to the federal budget.

5.4.2 Distribution of direct expenditures from the federal budget on different functions of government

For the purpose of analyzing the profile of different types of direct expenditures in individual subjects of the Federation, the categories of the functional classification were enlarged. The data obtained are presented in a statistical Appendix (Table A.4).

Analysis of the coefficients of variation of the specific index of expenditures (adjusted for the subsistence level) on different functions of government in individual subjects of the Federation showed that the most unevenly funded are regional expenditures

Table 5.8

Specific Direct Federal Expenditures on Production by Groups of Regions of Russia in 1998

Groups of regions	Specific direct expenditures on support of the production sector in % of the national average: nominal	Specific direct expenditures on support of the production sector in % of the national average: actual (adjusted for the subsistence level)	Direct expenditures on support of the production sector in relation to GRP (1996)
By economic areas	100	100	100
Northern	152	138	131
Northwestern	56	49	61
Central	252	193	249
including:			
Moscow and Moscow Oblast	467	346	350
not including Moscow and Moscow Oblast	26	159	200
Volga-Vyatka	24	30	33
Central Chernozem	13	18	19
Lower Volga	20	24	22
Northern Caucasus	76	105	144
Ural	28	32	27
Western Siberian	132	135	81
Eastern Siberian	34	32	30
Far East	143	93	109
Kaliningrad Oblast	4	4	6
Regions by level of development (specific GRP adjusted for the subsistence level)	**100**	**100**	**100**
Developed	33	36	67
Upper middle	64	72	93
Middle	30	30	35
Lower middle	85	89	80
Underdeveloped	278	213	163
By balance of financial flows	**100**	**100**	**100**
Consistent donors*	118	94	97
including:			
Moscow	793	576	430
not including Moscow	27	30	24
Inconsistent donors	49	50	59
Consistent recipients	100	105	131
By status	100	100	100
Oblasts	61	68	67
Territories	32	31	37
Republics	59	54	67
Autonomous regions	37	29	15
including:			
Khanty-Mansi and Yamal-Nenets	11	8	3
not including Khanty-Mansi and Yamal-Nenets	63	50	71
Moscow, St. Petersburg	535	391	344

Table 5.9

Table of Correlations

	FB expenditures per capita	FB expenditures per capita adjusted for the subsistence level	FB expenditures per capita on government administration	FB expenditures on government administration per bureaucrat	FB expenditures per capita on industry	FB expenditures per capita on agriculture	FB expenditures per capita on education	FB expenditures on education per student	FB expenditures per capita on public health	FB social expenditures per capita	FB social expenditures adjusted for the subsistence level	FB expenditures per capita on culture
FB* expenditures per capita	1											
FB expenditures per capita adjusted for the subsistence level	0.94	1										
FB expenditures per capita on government administration	0.80	0.69	1									
FB expenditures on government administration per bureaucrat	0.85	0.76	0.50	1								
FB expenditures per capita on industry	0.70	0.60	0.43	0.62	1							
FB expenditures per capita on agriculture	0.83	0.83	0.46	0.93	0.51	1						
FB expenditures per capita on education	0.68	0.65	0.51	0.66	0.37	0.64	1					
FB expenditures on education per student	0.22	0.06	0.51	0.20	0.32	0.08	0.44	1				
FB expenditures per capita on public health	0.82	0.76	0.51	0.87	0.55	0.83	0.73	0.19	1			
FB social expenditures per capita	0.75	0.75	0.30	0.90	0.49	0.94	0.54	–0.01	0.77	1		
FB social expenditures adjusted for the subsistence level	0.72	0.74	0.28	0.87	0.47	0.91	0.51	–0.04	0.73	1.00	1	
FB expenditures per capita on culture	0.61	0.62	0.20	0.75	0.39	0.76	0.55	–0.03	0.80	0.77	0.74	1

* FB — federal budgetary

Table 5.10

Federal Subsidy of the Coal Industry, % of Total for Russia

Region	Coal production	Federal subsidies of the coal industry
Kemerovo Oblast	44	35
Krasnoyarsk Territory	16	0.3
Komi Republic	8	15
Irkutsk Oblast	7	0.3
Rostov Oblast	5	21
Chita Oblast	4	1
Maritime Territory	4	5
Republic of Sakha (Yakutia)	4	2

on mitigating the consequences of natural and technogenic disasters. This is explained by the territorial localization of emergency situations. Expenditures on basic research vary almost as much, which is due to the location of federal scientific centers.

It follows from the data in Table 5.7 that expenditures on the category "*Government administration and local self-government*" (i.e., on territorial subdivisions of federal agencies) vary moderately in individual territories. The ten regions with the highest expenditures included nine regions representing sparsely settled territories of the Far North, where it is much more expensive to maintain government institutions, on account of the severe climatic conditions and enormous distances between population centers. The groups of leaders also included Moscow, where, for a number of reasons, there is a high portion of federal bureaucrats in the population. The data on expenditures per government employee in Moscow are quite indicative: they are more than three times higher than the national average. The specific expenditures on federal agencies are lowest in the subjects of the Federation that have received the greatest degree of autonomy within Russia: Bashkiria, Tatarstan, and Ingushetia. Such donor regions as Moscow, Samara, and Leningrad Oblasts, Krasnodar Territory, and St. Petersburg are also this category.

Calculations showed that, on the whole, expenditures on the government correlate to the greatest degree with expenditures on education and public health.

The research showed that the total expenditures *on support for the production sector* (industry, power generation, construction, transportation, roads, and communications) in individual regions of Russia varies more than twice as much as expenditures on maintaining government agencies. As we can see from Table 5.8, the portion of subsidies going to the production sector in the gross regional product is higher in underdeveloped, poor, and subsidized regions. We were also able to establish a high correlation between federal budgetary expenditures on the production sector and specific social expenditures (Table 5.9). The coefficient of correlation was 0.5.

To make them more informative, the expenditures on support of production were adjusted for the index of gross industrial output in the research. Analysis showed that support of enterprises in the production sector is selective. It is concentrated in a fairly

Table 5.11

Specific Direct Expenditures from the Federal Budget on Support for Agriculture by Groups of Regions of Russia in 1998 (%)

Groups of regions	Specific direct expenditures on support for agriculture in % of the national average: nominal	Specific direct expenditures on support for agriculture in % of the national average: actual (adjusted for the subsistence level)	Direct expenditures on support for agriculture in relation to GRP (1997)
By economic areas	**100**	**100**	**100**
Northern	19	17	16
Northwestern	16	15	17
Central	386	290	381
including:			
Moscow and Moscow Oblast	728	533	545
not including Moscow and Moscow Oblast	27	203	265
Volga-Vyatka	20	24	27
Central Chernozem	26	37	38
Lower Volga	40	48	42
Northern Caucasus	51	68	96
Ural	13	15	13
Western Siberian	16	16	10
Eastern Siberian	32	31	28
Far East	32	23	25
Kaliningrad Oblast	22	25	36
Regions by level of development (specific GRP adjusted for the subsistence level)	**100**	**100**	**100**
Developed	51	59	103
Upper middle	30	35	44
Middle	29	34	33
Lower middle	24	29	23
Underdeveloped	390	286	229
By balance of financial flows	100	100	100
Consistent donors*	165	126	136
including: Moscow	1261	917	685
not including Moscow	17	20	15
Inconsistent donors	43	53	51
Consistent recipients	32	37	42
By status	**100**	**100**	**100**
Oblasts	27	32	29
Territories	38	46	44
Republics	24	29	28
Autonomous regions	26	24	11
including:			
Khanty-Mansi and Yamal-Nenets	5	3	1
not including Khanty-Mansi and Yamal-Nenets	48	46	55
Moscow, St. Petersburg	817	594	525

limited group of regions and correlates to the greatest degree with social expenditures from the federal budget.

The research showed that most of the industrially developed regions of European Russia practically do not receive subsidies from the federal budget. The prevailing opinion that Russia now has no effective industrial policy aimed at promoting economic growth is confirmed by the list of regions that receive support for the production sector. It included Ingushetia (and, to a lesser degree, other regions of the Caucasus: Karachaevo-Cherkessia, Dagestan, and Kabardino-Balkaria), and also Moscow and a group of regions with a developed coal industry: Rostov, Sakhalin, and Kemerovo Oblasts, and the Komi Republic (Table 5.10). Federal budgetary expenditures on support for the production sector are not distributed on the basis of economic criteria and are used inefficiently. Inefficient production processes receive funding, while efficient enterprises are deprived of budgetary support.

The situation in the coal industry differs radically from most other branches of the production sector. The main expenditures on restructuring the industry are made in basins where coal production is inefficient and dropping, which explains the gap between the regions' percentage of coal production and subsidies received from the federal budget for supporting the coal industry.

Expenditures on the category "*Agriculture and fishing*" vary significantly in individual territories. However, even here, either territories of the North and the Far East, or the republics of the Northern Caucasus are predominant among the recipient regions. In this case as well, expenditures on support for agriculture correlate to the greatest degree with social expenditures, which is one more argument in favor of the hypothesis that they are primarily social expenditures, rather than economic support (Table 5.11).

On the whole, expenditures for *social purposes* are distributed most evenly among the territories (Map 12), which is apparently explained by the fact that they are strictly tied to institutions in the social sphere, which were formerly distributed among the territories based on the stated policy of providing at least a minimum level of common social standards for the whole population (Table 5.12).

However, the situation is different with respect to individual types of social expenditures. For instance, *expenditures on education* include mostly higher education, and also partly secondary and specialized secondary education (educational institutions turned over to subjects of the Federation). In this case, the expenditures go to traditional scientific and production centers. This explains the high specific level of them in Moscow, Tomsk, St. Petersburg, Novosibirsk, and such regional capitals as Khabarovsk, Krasnoyarsk, and Vladivostok. On the whole, our attention is drawn to the relatively high level of per capita expenditures on education in Siberia and the Far East, which may be explained by the age structure of the population that was established before the reforms began, with a higher than normal percentage of people of working (and childbearing) age and children.

Data on the amount of federal budgetary expenditures per student in higher educational institutions primarily demonstrate the effect of natural climatic factors, which can be judged by the portion of agriculture in the GRP (there is an inverse relationship

Table 5.12

Specific Direct Expenditures from the Federal Budget for Social Purposes (Adjusted for the Subsistence Level) by Groups of Regions of Russia in 1998 (%)

Groups of regions	Specific direct expenditures for social purposes (adjusted for the subsistence level) in % of the national average: nominal	actual (adjusted for the subsistence level)	Direct expenditures for social purposes (adjusted for the subsistence level) in relation to GRP (1996)
By economic areas	**100**	**100**	**100**
Northern	49	42	42
Northwestern	89	75	97
Central	303	233	299
including:			
Moscow and Moscow Oblast	554	407	415
not including Moscow and Moscow Oblast	40	178	227
Volga-Vyatka	37	46	50
Central Chernozem	38	53	55
Lower Volga	34	41	36
Northern Caucasus	50	66	96
Ural	35	40	34
Western Siberian	52	51	32
Eastern Siberian	65	65	58
Far East	68	51	52
Kaliningrad Oblast	43	50	72
Regions by level of development (specific GRP adjusted for the subsistence level)	**100**	**100**	**100**
Developed	56	61	114
Upper middle	47	52	68
Middle	56	56	65
Lower middle	44	51	42
Underdeveloped	308	231	180
By balance of financial flows	100	100	100
Consistent donors*	151	124	124
including: Moscow	953	693	517
not including Moscow	43	47	38
Inconsistent donors	47	52	56
Consistent recipients	51	55	66
By status	100	100	100
Oblasts	44	50	48
Territories	55	60	64
Republics	36	41	42
Autonomous regions	31	28	13
including:			
Khanty-Mansi and Yamal-Nenets	11	7	3
not including Khanty-Mansi and Yamal-Nenets	51	48	58
Moscow, St. Petersburg	661	484	424

Table 5.13

Regions with Greatest and Least Federal Expenditures on Education per Student

Regions	Rubles	Regions	Rubles
Sakhalin Oblast	19,609	Republic of Bashkortostan	25
Jewish Autonomous Oblast	13,658	Republic of Tatarstan	2,445
Republic of Tyva	13,117	Moscow Oblast	2,513
Magadan Oblast	12,924	Volgograd Oblast	2,590
Chita Oblast	11,252	Stavropol Territory	2,651
Murmansk Oblast	11,180	Ulyanovsk Oblast	3,063
Kamchatka Oblast	10,717	Vologda Oblast	3,111
Arkhangelsk Oblast	10,224	Republic of Dagestan	3,158
Orenburg Oblast	10,075	Samara Oblast	3,180
Komi Republic	9,402	Republic of Ingushetia	3,204

Table 5.14

Regions with Greatest and Least Federal Expenditures on Education per Student, Adjusted for the Subsistence Level

Regions	Rubles	Regions	Rubles
Orenburg Oblast	13,152	St. Petersburg	3,163
Jewish Autonomous Oblast	12,823	Altai Territory	6,067
Sakhalin Oblast	11,795	Amur Oblast	5,868
Kurgan Oblast	11,391	Astrakhan Oblast	6,268
Republic of Tyva	10,511	Belgorod Oblast	4,906
Tambov Oblast	9,346	Bryansk Oblast	7,008
Chita Oblast	9,123	Vladimir Oblast	8,433
Komi Republic	8,773	Volgograd Oblast	3,030
Arkhangelsk Oblast	8,683	Vologda Oblast	3 229

between these indices). However, when we compare the expenditures for regions belonging to the same climatic zone, for example, Vladimir and Smolensk Oblasts (expenditures on the order of 7,500 rubles per student) with Vologda or Ulyanovsk Oblast (3,000 rubles per student), obvious disproportions show up (Tables 5.13 and 5.14). So, expenditures in the neighboring Jewish Autonomous Oblast and Amur Oblast, or in Arkhangelsk and Vologda Oblasts differ by two times. The reasons for such seemingly hard-to-explain differences require additional study, but the very fact of their existence indicates the lack of a clear regional policy in the educational sphere.

Expenditures on the category "*Culture*" were sharply tilted in favor of Moscow and St. Petersburg, where the most important federal cultural institutions are concentrated. However, expenditures for these purposes are unevenly distributed even in relation to other regions. In our view, the differences by an order of magnitude in expenditures on culture between Pskov and Novgorod Oblasts have no reasonable explanation.

Table 5.15

Regions with Greatest and Least Specific Expenditures on Public Health from the Federal Budget

Regions	Rubles	Regions	Rubles
Moscow	315.7	Republic of Bashkortostan	0.9
St. Petersburg	110.3	Republic of Ingushetia	2.7
Chukotka Autonomous Region	98.2	Republic of Dagestan	4.0
Tomsk Oblast	78.0	Vladimir Oblast	4.4
Evenk Autonomous Region	71.7	Republic of Tatarstan	4.7
Khabarovsk Territory	66.3	Tula Oblast	4.9
Sakhalin Oblast	64.3	Tambov Oblast	5.6
Novosibirsk Oblast	60.2	Belgorod Oblast	5.6
Koryak Autonomous Region	58.1	Republic of North Osetia	5.8
Arkhangelsk Oblast	56.7	Ulyanovsk Oblast	5.9

Table 5.16

Regions with Greatest and Least Specific Expenditures on Public Health from the Federal Budget, Adjusted for the Subsistence Level

Regions	Rubles	Regions	Rubles
Republic of Bashkortostan	1.2	Moscow	229.4
Republic of Ingushetia	3.1	St. Petersburg	88.7
Vladimir Oblast	5.5	Tomsk Oblast	80.2
Republic of Dagestan	5.8	Kaluga Oblast	66.0
Tula Oblast	6.3	Stavropol Territory	57.4
Republic of North Osetia	6.5	Khabarovsk Territory	56.1
Penza Oblast	6.7	Rostov Oblast	55.1
Republic of Tatarstan	6.7	Novosibirsk Oblast	51.6
Khanty-Mansi Autonomous Region	7.2	Ivanovo Oblast	51.4
Tyumen Oblast	7.3	Arkhangelsk Oblast	48.2

The uneven distribution of expenditures on *public health* is reminiscent of the pattern of expenditures on culture. The pattern is extremely chaotic in the European part of Russia, where specific expenditures on public health in regions with similar funding conditions differ by ten times or more (Tables 5.15 and 5.16).

Expenditures on *social policy* are perhaps the most "spread-out" in individual territories (Table 5.17). The political aspect of these expenditures is obvious. The Northern Caucasus region, with its ethnic problems, can serve as an example. As in the case of expenditures on support for industry and agriculture, which, as was already pointed out, are called upon in Russia to perform functions that are not inherent in them, such politicization of social policy can aggravate relations between regions.

In particular, our attention is drawn to the level of expenditures on social support for the population in Moscow and Moscow Oblast, which is five times higher than the national average. With 10.4% of the country's population and 13.9% of national household

Table 5.17

Specific Direct Expenditures from the Federal Budget for Social Purposes (Adjusted for the Subsistence Level) by Groups of Regions in 1998

Groups of regions	Specific direct expenditures for social purposes (adjusted for the subsistence level), rubles: nominal	Specific direct expenditures for social purposes (adjusted for the subsistence level), rubles: actual (adjusted for the subsistence level)	Direct expenditures for social purposes subsistence level) as % of GRP (1996)
Average for Russia	*277.5*	*277.5*	*2.24*
By economic areas	**277.5**	**277.5**	**2.24**
Northern	135	115	0.94
Northwestern	247	209	2.18
Central	841	647	6.70
including:			
Moscow and Moscow Oblast	1,537	1,130	9.28
not including Moscow and Moscow Oblast	110	495	5.07
Volga-Vyatka	103	128	1.13
Central Chernozem	105	147	1.22
Lower Volga	94	115	0.79
Northern Caucasus	140	184	2.14
Ural	96	112	0.76
Western Siberian	143	142	0.71
Eastern Siberian	180	179	1.30
Far East	188	143	1.16
Kaliningrad Oblast	120	138	1.60
Regions by level of development (specific GRP adjusted for the subsistence level)	**277**	**277**	**2.24**
Developed	157	169	2.54
Upper middle	131	144	1.53
Middle	155	156	1.45
Lower middle	123	141	0.93
Underdeveloped	854	641	4.04
By balance of financial flows	277	277	2.24
Consistent donors*	420	343	2.78
including:			
Moscow	2,645	1,922	11.58
not including Moscow	120	130	0.86
Inconsistent donors	129	145	1.26
Consistent recipients	141	153	1.48
By status	277	277	2.24
Oblasts	121	137	1.07
Territories	153	166	1.42
Republics	101	115	0.93
Autonomous regions	86	77	0.28
including:			
Khanty-Mansi and Yamal-Nenets	32	21	0.06
not including Khanty-Mansi and Yamal-Nenets	142	133	1.29
Moscow, St. Petersburg	1,833	1,342	9.50

income, these already prosperous subjects of the Federation receive almost half of federal expenditures on social protection of the population.

5.5 BASIC CONCLUSIONS AND SUGGESTIONS

The availability of information from the Federal Treasury on the regional profile of funding of direct expenditures from the federal budget enabled us to apply it to regional research. Data on funding of various types of expenditures (monetary registers, clearing registers, nonmonetary setoffs), on the distribution of expenditures on different functions of government, and on funding of federal programs and other types of direct expenditures were analyzed for the very first time in a cross section of subjects of the Federation.

The analysis that was conducted enabled us to formulate a number of preliminary conclusions and suggestions:

- In spite of the fact that complete information on the territorial profile of federal expenditures is still lacking, the available data are sufficiently complete, reliable, and informative.
- At present, direct territorial expenditures from the federal budget are not planned and not analyzed in a regional profile, although the necessary prerequisites to do this are available.
- The chaotic nature of the distribution of federal expenditures and the lack of a clear regional policy lead to sharp territorial disproportions that potentially intensify tensions in relations between the Center and the regions, split up the economic space of Russia, and complicate reforms in the regions.
- The high concentration of territorial expenditures that was found in Moscow is alarming. This may be partially due to technical factors. However, such a concentration of federal expenditures in the most prosperous region reflects excessive centralization of financial flows and the lack of a clear regional policy.
- The portion of program expenditures (they are of a targeted nature and are selected on a competitive basis, the outcome of which can be checked in audits) in all direct expenditures in Russia seems too low (both in the law on the federal budget and, to an even greater degree, in its practical execution) when compared with countries of the Organization for Economic Cooperation and Development or transitional economies. This makes it hard to check the expediency and efficiency of federal budgetary expenditures.
- The noticeable correlation that was found between expenditures for social purposes and expenditures on support for agricultural production and industry allows us to draw the conclusion that there is no effective industrial or agrarian policy at the federal level, and production subsidies are used as a way of alleviating social and ethnic tensions. This approach is considerably less justified than direct social expenditures.
- The problems to be solved by the financial tools of budgetary funding should be more clearly distinguished, leaving the solution of problems of budgetary equalization to financial aid; and implementation of investment programs with clearly defined schedules and goals, to federal programs. Solution of specific social problems or achievement of industry standards should be assigned to other territorial expenditures.

CHAPTER 6

The Federal Budget as a Source of Investments and Regional Investment Policy

6.1 BASIC FEATURES OF CURRENT REGIONAL INVESTMENT POLICY

In the conditions of the USSR's planned economy, for decades the state budget served as the dominant source of funding for capital investments. The expediency of their distribution among individual regions of the country was determined unilaterally by directive, in the interests of development of material production. The deep drop in investments that struck the Russian economy in the 1990's preserved many negative phenomena in the socioeconomic situation in the country as a whole, as well as its individual territories. There was a sharp reduction in the government's participation in financing of investments in fixed capital. On the other hand, with the development of federative relations, the budgets of subjects of the Federation and municipal entities began to play a new and more important role as a source of funding for capital investments. Foreign investments became another new source. Though the amount of foreign investments is still extremely low, they have grown considerably in comparison with past years. Enterprises' internal funds have become the primary source of investments in fixed capital. All of these changes have also had a serious effect on regional investment policy.

Unfortunately, it has to be said that regional policy in the field of development problems has not yet been set forth in the form of any unified regulatory act of the Russian Federation. The general document regulating the activity of federal authorities in relation to regional development policy is the decree of the President of the Russian Federation No. 803 of June 3, 1996, which stated the "Basic provisions of regional policy in the Russian Federation." This decree set forth the goals and objectives of regional policy and outlined ways of achieving them. At the same time, as practice shows, the solution of most regional problems in the Russian Federation is not based on this decree, but primarily on other regulatory documents.

Diverse forms of investment support for the regions have already become widespread in Russia in past years. In this case, the number of special resolutions on questions of socioeconomic development of the regions (which, as a rule, include an investment component) that were adopted by the Government and President of the Russian Federation was greater at the very beginning of the economic transformations that in later years.

There are also other ways of distributing investments from the federal budget (through the systems of various targeted budgetary funds, indirectly through participation in the activity of state enterprises, etc.). Credits granted by the International and European Banks for Reconstruction and Development (IBRD and EBRD) play a special role here.

For all of their shortcomings, the official statistics do make it possible to conduct a detailed analysis of the pattern of investments in fixed capital appropriated from the federal budget in the last few years for individual regions of the country and the funding of targeted programs, and to draw conclusions about how well the actual steps taken to implement the basic provisions of regional investment policy fit the stated goals and objectives.

6.2 FEDERAL TARGETED PROGRAMS AS A TOOL FOR DISTRIBUTING INVESTMENTS AMONG THE REGIONS OF RUSSIA

6.2.1 General information

Only two federal targeted programs for socioeconomic development of the country's regions had been adopted prior to the end of 1995. A program for the Kurile Islands (Sakhalin Oblast) was adopted in 1993, and one for Yakutia in February 1995. A program for sociocultural development of Tver Oblast was also being carried out. However, the process of developing and adopting regional programs began to take off in December 1995. As a result, the total number of approved regional development programs had reached 32 by the beginning of 1999. In addition, at the time when the research was being conducted, several more regional programs were in the development and approval stage.

In 1998, programs were approved for development of Chelyabinsk, Kostroma, and Kurgan Oblasts, the Komi Republic, the Republics of Dagestan and Ingushetia, and Stavropol Territory. The "Siberia" program was also adopted, which encompasses 19 regions (see sidebar 6.1). Of the eight newly authorized programs, six were included in the federal budget for 1999. Several more programs are being developed pursuant to resolutions of the Government of the Russian Federation: for Chita, Magadan, and Murmansk Oblasts, the Koryak and Taimyr Autonomous Regions, and the North Caucasus economic area.

The Ministry of the Economy of Russia continues to receive proposals for development programs from regional administrations.

As a rule, federal targeted programs for socioeconomic development of the regions play a coordinating role in relation to other federal and regional programs being carried out in the territory of subjects of the Federation. Thus, in conditions of restructuring of the economy, the government is pursuing an active policy in regional and local labor markets. It is aimed at eliminating the threat of rising unemployment and underemployment,

Sidebar 6.1 ***The "Siberia" program***

The federal targeted program "Siberia" is aimed at:

- solving major geostrategic, political, economic, social, environmental, and scientific and technical problems at the federal level
- comprehensive integration of the republics, territories, oblasts, and autonomous regions of Siberia and stimulation of their interaction with other regions of Russia, and economic cooperation with foreign countries, primarily with members of the Commonwealth of Independent States (CIS) and countries of the Asiatic Pacific Ocean region
- creating a more efficient mechanism for the macroregion's economic self-development, taking into account its distinctive characteristics.

The objective is to use the advantages of Siberia's economic and geographic position to strengthen Russia's role in the world economic system and reinforce the country's economic space. It is proposed to modernize old transportation lines within Russia and create new ones (the Trans-Siberian Railroad (Transsib), the Northern Siberian Railroad (Sevsib), and the Baikal-Amur Mainline), as well as transportation outlets to world markets. Russia's new geopolitical situation has brought up the problem of using Siberian resources to replace the direct access to many types of strategic mineral raw material in other CIS countries that has now been lost. This problem is of a macroregional nature. It concerns the whole Siberian economic space and is not limited to individual regions of Siberia.

So, the following problems need to be solved within the scope of this program:

- strengthening the economic integration of regions in the territory of Siberia
- improving the mechanism for interaction of members of the interregional association "Siberian Agreement" in the economic sphere
- improving the mechanism for accumulation and use of resources for implementing the program, taking into account the interests of its participants
- eliminating excessive differences in the level of economic development and standard of living within Siberia
- carrying out projects and activities aimed at increasing the efficiency of business complexes in individual subjects of the Federation by strengthening interregional production ties between industries within Siberia using progressive forms of territorial organization of production forces
- developing projects for forming a new zone of economic development of Siberia in the Near North, for the purpose of prudent resource management and solving environmental and other problems of strategic significance

- consolidating the efforts of members of the interregional association in the process of forming transportation and telecommunications systems in Siberia, and creating new transportation outlets to the world market
- forming a coordinated policy for the regions of Siberia to attract foreign investments and foreign trade, particularly with CIS countries and China.

According to specialists at the Ministry of the Economy, the presence of a serious scientific and technological reserve in the form of projects ready to be implemented is an important distinctive feature of the "Siberia" targeted program. Within the scope of this program, a regional scientific and technical program should become the main channel for working out solutions to key problems and scenarios for the region's economic development, and the analytic and scientific coordinating center for targeted federal and regional programs to be carried out in Siberia.

The most important interregional projects, which will involve regional funds, along with federal budgetary funds, are reconstruction of the Trans-Siberian Railroad (Transsib), and providing a new outlet to the world market for the regions of Central Siberia by organizing mixed "river-sea" transportation along the "Enisei-Northern Sea Route." It is also proposed to create a unified siting plan for airports and passenger and freight terminals, to finish construction of the Northern Siberian Railroad, support and retool enterprises of the military-industrial complex within the scope of the Siberian regional program "Arms Production and Conversion," develop the internal food supply in regions of Siberia, finish setting up a unified power system in Siberia, and preserve Siberia's unique scientific potential.

supporting promising industries and production processes, taking into account the regions' strategic significance and the country's geopolitical interests, creating new, economically efficient jobs, and regulating internal and external migration.

The federal budget's participation in solving problems of the regions' socioeconomic development by the method of targeted programs is not the main source of funding for program activities. In most programs, the federal budget is committed to no more than a 20% share; and in the latest programs, 8–10% of the total need for funding of the programs' activities (see sidebar 6.2). The programs are supposed to be funded mainly from extrabudgetary sources. The portion of funding from regional and local budgets is usually not very large (no more than 20–30%), since the programs are carried out, as a rule, in regions with a subsidized budget.

The programs are characterized by different scales of the problems to be solved (from comprehensive socioeconomic development to individual regional issues). They also differ in their government clients, schedules, and, of course, amount of funding. Regional development programs may cover the territory of one subject of the Federation, or they may be of a local (for example, the resort city Sochi, or the historical center St.

Sidebar 6.2 ***Funding of federal targeted programs for socioeconomic development of the regions in 1998***

Unfortunately, federal targeted programs for socioeconomic development of the regions with all types of funding sources are far behind schedule. Their funding from the federal budget is sharply reduced from year to year. The law "On the federal budget in 1998" called for federal participation in funding of 139 federal programs and subprograms, with total funding of 36.9 billion rubles. This included 19 regional development programs, with total federal funding of 1.28 billion rubles. The actual funding of programs from the federal budget amounted to 537.7 million rubles, or 56% of the specified limits (not including the programs for development of Yakutia and the Lower Angara region of Krasnoyarsk Territory). Just four programs were funded to a significant extent from the federal budget, all of them for republics of the Russian Federation: Chuvashia (100%), Kalmykia (99%), Mordovia (88%), and Buryatia (84%).

In this case, according to data from the Ministry of Federation and Nationality Affairs of the Russian Federation, the funding limits specified for 1998 for federal budgetary expenditures on implementing federal targeted programs for development of the regions were reached only at the end of the year, thanks to targeted funding begun in December 1998, after the Government of the Russian Federation adopted resolution No. 1461 "On additional measures to execute the federal budget."

The total volume of work done on all programs in 1998 was 5.62 billion rubles. Work done at the expense of the federal budget accounted for 11%; at the expense of subjects of the Federation, 20%; and from extrabudgetary sources, 69%. The last two sources had a considerable share in programs for economic and social development of Krasnodar Territory and Rostov Oblast (100% each), Astrakhan Oblast and St. Petersburg (99% each), Sochi (89%), Chuvashia (83%), and Kalmykia (80%).

Petersburg) or interregional nature. The latter group includes the federal targeted programs "Siberia" and "The Far East," as well as a program for the North Caucasus that is in the development stage. It is noteworthy that when programs of an interregional nature are adopted, interregional associations for economic interaction of subjects of the Federation play an active role in developing them and coordinating the interests of different regions. Therefore, it is no accident that the territories covered by the "Siberia" program and the ones belonging to the corresponding associations "overlap" each other in three regions of Transbaikal.

On the whole, federal targeted regional development programs completely or partially cover the territory of 51 subjects of the Federation, including some regions in more than one program. The programs that have already been approved cover the territory of the whole Asiatic part of Russia, the North Caucasus, and individual regions in the European part of the country. The only major economic area in which not a single federal targeted regional development program is underway is the Central Chernozem region. However, this does not mean that there are no federal targeted programs being implemented in subjects of the Federation in that area.

In addition to regional development programs, the investment resources that actually go to particular subjects of the Federation may also be distributed as part of other federal targeted programs aimed at solving urgent issues in the social sphere, developing basic industries and infrastructure, crime prevention, etc. We have to take into account the purely regional orientation of 12 environmental programs (for example, in the Baikal Basin, the cities of Chapaevsk and Nizhnii Tagil, etc.) and 5 disaster relief programs (in the zone of the Chernobyl catastrophe, Ural regions that suffered from the activity of the "Mayak" production association, etc.). Thus, the total number of federal programs more or less tied to individual regions is close to 50. But other federal targeted programs are also implemented in specific territories, which means that they have to be linked with specific regions.

There are still no summary reports on the implementation of individual programs in specific regions. More than once, representatives of various government agencies at the federal level have already pointed out the need to compile a unified register for carrying out programs in individual regions of the country. Attempts to do this have been made, for example, by the Ministry of the Economy.

In spite of the positive experience of implementing federal targeted regional development programs, the shortage of money is making it necessary to reduce the amount of funding that they will receive in the future. The federal budget for 1999 calls for funding of 26 programs for socioeconomic development of the regions, for which 1.28 billion rubles has been appropriated. The reduction in government support for federal targeted programs will cut off fulfillment of a number of projects, freeze money already invested in priority investment projects, and provoke a sharply negative reaction from the regions.

Difficulties in funding programs from the federal budget have negative consequences far exceeding the budget's quantitative share among funding sources. In most cases, it is precisely the federal funds that play a decisive role in attracting other sources of money, i.e., they stimulate all investment activity in the region, prompting regional authorities to engage in strategic planning of their territories' development.

According to the forecast for the country's socioeconomic development in 1999 and the parameters of socioeconomic development up to 2001 developed by the Ministry of the Economy, in the current conditions most federal targeted programs will be frozen. It is also likely that resolutions of the President and Government of the Russian Federation connected with development and environmental remediation of the regions, such as the North Caucasus (including Dagestan), the Far East and Transbaikal, Kamchatka, the Kurile Islands, and the cities of Chapaevsk, Cherepovets, Nizhnii Tagil, etc. will no longer be carried out. It is expected that previously developed mechanisms using the

Table 6.1

Variation of Federal Budgetary Expenditures Per Capita (not including Moscow), %

Type of expenditures	Disregarding the subsistence level	Adjusted for the subsistence level
Direct expenditures	52.4	40.6
Expenditures on funding of programs	86.4	100.0
Expenditures on financial aid	115.3	101.0
Direct expenditures – expenditures on funding of programs	56.0	41.0
Direct expenditures + expenditures on financial aid – expenditures on funding of programs	74.9	56.7
Direct expenditures + expenditures on financial aid	71.6	54.6

Development Budget and competitive placement of federal investments will become key tools of government investment.

6.2.2 Territorial distribution of expenditures on federal programs in 1998

The portion of program expenditures (represented primarily by federal targeted programs) in the federal budget for 1998 was not very high. Of the total amount of expenditures planned for the year, which was 499.9 billion rubles, 37.3 billion rubles, or 7.4%, was supposed to go to funding of federal targeted programs. In practice, program expenditures were funded at a considerably lower level than expenditures as a whole. While the latter were funded at 76.3% of the planned level, targeted programs were only funded at 21.2%.

In 1998, 7.9 billion rubles, or 7.4% of all territorially oriented expenditures from the federal budget, was spent on funding of federal programs for all direct recipients of federal budgetary funds.

In 1998, funding of programs was characterized by strong territorial differentiation. The coefficient of variation of per capita program expenditures in individual regions (with the exception of Moscow) was 86.4%, while the analogous coefficient for all other types of direct expenditures was 56.0% (Table 6.1).

As in the previous year, funding of federal programs in 1998 made up an appreciable portion of all expenditures in regions with a high level of per capita expenditures, as well as a low one. A regional profile of funding of federal programs is presented in Table 6.2.

In 1998, a high portion of expenditures on programs was noted in a number of oblasts in the central part of Russia that are in the Chernobyl zone (Kaluga, Tula, and Orlov Oblasts). Other noticeable objects of federal programs are subsidized and problem republics of the North Caucasus (Ingushetia, Kabardino-Balkaria, and Karachaevo-Cherkessia), and regions in which specific federal programs are localized (St. Petersburg,

Table 6.2

Portion of Expenditures on Implementing Federal Programs in Regions with Different Levels of Direct Federal Expenditures

Specific direct expenditures from the federal budget, rubles/person	Portion of expenditures on implementing federal programs in relation to all direct expenditures from the federal budget			
	< 5%	5–10%	10–20%	> 20%
< 300		Sverdlovsk, Yaroslavl, Vologda, Nizhegorod, Kirov, Samara, and Penza Oblasts, Marii El Republic, Udmurt and Chuvash Republics	Smolensk, Tambov, Ulyanovsk, Lipetsk, and Novgorod Oblasts, Republics of Dagestan and Tatarstan, Krasnodar Territory	Republic of Bashkortostan
250–400	Tyumen and Perm Oblasts	Republic of Adygeya, Ivanovo, Tver, Kostroma, Kurgan, Omsk, and Orenburg Oblasts	Chelyabinsk, Voronezh, Kaliningrad, Leningrad, and Moscow Oblasts, Altai and Stavropol Territories, Amur and Astrakhan Oblasts	Ryazan, Kursk, Pskov, and Belgorod Oblasts
400–1000	Tomsk and Chita Oblasts, Altai Republic, Jewish Autonomous Oblast, Kemerovo and Murmansk Oblasts, Republic of Buryatia, Komi Republic, Republic of Tyva, Krasnoyarsk, Maritime, and Khabarovsk Territories	Novosibirsk Oblast, Republics of Kalmykia, Karelia, Mordovia, North Osetia, and Sakha (Yakutia), Arkhangelsk Oblast	Rostov and Saratov Oblasts, St. Petersburg, Karachaevo-Cherkess Republic, Irkutsk and Orlov Oblasts, Kabardino-Balkar Republic	Tula and Kaluga Oblasts, Republic of Ingushetia
> 1000	Kamchatka and Magadan Oblasts	Sakhalin Oblast, Moscow		

Table 6.3

Changing Structure of Sources of Investments in Fixed Capital, in Actual Prices

Amount of capital investments	1994	1995	1996	1997	1998
Total, billion rubles	108.8	267.0	376.0	408.8	402.4
including, in %					
federal budget	13.4	10.1	9.9	10.2	—
regional and local budgets	10.6	10.3	10.2	10.5	—
sources other than government budgets	74.0	78.2	79.9	79.3	—

Irkutsk). A contrasting situation is observed in such regions of the Far North as Kamchatka, Magadan, and Sakhalin Oblasts, where the level of direct federal expenditures is high, but these expenditures are not made as part of specific programs.

6.3 DISTRIBUTION OF INVESTMENTS FROM THE FEDERAL BUDGET IN INDIVIDUAL REGIONS OF RUSSIA IN 1994–1998

Analysis of the distribution of investments in fixed capital in 1994–1998 demonstrated, first of all, the heavy concentration of investments in a small group of regions. It was found that the direction of investments from the federal budget in 1994–1997 was quite steady. The coefficients of correlation between series of absolute values of capital investments from the federal budget in the actual prices at that time for a cross section of 88 regions (not including the Republic of Chechnya) were 0.98–0.99 for any combination of years. Taking into account the extremely high differences between regions in population, industrial output, etc., such stability indicates most likely indicates that the direction of capital investments corresponds, in general, to the regions' financial and economic potential.

In this case, the ratios of different sources in the overall amount of investments in fixed capital practically did not change during the period under consideration (Table 6.3 and Figure 6.1). The federal budget's share was about 10% (only in 1994 was it higher: 13%). The regional and local budgets' share was approximately the same: 10–11%. The main sources of investments in fixed capital were not from federal, regional, or local budgets, but from enterprises' and organizations' internal funds.

The correlation between the amounts of investments going to the regions from the budgets of different levels was consistently positive. However, the interdependence of these indices is diminishing. In 1994, the coefficient of correlation was 0.84; in 1995, 0.85; in 1996, 0.78, and in 1997, 0.59. This indicates that with the development of federative relations the behavior of government authorities at different levels and agencies of local self-government is becoming more and more independent.

Analysis of the total amount of capital investments from all sources demonstrates a number of general patterns and distinctive characteristics of the country's "investment

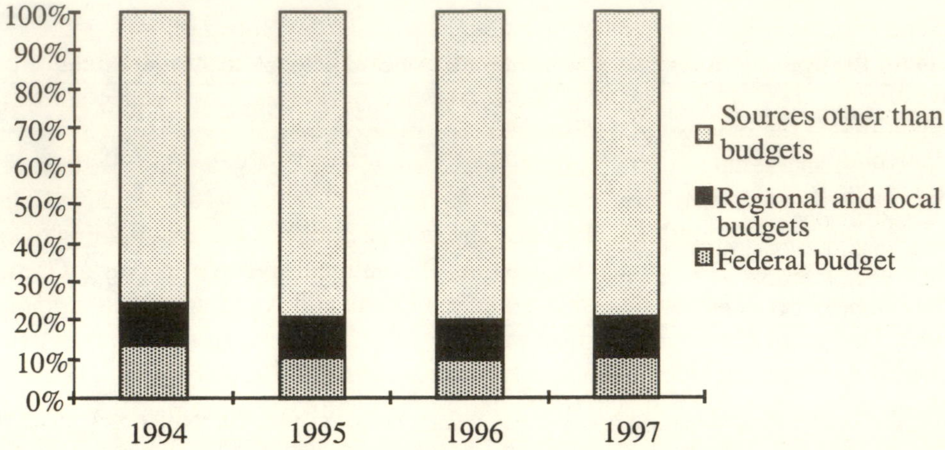

Figure 6.1. **Structure of funding sources for investments in fixed capital in Russia in 1994–1997.**

space." For instance, in 1997 the largest amounts of capital investments went to regions with a well developed industrial base. These are Tyumen Oblast (together with its autonomous regions, 14.5% of the amount for Russia) and Moscow plus Moscow Oblast. The amount of investments in the main Russian oil-producing region and in the capital region exceeded the total amount of investments in any large economic area of the country. Moscow alone accounted for 12.3% of Russian capital investments, and the Khanty-Mansi and Yamal-Nenets Autonomous Regions of Tyumen Oblast accounted for 7.8% and 5.9%, respectively. Moscow Oblast received significantly less investments (3.3%), although it did surpass all other subjects of the Federation. Following it on the list of leaders in capital investments came Tatarstan, Sverdlovsk Oblast, Bashkiria, St. Petersburg, Krasnoyarsk and Krasnodar Territories, and Samara Oblast (2–3% each). The second ten top regions included several more industrially developed oblasts, some of them with a high portion of extractive industries: Kemerovo, Chelyabinsk, Perm, Nizhegorod, Orenburg, Irkutsk, Rostov, Saratov, and Volgograd Oblasts, and also Yakutia (in descending order). The top 20 regions (including the two autonomous regions that are part of Tyumen Oblast) accounted for almost two thirds of the country's capital investments.

The ten last-place regions (the Republic of Chechnya was disregarded) included eight underdeveloped autonomous regions of the Far North, Altai, and Tyva. The total amount of capital investments in these regions in 1997 was only 0.26% of the total for Russia. The next 10 regions at the bottom of the list for receiving investments in fixed capital included two other national regions in the southern part of Siberia (Khakasia and the Jewish Autonomous Oblast), most of the republics of the North Caucasus (with the exception of Dagestan), and Kalmykia, plus several depressed regions in the European part of the country: Bryansk, Ivanovo, and Pskov Oblasts. The total amount of capital investments in the 20 last-place regions was 1.85% of the total for Russia.

The extremely low amounts of investments in underdeveloped regions of the country explain the consistent lack of sources other than budgetary ones for funding of capital investments. Therefore, for most underdeveloped territories, it is precisely the federal budget that is the main source of investments in fixed capital.

So, with an average of 10.3%, the federal budget's share of capital investments from all sources was more than two thirds in Ingushetia, half in Tyva, and about half in Kalmykia and the Chukotka Autonomous Region. The federal budget's share in funding of capital investments was 3.5–4.5 times higher than the national average in North Osetia and Altai, the Jewish Autonomous Oblast, and the Evenk and Aga Buryat Autonomous Regions. The list of regions with a high portion of the federal budget (more than twice the national average) included the Taimyr Autonomous Region, Adygeya, and also three oblasts in the Far East: Amur, Kamchatka, and Sakhalin. In addition, Moscow was one such region; the federal budget's share there was more than one quarter of all capital investments. All of the regions with high values of this index, with the exception of the Russian capital, are either underdeveloped, or far from the main zone of settlement in the country. Therefore, it is hard to overestimate the significance that federal investments have for them.

At the same time, the presence of Moscow in the upper part of the list confirms the higher than normal role of the flow of federal investments into this region, which is the most efficient one from the point of view of receiving a return on capital investments. Due to the great significance of federal investments in the Russian capital and the large amount of capital investments in it, the federal budget's share as a source of capital investments in the central economic area is also rather high: 21.3%. These values are closer to the national average for other large economic areas.

In 1997, the lowest portion of the federal budget in the total amount of investments was noted in highly industrialized regions, including ones where extractive industries are predominant. The large role of vertically integrated companies of national significance had an effect. These regions included, first of all, Tyumen Oblast as a whole, as well as its individual autonomous regions, and three republics with a protectionist policy in relation to letting in capital from outside of the region: Bashkiria, Tatarstan, and Yakutia. Besides these regions, in 1997 the federal budget's share was less than 5% (or less than half of the national average) in Udmurtia, and Samara, Orenburg, and Yaroslavl Oblasts.

As was already noted, during the period from 1994 through 1997, the main directions of capital investments from various sources in individual regions of the country were quite steady. Therefore, analysis of investments coming from all funding sources, including federal budgetary funds, in a cross section of subjects of the Federation during the period under consideration yields practically no new conclusions. The list of regions that receive investments from all sources is practically unchanged. This is true of both the upper and lower parts of the list. Sorting of the regions by the federal budget's share in the total amount of capital investments produces similar results. Only Chechnya's place in these lists particularly stands out, which is connected with objective difficulties of evaluating capital investments in this republic (Sidebar 6.3).

Sidebar 6.3 ***The Chechen Republic and investments in fixed capital from the federal budget***

As a rule, official data on practically any index for the Chechen Republic are either completely missing or have values that are extremely hard to explain. Data on investments in fixed capital in recent years are fragmentary. The official sources give figures for investments in Chechnya only for 1995 and 1996, i.e., while combat was going on there. In this case, the amount of investments going to Chechnya from the federal budget in 1995 was more than one fifth of all federal investments in Russia. The Republic of Chechnya was in second place (after Moscow) among regions of the country in the amount of investments from the federal budget. In 1996, the republic had a considerably lower position (just 1.7% of all investments from the federal budget). In 1995, the per capita federal investment in this region exceeded the national average by more than 35 times (!); and in 1996, by almost 2.9 times. In this case, according to data from the Russian Statistical Agency, there were practically no other sources of funding for capital investments in 1995 or 1996. In these years, the federal budget's share was 98% of all investments in Chechnya.

Analysis of the distribution of capital investments from the federal budget proper in 1994–1997 may indicate certain points in the geography of the federal budget's investment expenditures that are worthy of attention. The leaders and last-place regions in amounts of investments from the federal budget are given in Tables 6.4 and 6.5, and also on Map 13.

First of all, a significant part of federal financial resources is spent on capital investments in the Russian capital (Sidebar 6.4).

The second distinctive feature of the distribution of investments from the federal budget by regions is the consistently high amount of investments going to the most industrially developed regions, primarily those specializing in raw materials. Thus, the list of leading regions traditionally includes Tyumen, Sverdlovsk, Rostov, and Kemerovo Oblasts. In 1994, 1996, and 1997, the latter one held third or fourth place in Russia (Figure 6.4). It gets onto this list as the country's main coal-producing region. As is known, coal production is one of the most capital-intensive industries.

Even in the conditions of the drop in industrial production, a number of regions that are still actually areas of new economic development can be singled out as a special group with relatively high amounts of investments from the federal budget. In addition to Tyumen Oblast, with its autonomous regions, these include the Komi Republic, and Amur and Chita Oblasts. In this case, extremely high absolute indices, with average or even low population, as a rule, give these regions high per capita indices. Higher than normal per capita indices are also noted in regions of the Far North with low

Table 6.4

Leading Regions in Amount of Investments in Fixed Capital Received from the Federal Budget in 1994–1997, % Based on Data for Russia as a Whole

	1994			1995			1996			1997	
1	Moscow	25.92	1	Moscow	23.35	1	Moscow	24.49	1	Moscow	31.94
2	Moscow Oblast	7.71	2	Chechen Republic	20.50	2	Moscow Oblast	4.32	2	Moscow Oblast	4.90
3	Kemerovo Oblast	4.53	3	Moscow Oblast	5.95	3	St. Petersburg	2.73	3	Kemerovo Oblast	4.03
4	St. Petersburg	4.20	4	St. Petersburg	3.17	4	Kemerovo Oblast	2.65	4	Sverdlovsk Oblast	3.26
5	Novosibirsk Oblast	2.12	5	Stavropol Territory	2.18	5	Sverdlovsk Oblast	2.46	5	Tyumen Oblast*	3.08
6	Republic of Dagestan	2.12	6	Tyumen Oblast*	1.97	6	Rostov Oblast	2.46	6	St. Petersburg	2.90
7	Irkutsk Oblast*	2.02	7	Maritime Territory	1.83	7	Tyumen Oblast*	2.41	7	Chelyabinsk Oblast	1.97
8	Bryansk Oblast	1.98	8	Sverdlovsk Oblast	1.62	8	Irkutsk Oblast*	2.08	8	Rostov Oblast	1.90
9	Maritime Territory	1.94	9	Altai Territory	1.51	9	Novosibirsk Oblast	1.85	9	Novosibirsk Oblast	1.83
10	Rostov Oblast	1.87	10	Irkutsk Oblast*	1.42	10	Amur Oblast	1.84	10	Komi Republic	1.56
11	Chita Oblast*	1.82	11	Krasnodar Territory*	1.37	11	Krasnodar Territory	1.72	11	Perm Oblast	1.52
12	Altai Territory	1.76	12	Bryansk Oblast	1.29	12	Chechen Republic	1.68	12	Sakhalin Oblast	1.47
13	Sverdlovsk Oblast	1.73	13	Chelyabinsk Oblast	1.25	13	Khabarovsk Territory	1.65	13	Republic of Dagestan	1.41
14	Krasnodar Territory	1.64	14	Krasnoyarsk Territory*	1.13	14	Komi Republic	1.55	14	Amur Oblast	1.37
15	Tyumen Oblast*	1.58	15	Khabarovsk Territory	1.02	15	Kabardino-Balkar Republic	1.51	15	Saratov Oblast	1.33
16	Chelyabinsk Oblast	1.56	16	Republic of Dagestan	1.02	16	Tula Oblast	1.50	16	Khabarovsk Oblast	1.29
17	Khabarovsk Territory	1.53	17	Rostov Oblast	1.00	17	Maritime Territory	1.42	17	Krasnoyarsk Territory	1.26
18	Nizhegorod Oblast	1.48	18	Sakhalin Oblast	0.97	18	Krasnoyarsk Territory*	1.40	18	Stavropol Territory	1.24
19	Murmansk Oblast	1.40	19	Murmansk Oblast	0.94	19	Saratov Oblast	1.39	19	Krasnodar Territory	1.23
20	Amur Oblast	1.36	20	Nizhegorod Oblast	0.94	20	Chita Oblast	1.31	20	Irkutsk Oblast*	1.16

* Including autonomous regions.

Note: There are no data on the Chechen Republic for 1994 and 1997.

Table 6.5

Last-Place Regions in Amount of Investments in Fixed Capital Received from the Federal Budget in 1994–1997 (% of Data for Russia as a Whole)

	1994			1995			1996			1997	
1	Aga Buryat Autonomous Region	0.01	1	Aga Buryat Autonomous Region	0.01	1	Aga-Buryat Autonomous Region	0.02	1	Koryak Autonomous Region	0.02
2	Evenk Autonomous Region	0.04	2	Ust-Orda Buryat Autonomous Region	0.03	2	Komi-Permyak Autonomous Region	0.03	2	Komi-Permyak Autonomous Region	0.02
3	Komi-Permyak Autonomous Region	0.05	3	Republic of Ingushetia	0.04	3	Evenk Autonomous Region	0.04	3	Evenk Autonomous Region	0.02
4	Koryak Autonomous Region	0.05	4	Nenets Autonomous Region	0.06	4	Nenets Autonomous Region	0.06	4	Ust-Orda Buryat Autonomous Region	0.03
5	Nenets Autonomous Region	0.06	5	Evenk Autonomous Region	0.06	5	Koryak Autonomous Region	0.08	5	Taimyr Autonomous Region	0.04
6	Taimyr Autonomous Region	0.06	6	Komi-Permyak Autonomous Region	0.06	6	Kostroma Oblast	0.09	6	Aga Buryat Autonomous Region	0.05
7	Ust-Orda Buryat Autonomous Region	0.09	7	Taimyr Autonomous Region	0.06	7	Ust-Orda Buryat Autonomous Region	0.10	7	Nenets Autonomous Region	0.09
8	Magadan Oblast	0.12	8	Koryak Autonomous Region	0.07	8	Jewish Autonomous Oblast	0.11	8	Republic of Adygeya	0.15
9	Novosibirsk Oblast	0.14	9	Magadan Oblast	0.07	9	Novgorod Oblast	0.12	9	Altai Republic	0.16
10	Karachaevo-Cherkess Republic	0.16	10	Karachaevo-Cherkess Republic	0.10	10	Republic of Tyva	0.13	10	Kostroma Oblast	0.17
11	Altai Republic	0.18	11	Novgorod Oblast	0.10	11	Taimyr Autonomous Region	0.13	11	Magadan Oblast	0.19
12	Republic of Mordovia	0.20	12	Jewish Autonomous Oblast	0.11	12	Republic of Kalmykia	0.21	12	Marii El Republic	0.19
13	Republic of Kalmykia	0.20	13	Altai Republic	0.11	13	Marii El Republic	0.22	13	Republic of Tyva	0.20
14	Republic of Tyva	0.21	14	Republic of Mordovia	0.15	14	Altai Republic	0.24	14	Karachaevo-Cherkess Republic	0.20
15	Republic of Bashkortostan	0.21	15	Ivanovo Oblast	0.18	15	Yaroslavl Oblast	0.26	15	Udmurt Republic	0.23
16	Chukotka Autonomous Region	0.24	16	Republic of Kalmykia	0.18	16	Republic of Khakasia	0.26	16	Republic of Khakasia	0.23
17	Kostroma Oblast	0.24	17	Marii El Republic	0.21	17	Kurgan Oblast	0.26	17	Ivanovo Oblast	0.24
18	Jewish Autonomous Oblast	0.25	18	Chuvash Republic	0.22	18	Chukotka Autonomous Region	0.26	18	Yaroslavl Oblast	0.25
19	Marii El Republic	0.27	19	Republic of Khakasia	0.24	19	Republic of Karelia	0.26	19	Chukotka Autonomous Region	0.27
20	Tomsk Oblast	0.30	20	Republic of Adygeya	0.24	20	Penza Republic	0.27	20	Kurgan Oblast	0.27

Note: There are no data on the Chechen Republic for 1994 or 1997.

Sidebar 6.4 ***Moscow and investments***

Moscow's share of the total amount of investments from the federal budget is significantly more than the Russian capital's share of the country's population and industrial output. It rose noticeably in 1997, the city's 850th anniversary year, when it was almost one third of federal investments. In 1994–1996, it was only at the level of one fourth. At the same time, a certain reduction was noted in the share of Moscow Oblast, which consistently holds second place on the list of Russian regions with respect to their share of investments from the federal budget (Figure 6.2).

It is better to compare the Russian capital's positions in the amount of investments from the federal budget with a number of indices characterizing Moscow's financial potential as a region; for example, with collected tax payments. Then Moscow's positions in the budget's income and expenditure components will approximately coincide. The Russian capital's share of tax receipts to the federal budget in 1997 was 30.9%.

In this case, Moscow's share of investments from the federal budget is considerably lower than, for example, its share of commercial banks' assets and capital, bank credits, stock-exchange turnover, etc. (Figure 6.3). Its share of the total number of commercial banks in the Russian Federation steadily increased up until 1998, exceeding one third. Moscow banks' share of the total assets of the one hundred largest banks in the country also rose steadily in 1994–1997, exceeding nine tenths. During these years, the capital's banks issued from one half to three fourths of all ruble credits and more than four fifths of foreign-currency credits in the country. By the beginning of 1998, almost 94% of the investment portfolio of all Russian banks was concentrated in the capital's banks (this includes investments in promissory notes, stock, participation in subsidiary companies, etc.). Moscow banks' share in total bank investments in government securities for all of Russia was almost 99%. The turnover on Moscow stock exchanges was more than nine tenths of the turnover for all of the exchanges in the country.

population, primarily autonomous regions, which are not distinguished by high absolute values.

Table A.5 of the statistical appendix shows per capita investments from the federal budget, in actual prices at the time, for individual regions of Russia, and the leaders and last-place regions in per capita investments from the federal budget are presented in Tables 6.6 and 6.7.

Due to the need to solve geopolitical problems at the federal level, a number of densely populated North Caucasian regions of Russia are also distinguished by high amounts of federal investments, not just in absolute indices, but also per capita (Figure 6.4). In

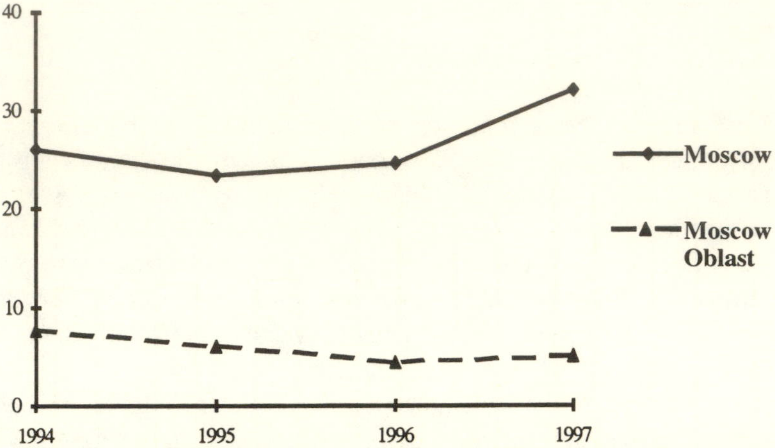

Figure 6.2. **Moscow's and Moscow Oblast's share of the total amount of investments in fixed capital from the federal budget** (%)

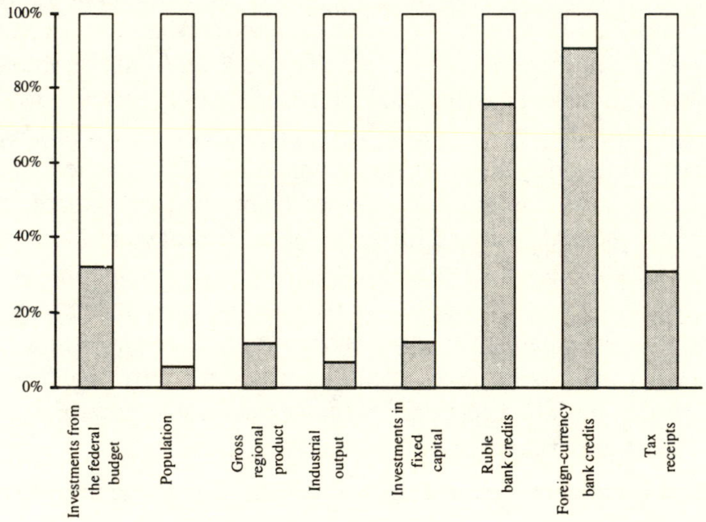

Figure 6.3. **Moscow's share of basic socioeconomic and financial indices for all of Russia in 1997** (%)

addition to the special case of Chechnya, which has been described and singled out, high amounts of federal investments went to Dagestan in almost all of the years under consideration, and to Kabardino-Balkaria in individual years. In relation to the population, amounts significantly greater than the national average were observed in 1994 in the Republics of Ingushetia, Adygeya, and Dagestan (1.5–1.8 times higher than the national average). In 1995, the leader was Stavropol Territory (1.2 times); in 1996, Ingushetia

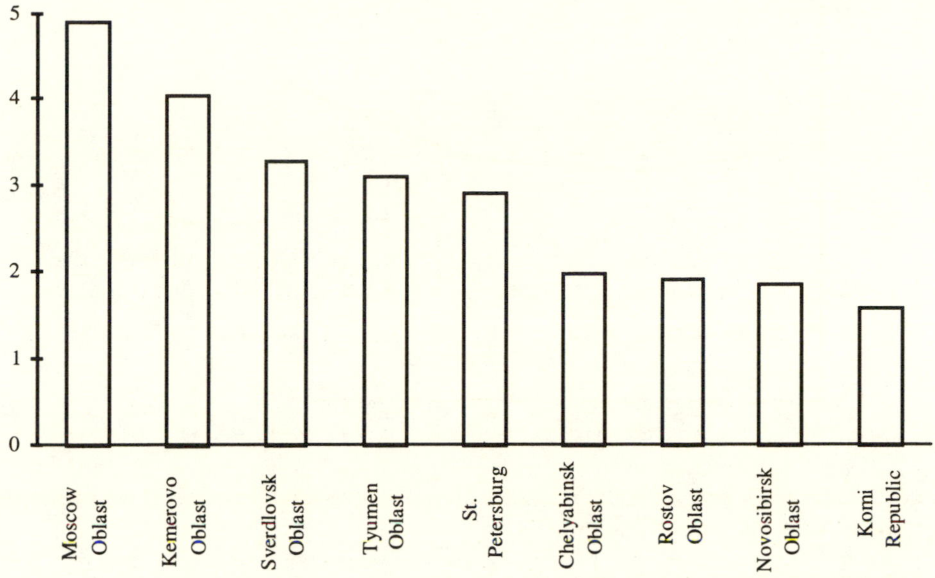

Figure 6.4. **Leading regions with respect to amount of investments in fixed capital**

and Kabardino-Balkaria (4.1 and 2.9 times, respectively). In 1997, North Osetia was the leader (1.2 times higher than the national average).

On the other hand, any characteristics of the distribution of investments in fixed capital from the federal budget indicate that most "Russian" Oblasts in the European part of the country are actually underfunded, as are three republics in the Volga-Vyatka economic area (the Marii El Republic, Mordovia, and Chuvashia). In recent years, the lowest per capita indices of the distribution of investments among large economic areas have been for the Volga-Vyatka, Lower Volga, and Central Chernozem areas.

It is worthwhile to distinguish two more groups of regions. The first one includes the republics that most actively champion the idea of their own sovereignty and rely on their internal, fairly strong, economic potential (Tatarstan and Bashkiria). The second group is made up of the most underdeveloped regions, which have no major investment projects (the Aga Buryat, Komi-Permyak, and Ust-Orda Buryat Autonomous Regions).

It is noteworthy that in 1995 Ingushetia had a very low amount of federal investments (lower than in other years and in comparison with other North Caucasian republics). This most likely indicates either diversion of money to try to straighten out the situation in Chechnya, or inaccuracy of the statistical reporting procedures due to combat.

In 1998, the data for which need additional processing, funding of investments from the federal budget remained unsatisfactory. As before, investment activity in the regions was carried out mostly at the expense of enterprises' internal funds and the consolidated budgets of subjects of the Federation.

As before, the largest share of investments in fixed capital (from all funding sources) went to Moscow and Moscow Oblast (16.2% and 4.8% of all capital investments,

Table 6.6

Leading Regions in Specific Investments in Fixed Capital from the Federal Budget (Number of Times More Than the National Average)

	1994			1995			1996			1997	
1	Moscow	4.43	1	Chechen Republic	35.06	1	Chukotka Autonomous Region	4.26	1	Moscow	5.46
2	Chukotka Autonomous Region	3.83	2	Evenk Autonomous Region	4.27	2	Taimyr Autonomous Region	4.25	2	Republic of Ingushetia	5.40
3	Evenk Autonomous Region	2.79	3	Chukotka Autonomous Region	4.15	3	Moscow	4.18	3	Chukotka Autonomous Region	4.32
4	Koryak Autonomous Region	2.40	4	Moscow	3.99	4	Republic of Ingushetia	4.12	4	Yamal-Nenets Autonomous Region	3.67
5	Yamal-Nenets Autonomous Region	2.36	5	Koryak Autonomous Region	3.29	5	Yamal-Nenets Autonomous Region	3.75	5	Sakhalin Oblast	3.35
6	Kemerovo Oblast	2.19	6	Sakhalin Oblast	2.21	6	Koryak Autonomous Region	3.38	6	Jewish Autonomous Oblast	3.18
7	Chita Oblast	2.08	7	Taimyr Autonomous Region	2.04	7	Evenk Autonomous Region	3.13	7	Nenets Autonomous Region	2.66
8	Kaliningrad Oblast	2.03	8	Yamal-Nenets Autonomous Region	1.91	8	Chechen Republic	2.88	8	Komi Republic	1.95
9	Taimyr Autonomous Region	2.03	9	Nenets Autonomous Region	1.74	9	Kabardino-Balkar Republic	2.82	9	Kemerovo Oblast	1.95
10	Bryansk Oblast	1.98	10	Republic of Tyva	1.40	10	Amur Oblast	2.62	10	Amur Oblast	1.95
11	Murmansk Oblast	1.98	11	Kamchatka Republic	1.36	11	Kamchatka Oblast	2.56	11	Republic of Kalmykia	1.90
12	Amur Oblast	1.94	12	Moscow Oblast	1.33	12	Nenets Autonomous Region	1.99	12	Kamchatka Oblast	1.89
13	Sakhalin Oblast	1.87	13	Murmansk Oblast	1.33	13	Komi Republic	1.93	13	Evenk Autonomous Region	1.80
14	Nenets Autonomous Region	1.81	14	Bryansk Oblast	1.29	14	Sakhalin Oblast	1.81	14	Tyumen Oblast	1.44
15	Republic of Ingushetia	1.77	15	Republic of Buryatia	1.28	15	Altai Republic	1.77	15	Taimyr Autonomous Region	1.35
16	Jewish Autonomous Oblast	1.76	16	Kaliningrad Oblast	1.27	16	Orlov Oblast	1.65	16	Khanty-Mansi Autonomous Region	1.28
17	Republic of Buryatia	1.76	17	Stavropol Territory	1.21	17	Magadan Oblast	1.57	17	Khabarovsk Territory	1.21
18	Moscow Oblast	1.73	18	Maritime Territory	1.20	18	Khabarovsk Territory	1.55	18	Altai Republic	1.21
19	Republic of Adygeya	1.53	19	Komi Republic	1.13	19	Chita Oblast	1.50	19	Republic of North Osetia	1.17
20	Republic of Dagestan	1.49	20	Tomsk Oblast	1.10	20	Republic of Buryatia	1.49	20	Moscow Oblast	1.10

Note: There are no data on the Chechen Republic for 1994 or 1997.

Table 6.7

Last-Place Regions in Specific Amount of Investments in Fixed Capital from the Federal Budget (Number of Times More Than the National Average)

	1994			1995			1996			1997	
1	Republic of Bashkortostan	0.08	1	Aga Buryat Autonomous Region	0.12	1	Kostroma Oblast	0.17	1	Republic of Bashkortostan	0.16
2	Republic of Tatarstan	0.13	2	Republic of Tatarstan	0.13	2	Novgorod Oblast	0.24	2	Komi-Permyak Autonomous Region	0.19
3	Aga Buryat Autonomous Region	0.19	3	Orenburg Oblast	0.18	3	Penza Oblast	0.25	3	Udmurt Republic	0.20
4	Novgorod Oblast	0.27	4	Perm Oblast	0.19	4	Udmurt Republic	0.26	4	Yaroslavl Oblast	0.26
5	Republic of Mordovia	0.31	5	Republic of Ingushetia	0.20	5	Yaroslavl Oblast	0.26	5	Ust-Orda Autonomous Region	0.26
6	Omsk Oblast	0.31	6	Novgorod Oblast	0.20	6	Nizhegorod Oblast	0.27	6	Vladimir Oblast	0.26
7	Saratov Oblast	0.33	7	Ivanovo Oblast	0.21	7	Vladimir Oblast	0.29	7	Republic of Tatarstan	0.28
8	Orenburg Oblast	0.35	8	Udmurt Republic	0.22	8	Komi-Permyak Autonomous Region	0.30	8	Ivanovo Oblast	0.29
9	Kirov Oblast	0.36	9	Republic of Mordovia	0.23	9	Republic of Bashkortostan	0.30	9	Kirov Oblast	0.29
10	Volgograd Oblast	0.37	10	Republic of Bashkortostan	0.23	10	Chuvash Republic	0.32	10	Ulyanovsk Oblast	0.30
11	Tomsk Oblast	0.41	11	Chuvash Republic	0.24	11	Orenburg Oblast	0.32	11	Penza Oblast	0.32
12	Voronezh Oblast	0.42	12	Vladimir Oblast	0.24	12	Belgorod Oblast	0.33	12	Kostroma Oblast	0.32
13	Vologda Oblast	0.43	13	Volgograd Oblast	0.26	13	Leningrad Oblast	0.34	13	Samara Oblast	0.33
14	Khanty-Mansi Autonomous Region	0.44	14	Voronezh Oblast	0.27	14	Kurgan Oblast	0.34	14	Orenburg Oblast	0.35
15	Kostroma Oblast	0.44	15	Yaroslavl Oblast	0.28	15	Volgograd Oblast	0.37	15	Voronezh Oblast	0.36
16	Komi-Permyak Autonomous Region	0.47	16	Penza Oblast	0.29	16	Ryazan Oblast	0.37	16	Kurgan Oblast	0.36
17	Krasnodar Territory	0.48	17	Omsk Oblast	0.30	17	Aga Buryat Autonomous Region	0.37	17	Krasnodar Territory	0.36
18	Lipetsk Oblast	0.48	18	Saratov Oblast	0.31	18	Ulyanovsk Oblast	0.38	18	Marii El Republic	0.37
19	Yaroslavl Oblast	0.49	19	Kursk Oblast	0.32	19	Kursk Oblast	0.39	19	Nizhegorod Oblast	0.38
20	Udmurt Republic	0.50	20	Ust-Orda Buryat Autonomous Region	0.33	20	Smolensk Oblast	0.39	20	Kursk Oblast	0.39

respectively), and also to Tyumen Oblast (11.2%, of which 6.5% went to the Khanty-Mansi Autonomous Region and 3.7% to the Yamal-Nenets Autonomous Region). In 1998, Tatarstan and St. Petersburg each "absorbed" 3.6% of the total amount of investments for the whole country. The ten leading regions also included several with strong economic potential (in descending order): Bashkiria, Sverdlovsk and Samara Oblasts, Krasnodar Territory, and Kemerovo Oblast.

On the other hand, the 10 subjects of the Federation with the least investments (in absolute terms) accounted for only 0.26% of all of the country's capital investments. In 1998, they included Tyva and Altai, the Jewish Autonomous Oblast, and the Koryak, Aga Buryat, Evenk, Taimyr, Ust-Orda Buryat, Komi-Permyak, and Chukotka Autonomous Regions. The 20 last-place regions accounted for a little bit more than 2% of investments. Data on the Chechen Republic in 1998 were not taken into account.

According to data from the Ministry of the Economy, of the total amount of the minimum guaranteed limits of budget obligations allocated to subjects of the Federation, in the first nine months of 1998 only 10.8% was funded. In this case, the level of funding for individual regions was not the same. For 23 of them, the budget obligations were not fulfilled at all. This includes several oblasts in the European part of the country (Kaluga, Orlov, Kursk, and Lipetsk) and a number of regions in the Far East (Yakutia, Khabarovsk Territory, Magadan Oblast, and the Koryak Autonomous Region).

Beginning in 2000, there may be significant adjustments in the amounts of funding of regional programs at the expense of federal budgetary funds. The federal budget's limited possibilities will have an effect. The planned audit of all approved federal targeted programs also has to be taken into account. It will be aimed at reducing the number of programs and ensuring that the ones that are left are funded for comprehensive and systematic solution of the most acute socioeconomic problems. Primary attention is supposed to be given to programs that the government has pledged to support under all circumstances (disaster relief, crime prevention, keeping industrial facilities safe). According to the Ministry of the Economy's forecast, the amount of funding of federal targeted programs from the federal budget in 2001 will be 18 billion rubles, which is significantly less than in 2000. To a certain extent, this is connected with the end of the period for carrying out almost 100 programs. In the section of the budget "Federal programs for socioeconomic development of the regions," just 28 programs are on the list of programs proposed for funding from the federal budget in 2000–2001.

Thus, the geographic distribution of investments in fixed capital from the federal budget in recent years indicates that the country is actually continuing to develop extensively thanks to regions of new development and border territories. On the whole, the priority direction of federal money is still to multinational subjects of the Federation (republics and autonomous regions). The Russian capital "absorbs" federal investments extremely actively.

At the same time, the traditionally developed regions, primarily in the European part of the country, remain "underfunded." There is no question that at present, with the catastrophic drop in production, the "load" on fixed assets is reduced. However, we must not forget that, in the absence of investments, increasing wear and obsolescence of equipment can only aggravate the drop in production.

Meanwhile, according to the Ministry of the Economy's forecasts, the decline in investment activity is expected to continue in all large economic areas of the country, with a decrease in the share of federal budgetary funds in the total amount of investments. The main source of funding for capital investments will still be enterprises' internal funds. In relation to the level of 1997, investments are expected to grow in only eight subjects of the Federation: Nizhegorod, Novgorod, Sakhalin, Tula, and Orenburg Oblasts, the Marii El Republic, Moscow, and St. Petersburg. The sharpest drop is predicted in regions in the Asiatic part of the country, where a significant reduction in funds from the federal budget will not be compensated by other funding sources.

6.4 PROJECTS OF THE INTERNATIONAL AND EUROPEAN BANKS FOR RECONSTRUCTION AND DEVELOPMENT IN RUSSIA

A large role in the investment process in the regions is played by loans received within the scope of the projects of international and foreign organizations, primarily the International and European Banks for Reconstruction and Development (IBRD and EBRD). The total amount of loans as of January 1, 1998, for these two banks' projects in Russia was $5,716.5 million. These organizations' credits are intended for development of the production infrastructure proper (so-called coal and oil loans, etc.), and also for solving various issues in the social sphere, environmental problems, etc. The only credit formally aimed at comprehensive support of regional programs is a loan for development of the regional social infrastructure (Sidebar 6.5).

According to the resolution of the Government of the Russian Federation No. 395 of April 3, 1996, "On approval of the procedure for working with programs financed by IBRD loans," investment projects may be initiated by either federal or regional executive authorities. However, according to the IBRD's rules, only the government of the borrowing country can act as the borrower and the guarantor of the loan (it is also customary for the government to fund part of the loan's repayment). Therefore, the responsibility for implementing the projects to be carried out at the expense of IBRD and EBRD credits rests not with the executive authorities of subjects of the Federation, but with the Government of the Russian Federation.

At the beginning of 1998, $1,808.1 million had been spent, or 31.6% of the total amount of loans from international banks. The portion of the funds that had been used in individual subjects of the Federation was sharply differentiated: from 0 to almost 100%. This is connected with the fact that the projects being implemented in the regions are in different stages of fulfillment. In this case, our research did not reveal any clear pattern in the distribution of regions in this regard. Thus, most of the loan money had been used in Kostroma (97.5%) and Pskov Oblasts (91%). About four fifths of the loans had already been used in Smolensk and Saratov Oblasts, and in North Osetia. At the same time, in Kabardino-Balkaria, Krasnoyarsk Territory, Leningrad Oblast, and the Jewish

Sidebar 6.5 ***Project for support of the regional social infrastructure***

In 1994, the IBRD approached the Government of the Russian Federation with a proposal about preparing a project for support of the regional social infrastructure. This idea came up in the course of discussions between the bank's representatives and the Russian government devoted to the concepts of projects capable of supporting the decentralization of state power, which were aimed at providing the basic minimum of social services and solving additional problems appearing in connection with the fact that departmental facilities with a social function were passing into state ownership. The project was prepared in 1994–1996, and a loan agreement between the Government of the Russian Federation and the IBRD was executed in August 1996.

In order to simplify the project's development and especially its implementation, subprojects were included in it for just two regions: Novosibirsk and Rostov Oblasts. On the one hand, they are fairly representative of a large number of oblasts, and on the other hand, they differ sharply from each other from the point of view of their geographic location and economic situation. The decision to limit the project to two oblasts (a version with three oblasts was originally considered) made it less complicated and allowed it to be prepared more quickly as a demonstration project. This did not decrease the benefits obtained, due to differences between the regions. Although the project's general management is done by federal ministries, the responsibility for carrying out its specific components rests with the administrations of Novosibirsk and Rostov Oblasts. This project became the IBRD's first credit in conditions where the main responsibility for implementing the project was entrusted to regional administrations.

The project's basic objectives consist in the following:

- to prevent further deterioration of the social infrastructure by financing the reconstruction of top-priority public-health, educational, water-supply, and sewerage facilities, and also new construction of such facilities on a limited scale
- to increase the efficiency of managing government resources
- to stimulate development of the private sector
- to make a contribution to the government policy of decentralization by encouraging participation, including that of nongovernmental organizations, in the process of making decisions concerning the project.

The loan is financing small investment projects in the educational, public-health, water-supply, and sewerage systems. It is aimed at introducing new mechanisms for managing the budget and finances in two oblasts of Russia.

The project's total cost is estimated as $288.1 million, of which $200 million is loan money and the rest is allocated by the Russian side. The repayment period is 17 years, including a five-year grace period. The two oblasts participating in the project received credits of $193 million (half as a grant, the rest as a loan with variable interest up to 2.5%, which is more than the IBRD's lending rate with a repayment period of 12 years and a three-year grace period).

Table 6.8

Leading Regions in Amount of Loans from the International and European Banks for Reconstruction and Development as of January 1, 1998 (% of Total for Russia)

Total amount of loans			Loans used		
1	Moscow	42.14	1	Tyumen Oblast*	35.40
2	Tyumen Oblast*	23.56	2	Moscow	32.93
3	Tomsk Oblast	4.70	3	Komi Republic	5.42
4	St. Petersburg	4.41	4	St. Petersburg	4.15
5	Komi Republic	2.84	5	Tomsk Oblast	3.91
6	Rostov Oblast	2.38	6	Omsk Oblast	2.10
7	Novosibirsk Oblast	1.69	7	Sverdlovsk Oblast	1.65
8	Ryazan Oblast	1.25	8	Samara Oblast	1.63
9	Orenburg Oblast	1.22	9	Rostov Oblast	1.46
10	Omsk Oblast	1.17	10	Novgorod Oblast	1.22
11	Vologda Oblast	1.15	11	Tver Oblast	0.87
12	Sverdlovsk Oblast	1.13	12	Vologda Oblast	0.80
13	Vladimir Oblast	1.13	13	Pskov Oblast	0.78
14	Tver Oblast	1.08	14	Kostroma Oblast	0.75
15	Nizhegorod Oblast	1.05	15	Nizhegorod Oblast	0.73
16	Republic of Karelia	0.72	16	Smolensk Oblast	0.70
17	Novgorod Oblast	0.68	17	Republic of Mordovia	0.59
18	Samara Oblast	0.64	18	Republic of North Osetia	0.51
19	Kaluga Oblast	0.60	19	Moscow Oblast	0.44
20	Moscow Oblast	0.57	20	Maritime Territory	0.34

* Including autonomous regions.

Autonomous Region, the international banks' projects had been approved, but their implementation had not begun.

On the whole, at the beginning of 1998 the IBRD and EBRD projects covered 64 subjects of the Federation (if autonomous regions are not counted separately). Only 15 regions had not received credits. The distribution of loans received from international banks is shown on Maps 14 and 15.

Thus, the distribution of international bank credits in individual regions of the country is characterized by even greater differentiation than the distribution of capital investments from the federal budget. The lion's share of IBRD and EBRD credits goes to two regions: Moscow and Tyumen Oblast (including its autonomous regions). At the beginning of 1998, they accounted for about two thirds of the credits that had been allocated and already used (Table 6.8). In this case, the Russian capital's share in the total amount of loans was more than one third.

The high portion of credits provided to the Russian capital partially blurs the pattern of distribution of international credit funds by regions. In reality, the financial resources received in Moscow are later redistributed among other regions.

At the same time, the indices characterizing Tyumen Oblast do indicate that these credits go primarily to development of raw-material industries. This is confirmed by the

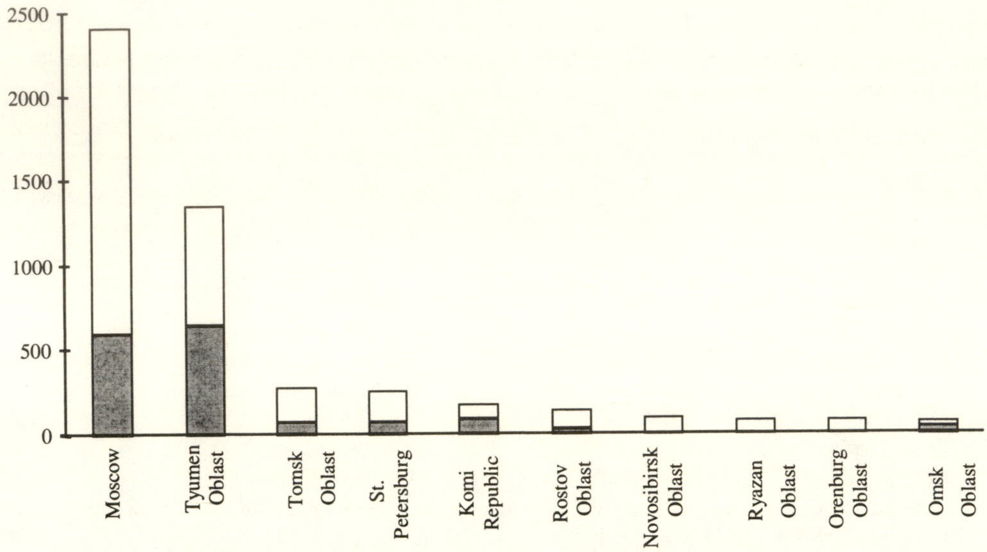

Figure 6.5. **Ten regions with largest total amount of IBRD and EBRD loans as of January 1, 1998, million dollars.** *Note:* The portion of loan money already used is shaded.

fact that the top five regions in the amount of credits (in the total amount of loans, as well as those that have already been used) included Tomsk Oblast, where, as in Tyumen, one of the oil loans is being used, and the Komi Republic, which is receiving considerable financial resources for mitigating the oil-pipeline accident near Usinsk. St. Petersburg is also one of the five leading regions.

The high concentration of credits received from the IBRD and EBRD in just a few regions is confirmed by the fact that at the beginning of 1998 just ten regions accounted for more than 85% of the allocated loans and about 90% of those that have already been used. The top twenty regions accounted for more than 94% and 96%, respectively. The leading regions in the total amount of international bank loans are shown in Figure 6.5.

It is noteworthy that the IBRD and EBRD credits hardly reach the republics of the Russian Federation. Their total share in the amount of international bank loans is just 4.9% (including 2.8% for the Komi Republic), and 7.2% of the loans that have already been used (5.4% for the Komi Republic). The credits do not reach such republics as Tatarstan, Yakutia, Kalmykia, Ingushetia, Karachaevo-Cherkessia, Altai, Tyva, and also Chechnya.

The importance of IBRD and EBRD loans for development of the fuel and raw-material industries stands out clearly when we look at the per capita amounts for individual regions of the country. For instance, the total amount of loans provided to Tyumen Oblast per capita is more than 11 times higher than the national average; the figure for Tomsk Oblast is 6.4 times higher than the average; and for the Komi Republic, 3.6 times higher. The per capita indices for Moscow (7.2 times higher than the national average) are quite high. Other regions that have received higher than average loans are the Republic of Karelia, St. Petersburg, and Ryazan, Novgorod, Vladimir and Vologda Oblasts (1.0–1.4 times higher than the national average). In all the rest of the regions, this index is below the national average.

The amounts of credits used by the beginning of 1998 are similar. Tyumen Oblast is in first place (its index is 16.5 times higher than the national average); then come Komi (6.8), Moscow (5.6), and Tomsk Oblast (5.4 times higher than the national average). Following considerably behind the leaders are Novgorod Oblast (2.4), and also Omsk, Pskov, and Kemerovo Oblasts, St. Petersburg, and North Osetia (all 1.1–1.4 times higher than the national average).

The large loans received for development of the fuel and raw-material industries cannot help but cause additional concern. It is noteworthy that the oil loans are so large in comparison with other IBRD and EBRD credits that, even with their gigantic size, Tyumen and Tomsk Oblasts are in the top ten regions with respect to the amount of loans in relation to area. As an analysis conducted at the Ministry of the Economy shows, the efficiency of investments, figured as the ratio of total industrial output to the amount of investments over a number of previous years, is extremely low precisely in Tyumen and Tomsk Oblasts, and also in the Nenets Autonomous Regions, which may be partly explained by the fact that their industries are very capital-intensive.

The high level of inflation does not permit direct comparison of the amounts of international bank loans with domestic capital investments figured in actual ruble prices. However, some general conclusions can be drawn from correlation analysis. On the whole, the financial resources distributed among individual regions of the country within the scope of IBRD and EBRD projects duplicate, to a significant extent, the distribution of investments in fixed capital from all funding sources.

Correlation analysis between indices characterizing the distribution of international loans and cumulative investments during 1994–1997 showed that the loans go precisely to the regions that also receive other investments. For a sample of regions with or without Moscow, and also without the autonomous regions and Chechnya, the values of the coefficients of correlation for the total amount of loans and loans used by the end of 1997 were 0.85–0.91. At the same time, the distribution of capital investments from the federal budget does not duplicate so clearly the pattern of international loans in individual regions of the country. The coefficients of correlation for cumulative investments from the federal budget and IBRD loans in individual regions are 0.87 and 0.70, respectively, for the total amount of loans and those that have been used. Disregarding Moscow, which significantly alters the pattern of regional redistribution of financial resources, the coefficients of correlation drop to 0.30 and 0.28, respectively.

This situation is explained primarily by the higher than average amounts of federal capital investments in eastern regions of the country, and also in republics of the Russian Federation, whose share of international loans is extremely low.

6.5 CONCLUSIONS

Thus, regional policy in the investment sphere is actually manifested in coordination of different directions of capital investments from a number of sources. Different forms of investment support of the regions have been put to practical use in Russia during the years of economic transformations. The most common practice is to adopt and implement federal targeted programs for socioeconomic development of the regions.

At present, more than 30 regional federal targeted programs "cover" the territory of more than half of all subjects of the Federation. These programs differ in their coverage of territory (from local to interregional), the scale of problems to be solved, schedule, and amount of funding, and they have different government clients. As a rule, a shortage of money for implementing the programs has made itself felt in recent years, as a result of which they are underfunded. In spite of the fact that a number of new programs are presently being developed and approved, the idea that the number of programs themselves and the amounts of funding that they receive need to be reduced is expressed more and more often in various official documents and scientific discussions.

Analysis of the distribution of investments in fixed capital from all funding sources in recent years demonstrates their heavy concentration in a limited number of regions of the country. It was found that the distribution of investments in individual regions is highly stable in different years, and the portion of the federal budget going to funding of them is relatively stable. The two main regions attracting investments in Russia are the capital region and Tyumen Oblast, with its autonomous regions. Large amounts of capital investments are also distributed in other highly industrialized regions. In absolute terms, extremely little investment goes to underdeveloped autonomous regions of the Far North, and also to most autonomous entities of the North Caucasus and Southern Siberia. As a rule, the federal budget plays a more important role for them as a source of funding for capital investments than it does for other regions. In most such regions the per capita distribution of investments from the federal budget is considerably higher than the national average. Official statistical data demonstrate the special position of the Chechen Republic in the distribution of federal investments, which needs additional analysis.

The lion's share of investments in fixed capital from the federal budget goes to Moscow. Moscow's share of investments from the federal budget significantly exceeds its share of Russia's population and basic indices of its socioeconomic development. However, this share is comparable to and, in some cases, even lower than indices characterizing Moscow's financial potential.

IBRD and EBRD loans play a large role in the investment process in regions of the country. By the beginning of 1998, these organizations' projects extended to 64 subjects of the Russian Federation (if autonomous regions are not counted separately). The distribution of international bank credits in individual regions is highly differentiated. Two thirds of the credits that have been allocated and already used went to Moscow and Tyumen Oblast. Taking into account analysis of the distribution of investments in fixed capital from all funding sources in individual regions, we can draw the conclusion that the compensatory significance of IBRD and EBRD credits should not be overestimated. At the same time, for example, international bank credits hardly reach eastern regions of the country, where the amounts of federal capital investments are relatively higher than in other regions.

CHAPTER 7

Extrabudgetary Funds as a Channel for Territorial Redistribution of Public Finances

7.1 STATEMENT OF THE PROBLEM

Traditionally, research devoted to financial interrelations between the Center and the regions only deals with their budgetary component. However, this approach is limited and cannot provide a complete idea of the regions' financial independence and their reliance on redistribution of money among subjects of the Federation. In essence, the revenues and expenditures of extrabudgetary funds differ little from budgetary revenues and expenditures. This is partly confirmed by the continuing debate about the advisability of including extrabudgetary funds in the budget.

This chapter looks at the contribution that four social extrabudgetary funds make to the territorial redistribution of public finances. They are the Pension Fund of the Russian Federation, the Social Insurance Fund of the Russian Federation, the State Employment Fund of the Russian Federation, and mandatory medical insurance funds (the Federal Mandatory Medical Insurance Fund and territorial mandatory medical insurance funds of subjects of the Russian Federation). Data on road funds (the Federal Road Fund and territorial road funds of subjects of the Russian Federation), which are formally targeted budgetary funds, but are essentially extrabudgetary, are also included in the analysis.[1]

First we will consider some general questions concerning extrabudgetary funds. Characteristics of their role in the Russian financial system are given, and the composition of revenues and expenditures for Russia as a whole is analyzed. Then we will look at the geography of extrabudgetary funds in detail. There are differences between regions in the distribution of revenues between their central and territorial divisions, and also differences in the per capita collection of insurance payments (taxes) and expenditures. It is established that the extrabudgetary funds' territorial divisions depend on redistribution of money from the Center, and the composition of their expenditures is analyzed.

[1] Hereinafter, by extrabudgetary funds we mean all five of the funds mentioned.

7.2 EXTRABUDGETARY FUNDS' REVENUES AND EXPENDITURES IN 1996–1998

7.2.1 Ratio of budgetary and extrabudgetary financial flows

Financial flows within the framework of extrabudgetary funds form a significant part of all financial flows between the Center and the regions. Table 7.1 gives the results of comparison of the extrabudgetary funds' revenues and expenditures with those of the consolidated budget (the total amount of the federal, regional, and local budgets). Since the most complete data on extrabudgetary funds are from 1998, that year was selected for the analysis.

The extrabudgetary funds' revenues and expenditures make up almost half of the consolidated budget's revenues and expenditures. Thus, financial flows comparable to half of the budgetary flows remain unstudied in traditional research. Extrabudgetary funds also play a very significant role in providing social services: they account for almost half of such expenditures.

7.2.2 Composition of extrabudgetary funds' revenues and expenditures

The main source of revenue for the social extrabudgetary funds is mandatory insurance premiums paid by employers, which are figured as a percentage of the accrued payroll fund. Insurance premiums to the Pension Fund of the Russian Federation are also paid by individuals.

The rate of deductions for extrabudgetary funds is set in federal laws adopted each year. The base rates have remained stable in recent years. In 1996–1998, they were (in percent of the accrued payroll fund):

- to the Pension Fund of the Russian Federation: 28% for employers and 1% for workers
- to the Social Insurance Fund of the Russian Federation: 5.4%
- to mandatory medical insurance funds: 3.6%
- to the State Employment Fund of the Russian Federation: 1.5%.

Thus, the aggregate amount of deductions to the social extrabudgetary funds was 38.5% of the payroll fund for employers, and 39.5% taking into account the 1% that workers pay to the Pension Fund.

Management of the Pension Fund, the State Employment Fund, and the Social Insurance Fund of the Russian Federation is strictly centralized. These funds have divisions in the subjects of the Federation; these divisions report to the central agencies and do not have any independent authority or sources of funding. The mandatory medical insurance funds have a two-level structure, so there is a clear delineation of revenues here. The premium rate for the federal fund is 0.2%; and for the territorial funds, 3.4% (total 3.6%).

The road funds also have a two-level structure. Road taxes are their main source of revenues. The Federal Road Fund of the Russian Federation gets the tax on sales of fuels

Table 7.1

Ratio of Revenues/Expenditures of the Consolidated Budget and Extrabudgetary Funds in 1998 (%)

Funds	**Ratio of funds' revenues to budgetary revenues**	**Ratio of funds' expenditures to budgetary expenditures**	**Ratio of funds' expenditures to budgetary social expenditures**
Pension Fund of the Russian Federation	25.4	22.2	69.9
Social Insurance Fund of the Russian Federation	5.0	4.1	13.0
State Employment Fund of the Russian Federation	1.3	1.1	3.6
Mandatory medical insurance funds*	4.8	4.2	13.3
Road funds*	10.8	12.3	
Total for social funds	36.4	31.6	99.7
Total for all funds	47.2	44.0	

* Federal and territorial.

and lubricants, and excise taxes from the sale of cars for individuals' personal use. The territorial road funds get the tax from owners of transportation vehicles and the tax on purchase of motor vehicles (except for cars purchased by individuals for their personal use). The tax on highway users is divided between the federal and territorial funds. It is credited to the Federal Road Fund at the rate of 0.5%; and to the territorial funds, at the rate of 2.0%. Regional legislative (representative) authorities have the right to raise or lower the tax rate, but by no more than 50% of the federal tax rate. The tax on highway users makes up the greater part of all tax receipts to the road funds. In 1997–1998, it provided about 80% of the road funds' receipts. A little bit more than 10% comes from the tax on sales of fuels and lubricants.

Other sources from which the social extrabudgetary funds, as well as the road funds, are formed are money transferred from the regional and federal budgets, fines and penalties, interest on deposits and other financial investments, loans, and some other sources. Since revenues are redistributed from financially more prosperous regions to less prosperous ones within the framework of extrabudgetary funds, as well as the budget itself, financial aid from the Center plays an appreciable role in the revenues of the territorial divisions in a number of regions.

The composition of the extrabudgetary funds' revenues for Russia as a whole is presented in Table 7.2. As analysis of the data from 1996–1998 shows, the portion of insurance premiums (or taxes for the road fund) amounted to at least four fifths for all of the funds (with the exception of the territorial ones) in all of the years. During the period under consideration, the trend is toward an increase in this portion of the funds' revenues.

The composition of the extrabudgetary funds' expenditures is not as uniform as that of their revenues. The main groups of the social extrabudgetary funds' expenditures (Table 7.3) are pension and benefit payments to individuals, and also funding of social programs and functions conducted by the funds' executive directors. And while, for example, almost all of the Pension Funds' money is spent on payment of pensions and benefits, this sort of funding is not done at all by the mandatory medical insurance funds.

The road funds' main expenditures go to maintenance, repair, reconstruction, and construction of general-use highways (Table 7.4). The Federal Road Fund pays for federal highways, and the territorial funds primarily pay for regional one.

7.3 TERRITORIAL CHARACTERISTICS OF THE FORMATION OF EXTRABUDGETARY FUNDS IN 1997–1998

7.3.1 Distribution of revenues between the Center and the regions

The data for 1998 show noticeable regional differences in how the insurance premiums to the social funds (Table 7.5) and also road taxes (Table 7.6), are divided between the Center and subjects of the Federation.

Table 7.2

Composition of Extrabudgetary Funds' Revenues in 1996–1998 (%)

Funds	Insurance premiums (taxes) 1996	1997	1998	From regional budgets 1997	1998	From the federal budget 1997	1998	Fines and penalties 1997	1998	Other revenues 1997	1998
Pension Fund of the RF	87.4	84.7	89.4	0.0	0.0	12.9	8.9	2.1	1.3	0.3	0.3
Social Insurance Fund of the RF	88.7	89.7	94.0	0.0	0.0	0.7	1.6	7.4	1.4	2.2	3.0
State Employment Fund of the RF	84.4	90.3	93.1	0.2	0.3	2.7	0.1	0.0	1.8	6.8	4.8
Federal MMIF*	95.7	95.5	87.3	0.0	0.0	0.0	0.0	2.9	3.3	1.6	9.3
Territorial MMIF	*60.0*	*60.7*	*62.7*	*23.0*	*23.3*	*0.0*	*0.0*	*6.3*	*5.8*	*10.0*	*8.2*
Federal Road Fund of the RF	n.d.	98.8	99.1	0.0	0.0	0.0	0.0	0.0	0.0	1.2	0.9
Territorial road funds	*n.d.*	*n.d.*	*83.0*	*n.d.*	*0.0*	*n.d.*	*0.0*	*n.d.*	*0.0*	*n.d.*	*16.9*

* MMIF—mandatory medical insurance fund.

Table 7.3

Composition of Social Extrabudgetary Funds' Expenditures in 1997–1998 (%)

Funds	Pension and benefit payments to individuals		Social programs and functions		Fund's executive management		Other expenditures	
	1997	1998	1997	1998	1997	1998	1997	1998
Pension Fund of the RF	97.7	96.1	0.0	0.0	0.9	0.9	1.4	3.0
Social Insurance Fund of the RF	73.4	67.8	21.3	27.8	3.8	3.9	1.5	0.6
State Employment Fund of the RF	62.0	59.8	6.5	6.1	16.7	19.4	14.8	14.7
Federal MMIF	0.0	0.0	92.8	90.6	1.7	2.0	5.5	7.4
Territorial MMIF	0.0	0.0	94.3	94.1	2.9	3.1	2.8	2.8

Table 7.4

Composition of Road Funds' Expenditures in 1997–1998 (%)

	Federal Fund		Territorial funds
Expenditure items	**1997**	**1998**	**1998**
Repair and maintenance of highways	25.3	27.6	39.5
Construction and reconstruction of highways	15.1	34.1	34.1
Grants and subsidies	54.8	34.9	0
Other expenditures	4.8	3.3	16.4

Table 7.5

Territorial Divisions of Social Extrabudgetary Funds' Share of Insurance Premiums in 1998

Share of premiums	Regions	Population
Less than 60%	Kabardino-Balkar Republic, Republic of Dagestan, Ivanovo and Tula Oblasts, Altai Territory, Voronezh and Penza Oblasts	12.6 million people, or 8.6%
60–70%	Kirov Oblast, Chuvash Republic, Smolensk Oblast, Marii El Republic, Rostov, Kursk, Vladimir, and Kostroma Oblasts, Jewish Autonomous Oblast, Belgorod and Novgorod Oblasts	15.5 million people, or 10.5%
70–80%	Saratov Oblast, Republic of Buryatia, Kemerovo, Lipetsk, Volgograd, Yaroslavl, and Orenburg Oblasts, Republic of Khakasia, Aga Buryat Autonomous Region, Kaliningrad Oblast, Republic of Karelia, Arkhangelsk Oblast, Republic of Ingushetia	18.5 million people, or 12.6%
80–95%	Chelyabinsk and Moscow Oblasts, Altai, Udmurt, and Komi Republics, Leningrad, Tyumen, Sverdlovsk, Irkutsk, Bryansk, and Vologda Oblasts, Maritime Territory, St. Petersburg, Tambov Oblast	34.6 million people, or 23.5%
95–100%	Republic of Sakha (Yakutia), Ulyanovsk, Amur, and Pskov Oblasts, Khabarovsk Territory, Republic of Mordovia, Krasnoyarsk Territory, Chita Oblast, Krasnodar Territory, Astrakhan Oblast, Republic of Adygeya, Novosibirsk and Omsk Oblasts, Yamal-Nenets Autonomous Region, Murmansk, Samara, and Tomsk Oblasts, Ust-Orda Buryat Autonomous Region, Kamchatka and Perm Oblast	31.8 million people, or 21.6%

Table 7.6

Share of Road Taxes Credited to Territorial Road Funds in 1998

Share of taxes	Regions	Population
Less than 50%	Aga Buryat Autonomous Region, Republics of Ingushetia and Kalmykia, Altai Republic, Omsk Oblast	3.1 million people, or 2.1%
50–65%	Moscow, Leningrad, and Kaliningrad Oblasts, Republic of Tyva, Karachaevo-Cherkess Republic, Astrakhan Oblast, Khabarovsk Territory, Moscow, Smolensk and Orenburg Oblasts	24.5 million people, or 16.7%
65–75%	Koryak Autonomous Region, Kamchatka Oblast, Komi-Permyak Autonomous Region, Yaroslavl and Sakhalin Oblasts, St. Petersburg, Republic of Adygeya, Stavropol Territory, Kaluga Oblast, Komi Republic, Magadan and Perm Oblasts, Maritime Territory, Marii El and Chuvash Republics, Irkutsk and Novgorod Oblasts, Nenets Autonomous Region, Tula Oblast, Chukotka Autonomous Region, Rostov, Ryazan, Volgograd, Vologda, and Tyumen Oblasts, Evenk Autonomous Region, Bryansk, Vladimir, Lipetsk, and Novosibirsk Oblasts, Republic of Buryatia	44.7 million people, or 30.4%
75–85%	Chita, Orlov, and Samara Oblasts, Republic of Mordovia, Khanty-Mansi Autonomous Region, Pskov and Tomsk Oblasts, Republic of North Osetia, Tver and Kirov Oblasts, Taimyr Autonomous Region, Kabardino-Balkar Republic, Murmansk Oblast, Krasnodar Territory, Udmurt Republic, Voronezh, Nizhegorod, and Kurgan Oblasts, Republic of Khakasia, Krasnoyarsk Territory, Ulyanovsk Oblast, Republic of Karelia, Jewish Autonomous Oblast, Altai Territory, Saratov, Sverdlovsk, and Tambov Oblasts	46.8 million people, or 31.8%
85–100%	Ivanovo, Penza, Chelyabinsk, Belgorod, and Amur Oblasts, Republic of Sakha (Yakutia), Kursk and Kostroma Oblasts, Ust-Orda Buryat and Yamal-Nenets Autonomous Regions, Arkhangelsk Oblast, Republic of Dagestan, Kemerovo Oblast, Republics of Tatarstan and Bashkortostan	27.2 million people, or 18.5%

A particularly low share of insurance premiums goes to Kabardino-Balkaria (27%) and Dagestan (36%), while the Aga Buryat Autonomous Region receives an extremely low share of road taxes (8%). In 1998, the insurance premiums were completely credited to the territorial divisions in Tomsk, Kamchatka, and Perm Oblasts, and in the Ust-Orda Buryat Autonomous Region, while road taxes went entirely to the territorial divisions in Tatarstan and Bashkiria.

In our view, the regional differences in how insurance premiums and road taxes are distributed between the Center and the regions are hard to explain. Both highly developed and underdeveloped territories turned up in various categories with respect to the regional share.

7.3.2 Differences between regions in per capita premiums and taxes

As with other taxes, the differences between regions in collection of insurance premiums and road taxes are determined primarily by the difference in price levels. Tables 7.7 and 7.8 classify the regions according to the per capita revenues of their territorial divisions of extrabudgetary funds, taking into account the subsistence level. The differences between regions are also reflected on Map 16.

To a significant extent, the rest of the factors influencing the differences between regions in per capita collections of insurance premiums and road taxes are the same as for other taxes. The primary ones are differences in the level of regional development and regional laws on concessions with respect to paying taxes to the extrabudgetary funds. As a consequence, the coefficients of correlation between the amounts of tax collections going to regional budgets and to social extrabudgetary funds and road funds in 1998 were approximately 0.8. This means that, for the most part, the disproportions in specific taxes correspond to disproportions in per capita insurance premiums and road taxes (Figure 7.1). However, there are certain deviations. It must also be noted that, on the whole, the extreme values of specific collections to extrabudgetary funds in 1998 differed somewhat less than per capita taxes. In the former case, the maximum value was 3.5 times more than the average; and in the latter case, 7 times more.

The considerable differences between per capita payments to the extrabudgetary funds' territorial divisions and to regional budgets are most likely explained primarily by subjective factors.

7.3.3 Distribution of financial aid among the regions

The considerable differences between regions in per capita payments to the extrabudgetary funds (adjusted for the subsistence level) result in similar differences in their ability to pay for their expenditures with their own revenues. These differences will not change significantly in the near future. This is confirmed by the Ministry of the Economy's forecast for 2000 (Figure 7.2). While six regions (Dagestan, the Aga Buryat and Ust-Orda Buryat Autonomous Regions, North Osetia, Bryansk Oblast, and Karachaevo-Cherkessia) cannot satisfy even half of their need for expenditures from the social extrabudgetary funds with their own revenues, in the Khanty-Mansi Autonomous Region internal revenues exceed expenditures by approximately 2.5 times; and in the Yamal-Nenets Autonomous Region, by more than three times.

Table 7.7

Specific Insurance Premiums Going to Territorial Divisions of Social Extrabudgetary Funds in 1998, Adjusted for the Subsistence Level

Premiums/person, % of average for Russia	Regions	Population
Less than 50%	St. Petersburg, Kabardino-Balkar Republic, Republics of Dagestan and Ingushetia, Aga Buryat Autonomous Region, Republic of North Osetia, Ust-Orda Buryat Autonomous Region, Republic of Tyva	9.1 million people, or 6.2%
50–70%	Marii El and Karachaevo-Cherkess Republic, Altai Territory, Penza Oblast, Republic of Mordovia, Chuvash Republic, Ivanovo Oblast, Chukotka, Komi-Permyak, and Koryak Autonomous Regions, Stavropol Territory, Kirov Oblast, Republic of Khakasia	14.1 million people, or 9.6%
70–85%	Chita and Bryansk Oblast, Republic of Adygeya, Jewish Autonomous Oblast, Rostov, Tambov, Omsk, Kurgan, Voronezh, and Volgograd Oblasts, Republic of Kalmykia, Tver and Novosibirsk Oblasts, Republic of Sakha (Yakutia), Saratov Oblast, Republic of Buryatia, Smolensk, Pskov, Arkhangelsk, Kemerovo, Kostroma, and Ryazan Oblasts	35.5 million people, or 24.1%
85–100%	Kursk, Vladimir, and Amur Oblasts, Evenk Autonomous Region, Udmurt Republic, Tula, Astrakhan, Orlov, Ulyanovsk, Tyumen, Kaluga, and Sakhalin Oblasts, Altai Republic, Sverdlovsk, Orenburg, Novgorod, Yaroslavl, and Kamchatka Oblasts, Krasnodar Territory	28.6 million people, or 19.5%
100–150%	Republic of Karelia, Maritime Territory, Chelyabinsk and Kaliningrad Oblast, Republic of Bashkortostan, Belgorod, Murmansk, Nizhegorod, Moscow, Tomsk, Irkutsk, and Lipetsk Oblasts, Republic of Tatarstan, Khabarovsk Territory, Vologda and Perm Oblasts, Komi Republic, Samara Oblast, Krasnoyarsk Territory, Nenets Autonomous Region	46.5 million people, or 31.6%
More than 150%	Moscow, Yamal-Nenets and Khanty-Mansi Autonomous Region, Leningrad Oblast, Taimyr Autonomous Region	12.5 million people, or 8.5%

Table 7.8

Specific Tax Receipts Going to Territorial Road Funds in 1998, Adjusted for the Subsistence Level

Taxes/person, % of average for Russia	Regions	Population
Less than 20%	Republics of Ingushetia and Tyva, Aga Buryat Autonomous Region, Karachaevo-Cherkess Republic, Ust-Orda Buryat Autonomous Region, Republics of Dagestan and North Osetia	4.0 million people, or 2.8%
20–50%	Koryak, Evenk, Taimyr, Chukotka, and Komi-Permyak Autonomous Regions, Chita Oblast, Kabardino-Balkar Republic, Stavropol Territory, Jewish Autonomous Oblast, Marii El Republic, Republic of Adygeya, Chuvash Republic, Astrakhan Oblast	8.8 million people, or 6.0%
50–70%	Republic of Khakasia, Smolensk Oblast, Republic of Buryatia, Altai Republic, Republic of Sakha (Yakutia), Rostov, Magadan, Bryansk, Moscow, Kirov, Kamchatka, and Vladimir Oblasts, Altai Territory, Kaluga Oblast, Republic of Kalmykia, Orlov and Novosibirsk Oblasts, Maritime Territory, Sakhalin, Ivanovo, and Ryazan Oblasts, Republic of Mordovia, Tula, Kaliningrad, and Penza Oblasts	38.6 million people, or 26.3%
70–100%	Khabarovsk Territory, Pskov, Amur, and Volgograd Oblasts, Krasnodar Territory, Leningrad, Novgorod, Irkutsk, Kurgan, and Voronezh Oblasts, Republic of Karelia, Tyumen, Murmansk, Tver, and Tambov Oblasts, Udmurt Republic, Arkhangelsk, Orenburg, and Vologda Oblasts	32.5 million people, or 22.1%
100–120%	Kemerovo, Ulyanovsk, and Saratov Oblasts, St. Petersburg, Nenets Autonomous Region, Yaroslavl, Chelyabinsk, Kostroma, Kursk, Sverdlovsk, and Tomsk Oblasts	25.0 million people, or 17.0%
130–152%	Krasnoyarsk Territory, Nizhegorod, Omsk, Lipetsk, and Belgorod Oblasts, Komi Republic, Perm and Samara Oblasts	18.9 million people, or 12.9%
More than 200%	Republics of Tatarstan and Bashkortostan, Moscow, Yamal-Nenets and Khanty-Mansi Autonomous Regions	18.4 million people, or 12.5%

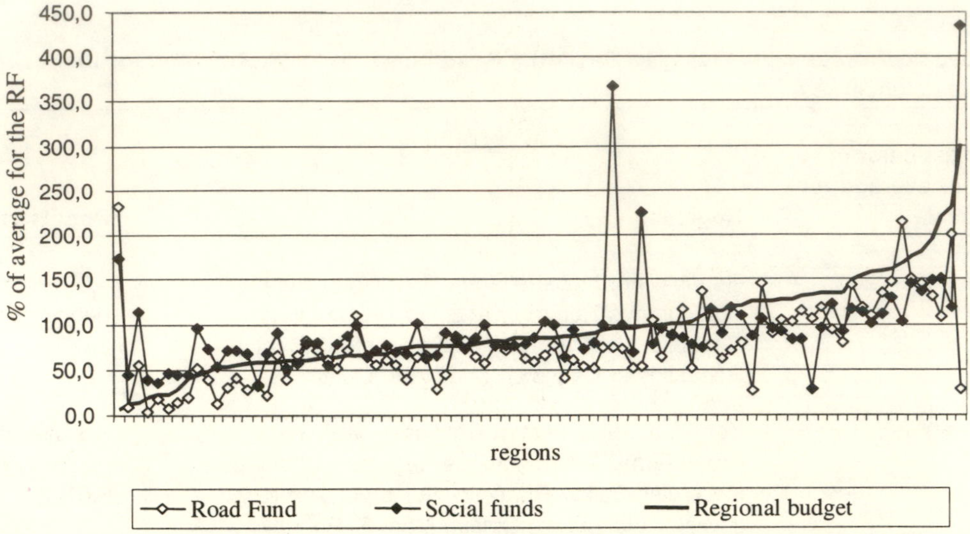

Figure 7.1. **Per capita collection of taxes and insurance premiums to regional budgets and territorial divisions of extrabudgetary funds in 1998, adjusted for the subsistence level.** *Note:* To make the graph easier to read, data for the Yamal-Nenets and Khanty-Mansi Autonomous Regions are not shown.

Naturally, the different levels of support of the extrabudgetary funds' territorial divisions with their own revenues lead to considerable differences between the regions in the portion of financial aid from the central divisions in their revenues (Table 7.9)

In contrast to the process of distributing financial aid among the regional budgets, the process of distributing financial aid among the extrabudgetary funds' territorial divisions is not widely discussed. Unfortunately, the authors of this research do not know the procedures that are used to calculate how much money goes to the territorial divisions.

The redistribution effect from the Center providing money to the extrabudgetary funds' territorial divisions is even less significant than that from appropriation of financial aid to the regional budgets. Available data enable us to evaluate the results of equalization in a cross section of all of the regions on the example of the State Employment Fund of the Russian Federation in 1998 (Figure 7.3). From the graph, we can see that there is almost no equalization of the specific revenues of the fund's territorial divisions.

Calculations for all of the funds for a sample of regions produce similar results, which indicates that financial aid is not provided to the regions on an objective basis.

7.3.4 Expenditures of extrabudgetary funds' territorial divisions

The situation with differences between regions in per capita expenditures of the extrabudgetary funds' territorial divisions, adjusted for the subsistence level, is similar

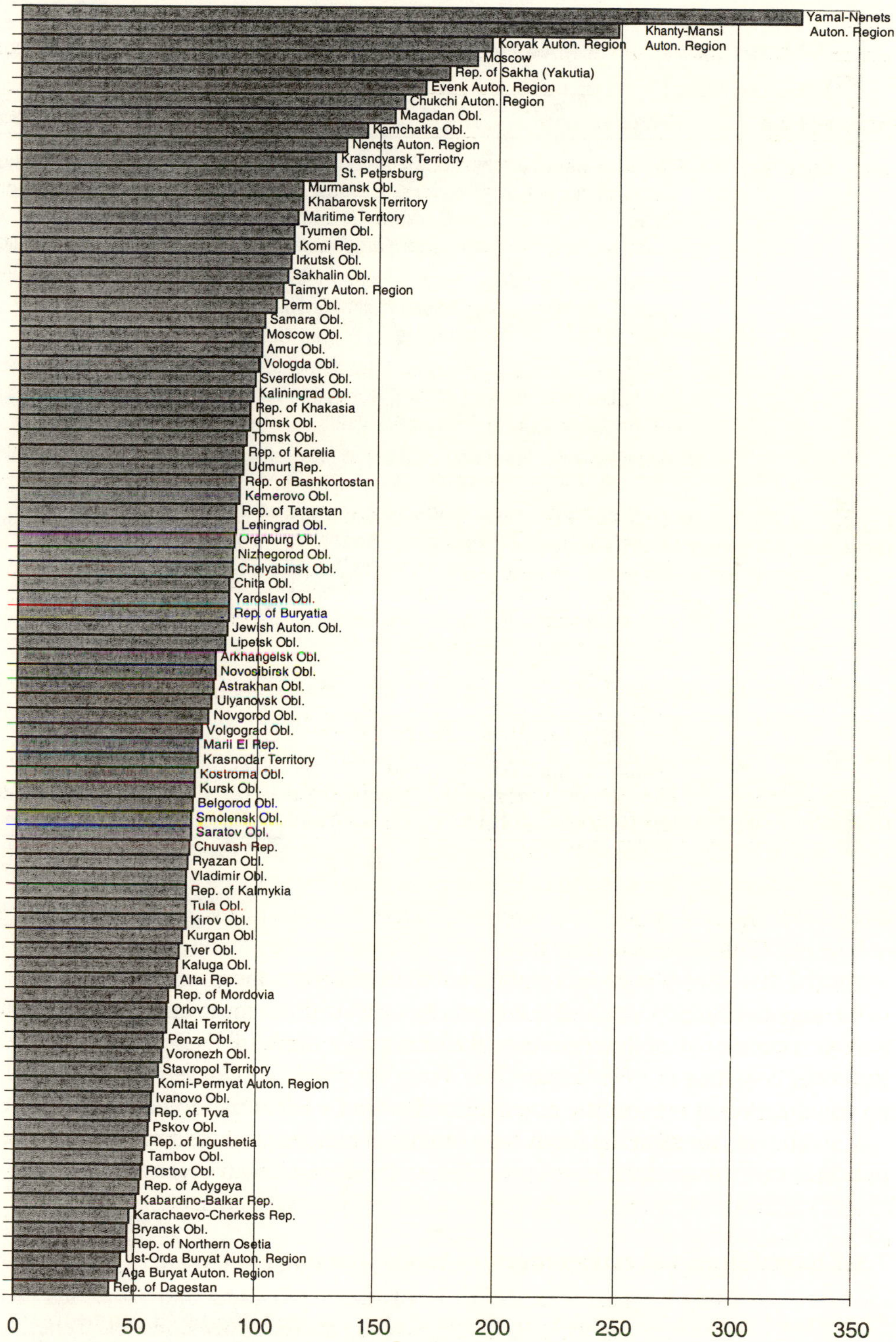

Yamal-Nenets Auton. Region
Khanty-Mansi Auton. Region
Koryak Auton. Region
Moscow
Rep. of Sakha (Yakutia)
Evenk Auton. Region
Chukchi Auton. Region
Magadan Obl.
Kamchatka Obl.
Nenets Auton. Region
Krasnoyarsk Terriotry
St. Petersburg
Murmansk Obl.
Khabarovsk Territory
Maritime Territory
Tyumen Obl.
Komi Rep.
Irkutsk Obl.
Sakhalin Obl.
Taimyr Auton. Region
Perm Obl.
Samara Obl.
Moscow Obl.
Amur Obl.
Vologda Obl.
Sverdlovsk Obl.
Kaliningrad Obl.
Rep. of Khakasia
Omsk Obl.
Tomsk Obl.
Rep. of Karelia
Udmurt Rep.
Rep. of Bashkortostan
Kemerovo Obl.
Rep. of Tatarstan
Leningrad Obl.
Orenburg Obl.
Nizhegorod Obl.
Chelyabinsk Obl.
Chita Obl.
Yaroslavl Obl.
Rep. of Buryatia
Jewish Auton. Obl.
Lipetsk Obl.
Arkhangelsk Obl.
Novosibirsk Obl.
Astrakhan Obl.
Ulyanovsk Obl.
Novgorod Obl.
Volgograd Obl.
Marii El Rep.
Krasnodar Territory
Kostroma Obl.
Kursk Obl.
Belgorod Obl.
Smolensk Obl.
Saratov Obl.
Chuvash Rep.
Ryazan Obl.
Vladimir Obl.
Rep. of Kalmykia
Tula Obl.
Kirov Obl.
Kurgan Obl.
Tver Obl.
Kaluga Obl.
Altai Rep.
Rep. of Mordovia
Orlov Obl.
Altai Territory
Penza Obl.
Voronezh Obl.
Stavropol Territory
Komi-Permyat Auton. Region
Ivanovo Obl.
Rep. of Tyva
Pskov Obl.
Rep. of Ingushetia
Tambov Obl.
Rostov Obl.
Rep. of Adygeya
Kabardino-Balkar Rep.
Karachaevo-Cherkess Rep.
Bryansk Obl.
Rep. of Northern Osetia
Ust-Orda Buryat Auton. Region
Aga Buryat Auton. Region
Rep. of Dagestan
0
50
100
150
200
250
300
350

Figure 7.2. **Ratio of revenues to expenditures of social extrabudgetary funds' territorial divisions in 2000 (forecast) (%).**

Table 7.9

Portion of Financial Aid in the Revenues of Extrabudgetary Funds' Territorial Divisions in 1998

Portion of aid	Regions	Population
Less than 5%	Yamal-Nenets Autonomous Region, Republic of Sakha (Yakutia), Krasnoyarsk Territory, Chita Oblast, St. Petersburg, Samara Oblast, Maritime Territory, Perm, Irkutsk, and Kamchatka Oblasts	30.4 million people, or 20.7%
5–10%	Khabarovsk Territory, Komi Republic, Murmansk, Rostov, Tyumen, Astrakhan, Kaliningrad, Moscow, Vologda, and Tomsk Oblasts	20.4 million people, or 13.9%
10–20%	Sverdlovsk, Amur, Leningrad, Novosibirsk, and Chelyabinsk Oblasts, Udmurt Republic, Volgograd, Arkhangelsk, and Orenburg Oblasts	21.8 million people, or 14.8%
20–35%	Altai Republic, Republic of Karelia, Yaroslavl Oblast, Republics of Khakasia and Buryatia, Lipetsk and Belgorod Oblasts, Aga Buryat Autonomous Region, Omsk Oblast, Jewish Autonomous Oblast, Ulyanovsk, Vladimir, Saratov, and Kursk Oblasts, Krasnodar Territory, Novgorod, Kemerovo, and Kurgan Oblasts, Republic of Mordovia, Stavropol Territory, Chuvash Republic	31.3 million people, or 21.3%
35–50%	Marii El Republic, Penza, Pskov, Smolensk, and Kirov Oblasts, Altai Territory, Republic of Ingushetia, Voronezh, Kostroma, Ivanovo, Tambov, and Tula Oblasts, Republic of Adygeya, Bryansk Oblast	18.4 million people, or 12.5%
More than 50%	Republic of Dagestan, Kabardino-Balkar and Ust-Orda Buryat Autonomous Regions	3.0 million people, or 2.1%

to that with regional budgetary expenditures: the disproportions are enormous and hard to explain (Table 7.10 and Map 17).

The differences between regions in the composition of expenditures by the extrabudgetary funds' territorial divisions are significant. In conducting the research, we used data on the composition of expenditures by territorial divisions of the State Employment Fund and the Social Insurance Fund of the Russian Federation for 1998. It is the most differentiated on the average for Russia (see Table 7.3). Therefore, we can expect that significant differences between regions in the composition of expenditures may be found in precisely these two funds. The directions of spending by the other funds' territorial divisions, on the other hand, are relatively uniform in individual subjects of the Federation.

The most interesting thing in the composition of expenditures is the percentage of pension and benefit payments and funding of social programs and functions (Tables 7.11 and 7.12). We can assume that the higher the portion of pensions and benefits, the less favorable the situation in the region is. In fact, the more money that has to be spent

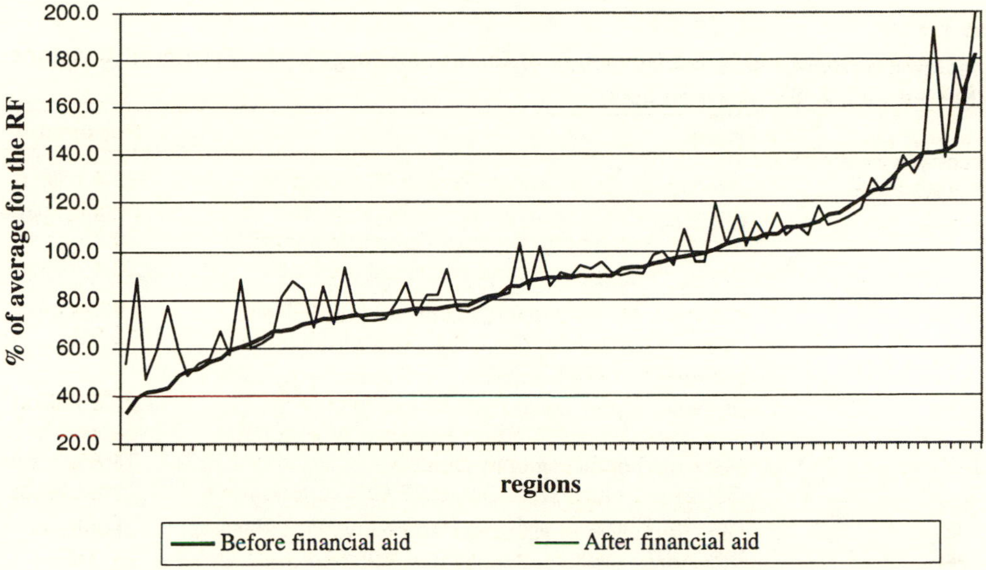

Figure 7.3. **Revenues of territorial divisions of the Employment Fund before and after money was provided from the Center in 1998.** *Note:* To make the graph easier to read, no data are shown for Moscow or the Yamal-Nenets and Khanty-Mansi Autonomous Regions, where the revenues of extrabudgetary funds' territorial divisions are 2, 2.5, and 3 times more, respectively, than the national average, both before and after financial aid is provided.

on mandatory payments to individuals, the less that is left for funding occupational training and retraining of unemployed workers, programs to save jobs and create additional or new ones, and development of business activity (the State Employment Fund of the Russian Federation), or for public health and spa services for the population (the Social Insurance Fund of the Russian Federation).

Like the differences in per capita revenues, the differences between regions in the composition of expenditures result from random factors. As for the State Employment Fund, the research revealed some relationship between the portion of expenditures on income support and the official level of unemployment (Figure 7.4). However, the dependence is very slight (the coefficient of correlation is 0.39).

Calculations also showed that the portion of benefit payments to individuals from territorial divisions of the State Employment Fund and the Social Insurance Fund hardly correlate with each other at all (the coefficient of correlation is 0.31). In our view, the distribution of regions by types is almost unexplainable and is most likely brought about primarily by subjective factors.

7.4 CONCLUSIONS AND SUGGESTIONS

The financial flows within the framework of the extrabudgetary funds are commensurable with the budgetary financial flows. However, very little attention is paid to the

Table 7.10

Specific Expenditures of Social Extrabudgetary Funds' Territorial Divisions in 1998, Adjusted for the Subsistence Level

Expenditures/person, % of average for Russia	Regions	Population
Less than 75%	St. Petersburg, Aga Buryat and Koryak Autonomous Regions, Chita Oblast, Chukotka Autonomous Region, Ingush Republic, Republic of Sakha (Yakutia), Magadan and Amur Oblasts, Republic of Tyva	9.3 million people, or 6.1%
75–90%	Marii El Republic, Republics of Khakasia and Dagestan, Kamchatka Oblast, Evenk Autonomous Region, Republic of North Osetia, Tyumen and Novosibirsk Oblast, Republic of Buryatia, Ust-Orda Buryat Autonomous Region	9.8 million people, or 6.7%
90–100%	Republic of Kalmykia, Maritime Territory, Arkhangelsk Oblast, Altai Territory, Sakhalin Oblast, Moscow, Penza Oblast, Kabardino-Balkar Republic, Kirov and Volgograd Oblasts, Jewish Autonomous Oblast, Astrakhan Oblast, Chuvash Republic, Saratov, Omsk, and Sverdlovsk Oblasts, Udmurt and Karachaevo-Cherkess Republics, Republic of Mordovia	37.7 million people, or 25.6%
100–110%	Republic of Karelia, Stavropol Territory, Murmansk Oblast, Khabarovsk Territory, Khanty-Mansi Autonomous Region, Kaliningrad, Orenburg, Irkutsk, Kurgan, and Kemerovo Oblasts, Altai Republic	17.5 million people, or 11.9%
110–125%	Nenets Autonomous Region, Tomsk and Chelyabinsk Oblasts, Republic of Bashkortostan, Tver Oblast, Komi-Permyak Autonomous Region, Moscow, Kostroma, Voronezh, Ulyanovsk, and Vladimir Oblasts, Yamal-Nenets Autonomous Region, Yaroslavl, Vologda, Rostov, Ivanovo, Smolensk, Pskov, Kursk, and Ryazan Oblasts, Krasnoyarsk Territory, Perm Oblast	43.0 million people, or 29.3%
More than 125%	Krasnodar Territory, Kaluga Oblast, Republic of Adygeya, Tambov Oblast, Komi Republic, Republic of Tatarstan, Nizhegorod, Novgorod, Bryansk, Tula, Lipetsk, Belgorod, Samara, and Orlov Oblasts, Taimyr Autonomous Region, Leningrad Oblast	29.2 million people, or 19.9%

Table 7.11

Portion of Expenditures on Income Support in Total Expenditures of Territorial Divisions of the State Employment Fund of the Russian Federation in 1998

Portion of expenditures	Regions	Population
Less than 50%	Moscow, Orenburg Oblast, Evenk Autonomous Region, Republic of Sakha (Yakutia), Ust-Orda Buryat Autonomous Region, Smolensk, Chelyabinsk, Belgorod, Lipetsk, and Rostov Oblasts, Yamal-Nenets Autonomous Region, Omsk Oblast	26.7 million people, or 18.1%
50–60%	Kaliningrad and Orlov Oblasts, St. Petersburg, Aga Buryat Autonomous Region, Magadan Oblast, Udmurt Republic, Komi-Permyak Autonomous Region, Tyumen and Ivanovo Oblasts, Chukotka Autonomous Region, Maritime Territory, Khanty-Mansi Autonomous Region, Volgograd, Amur, and Kemerovo Oblasts, Karachaevo-Cherkess Republic, Moscow Oblast	28.7 million people, or 19.5%
60–65%	Altai Territory, Republics of Khakasia and Tyva, Taimyr Autonomous Region, Tver, Voronezh, and Ryazan Oblasts, Krasnoyarsk and Khabarovsk Territories, Altai Republic, Kaluga Oblast	14.9 million people, or 10.1%
65–70%	Penza, Kurgan, Pskov, and Ulyanovsk Oblasts, Stavropol Territory, Novosibirsk Oblast, Republic of Adygeya, Koryak Autonomous Region, Republic of Buryatia, Tambov and Sakhalin Oblasts, Jewish Autonomous Oblast, Novgorod Oblast, Marii El Republic, Bryansk, Perm, and Tomsk Oblasts, Republic of Kalmykia, Komi Republic	22.4 million people, or 15.2%
70–75%	Chita, Saratov, and Nizhegorod Oblasts, Republic of North Osetia, Kirov, Kursk, Vologda, and Kamchatka Oblasts, Republic of Dagestan, Irkutsk and Astrakhan Oblasts, Nenets Autonomous Region, Krasnodar Territory, Arkhangelsk, Tula, Sverdlovsk, Yaroslavl, Murmansk, and Kostroma Oblasts, Chuvash Republic	36.3 million people, or 24.7%
More than 75%	Vladimir and Leningrad Oblasts, Kabardino-Balkar Republic, Republic of Mordovia, Samara Oblast, Ingush Republic, Republic of Karelia	9.4 million people, or 6.4%

Table 7.12

Portion of Expenditures on Benefit Payments in Total Expenditures of Territorial Divisions of the Social Insurance Fund of the Russian Federation in 1998

Portion of expenditures	Regions	Population
Less than 70%	Tyumen, Moscow, and Astrakhan Oblasts, St. Petersburg, Kaliningrad, Kursk, Orlov, Bryansk, and Samara Oblasts, Republic of Adygeya, Smolensk and Nizhegorod Oblasts, Ingush Republic	27.3 million people, or 18.5%
70–75%	Maritime Territory, Novgorod, Kurgan, and Kostroma Oblasts, Krasnodar Territory, Leningrad and Ryazan Oblasts, Aga Buryat Autonomous Region, Tver Oblast, Jewish Autonomous Oblast, Vladimir, Ivanovo, Saratov, Kaluga, Kirov, and Penza Oblasts, Stavropol Territory	27.4 million people, or 18.5%
75–80%	Chita, Rostov, Murmansk, Chelyabinsk, and Tula Oblasts, Kabardino-Balkar Republic, Yaroslavl, Belgorod, and Novosibirsk Oblasts, Marii El Republic, Sverdlovsk and Voronezh Oblasts, Karachaevo-Cherkess Republic, Republic of Kalmykia, Pskov Oblast, Krasnoyarsk Territory, Khanty-Mansi and Yamal-Nenets Autonomous Regions, Khabarovsk Territory, Tomsk and Perm Oblast, Udmurt Republic, Magadan Oblast, Nenets Autonomous Region, Kamchatka Oblast, Republic of North Osetia, Lipetsk and Vologda Oblasts, Taimyr Autonomous Region	48.7 million people, or 33.1%
80–85%	Republic of Khakasia, Altai Republic, Altai Territory, Orenburg, Kemerovo, Tambov, and Ulyanovsk Oblasts, Republic of Mordovia, Evenk Autonomous Region, Komi Republic, Buryatia, Ust-Orda Buryat and Komi-Permyak Autonomous Regions, Amur Oblast, Chukotka Autonomous Region, Sakhalin Oblast, Chuvash Republic	18.0 million people, or 12.3%
More than 85%	Republic of Tyva, Koryak Autonomous Region, Arkhangelsk Territory, Republics of Dagestan and Karelia	4.7 million people, or 3.2%

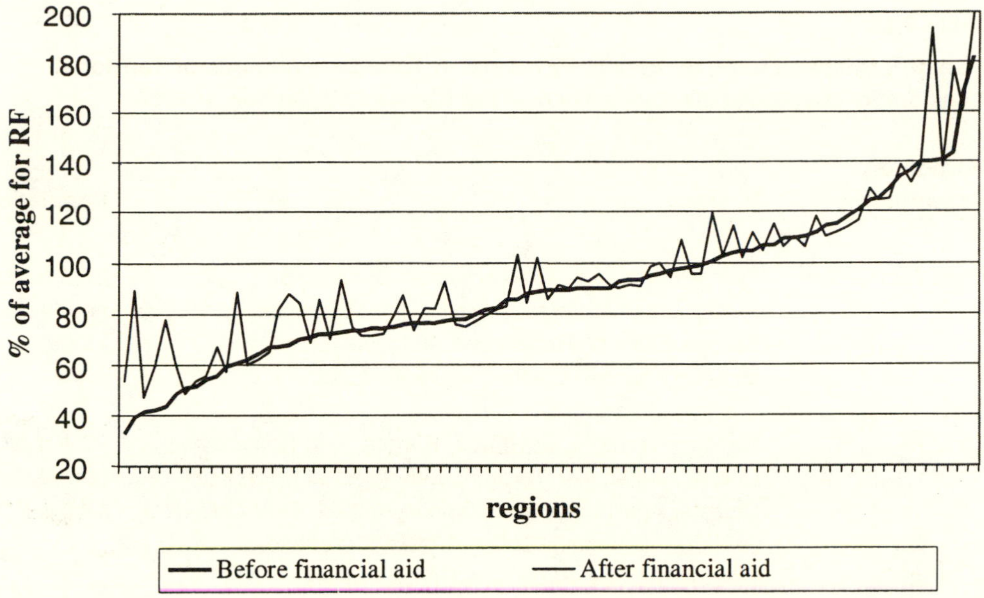

Figure 7.4. **Ratio between portion of expenditures on income support in expenditures of territorial divisions of the State Employment Fund and the official level of unemployment in 1998.**

composition of revenues and expenditures of the extrabudgetary funds' territorial divisions, or to the interaction of their central and regional divisions. As a result, the scale of redistribution of money within the framework of the extrabudgetary funds, and the criteria and principles on which such redistribution is based remain unknown to the general public. Certainly, the reform of financial interrelations between the Center and the regions cannot be complete without improving the mechanisms by which financial aid is provided to the territories through the extrabudgetary funds. To accomplish this objective, it is necessary, first of all, to include information about the extrabudgetary funds in the general system of monitoring of regional finances.

The territorial structure of the extrabudgetary funds is largely analogous to the budgetary structure. Like the regional budgets, the territorial divisions of the extrabudgetary funds are characterized by enormous differences in per capita tax collections and insurance premiums, and in the portion of these revenues that stays in the territory. There are also significant regional differences the structure of per capita tax collections and insurance premiums. It is perfectly obvious that, as in the budget itself, financial interrelations between the Center and the regions within the framework of the extrabudgetary funds are distinguished by a certain degree of subjectivity, and that the effect of trying to equalize the revenues available to the territorial divisions is insignificant. Therefore, the goals and objectives of improving the mechanisms by which financial aid is provided to territorial divisions of the extrabudgetary funds are the same as they are for reforming interbudgetary relations.

CHAPTER 8

Geography of Public Finances

8.1 STATEMENT OF THE PROBLEM

Analysis of the revenues and expenditures of budgets and extrabudgetary funds is no less interesting than generalization of information on public finances, such as the balance of financial flows described in Chapter 2. By adding up the revenues and expenditures of regional and local budgets, plus the federal budgetary revenues and expenditures "connected" with a particular territory, we can get the so-called consolidated budget of a region.[1] The region's expanded budget is obtained by adding to the consolidated budget the revenues and expenditures of the extrabudgetary funds. The balance of financial flows can and should be used mainly to characterize the interrelations between the Center and subjects of the Federation. Analysis of the consolidated and expanded budgets provides new information on a number of aspects of public finances, including:

- the extent to which subjects of the Federation are subsidized (which is calculated for both the consolidated and expanded budgets)
- the ratio of federal and regional expenditures in a region
- the ratio of the budgetary and extrabudgetary components of public finances in a region
- the portion of all revenues collected in a region (going to the budgets of all levels and to the extrabudgetary funds) in the gross regional product
- the structure of all expenditures (budgetary and extrabudgetary) in a region, including the ratio of the "production" and "social" components of public finances.

In this chapter, we will first look at the regions' consolidated budgets, then their expanded budgets. The same statistical data were used to compile the regions' consolidated budgets as to compile the balance of financial flows, and the federal budget's revenues and direct expenditures are taken into account to the same degree (see Chapter 2). Although we did encounter a shortage of data on the extrabudgetary funds in

[1] In contrast to a region's consolidated budget, a regional consolidated budget is understood to mean the sum of the regional and local budgets.

preparing this chapter, the regions' expanded budgets can still be calculated, at least tentatively.

8.2 A REGION'S CONSOLIDATED BUDGET

8.2.1 Model of a region's consolidated budget

The most important factor determining the dependence of regional budgets on financial aid from the federal budget, the structure of regional expenditures, and the Federation's direct expenditures in individual territories, and a number of other indices, is how revenues and expenditures are divided between the federal and regional budgets. Therefore, in order to get a complete idea of the budget sphere in individual regions it is necessary to put together and analyze a consolidated budget for a region, by which we mean the revenues and expenditures of budgets at all levels (federal, regional, and local) "connected" to the territory of a particular subject of the Federation.

The equation for a region's consolidated budget can be represented as follows:

$$R - E = S + D,$$

where R is the revenues (tax and nontax) collected in the region's territory and credited to the budgets of all hierarchical levels (federal, regional, and local);

E is expenditures from the budgets of all levels (federal, regional, and local) in the region's territory not connected with redistribution of revenues between the budgets of different levels;

S is the balance (absolute value) of budgetary financial flows between the Center and the regions; for donor regions, the balance of financial flows is negative; for recipient regions, it is positive;

D is the difference between the consolidated regional budget's revenues and expenditures (the deficit). The difference between the deficit indicated in statistical reports on the execution of regional budgets and the remainder of loans provided from the federal budget not repaid at the end of the year should be used as this index. In this research, loans from the federal budget that are not repaid are considered a mechanism of financial aid to regional budgets and, accordingly, are part of the balance of budgetary financial flows between the Center and the regions.

The meaning of this formula is fairly simple. In the territory of a region, on the one hand, a certain amount of revenue is collected (going to the budgets of all levels). On the other hand, particular expenditures (not including internal transfers) are funded, also from the budgets of all levels, in the region's territory. First of all, the difference between the total revenues collected in the region and the expenditures that are made is expressed in the regional budget's deficit, and secondly, it is compensated by redistribution of money between regions in the form of financial aid to the regional budgets from the federal budget, as well as direct expenditures from the federal budget that are disproportional to the revenues credited to the federal budget from the region's territory.

The formula for a consolidated budget can be represented in greater detail as follows:

$$R_{fb} + R_{rb} + R_{lb} - E_{fb} - E_{rb} - E_{lb} = F + B + D_{rb} + D_{lb},$$

where R_{fb} is tax and nontax revenues collected in the region's territory and credited to the federal budget;

R_{rb} is tax and nontax revenues collected in the region's territory and credited to the regional budget (the regional budget's internal revenues);

R_{lb} is tax and nontax revenues collected in the region's territory and credited to local budgets (the local budgets' internal revenues);

E_{fb} is direct expenditures from the federal budget in the region;

E_{rb} is expenditures from the regional budget not including internal transfers (i.e., not including financial aid to local budgets);

E_{lb} is expenditures from local budgets not including internal transfers (i.e., not including expenditures on transfer of budgetary funds to other budgets);

F is financial aid to regional budgets from the federal budget;

B is the balance of financial flows between the Center and the regions, i.e., the difference between revenues collected in the region's territory and credited to the federal budget and total expenditures from the federal budget in the region (the sum of financial aid to regional budgets and direct expenditures);

D_{rb} is the regional budget's deficit (budget loans are included in financial aid from the federal budget);

D_{lb} is the local budgets' deficit.

We should pay particular attention to the division of expenditures into expenditures not including internal transfers and expenditures on providing financial aid to budgets at lower levels. Excluding the latter from the total amount of expenditures makes it possible, first of all, to avoid double counting: the federal budget's expenditures on financial aid, being regional budgets' revenues at the same time, go to funding of various functions from the regional budgets. The same thing is true of regional and local budgets. Expenditures on providing financial aid characterize interbudgetary relations to a greater degree than they do expenditures as such.

Hereinafter, by the expenditures of a consolidated budget we will mean expenditures not including internal transfers.

Quite a bit of attention has traditionally been given to problems concerning the total amount of revenues collected in a region (i.e., the tax potential of subjects of the Federation), and they are not analyzed in detail in this study. Questions concerning the expenditure part of consolidated regional budgets (not including internal transfers) have not been studied previously and are analyzed for the first time in this research.

8.2.2 Ratio of revenues and expenditures of the regions' consolidated budgets

The ratio of revenues and expenditures (not including internal transfers) of the regions' consolidated budgets is one of the indices (along with indices of the balance of financial flows between the federal budget and the territories, and the portion of financial aid in the regional budgets' revenues) that show how independent subjects of the Federation are in regard to their budgets.

Although the very concept of a region's consolidated budget is purely theoretical, the meaning of this parameter is simple. The ratio of a consolidated budget's revenues and expenditures shows whether or not a particular region could exist as an independent subject and, if so, what its budget deficit or surplus would be (for example, if the ratio of revenues to expenditures is 80%, the region's consolidated budget deficit would be 20%).

As we already said in the chapter on the extrabudgetary funds, the territorial road and environmental funds and the fund for replacement of the mineral raw-material base in the regions can be targeted budgetary funds or extrabudgetary funds.[2] So the formal use of data on the regional budgets' revenues and expenditures in the calculations will not provide fully comparable data on the consolidated budgets of subjects of the Federation. Therefore, regardless of whether or not these funds are consolidated in the regions, the expenditures of targeted budgetary funds were excluded from the calculations when compiling the regions' consolidated budgets.

On the average for the regions, the ratio of revenues to expenditures in their consolidated budgets was 108% in 1998, and 115% in 1999.[3] There were 21 and 32 regions in 1998 and 1999, respectively, where revenues exceeded expenditures (so-called unsubsidized regions). Differences between regions in the ratio of their consolidated budgets' revenues to expenditures are presented in Figure 8.1. Novosibirsk Oblast was the only region to move from unsubsidized in 1998 to subsidized in 1999 (it went from being a donor region to a recipient region). Accordingly, there were 20 consistently unsubsidized subjects of the Federation in 1998–1999, and 12 new ones became unsubsidized in 1999. On the whole, however, the differences between regions were relatively constant (the coefficient of correlation between the indices for 1998 and 1999 was 0.9). The greatest changes were primarily for less populated and economically underdeveloped autonomous regions and republics in the southern part of Russia. In most regions, as for Russia as a whole, the ratio of revenues to expenditures rose in 1999 in comparison with 1998. Among relatively large regions, a noticeable reduction in the

---

[2] We will recall that these funds' revenues and expenditures were taken into account in compiling the balance of financial flows, since the federal road and environmental funds and the fund for replacement of the mineral raw-material base are targeted budgetary funds.

[3] The data on expenditures of the regional budgets, as well as the federal budget, and also on the regional budgets' tax and nontax revenues, are final for 1998 (Ministry of Finance of the Russian Federation), and the data on the regional budget's revenues are up to date (Ministry of Taxes and Duties of the Russian Federation). All data for 1999 are preliminary.

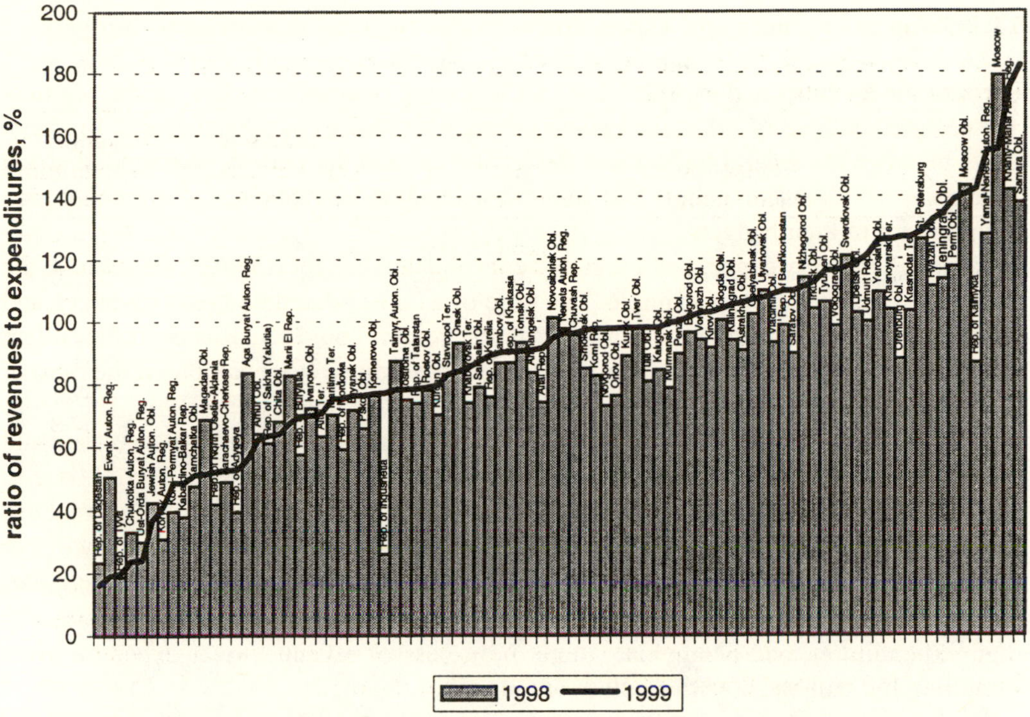

Figure 8.1 **Distribution of subjects of the Federation by ratio of their consolidated budget's revenues to expenditures (not including internal transfers) in 1998–1999.**

ratio of revenues to expenditures (by more than 15%) was only characteristic of the Marii El Republic and Magadan Oblast.

Although there were somewhat fewer of the regions we called unsubsidized than there were donor regions, nevertheless the number of them is much larger than 10 (as we already said in Chapter 2, that is the number of subjects of the Federation that are traditionally considered donors to the federal budget). In 1999, more than a third of the subjects of the Federation were unsubsidized, with about 57% of Russia's population living in those regions (41% in consistently unsubsidized regions).

The leader in the ratio of revenues to expenditures in 1998 was Moscow (179%), followed by Moscow Oblast (144%), and then the Khanty-Mansi Autonomous Region and Samara Oblast. In 1999, Samara Oblast moved into first place (182%), and Moscow held third place after the Khanty-Mansi Autonomous Region. For the most part, the differences between subjects of the Federation correspond to prevailing ideas about disproportions in the level of the regions' economic development. The unsubsidized regions are mostly large, industrially developed ones, and oil- and gas-producing autonomous regions. As expected, the ones in the worst shape are republics of the North

Table 8.1

Ratio of Revenues to Expenditures of the Regions' Consolidated Budgets in Different Parts of the Country in 1998–1999

Area	Population, million people	Share of population, %	Revenues to expenditures in 1998, %	Revenues to expenditures in 1999, %
Central	37.4	25.6	141.5	137.0
Northwestern	14.6	10.0	101.5	111.0
North Caucasus	21	14.4	77.2	87.5
Volga	32.1	22.0	99.1	113.1
Ural	12.7	8.7	122.5	141.4
Siberia	20.9	14.3	86.7	92.1
Far East	7.3	5.0	65.3	67.8

Caucasus and Southern Siberia, and most of the autonomous regions. At the same time, there are some striking exceptions. These include Tatarstan, where revenues are less than expenditures, and Kalmykia, where the excess of revenues over expenditures is such that this republic held third place among all of the regions.

When we look at the ratio of revenues and expenditures of the regions' consolidated budgets, we must also remember that both the numerator and the denominator of this index are affected not only by objective factors, but also by subjective ones. As applied to direct expenditures from the federal budget, this was shown in Chapter 4, and the situation is similar with regional expenditures. Revenues not only depend on the level of a region's economic development, but also on the authorities' efforts to collect taxes (primarily the efforts of regional authorities). This means that, in a number of cases, if federal or regional authorities wish to do so, revenues can be increased and spending can be cut, so that a subject of the Federation goes from being a subsidized region to an unsubsidized one.

The concentration of problem regions in the North Caucasus, Siberia, and the Far East is illustrated by data on the ratio of revenues to expenditures of the regions' consolidated budgets in different parts of the country (Table 8.1). The Central, Northwestern, and Ural parts of the country, and the Volga area in 1999, are unsubsidized. In the Far Eastern area of the country, there is not a single unsubsidized region (just as there is not one donor with respect to the balance of financial flows taking into account direct expenditures from the federal budget).

Analysis of the data for different parts of the country also enables us to answer the question of whether or not the subjects of the Federation should be enlarged, which is periodically raised in scientific publications and the mass media. One of the arguments put forth in favor of merging regions into larger units is that it would create self-sufficient subjects of the Federation that do not require such large-scale financial aid from the federal budget as they presently do, or not need it at all. The presence of subsidized, as well as unsubsidized areas of the country indicates that no enlargement of subjects of the Federation is capable of fully solving the problem of regions that have to be subsidized. The reason for this lies in the considerable territorial concentration of highly subsidized subjects of the Federation.

Including autonomous regions as part of their respective oblasts (territories) also only half solves the problem of subsidies. If we disregard Tyumen Oblast, with the Khanty-Mansi and Yamal-Nenets Autonomous Regions, which are themselves the most financially prosperous, revenues exceed expenditures in subjects of the Federation combined with their autonomous regions only in Perm and Irkutsk Oblasts, and in Krasnoyarsk Territory. In Arkhangelsk, Kamchatka, and Chita Oblasts, revenues are less than expenditures even without the autonomous regions, with the situation in the Nenets Autonomous Region being even better than in Arkhangelsk Oblast. Chita Oblast was also characterized by a higher rate of subsidy than the Aga Buryat Autonomous Region in 1998.

Such a result, in which financial self-sufficiency can be achieved only for individual consolidated regions, is entirely predictable. The problem of redistribution of budgetary revenues exists to one degree or another in any country, and Russia is no exception to this rule.

8.2.3 Ratio of federal and regional expenditures

One of the basic characteristics of the regions' consolidated budgets can be the ratio of federal and regional expenditures (not including internal transfers) in the territory of a subject of the Federation. For Russia as a whole, direct federal expenditures connected to a particular territory make up a little bit more than one fifth of the regional budgets' expenditures[4] (17.5% in 1998 and 22.0% in 1999). Individual regions differ noticeably in this index (data for 1999 are presented in Table 8.2).

The proportions between federal and regional expenditures in individual subjects of the Federation remained fairly stable in 1998–1999 (coefficient of correlation 0.88). In the overwhelming majority of regions, the portion of federal expenditures in 1999 rose in comparison with 1998.[5] This increase was most significant in economically underdeveloped republics: Dagestan (by 20%), Ingushetia (by 16%), the Republics of Kalmykia, Altai, and Tyva, and the Ust-Orda Buryat Autonomous Region (by 11–13%). In more prosperous regions, the maximum changes reached 8–10% (Komi Republic, Kaluga, Kostroma, Kurgan, and Amur Oblasts, and Moscow).

---

[4] Here and hereinafter, by regional budgets we mean the consolidated regional budgets, i.e., the sum of regional budgets proper and local budgets.

[5] The portion of federal expenditures dropped in only 8 regions (the Republics of Sakha (Yakutia) and North Osetia-Alania, Vologda, Bryansk, and Orlov Oblasts, and the Nenets, Khanty-Mansi, and Koryak Autonomous Regions), and only slightly at that.

Table 8.2

Portion of Direct Federal Expenditures in Total Amount of Expenditures (Not Including Internal Transfers) of the Regions' Consolidated Budgets in 1999 (%)

Portion of federal expenditures, %	Regions	Population
Less than 15	Khanty-Mansi Autonomous Region, Yamal-Nenets Autonomous Region, Republics of Bashkortostan and Tatarstan, Vologda Oblast, Republic of Sakha (Yakutia), Tyumen Oblast, Taimyr and Nenets Autonomous Regions, Samara Oblast, Koryak Autonomous Region, Orenburg and Leningrad Oblasts	20.8 million people, or 14.2%
15–20	Lipetsk Oblast, Krasnoyarsk Territory, Belgorod and Perm Oblasts, Udmurt Republic, Chelyabinsk, Volgograd, Yaroslavl, Nizhegorod, Novgorod, and Murmansk Oblasts, Evenk Autonomous Region, Irkutsk and Sverdlovsk Oblasts, Krasnodar Territory	35.8 million people, or 24.5%
20–25	Ulyanovsk Oblast, Republic of Khakasia, Saratov, Omsk, and Kirov Oblasts, Republic of Karelia, Altai Territory, Kabardino-Balkar Republic, Moscow and Kostroma Oblasts, Ust-Orda Buryat Autonomous Region, Chuvash Republic, Republics of Mordovia and Adygeya, Orlov, Ryazan, Kursk, Vladimir, and Penza Oblasts, Republic of Buryatia, Tver, Magadan, Voronezh, and Smolensk Oblasts, St. Petersburg, Astrakhan and Pskov Oblasts	42.8 million people, or 29.3%
25–30	Arkhangelsk, Kaliningrad, and Tomsk Oblast, Aga Buryat Autonomous Region, Tambov Oblast, Maritime Territory, Amur and Kemerovo Oblasts, Komi-Permyat Autonomous Region, Sakhalin and Ivanovo Oblasts, Marii El Republic, Karachaevo-Cherkess and Chukotka Autonomous Regions, Kurgan Oblast, Khabarovsk and Stavropol Territory, Komi Republic	20.8 million people, or 14.2%
More than 30	Kaluga and Kamchatka Oblasts, Republics of North Osetia-Alania and Kalmykia, Jewish Autonomous Oblast, Moscow, Tula and Novosibirsk Oblasts, Republic of Tyva, Bryansk, Chita, and Rostov Oblasts, Republics of Ingushetia and Dagestan, Altai Republic	25.8 million people, or 17.7%

To a significant extent, the differences between regions in the portion of federal expenditures in the total budgetary expenditures conform to certain patterns. A higher share of federal expenditures is characteristic of:

a) many economically underdeveloped regions, where the regional budgets' per capita expenditures are low;

b) Moscow, where educational and public-health institutions, scientific research institutes, cultural facilities, etc. funded from the federal budget are concentrated;
c) regions where there is a need for a larger scale of expenditures on specific items. These are Bryansk and Tula Oblasts, which receive a considerable amount of money for mitigating the consequences of emergency situations and natural disasters, Rostov Oblast, where expenditures for supporting the coal industry are high, and Novosibirsk Oblast, which is one of the three leading Russian scientific Centers.

On the other hand, the lowest portion of federal expenditures (no more than 5%) is noted in the Yamal-Nenets and Khanty-Mansi Autonomous Regions, and in Tatarstan and Bashkiria. The reasons for this are fairly obvious. These autonomous regions are the most financially prosperous and obviously have no special need for funding from the federal budget. Tatarstan and Bashkiria have special relationships with the Center. They keep a higher than normal portion of revenues in their own territory and, accordingly, have greater possibilities for funding from their regional budgets. Yakutia is another region with a lower than normal share of expenditures from the federal budget, apparently for the same reason.

The analysis that was conducted established an inverse relationship between the federal budget's share of the expenditures of a region's consolidated budget and the regional budget's per capita expenditures (adjusted for the subsistence level). The coefficient of correlation between these indices was –0.56 in 1998 and –0.54 in 1999. There is also a correlation between the federal budget's share in the total amount of expenditures and per capita direct expenditures from the federal budget adjusted for the subsistence level, but only a direct one (the higher per capita federal expenditures are, the higher the portion of them is). In 1998, the coefficient of correlation for this relationship was 0.64, and in 1999 it decreased to 0.43.

Based on the data cited and the indicated patterns, it is quite valid to say that the portion of federal expenditures in the total amount of budgetary expenditures depends to a significant extent on objective factors; however, the influence of subjective factors is also evident. Along with the obvious cases of a higher or lower than normal portion from the federal budget (Moscow, Khanty-Mansi and Yamal-Nenets Autonomous Regions, Bashkiria and Tatarstan, and financially prosperous regions with a low portion of expenditures from the federal budget, and on the other hand, the economically most backward regions with a high portion from it), there are facts that cannot be explained, in our view. For example, the very low portion of expenditures from the federal budget in the Koryak Autonomous Region, and on the other hand, the high portion in Kaluga Oblast, which has no particular problems.

8.2.4 Per capita expenditures of the regions' consolidated budgets

Since there are significant differences between subjects of the Federation in price levels, as in all of the preceding sections we will look at the specific values of expenditures

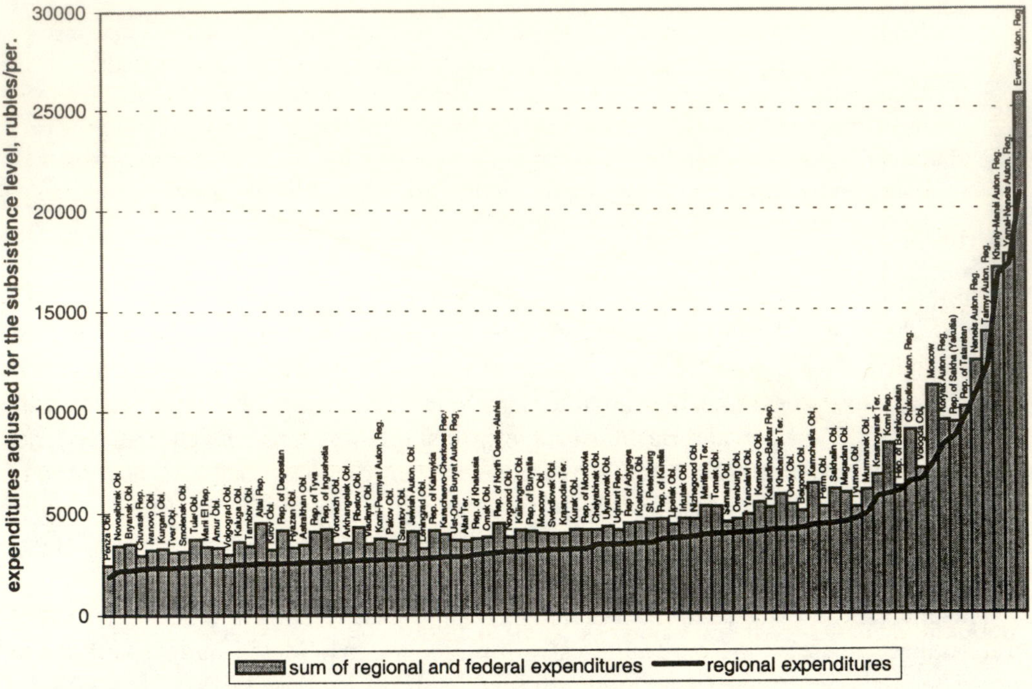

Figure 8.2 **Per capita expenditures from regional budgets and the regions' consolidated budgets, adjusted for the subsistence level, in 1999.**

from the regions' consolidated budgets adjusted for the regional values of the subsistence level.

When analyzing expenditures, two aspects of this problem are of the greatest interest: the scale of differences between regions in this index, and the increase or decrease in differences in per capita regional expenditures after federal expenditures are included.

The differences between regions in per capita expenditures from the regions' consolidated budgets are very high and only a little bit less than the differences in per capita expenditures from the regional budgets (Figure 8.2). So, for per capita regional expenditures (adjusted for the subsistence level) the ratio of the maximum value to the minimum was 12.2 times, and the mean deviation from the national average was 47.4%. For per capita expenditures from the consolidated regional budgets, these figures were 10.9 times and 41.1%, respectively. Since federal expenditures make up approximately one fifth of all expenditures, the differences between regions in per capita expenditures from the regions' consolidated budgets correspond, for the most part, to the differences in per capita regional expenditures, and to a much lesser degree to per capita direct federal expenditures.

Like the regional budgets' per capita expenditures, the per capita expenditures from the regions' consolidated budgets remain stable from year to year.

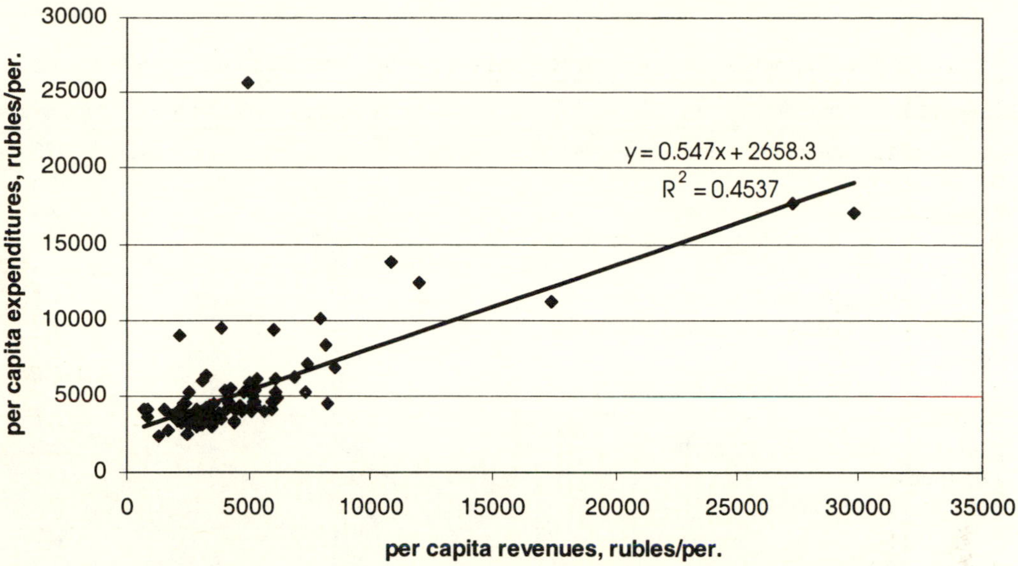

Figure 8.3 **Ratio of per capita revenues and expenditures of the regions' consolidated budgets, adjusted for the subsistence level, in 1999.**

In the final analysis, there is not much redistribution effect from all of the financial flows between the regions that are channeled through the federal budget (per capita federal expenditures are distributed among the regions more evenly than the regions' own expenditures). The coefficient of correlation between the total amount of revenues collected in a region's territory and total expenditures from the region's consolidated budget was 0.84 in 1998, and 0.67 in 1999 (0.85 without the Evenk Autonomous Region). Figure 8.3 demonstrates the close interrelation of the revenue and expenditure parts of the regions' consolidated budgets.

Per capita regional and federal expenditures are not statistically interrelated and thus do not supplement each other. In our opinion, it is impossible to give an unequivocal assessment of this situation. On the one hand, the objects of federal funding should not depend, for the most part, on the amount of regional expenditures. On the other hand, it may be that direct federal expenditures could be used more to equalize socioeconomic conditions in the regions.

8.2.5 Composition of expenditures of the regions' consolidated budgets

As with many other indices, the subjects of the Federation differ significantly from each other in the composition of expenditures from their consolidated budgets (Table 8.3).

The deviations from the average are partly objective. For example, Novosibirsk Oblast, one of the three largest scientific centers in Russia, has a very high portion of expendi-

Table 8.3

Composition of Expenditures from the Regions' Consolidated Budgets in 1999 (%)

Expenditure items	Average	Maximum	Minimum
Government administration and local self-government	5.7	13.3	2.5
Law enforcement	8.8	19.3	2.6
Basic research	1.6	9.6	0.0
Industry, power generation, and construction	4.0	24.4	0.3
Agriculture and fishing	5.0	16.3	0.3
Environmental protection	0.7	2.5	0.1
Transportation, roads, and communications	3.4	11.4	0.1
Housing and utilities	16.1	31.4	5.4
Prevention and mitigation of emergency situations	0.9	14.1	0.0
Education	19.2	31.0	9.8
Culture, art, and cinematography	2.3	4.6	1.0
Mass media	0.7	2.0	0.1
Public health and fitness	13.2	27.5	7.2
Social policy	6.1	13.7	1.6
Other expenditures	12.2	39.4	0.5

tures on basic research and scientific and technical progress. A higher than average portion of expenditures on government administration is characteristic of a number of sparsely populated subjects of the Federation. A considerable portion of expenditures on prevention and mitigation of emergency situations and natural disasters (more than 10%) is noted in Bryansk and Tula Oblasts, which suffered severely from the accident at the Chernobyl nuclear power plant. However, on the whole, the differences between regions are hard to explain, in our opinion.

The portions of production and social expenditures in the regions' consolidated budgets can be more informative. The former include expenditures on industry, power generation, construction, agriculture, fishing, transportation, roads, communications, and information systems. The latter are made up of expenditures on education, culture and art, mass media, public health and fitness, and social policy. The differences between regions in these two indices, and also their relationship with other expenditures, are reflected in Figure 8.4.

On the average for the subjects of the Federation in 1999, the portion of social expenditures was 41.6%; production expenditures, 12.4%; housing and utilities, 16.1% (the latter are fully funded from the regional budgets); and all of the remaining expenditures accounted for 29.9%. It is quite natural that the differences between regions in the portion of social expenditures are much smaller than the differences in the portion of production expenditures. In the former case, the extreme values are 55.7% (Ust-Orda Buryat Autonomous Region) and 22.6% (Evenk Autonomous Region); and in the latter. 32.1% (Yamal-Nenets Autonomous Region) and 4.2% (Koryak Autonomous Region). There is practically no interrelation between the portions of production and social expenditures in the total amount of expenditures (the coefficient of correlation in 1999 was –0.28).

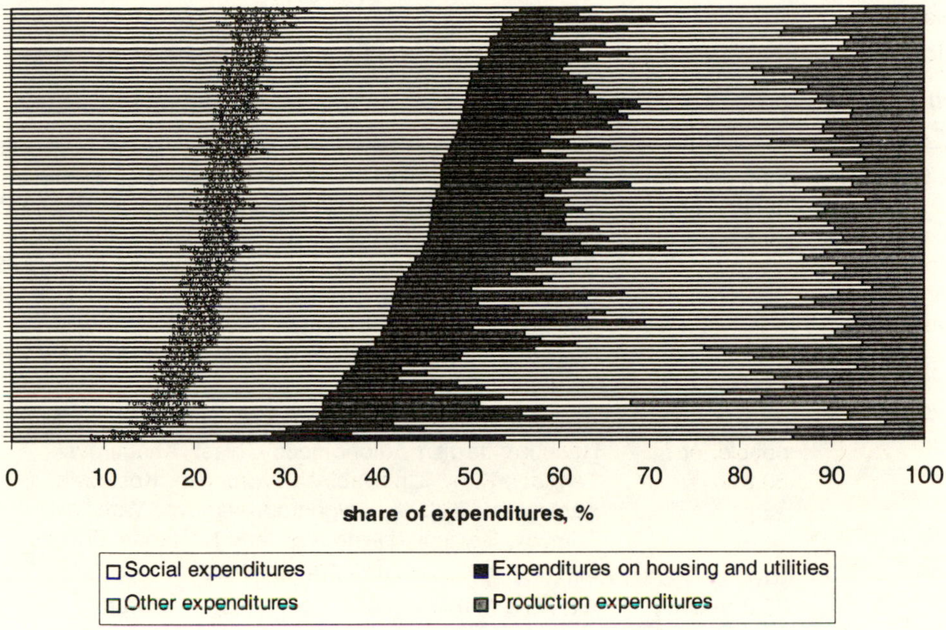

Figure 8.4 **Composition of expenditures from the regions' consolidated budgets in 1999.**

The main factor determining the differences between subjects of the Federation in the portion of social expenditures is the amount of per capita expenditures from the regions' consolidated budgets, adjusted for the subsistence level (the coefficient of correlation was –0.54). Social expenditures are more "obligatory" than production expenditures: the social sphere has top priority in the regions' spending. Therefore, the "poorer" a region is, the higher the share of social expenditures is and the less it can allow itself any other spending. The percentage of other expenditure items is of a more random nature.

8.2.6 Interrelations of socioeconomic indices with parameters of the regions' consolidated budgets

Per capita expenditures adjusted for the subsistence level only partly reflect the objectivity or subjectivity of differences between regions. Differences in the regions' economic and demographic structure, and the output of individual industries remain unaccounted for.

Of the presently available indices for evaluating how much the economy is subsidized, the following ratios are the most adequate:

a) production expenditures to gross regional product (Table 8.4). At the time when the research was done, data on the gross regional product had been published for 1998 only, and data on GRP are not given for the autonomous regions

Table 8.4

Ratio of Production Expenditures to Gross Regional Product in 1998 (%)

Portion of GRP, %	Population	Regions
less than 3	56.6 million people, or 38.8%	Irkutsk and Sverdlovsk Oblasts, Krasnoyarsk Territory, Samara, Novgorod, and Arkhangelsk Oblasts, Republic of Khakasia, Chita, Tomsk, Omsk, Murmansk, and Moscow Oblasts, Republic of Karelia, Amur, Vladimir, Leningrad, Belgorod, Penza, Novosibirsk, Kaliningrad, and Tver Oblasts, Republic of Buryatia, Smolensk, Nizhegorod, Ryazan, and Perm Oblasts, Udmurt Republic, Stavropol Territory
3–4	30.4 million people, or 20.8%	Altai Republic, Orenburg and Astrakhan Oblasts, Marii El Republic, Jewish Autonomous Oblast, Khabarovsk Territory, Kirov, Chelyabinsk, Voronezh, Kostroma, Kamchatka, Kaluga, Volgograd, Ivanovo, Yaroslavl, Tambov, Bryansk, Ulyanovsk, and Magadan Oblasts, Chuvash Republic, Tyumen Oblast
4–5	23.6 million people, or 16.2%	Altai and Maritime Territories, Vologda, Saratov, and Kurgan Oblasts, St. Petersburg, Tula, Lipetsk, and Pskov Oblasts, Krasnodar Territory
5–6	19.9 million people, or 13.6%	Moscow, Republic of Bashkortostan, Karachaevo-Cherkess Republic, Republics of Mordovia and Tatarstan, Kursk Oblast, Republic of North Osetia
more than 6	15.4 million people, or 10.6%	Republic of Tyva, Kabardino-Balkar Republic, Republics of Sakha (Yakutia) and Dagestan, Rostov, Orlov, and Sakhalin Oblasts, Komi Republic, Republic of Adygeya, Kemerovo Oblast, Republic of Kalmykia, Chukotka Autonomous Region, Ingush Republic

b) expenditures on agriculture to agricultural output (Table 8.5). It is almost impossible to evaluate the scale of budgetary support for industry, since in the budget reports expenditures on industry are combined with expenditures on construction, and in different regions either industry or construction may be supported, or both of them in varying proportions.

On the average for Russia, the ratio of production expenditures to the gross regional product in 1998 was 3.9%. Irkutsk and Sverdlovsk Oblasts (1.7–1.8%) stand out, on the one hand; and Kalmykia (10.0%), the Chukotka Autonomous Region (14.7%), and Ingushetia (22.8%), on the other. In the remaining regions, this index did not exceed 8.5%.

On the average for Russia, the level of budget support for agriculture from the budgets of all levels was 6 kopecks per ruble of agricultural output. It was more than a ruble in the Yamal-Nenets and Taimyr Autonomous Regions. In Yakutia and the Khanty-Mansi, Chukotka, and Nenets Autonomous Regions, it was 43–46 kopecks per ruble,

Table 8.5

Ratio of Expenditures on Agriculture and Fishing to Agricultural Output in 1999, Kopecks per Ruble of Output

Expenditures/ output, kopecks/ruble	Population	Regions
less than 3	26.8 million people, or 18.4%	Ust-Orda Buryat and Komi-Permyat Autonomous Republics, Penza and Leningrad Oblasts, Aga Buryat Autonomous Republic, Novosibirsk Oblast, Marii El and Altai Republics, Arkhangelsk Oblast, Rostov, Bryansk, Kamchatka, Pskov, Yaroslavl, Chita, Kostroma, and Amur Oblasts, Altai Territory, Kirov Oblast
3–5	63.7 million people, or 43.7%	Novgorod, Vladimir, Irkutsk, and Samara Oblasts, Krasnoyarsk Territory, Republic of Buryatia, Sverdlovsk, Chelyabinsk, Tver, Moscow, and Kemerovo Oblasts, Kabardino-Balkar Republic, Stavropol Territory, Chuvash Republic, Kaluga Oblast, Udmurt Republic, Smolensk and Voronezh Oblasts, Jewish Autonomous Oblast, Tula, Belgorod, Omsk, Kurgan, Tambov, Orenburg, Ryazan, Kaliningrad, Volgograd, and Nizhegorod Oblasts, Republic of Mordovia, Perm Oblast, Karachaevo-Cherkess Republic
5–8	24.3 million people, or 8.9%	Republic of Dagestan, Khabarovsk Territory, Astrakhan and Lipetsk Oblasts, Republics of Khakasia and Karelia, Maritime Territory, Ivanovo, Sakhalin, and Vologda Oblasts, Republic of Tyva, Tomsk Oblast, Republic of Adygeya, Krasnodar Territory, Saratov Oblast, Tyumen Oblast, Republic of North Osetia-Alania
8–12	13.2 million people, or 9.1%	Republic of Ingushetia, Orlov, Magadan, and Kursk Oblasts, Republic of Bashkortostan, Koryak and Evenk Autonomous Republics, Murmansk Oblast, Republic of Tatarstan, Ulyanovsk Oblast
more than 12	4.5 million people, or 3.1%	Komi Republic, Republics of Kalmykia and Sakha (Yakutia), Khanty-Mansi, Chukotka, Nenets, Taimyr, and Yamal-Nenets Autonomous Republics

and 15 kopecks in the Komi Republic. Outside of northern regions, the highest level of support for agriculture was in Kalmykia: 19 kopecks per ruble of output.

For the most part, the differences between regions in these two indices characterizing the level of government support for the economy do not show any pattern. Subjects of the Federation with a high or low level of economic development frequently fall into various categories. We can only note that, as a rule, the highest level of government support is typical of regions where the economy as a whole, or individual industries, are poorly developed, or production is associated with especially difficult conditions. This is primarily true of agriculture, where the leading positions in the scale of government support are mostly held by northern subjects of the Federation. The group of regions with the highest ratio of their consolidated budgets' expenditures to GRP includes regions with a high level of support for the coal industry: Rostov and Kemerovo Oblasts, and the Komi Republic.

8.3 A REGION'S "EXPANDED" BUDGET

8.3.1 Model of a region's "expanded" budget

In this research, a region's expanded budget is understood as the revenues and expenditures not only of the budgets of all levels, but also of targeted budgetary or extrabudgetary funds (road funds, environmental funds, and funds for replacement of the mineral raw-material base), and extrabudgetary social funds (the Pension Fund of the Russian Federation, Social Insurance Fund of the Russian Federation, State Employment Fund of the Russian Federation, mandatory medical insurance funds, and road funds). Since the revenues and expenditures of the extrabudgetary funds are essentially no different from budgetary revenues and expenditures, the "expanded" budget is what needs to be analyzed to get an idea of the aggregate tax burden in a region, the role of federal funding of particular expenditures in a region, and the degree to which a subject of the Federation depends on redistribution of revenues among the regions (through the federal budget and the central divisions of the extrabudgetary funds).

The equation for a region's expanded budget differs from the formula for the consolidated budget in that it includes the extrabudgetary funds' revenues and expenditures:

$$R - E + R_{ebf} - E_{ebf} = S + S_{ebf} + D + D_{ebf},$$

where R is the revenues collected in the region's territory and credited to the budgets of all hierarchical levels;

E is expenditures from the budgets of all levels in the region's territory that are not connected with redistribution of revenues between the budgets of different levels;

R_{ebf} is the total amount of payments to the extrabudgetary funds collected in the region's territory;

E_{ebf} is the extrabudgetary funds' expenditures in the region's territory;

S is the balance of budgetary financial flows between the Center and the regions;

S_{ebf} is the balance of financial flows between the extrabudgetary funds' central and territorial divisions. For donor regions, the balance of financial flows is negative; for recipient regions, it is positive.

D is the difference between expenditures and revenues of the consolidated regional budget (deficit);

D_{ebf} is the difference between expenditures and revenues of the extrabudgetary funds' territorial divisions.

Table 8.6

Components of Revenues and Expenditures of the Regions' "Expanded" Budgets in 1998–1999

Components of expanded budgets	Portion in revenues, %		Portion in expenditures, %	
	1998	1999	1998	1999
Budgets of all levels	64.3	64.2	60.9	59.0
Targeted budgetary and extrabudgetary funds	9.1	10.8	9.9	12.9
Extrabudgetary social funds	26.6	25.0	29.1	28.1

Since we did not have all of the necessary data on the extrabudgetary funds' revenues and expenditures, certain arbitrary decisions had to be made in the calculations:

- instead of the actual expenditures of regional targeted funds, we used the sum of these funds' revenues and federal expenditures on the item of targeted budgetary funds (the actual expenditures hardly differ much from this amount)
- the Pension Fund's revenues for 1998 include money received by the fund's territorial divisions from the federal budget, i.e., the money collected in the regions is somewhat overstated
- as the revenues of territorial divisions of the social insurance funds in 1998 we used the amount of insurance premiums going to the territorial divisions. The actual revenues were higher by the amount of money turned over to the fund's central division and the amount of the territorial divisions' other internal revenues (penalties, fines, etc.)
- the revenues of the territorial mandatory medical insurance funds and territorial divisions of the State Employment Fund were calculated as the difference between the total amount of revenues and the amount of financial aid from the center (in the former case, subsidies from the Federal Mandatory Medical Insurance Fund; in the latter, from the fund's central division). The actual revenues were higher by the amount of money turned over to the Center.

8.3.2 Ratio of budgetary and extrabudgetary components of the regions' "expanded" budgets

In Chapter 5, we considered the ratio of budgetary and extrabudgetary revenues and expenditures for Russia as a whole. Differences between regions in this indices are investigated in this section. Table 8.6 gives the average composition of revenues and expenditures for the regions' expanded budgets in 1998–1999. The data given here differ from those in Chapter 5, since not all revenues and expenditures (from the budgets, as well as extrabudgetary funds) can be "linked" to individual regions.

The distribution of regions by the portion of budgetary revenues and expenditures in the total amount of revenues and expenditures of their "expanded" budgets in 1999 is presented in Tables 8.7 and 8.8.

Table 8.7

Portion of Budgetary Revenues in Revenues of the Regions' "Expanded" Budgets in 1999

Portion, %	Population	Regions
65–78	29.6 million people, or 20.3%	Leningrad Oblast, Republic of Ingushetia, Moscow, Republics of North Osetia-Alania and Mordovia, Ryazan Oblast, Yamal-Nenets Autonomous Region, Orlov Oblast, Karachaevo-Cherkess and Kabardino-Balkar Republics, Tyumen and Moscow Oblasts, Republic of Kalmykia, Vologda, Voronezh, and Yaroslavl Oblasts
60–65	76.1 million people, or 52.1%	Krasnodar Territory, Bryansk, Rostov, Ulyanovsk, and Lipetsk Oblasts, Altai Territory, Samara Oblast, Khanty-Mansi Autonomous Region, Saratov, Orenburg, and Kursk Oblasts, Udmurt and Chuvash Republics, Tambov and Kirov Oblasts, Marii El Republic, Vladimir, Tver, Ivanovo, Kostroma, Perm, Tula, and Novosibirsk Oblast, St. Petersburg, Krasnoyarsk Territory, Evenk Autonomous Region, Irkutsk Oblast, Republic of Sakha (Yakutia), Penza Oblast, Republic of Bashkortostan, Stavropol Territory, Kurgan Oblast, Altai Republic, Komi-Permyat Autonomous Region, Volgograd Oblast, Republic of Tatarstan, Kaluga and Pskov Oblasts
55–60	32.6 million people, or 22.4%	Republic of Adygeya, Kaliningrad, Nizhegorod, and Smolensk Oblasts, Nenets Autonomous Region, Sakhalin and Kemerovo Oblasts, Khabarovsk Territory, Murmansk, Omsk, and Sverdlovsk Oblasts, Republic of Khakasia, Belgorod Oblast, Komi Republic, Chelyabinsk Oblast, Maritime Territory, Novgorod, astrakhan, Arkhangelsk, and Tomsk Oblasts
50–55	3.7 million people, or 2.5%	Republic of Buryatia, Koryak Autonomous Region, Republic of Karelia, Ust-Orda Buryat, Aga Buryat, and Taimyr Autonomous Regions, Chita and Kamchatka Oblasts
44–50	4.0 million people, or 2.7%	Magadan Oblast, Republic of Dagestan, Amur Oblast, Republic of Tyva, Chukotka Autonomous Region, Jewish Autonomous Oblast

If we look at the ratio of regional components of revenues and expenditures in the regions' expanded budgets, we can find a direct correlation between the portions of targeted (budgetary and extrabudgetary) funds only. There is no interrelation between the portions of budgetary revenues and expenditures and the portions of the social extrabudgetary funds' revenues and expenditures. In this case, the differences between regions in the portion of budgetary revenues in the total amount of the expanded budgets' revenues are hard to explain and are most likely random. For example, Moscow,

Table 8.8

Portion of Budgetary Expenditures in Expenditures of the Regions' "Expanded" Budgets in 1999

Portion, %	Population	Regions
65–81	16.0 million people, or 11.0%	Koryak, Evenk, and Ust-Orda Buryat Autonomous Regions, Republic of Sakha (Yakutia), Chukotka Autonomous Region, Leningrad and Magadan Oblasts, Moscow, Yamal-Nenets Autonomous Region, Republic of Ingushetia, Kamchatka, Vologda, and Tyumen Oblasts, Republic of Tyva, Nenets Autonomous Region
60–65	18.3 million people, or 12.5%	Republic of Tatarstan, Kabardino-Balkar Republic, Republic of Dagestan, Khabarovsk Territory, Taimyr Autonomous Region, Jewish Autonomous Oblast, Maritime Territory, Murmansk Oblast, Krasnoyarsk Territory, Sakhalin Oblast, Republic of North Osetia-Alania, Komi Republic, Chita Oblast
55–60	40.4 million people, or 27.7%	Khanty-Mansi Autonomous Region, Kemerovo, Amur, and Orlov Oblasts, Aga Buryat Autonomous Region, Irkutsk Oblast, Republic of Karelia, Karachaevo-Cherkess Republic, Republic of Bashkortostan, Tomsk Oblast, Republic of Buryatia, St. Petersburg, Republic of Adygeya, Novosibirsk Oblast, Republic of Khakasia, Altai Republic, Republic of Mordovia, Udmurt Republic, Moscow, Kaliningrad, Perm, Yaroslavl, and Kostroma Oblasts, Komi-Permyat Autonomous Region
50–55	51.9 million people, or 35.6%	Nizhegorod Oblast, Marii El Republic, Orenburg and Lipetsk Oblasts, Altai Territory, Arkhangelsk, Novgorod, and Samara Oblasts, Stavropol Territory, Chelyabinsk and Rostov Oblasts, Krasnodar Territory, Pskov, Omsk, Astrakhan, Sverdlovsk, Kursk, Saratov, and Ulyanovsk Oblasts, Chuvash Republic, Kaluga and Kirov Oblasts, Republic of Kalmykia, Belgorod Oblast
44–50	19.2 million people, or 13.2%	Volgograd, Kurgan, Smolensk, Tula, Tver, Vladimir, Ryazan, Bryansk, Ivanovo, Voronezh, Tambov, and Penza Oblasts

the Yamal-Nenets Autonomous Region, and the Kabardino-Balkar and Karachaevo-Cherkess Republics are all in the same group. Nevertheless, we can note that the groups of regions with the lowest portion of budgetary revenues include the regions that are economically least developed. The greater part of the funds' revenues is made up of the social extrabudgetary funds' revenues, the tax base for which is determined by the amount of accrued wages. In economically underdeveloped regions, the share of this tax base is disproportionately high in comparison with the tax base for other taxes, such as the profit tax, payments for use of natural resources, etc.

The differences between regions in the portion of budgetary expenditures in the total amount of their expanded budgets' expenditures are more easily explained. The less economically developed a region is, the higher the portion of the social extrabudgetary funds' expenditures is in it, and the lower the portion of budgetary expenditures and targeted funds' expenditures.[6] The increased portion of the social funds' expenditures is explained by the same factors as the higher portion of social expenditures in the total expenditures of the regions' consolidated budgets: the social sphere has top priority in the regions' spending. These patterns are also partly connected with the equalizing effect from redistribution of financial resources between the center and the regions. The disproportions between regions in the social funds' per capita revenues are less than for per capita budgetary revenues, and the scale of redistribution of financial resources between regions is comparatively high in the Pension Fund, the revenues and expenditures of which make up the greater part of the social funds' revenues and expenditures. The equalizing effect from financial aid to the regional budgets and territorial targeted funds is lower, and the initial disproportions in per capita revenues are higher.

8.3.3 Ratio of "expanded" budgets' revenues and expenditures

Since the role of extrabudgetary revenues and expenditures in the total revenues and expenditures is different in various regions, the ratio of revenues and expenditures of the regions' expanded budgets differs from the ratio of revenues and expenditures of their consolidated budgets (Figure 8.5).

While still quite significant, the differences between regions in the ratio of their expanded budgets' revenues and expenditures are still less than the differences in the ratio of their consolidated budgets' revenues and expenditures (the minimum value is higher, and the maximum one is lower).

On the average for the regions, the ratio of their expanded budgets' revenues to expenditures was 105.1% in 1998 and 109.3% in 1999 (these values are lower than those for the regions' consolidated budgets). In 1998, revenues exceeded expenditures in 17 regions; and in 1999, in 27 regions. Sixteen subjects of the Federation were consistently unsubsidized in these two years.

We should also note that the lists of unsubsidized regions according to their consolidated and expanded budgets do not nearly coincide. Thus, Voronezh, Kirov, Vladimir, Ulyanovsk, Saratov, Belgorod, Ryazan, and Volgograd Oblasts were unsubsidized according to the consolidated budget and subsidized according to the expanded one. The opposite situation took place in the Komi Republic, the Nenets Autonomous Region, and Murmansk Oblast. In 1999, 24 regions were unsubsidized according to the expanded budget as well as the consolidated one.

---

[6] The portion of social expenditures in the regions' expanded budgets in 1999 was 52.6% (in comparison to 41.6% in their consolidated budgets).

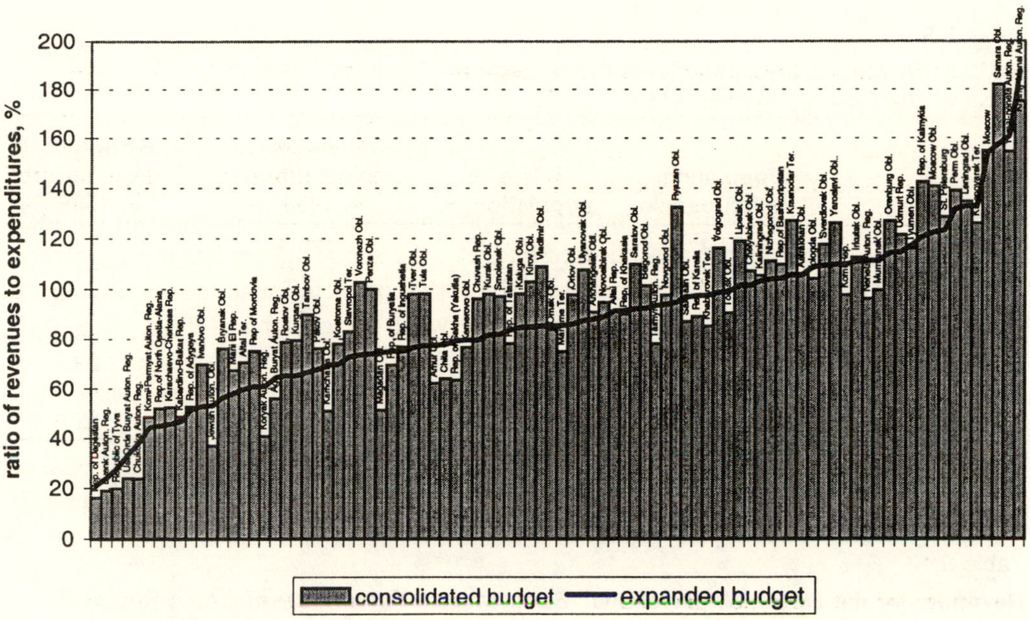

Figure 8.5 **Ratio of revenues to expenditures of the regions' consolidated and expanded budgets in 1999**

As in the case of the consolidated budget, the revenues of the regions' expanded budgets exceed their expenditures in the Central, Northwestern, and Ural parts of the country in both 1998 and 1999, and in the Volga area in 1999. On the whole, the North Caucasus, Siberia, and the Far east are problem areas (Table 8.9).

8.3.4 Revenues of the regions' "expanded" budgets as a percentage of GRP

The differences between regions in their "expanded" budgets' revenues as a percentage of GRP in 1998 (there are no data on GRP for 1999) are presented in Table 8.10. The extreme values of this index were 80% in Kalmykia, 48% in the Altai Republic, 46% in Moscow, 42% in St. Petersburg, and 40% in Kaliningrad Oblast; and at the other end of the scale, 22% in Kabardino-Balkaria and less than 20% in Dagestan. In the rest of the regions it was at least 24.5%

On the whole, the distribution of regions by types is rather random, though some patterns can be distinguished. The largest portion of revenues in GRP is characteristic of republics of the Russian "offshore" (Ingushetia, Kalmykia, Altai, and Kaliningrad Oblast), and also of those with the largest per capita revenues (Moscow and Tyumen Oblast, the data for which include the Khanty-Mansi and Yamal-Nenets Autonomous Regions). On

Table 8.9

Ratio of Revenues to Expenditures of the Regions' Expanded Budgets in Different Parts of the Country in 1998–1999

Areas	Population, million people	Share of population, %	Revenues to expenditures in 1998, %	Revenues to expenditures in 1999, %
Central	37.4	25.6	128.4	123.2
Northwestern	14.6	10.0	101.2	111.2
North Caucasus	21	14.4	75.2	77.3
Volga	32.1	22.0	96.0	104.1
Ural	12.7	8.7	123.8	139.7
Siberia	20.9	14.3	90.2	93.2
Far East	7.3	5.0	78.9	82.4

Table 8.10

Revenues of the Regions' "Expanded" Budgets as a Percentage of Gross Regional Product in 1998

Portion, %	Population	Regions
more than 35	24.9 million people, or 17.1%	Republic of Kalmykia, Altai Republic, Moscow, St. Petersburg, Kaliningrad and Moscow Oblasts, Republic of Ingushetia, Tyumen Oblast
32.5–35	18.7 million people, or 12.8%	Udmurt Republic. Nizhegorod, Novosibirsk, and Kaluga Oblasts, Komi Republic, Magadan, Kostroma, Samara, Omsk, Ryazan, and Sakhalin Oblasts
30–32.5	34.6 million people, or 23.7%	Saratov, Chelyabinsk, Kemerovo, Ivanovo, Sverdlovsk, and Astrakhan Oblasts, Khabarovsk Territory, Pskov, Penza, and Vladimir Oblasts, Maritime Territory, Republic of Bashkortostan, Orenburg and Yaroslavl Oblasts, Chukotka Autonomous Region, Volgograd Oblast
27.5–30	45.4 million people, or 45.4%	Tver Oblast, Republic of Karelia, Voronezh, Orlov, Chita, and Perm Oblasts, Krasnodar Territory, Lipetsk, Tula, Kirov, and Ulyanovsk Oblasts, Krasnoyarsk Territory, Belgorod and Tambov Oblasts, Republic of Tatarstan, Chuvash Republic, Rostov, Leningrad, Murmansk, Vologda, and Arkhangelsk Oblasts, Jewish Autonomous Oblast, Bryansk and Kurgan Oblasts, Republic of Khakasia
less than 27.5	22.3 million people, or 15.3%	Novgorod and Kursk Oblasts, Republic of North Osetia-Alania, Tomsk Oblast, Altai Territory, Irkutsk Oblast, Republic of Buryatia, Smolensk Oblast, Marii El Republic, Republics of Tyva and Sakha (Yakutia), Amur Oblast, Republic of Adygeya, Kamchatka Oblast, Republic of Mordovia, Stavropol Territory, Karachaevo-Cherkess and Kabardino-Balkar Republics, Republic of Dagestan

the other hand, the smallest portion of revenues in GRP is typical primarily of regions in the worst economic shape.

8.4 BASIC CONCLUSIONS

There are approximately as many regions in Russia that could be self-sufficient, i.e., get along without any additional aid from outside, as there are donor regions with respect to the financial balance taking into account the Federation's direct expenditures: about 30.

Nevertheless, the distribution of regions by degree of self-sufficiency differs, to a certain degree, from the distribution according to the percentage of funds returned to the region from the Center.

To a significant extent, the geography of expenditures from the consolidated budgets is subjective. There are large differences between subjects of the Federation in the composition of expenditures, the scale of subsidizing the economy, and support for the social sphere.

The differences between regions in the portion of social expenditures in their expanded budgets (including the extrabudgetary funds) are much smaller than the differences in the portion of social expenditures in their consolidated budgets.

In the near future, much more attention needs to be paid to coordinating the different directions and mechanisms of regional economic policy conducted by the Center.

CONCLUSION

What have we learned? Our analysis of financial flows between the Center and the regions largely enabled us to assess the current financial situation of the territories in a new way and to give details of the interrelations between federal authorities and subjects of the Federation. So as not to repeat the conclusions given at the end of each chapter, we will generalize the study's results in the form of three main theses.

First of all, we can confidently say that over the last 3–4 years there has been a much more numerous group of regions in Russia with a relatively favorable financial situation. We found that about 30 subjects of the Federation, with population equal to practically 50% of the country's entire population, credit more revenues to the federal budget than the federal budget spends in their territory. This means that in these territories the amount of revenues collected for all levels of the budget system is greater than its expenditures in that region.

Secondly, the country's budget system and its public finances cannot be considered manageable as long as, in addition to budgetary flows proper, there are financial flows between the budgets of all levels of government which are fed from the so-called extrabudgetary funds. Not only is the movement of this money virtually off-limits for consolidated accounting, but the amount of money involved is comparable to approximately half of all of the budgetary flows!

Thirdly, it has been shown on the basis of extensive factual data that the economic policy conducted by the Center in relation to subjects of the Federation does not provide any significant equalizing effect either in regard to meeting the regions' current spending requirements, or their investment needs. Analysis of management practice during the period from 1996 through 1999 clearly demonstrates the lack of attention to such an important element of the mechanism by which funds are distributed from the federal budget among the regions as direct expenditures from the federal budget. On the one hand, this circumstance undermines confidence in the objectivity of the federal authorities' policy, and on the other, it inevitably sharply reduces the effectiveness of that policy.

Undoubtedly, many of the questions that we have touched upon in this research need more detailed study in the future. But we can already talk about who might benefit from the recommendations set forth in this book. We will mention some institutions that could put our findings to practical use.

Legislative authority (the Federal Assembly of the Russian Federation). Thanks to the significantly expanded view of public finances constructed on the methodology of the overall financial balance, the State Duma of the Russian Federation and other participants in the budget process have the opportunity to work not only with traditional data on the federal budget, but also with information on the "expanded budget," which includes, for example, figures on the movement of money from the extrabudgetary funds. This puts into the hands of the deputies and members of the Federation Council data on the actual funding of expenditures items in a regional profile, which enables them to base their decisions on unique information about the execution of the federal budget. The Clearing House of the Russian Federation can be a natural user of such information, since its functions directly include such supervision.

Executive authority (the Government of the Russian Federation, and federal ministries and departments). As a result of the research that has been done, they have at their disposal, for the first time, relatively complete information on the territorial aspect of expenditures from the federal budget of Russia. For *the Government of the Russian Federation*, this can be both a tool and an information base that will help it revise or correct a number of industry spending priorities. In addition, the government is getting a useful base for analyzing the efficiency of individual ministries' work, and the ministries, in turn, will have the opportunity to evaluate regional aspects of their own industry policy. For *the Ministry of Federation and Nationality Affairs of the Russian Federation*, the results of the research can become a basis for determining key priorities of regional policy in the country. For *the Ministry of Finance of the Russian Federation*, familiarization with the results of the research will open up important new possibilities for developing the annual budgets and showing more clearly the bases for this procedure as a "budget list for the regions." This will provide arguments for defending its position in interbudgetary relations. We very much want to believe that *the Federal Treasury of the Russian Federation*, which has become a real player in the execution of the federal budget, can find in this research additional arguments in favor of strengthening its status and, at the same time, in favor of developing the treasury's technical infrastructure supporting the collection and processing of all of the information needed to perform the functions entrusted to it. Last, but not least, the methodology described in this book and the experience of calculating the "expanded" budget can help to obtain new data on the tax base in individual regions of the country that will be useful to *the Ministry of Taxes and Duties of the Russian Federation.*

Regional authorities in no way suffer from our research. The significantly larger number of stable regions does not at all refute the division of them into more or less solvent ones and poor territories to which the Federation is obligated to provide financial support. For the economically least fortunate regions, a clearer division of the groups only provides additional arguments for receiving transfers from the Fund for Financial Support of the Regions. And for the "nouveau riche" regions, which have appeared only sporadically on lists of the territories most attractive for investments, the results of the research provide an opportunity to actually raise their credit rating, provided, of course, that they present their case competently to the proper rating agencies.

International financial organizations (the International Bank for Reconstruction and Development, the International Monetary Fund, and the European Bank for Reconstruction and Development) may also be interested in the research data. First of all, these data give a more accurate idea of the real transparency of Russia's budget sphere, and also significantly increase the transparency of public finances, qualitatively improving former ideas about the balance of financial flows and the components and dynamics of expenditures in a regional profile, including data on the expanded budget (extrabudgetary funds, transfers, etc.). Secondly, in the course of the research conclusions were drawn about the obvious underestimation of the large number of regions in Russia with surplus revenues, three times more than the commonly known figure from the list of regions that are donors to the budget, which numerous investigations by these organizations' experts could not show or properly evaluate.

Corporate investors (investment banks, companies, etc.), by relying on a comprehensive accounting of the regions' financial interrelations with the budget system, can much more accurately assess a territory's tax potential, the regions' credit ratings, and their own financial risks if they invest money in these regions. This aspect of the question generally deserves separate consideration, since it includes more detailed analysis of how the financial mechanism operates, but from what has been published it is evident that the number of regions with a stable economy is significantly greater than what was formerly thought. In addition to everything else, this circumstance raises the prospect of transforming these territories into a special object of regional policy and consequently may induce federal authorities to take into account new systematic factors aimed at intensifying the territories' development potential.

Without exaggeration, we can say that, thanks to the publication of the results of this research, *academic science* is getting access to a vast array of information on public (federal and regional) finances and fiscal tools that was previously unavailable.

Compiling a complete balance of financial flows between the Center and the regions is an indispensable condition for understanding the economic and political factors that determine their interrelations on a wide range of issues. Therefore, we believe that it is necessary to take steps in the future to disseminate objective information about financial flows between the Center and the regions among government bureaucrats and independent experts, and also to promote the goal of improving the system for collecting and processing the relevant statistical data.

Appendix to Chapter 2

Table A.1

Balance of Financial Flows between the Center and the Regions in 1996–1998

	% return									Balance per capita (1996, 1997 in 1000 undenominated rubles/person, 1998 – rubles/person)								
	Balance with respect to financial aid			Balance including direct expenditures			Complete balance			Balance with respect to financial aid			Balance including direct expenditures			Complete balance		
Region	**1996**	**1997**	**1998**	**1996**	**1997**	**1998**	**1996**	**1997**	**1998**	**1996**	**1997**	**1998**	**1996**	**1997**	**1998**	**1996**	**1997**	**1998**
Republic of Karelia	115,0	202,1	89,6	230,7	350,3	206,3	195,2	235,9	153,7	–72,3	–402,2	43,3	–629,6	–985,3	–441,3	–669,1	–1051,0	–476,3
Komi Republic	34,3	22,9	9,6	105,8	76,4	103,9	98,6	71,0	87,2	1408,5	2014,6	966,1	–125,0	617,7	–42,1	32,3	824,9	185,4
Arkhangelsk Oblast	94,9	106,8	40,3	206,5	216,6	123,3	155,4	142,1	110,8	26,1	–36,6	346,1	–540,3	–623,8	–135,3	–502,1	–552,9	–106,2
Nenets Autonomous Region	76,0	127,3	47,9	93,3	189,9	89,2				572,9	–667,0	1246,7	159,8	–2195,0	258,2			
Vologda Oblast	74,9	97,4	22,3	124,4	152,9	68,2	117,0	126,4	66,7	154,4	15,9	410,2	–150,0	–327,5	167,8	–134,5	–262,4	285,3
Murmansk Oblast	119,3	193,5	112,0	223,7	317,0	163,1	220,9	317,7	154,2	–174,2	–875,3	–111,7	–1117,5	–2031,3	–589,1	–1114,3	–2070,4	–584,7
St. Petersburg	4,6	10,8	0,8	36,0	66,8	36,1	28,9	58,8	32,9	1553,0	1493,1	1832,5	1041,8	556,0	1180,4	1464,3	805,2	1461,3
Leningrad Oblast	10,6	29,9	14,5	32,3	57,2	47,7	42,5	69,1	53,8	828,6	736,3	885,7	627,4	449,5	542,0	714,8	498,0	580,5
Novgorod Oblast	102,4	160,8	172,2	148,4	233,7	235,6	125,4	173,4	151,8	–14,7	–346,4	–328,8	–301,4	–761,2	–617,7	–268,2	–718,6	–584,9
Pskov Oblast	181,4	195,0	136,5	239,4	262,2	217,0	279,7	347,8	321,7	–399,3	–498,9	–141,4	–683,6	–851,2	–453,6	–1071,1	–1492,7	–1038,4
Bryansk Oblast	54,7	47,2	46,0	140,5	154,7	193,0	221,5	272,0	299,7	305,6	376,0	266,4	–273,2	–389,6	–458,6	–844,6	–1396,7	–1147,1
Vladimir Oblast	63,2	72,5	60,0	92,8	125,7	99,4	79,2	97,6	91,5	257,3	166,4	271,8	50,6	–155,7	3,8	245,5	35,0	106,6

Ivanovo Oblast	158,4	218,8	97,1	215,7	294,7	183,3	142,0	153,2	130,2	–260,8	–504,9	10,6	–516,9	–827,4	–307,3	–410,0	–776,0	–314,3
Kaluga Oblast	88,0	87,6	72,9	135,6	149,8	134,3				87,7	98,0	204,3	–259,3	–392,6	–258,6			
Kostroma Oblast	316,4	152,9	119,4	371,3	195,7	186,3	214,6	142,5	133,0	–1103,1	–381,8	–105,7	–1382,8	–691,1	–471,3	–1382,8	–690,6	–470,4
Moscow	4,9	3,4	0,8	7,8	15,9	83,2				5932,9	8310,8	7968,2	5756,4	7229,8	1345,7			
Moscow Oblast	13,9	12,9	5,1	37,9	36,7	22,6	35,6	42,4	27,6	1306,9	1709,4	1849,2	943,0	1241,5	1508,5	1339,7	1382,2	1668,0
Orlov Oblast	76,0	148,5	73,8	166,6	255,3	196,0				191,3	–333,3	142,0	–529,9	–1066,9	–520,1			
Ryazan Oblast	44,2	52,1	23,1	83,0	103,4	63,3				437,7	433,9	730,6	133,6	–30,4	348,1			
Smolensk Oblast	35,9	48,8	62,8	76,3	97,2	121,6	86,0	100,4	112,2	388,0	356,9	177,2	143,3	19,3	–102,8	131,3	–5,7	–130,9
Tver Oblast	66,3	96,6	43,9	103,2	160,9	102,2				203,8	20,5	312,4	–19,5	–365,4	–12,2			
Tula Oblast	77,3	85,0	33,8	187,0	232,1	157,7	144,0	148,7	123,7	135,4	98,8	395,6	–519,0	–868,8	–344,7	–500,6	–842,0	–323,2
Yaroslavl Oblast	36,6	39,5	18,8	61,0	71,1	45,7	63,8	75,0	58,1	947,4	912,6	901,1	582,2	435,8	602,9	640,2	507,2	654,8
Marii El Republic	100,7	118,3	75,2	174,9	172,0	152,1	142,8	134,0	122,0	–3,5	–103,9	96,5	–404,5	–408,1	–202,6	–372,9	–406,9	–192,9
Republic of Mordovia	138,4	127,3	134,9	205,3	178,0	253,0	218,9	185,5	263,4	–238,0	–192,7	–122,1	–652,9	–550,2	–535,4	–753,0	–626,9	–670,9
Chuvash Republic	66,1	77,2	45,1	115,8	128,8	109,5	110,3	114,6	99,1	176,4	143,3	223,7	–82,2	–180,9	–38,7	–82,1	–173,2	8,1
Kirov Oblast	56,4	82,1	56,3	96,9	131,2	101,3	97,7	115,7	100,6	257,3	134,8	258,7	18,5	–234,5	–7,7	20,9	–233,8	–7,0
Nizhegorod Oblast	11,8	8,0	9,1	29,7	29,6	32,7				1302,1	1733,6	988,4	1038,2	1326,8	731,4			
Belgorod Oblast	20,5	18,3	28,1	61,2	64,1	84,7	55,6	74,1	82,4	598,9	629,9	426,8	291,9	276,8	91,0	558,0	362,1	202,8

Table A.1 (continued)

Balance of Financial Flows between the Center and the Regions in 1996–1998

	% return									Balance per capita (1996, 1997 in 1000 undenominated rubles/person, 1998 – rubles/person)								
	Balance with respect to financial aid			Balance including direct expenditures			Complete balance			Balance with respect to financial aid			Balance including direct expenditures			Complete balance		
Region	1996	1997	1998	1996	1997	1998	1996	1997	1998	1996	1997	1998	1996	1997	1998	1996	1997	1998
Voronezh Oblast	38,7	39,7	38,7	78,5	94,2	89,4	78,9	92,9	81,2	369,1	406,7	367,4	129,5	38,8	63,7	223,9	114,2	262,7
Kursk Oblast	26,8	82,7	32,8	66,7	145,5	93,2	75,7	117,0	92,5	476,6	110,0	443,8	216,6	–288,7	44,8	255,1	–240,9	90,2
Lipetsk Oblast	3,8	21,6	8,1	35,4	81,7	61,0	44,9	87,2	75,6	665,5	439,3	476,1	447,0	102,3	202,2	501,4	134,6	242,0
Tambov Oblast	62,8	88,6	71,5	131,8	144,1	135,5	202,6	282,0	250,8	185,0	58,3	122,3	–158,0	–226,2	–152,2	–589,7	–1041,6	–756,9
Republic of Kalmykia	139,9	79,9	46,1	196,7	116,6	79,7				–351,0	408,4	929,8	–849,9	–336,3	349,8			
Republic of Tatarstan	23,8	12,3	–5,1	57,4	12,3	24,8				446,7	978,5	377,4	249,7	978,1	270,1			
Astrakhan Oblast	111,9	86,5	73,1	182,5	141,9	130,6	195,6	151,4	126,5	–71,3	110,3	162,5	–495,4	–342,6	–184,8	–616,9	–492,8	–185,3
Volgograd Oblast	25,9	25,3	23,2	51,2	58,9	68,1	45,7	61,2	67,9	632,4	712,0	505,0	415,8	391,8	209,8	672,5	541,5	344,8
Penza Oblast	84,4	66,8	45,9	145,5	126,8	109,1	116,3	107,6	102,0	76,8	190,2	231,7	–223,4	–153,2	–38,7	–148,9	–100,5	–20,0
Samara Oblast	2,0	1,9	2,8	13,0	13,5	17,1	13,5	15,1	20,1	1941,1	3260,3	1668,4	1722,7	2876,0	1423,1	1716,1	2824,8	1373,5
Saratov Oblast	42,8	38,9	36,9	86,0	72,1	104,6	88,8	81,3	100,1	436,1	655,1	392,6	107,1	299,7	–28,8	118,6	319,4	–1,2
Ulyanov Oblast	34,7	35,5	27,9	70,7	72,0	65,0	98,6	124,9	114,6	436,4	550,4	491,3	195,7	238,5	238,6	9,4	–216,2	–104,3
Republic of Adygeya	214,5	236,1	474,8	316,2	324,0	621,2	417,0	452,3	746,7	–400,7	–616,1	–976,1	–756,4	–1014,3	–1357,1	–1142,0	–1732,5	–2007,2
Republic of Dagestan	579,7	630,2	1219,6	664,8	842,6	1567,8	207,7	237,7	248,2	–509,6	–968,3	–926,5	–600,1	–1356,1	–1214,7	–541,2	–1340,5	–1124,7

Ingush Republic	155,6	156,0	449,8	155,6	156,0	636,3	140,9	139,2	467,5	–658,7	–377,4	–1132,5	–658,7	–377,4	–1736,3	–578,8	–336,9	–1937,4
Kabardino-Balkar Republic	245,8	334,8	645,8	245,8	400,4	900,1	152,1	175,7	218,2	–484,2	–972,1	–1132,3	–484,2	–1243,6	–1659,8	–400,9	–1061,8	–1446,0
Karachaevo-Cherkess Republic	135,8	190,5	222,4	216,4	320,1	430,2				–131,6	–421,1	–303,5	–428,0	–1023,8	–819,1			
Republic of Northern Osetia	336,9	405,3	272,1	480,8	604,0	498,2				–720,8	–868,3	–557,8	–1158,6	–1433,8	–1290,9			
Krasnodar Territory	39,3	66,0	28,9	71,4	127,5	70,8	122,4	171,6	137,5	398,7	208,9	483,7	188,3	–169,3	198,5	–153,9	–477,5	–263,9
Stavropol Territory	56,2	65,8	68,8	88,0	108,8	124,3	115,3	183,9	192,0	303,9	220,2	171,3	83,5	–56,3	–133,7	–114,6	–591,4	–556,7
Rostov Oblast	69,4	55,9	44,4	178,4	168,2	155,8	144,8	133,5	127,5	177,4	257,3	283,9	–454,0	–398,0	–284,8	–324,1	–256,4	–177,0
Republic of Bashkor-tostan	0,1	0,0	0,0	0,1	0,0	8,7				710,5	867,7	488,9	710,5	867,7	446,1			
Udmurt Republic	51,7	58,8	48,2	87,9	83,1	75,8	89,7	86,7	80,4	491,2	576,5	561,4	122,6	236,0	262,6	122,6	237,1	265,1
Kurgan Oblast	94,0	141,4	118,3	161,1	227,5	241,0	206,9	339,1	310,1	32,4	–165,9	–52,1	–328,1	–510,6	–401,4	–623,8	–1147,2	–804,3
Orenburg Oblast	23,5	26,0	14,2	62,4	54,5	55,1	59,5	59,5	62,1	725,3	788,8	633,3	356,3	484,5	331,8	502,1	657,6	423,8
Perm Oblast	13,6	12,3	2,7	36,2	37,0	35,8	40,9	45,5	44,3	1336,3	1706,3	962,4	985,7	1225,6	634,4	914,4	1061,6	550,1
Komi-Permyat Autonomous Region	554,8	508,4	388,2	717,8	611,2	561,1				–940,8	–962,1	–743,7	–1277,8	–1204,4	–1189,9			

Table A.1 (continued)

Balance of Financial Flows between the Center and the Regions in 1996–1998

	% return									Balance per capita (1996, 1997 in 1000 undenominated rubles/person, 1998 – rubles/person)								
	Balance with respect to financial aid			Balance including direct expenditures			Complete balance			Balance with respect to financial aid			Balance including direct expenditures			Complete balance		
Region	1996	1997	1998	1996	1997	1998	1996	1997	1998	1996	1997	1998	1996	1997	1998	1996	1997	1998
Sverdlovsk Oblast	3,6	14,8	7,7	29,7	54,0	32,9	30,7	61,0	42,0	1468,6	1154,9	1074,2	1071,1	622,8	780,6	1157,5	660,3	809,1
Chelyabinsk Oblast	25,8	43,8	3,9	67,5	87,9	60,4	68,1	89,2	70,2	705,4	530,8	568,7	309,4	114,4	234,2	333,7	146,0	270,6
Altai Republic	404,0	210,6	64,0	637,2	290,3	116,3	571,7	301,6	119,0	–1148,4	–1012,5	501,3	–2029,2	–1742,4	–227,5	–2223,1	–2120,2	–305,0
Altai Territory	203,5	201,8	205,7	300,2	263,7	311,8	198,5	162,4	171,4	–432,4	–499,3	–322,4	–836,8	–803,3	–646,2	–815,7	–797,5	–637,6
Kemerovo Oblast	75,6	79,9	71,2	181,6	157,9	190,1	149,3	115,3	139,6	276,8	215,6	231,9	–927,2	–622,0	–725,6	–846,0	–367,9	–636,0
Novosibirsk Oblast	22,5	46,3	12,7	81,6	115,3	83,7	87,7	136,9	99,7	775,7	571,7	810,7	184,4	–162,6	151,6	125,8	–412,6	3,0
Omsk Oblast	30,9	24,9	21,7	55,3	52,3	63,4	49,2	68,8	66,6	1074,0	1071,5	645,2	695,5	680,2	301,5	1116,9	581,0	462,0
Tomsk Oblast	21,9	24,9	27,1	74,6	57,2	90,5	77,0	62,6	112,6	1292,7	1751,5	681,9	421,1	998,7	88,9	381,3	872,7	–117,6
Tyumen Oblast	25,1	33,6	33,3	35,8	61,0	63,9	35,1	61,0	57,7	1243,1	1198,3	775,3	1065,7	703,8	420,2	1141,8	754,7	643,6
Khanty-Mansi Autonomous Region	3,0	0,2	2,5	4,1	3,0	5,3				14152,6	16300,6	6594,9	13998,1	15840,5	6402,0			
Yamal-Nenets Autonomous Region	3,0	0,2	0,0	3,0	1,4	3,7	3,0	1,3	3,7	9755,1	15401,2	8115,2	9755,1	15210,6	7818,1	9784,7	17234,1	7833,5
Republic of Buryatia	189,4	264,8	174,8	317,3	345,4	287,5	226,6	190,2	183,1	–401,6	–773,8	–320,8	–975,8	–1152,4	–804,4	–902,1	–1015,2	–720,5

Republic of Tyva	1148,4	1273,2	1806,8	1655,8	1525,3	2500,5				−1883,1	−2590,5	−1560,7	−2794,5	−3147,0	−2195,1			
Republic of Khakasia	95,3	90,5	45,1	206,1	153,7	119,8	158,8	123,9	107,1	19,8	57,2	254,6	−446,3	−323,3	−91,7	−408,1	−294,7	−63,7
Krasnoyarsk Territory	13,9	27,5	4,5	61,3	87,8	59,1	58,2	83,0	58,5	820,2	830,0	879,2	368,5	139,6	376,8	426,2	209,2	398,9
Taimyr Autonomous Region	127,8	286,8	120,6	166,5	1108,0	246,4				−433,9	−1776,0	−224,6	−1036,8	−9581,4	−1593,7			
Evenk Autonomous Region	951,4	1311,7	475,4	951,4	1311,7	855,5				−5051,5	−12838,3	−3631,6	−5051,5	−12838,3	−7308,2			
Irkutsk Oblast	18,4	50,7	14,5	51,9	127,8	61,2	53,9	114,8	63,0	1223,7	414,0	827,8	721,2	−233,8	375,1	726,2	−169,3	400,1
Ust-Orda Buryat Autonomous Region	983,2	868,6	1399,3	1254,9	955,4	1597,0	1563,2	1434,3	2646,7	−1238,0	−1232,4	−1176,2	−1619,0	−1371,7	−1355,2	−2051,2	−2139,6	−2305,5
Chita Oblast	80,0	262,8	89,2	179,2	394,9	195,2	141,8	251,6	149,0	105,9	−583,1	45,9	−420,2	−1056,5	−404,1	−327,7	−935,5	−278,9
Aga Buryat Autonomous Region	2545,3	293,9	92,5	3966,1	336,4	116,1	978,0	238,9	113,1	−1734,8	−1133,8	84,9	−2742,7	−1382,2	−181,6	−2749,1	−1375,6	−180,2
Republic of Sakha (Yakutia)	157,0	216,8	54,0	198,5	272,7	127,2	194,1	249,5	112,4	−767,4	−1894,2	498,1	−1326,1	−2799,3	−295,0	−1306,5	−2699,5	−154,4
Jewish Autonomous Oblast	365,3	508,7	518,0	522,2	654,1	791,1	204,0	277,0	253,7	−777,5	−1388,0	−867,0	−1237,3	−1881,6	−1433,4	−994,0	−1593,6	−1262,4

Table A.1 (continued)

Balance of Financial Flows between the Center and the Regions in 1996–1998

Region	% return									Balance per capita (1996, 1997 in 1000 undenominated rubles/person, 1998 – rubles/person)								
	Balance with respect to financial aid			Balance including direct expenditures			Complete balance			Balance with respect to financial aid			Balance including direct expenditures			Complete balance		
	1996	1997	1998	1996	1997	1998	1996	1997	1998	1996	1997	1998	1996	1997	1998	1996	1997	1998
Chukchi Autonomous Region	418,0	407,8	993,2	652,9	569,9	1550,5				–4816,6	–7596,0	–4971,2	–8376,3	–11598,1	–8073,3			
Maritime Territory	66,7	110,5	114,6	162,9	187,2	206,0	152,7	180,6	185,1	294,1	–105,7	–91,1	–555,7	–882,0	–661,4	–500,0	–849,8	–617,8
Khabarovsk Territory	70,4	86,3	51,8	124,2	141,1	118,0	122,7	139,9	116,1	407,0	191,0	496,5	–332,8	–575,3	–185,8	–332,8	–575,3	–185,8
Amur Oblast	138,7	335,5	228,7	215,1	428,4	330,7	208,8	417,6	335,4	–363,2	–1094,1	–484,1	–1079,6	–1525,6	–867,8	–1077,5	–1675,5	–992,5
Kamchatka Oblast	152,6	262,0	239,1	308,6	414,0	403,0				–530,0	–1716,0	–1047,4	–2099,8	–3326,9	–2281,9			
Koryak Autonomous Region	885,7	519,7	1202,7	1130,8	887,7	1613,0				–6748,5	–6067,4	–4333,1	–8853,9	–11386,0	–5945,6			
Magadan Oblast	249,2	362,0	139,6	355,0	504,3	249,4				–2072,6	–2938,4	–481,7	–3542,8	–4534,6	–1815,8			
Sakhalin Oblast	129,1	95,4	74,6	236,5	148,4	177,2				–324,4	92,9	288,3	–1519,2	–967,4	–877,3			
Kaliningrad Oblast	58,0	52,2	16,8	58,0	65,5	66,6	49,4	68,1	55,7	265,2	340,1	526,5	265,2	245,5	211,0	394,4	269,7	439,6
Russian Federation	29,1	31,2	20,7	56,8	61,6	79,4				996,2	1165,6	1034,5	607,0	650,0	269,2			

Appendix to Chapter 3

Appendix A.2

Individual Characteristics of the Territorial Structure of Tax Potential, in %

	Tax burden in 1997 as % of		Taxes/person, taking into account the subsistence level, % of average for the Russian Federation			Federal budget's share of taxes			Regions' share of federal budget taxes			Share of increment in arrears (total)			Fulfillment of plan for collection of federal budget taxes		Portion of "cash money" in regional budget taxes		
Region	GRP	Payroll fund	1996	1997	1998	1996	1997	1998	1996	1997	1998	1996	1997	1998	1997	1998	1996	1997	III quarter of 1998
Republic of Karelia	17,1	44,5	48,0	46,0	53,1	24,0	16,8	18,2	0,2	0,1	0,2	24,9	24,1	3,2	43,3	110,9	57,2	54,2	59,8
Komi Republic	24,4	80,2	120,3	123,2	119,4	42,7	39,3	23,7	1,2	1,1	0,6	14,9	18,0	17,8	96,3	67,2	35,9	40,3	28,8
Arkhangelsk Oblast	18,7	50,8	46,2	47,3	52,7	28,1	23,2	26,6	0,4	0,3	0,4	20,3	10,2	20,6	56,4	117,3	39,3	29,1	33,8
Nenets Autonomous Region		109,6		147,7	159,2	37,0	25,1	30,1	0,1	0,0	0,1	-4,8	17,3	-14,2	115,6	111,8	84,4	66,5	85,4
Vologda Oblast	18,5	59,6	73,3	72,7	83,6	26,3	20,5	18,6	0,4	0,3	0,4	13,4	12,8	8,9	58,4	122,8	49,3	42,9	46,3
Murmansk Oblast	21,1	55,0	65,2	72,0	79,8	31,7	23,5	23,7	0,4	0,4	0,5	21,9	5,0	24,1	61,1	123,1	63,0	50,7	50,0
St. Petersburg	26,9	82,2	129,7	96,2	109,6	45,3	38,6	38,5	3,7	3,3	4,6	3,5	4,5	3,7	94,5	127,9	82,1	80,0	
Leningrad Oblast	23,5	78,5	85,2	77,1	76,7	39,2	38,2	37,3	0,8	0,7	0,9	13,4	5,8	11,6	94,3	113,3	63,7	47,3	54,8
Novgorod Oblast	19,7	64,7	66,3	59,2	61,8	33,1	26,9	23,6	0,2	0,2	0,2	6,1	6,5	9,6	75,6	117,0	74,8	66,9	66,4
Pskov Oblast	17,3	60,8	45,3	45,7	45,1	37,5	35,2	29,8	0,2	0,2	0,2	10,0	9,4	21,1	90,5	92,7	60,7	55,2	54,0

Bryansk Oblast	19,0	73,2	63,6	56,5	53,6	45,9	42,7	36,4	0,5	0,4	0,4	20,7	4,5	15,6	87,3	94,2	61,0	49,6	54,6
Vladimir Oblast	21,2	66,3	66,3	59,8	67,5	38,8	29,9	36,1	0,6	0,4	0,6	12,4	14,4	15,7	67,5	138,5	54,6	39,2	50,9
Ivanovo Oblast	19,3	58,2	47,5	45,4	47,0	35,4	28,5	29,8	0,3	0,2	0,2	21,0	24,6	25,4	50,1	105,0	42,4	33,0	41,2
Kaluga Oblast	21,0	67,8	69,1	66,3	70,1	41,1	36,7	37,4	0,4	0,4	0,4	11,0	10,2	8,5	87,6	109,6	70,6	63,3	68,3
Kostroma Oblast	21,4	82,4	59,1	75,8	85,9	32,4	28,1	23,2	0,2	0,2	0,2	19,4	17,7	19,8	83,4	93,9	45,1	45,0	22,4
Moscow	39,9	206,5	267,6	285,3	287,5	57,6	57,7	57,7	26,0	30,9	36,1	2,7	2,1	7,1	111,0	99,0	89,2	93,1	
Moscow Oblast	26,7	118,1	106,5	111,2	128,0	48,1	48,7	47,6	4,8	5,3	6,7	6,5	8,9	39,8	112,7	139,8	73,9	69,1	94,1
Orlov Oblast	19,4	70,7	74,5	62,2	67,9	47,2	35,7	29,1	0,3	0,3	0,3	5,9	6,2	9,6	70,8	94,5	66,9	52,8	
Ryazan Oblast	21,5	89,2	75,8	77,9	86,4	41,5	37,0	39,6	0,5	0,5	0,6	22,5	10,7	14,7	75,6	137,3	61,2	49,0	46,8
Smolensk Oblast	17,4	67,8	65,6	62,3	59,5	37,5	34,8	29,1	0,3	0,3	0,3	17,9	26,2	18,5	81,7	94,8	67,5	56,0	50,2
Tver Oblast	19,2	71,1	67,1	61,8	68,8	34,7	29,9	28,2	0,5	0,4	0,5	16,7	22,3	20,4	65,3	105,6	59,6	48,3	50,8
Tula Oblast	20,1	59,6	69,1	62,8	70,0	35,2	34,4	31,3	0,5	0,5	0,6	16,5	21,3	15,3	65,0	115,8	72,4	72,1	71,7
Yaroslavl Oblast	22,7	92,2	102,5	98,3	99,9	50,7	41,8	36,4	1,0	0,8	0,8	15,1	20,9	13,4	86,7	107,1	58,3	46,6	39,2
Marii El Republic	17,1	61,3	44,7	38,5	42,7	40,8	37,9	29,6	0,2	0,2	0,2	12,9	14,0	19,5	76,3	86,7	37,9	38,8	29,4
Republic of Mordovia	19,0	75,7	47,6	55,9	50,6	44,5	35,5	24,5	0,3	0,3	0,2	7,7	11,6	32,2	93,0	117,0	41,3	35,4	44,6
Chuvash Republic	22,7	79,1	64,6	60,6	58,3	33,1	31,0	25,3	0,3	0,3	0,3	6,8	6,5	20,7	84,7	97,6	32,4	18,0	35,4
Kirov Oblast	18,4	66,5	52,1	49,9	54,2	36,5	35,0	31,5	0,5	0,5	0,5	18,0	19,9	14,9	87,2	109,9	46,3	41,3	46,7

Appendix A.2 (continued)

Individual Characteristics of the Territorial Structure of Tax Potential, in %

Region	Tax burden in 1997 as % of		Taxes/person, taking into account the subsistence level, % of average for the Russian Federation			Federal budget's share of taxes			Regions' share of federal budget taxes			Share of increment in arrears (total)			Fulfillment of plan for collection of federal budget taxes		Portion of "cash money" in regional budget taxes		
	GRP	Payroll fund	1996	1997	1998	1996	1997	1998	1996	1997	1998	1996	1997	1998	1997	1998	1996	1997	III quarter of 1998
Nizhegorod Oblast	25,9	99,7	117,7	120,8	122,2	50,9	48,2	34,1	2,6	2,8	2,1	20,9	10,4	17,4	98,3	93,3	59,9	51,6	
Belgorod Oblast	18,3	70,2	85,9	72,4	87,0	37,9	33,0	26,6	0,5	0,5	0,5	11,4	13,4	16,5	76,5	116,7	62,4	55,8	55,9
Voronezh Oblast	17,4	69,8	66,2	58,3	66,0	38,3	36,1	35,1	0,7	0,7	0,8	15,3	21,0	25,6	76,2	115,0	56,5	42,4	41,4
Kursk Oblast	17,3	70,8	73,8	67,3	77,3	38,3	32,3	33,3	0,4	0,4	0,5	19,7	17,5	32,2	60,1	112,7	32,8	29,3	41,4
Lipetsk Oblast	20,4	72,1	106,3	86,9	96,4	27,9	21,2	21,7	0,4	0,3	0,3	3,2	1,8	10,7	63,4	86,6	77,1	66,2	
Tambov Oblast	19,2	63,2	63,4	53,3	57,1	37,3	31,3	31,6	0,3	0,2	0,3	8,2	15,7	10,0	67,5	101,3	48,4	41,1	40,4
Republic of Kalmykia	52,7	136,5	56,0	92,8	95,1	58,7	67,3	63,8	0,1	0,3	0,3	12,5	7,3	18,0	131,6	78,0	57,2	68,0	34,8
Republic of Tatarstan	25,0	105,0	140,7	159,3	131,5	19,0	24,6	11,1	1,1	1,7	0,7	13,4	7,6	23,5	68,0	41,5	44,2	43,2	
Astrakhan Oblast	18,9	70,8	48,0	59,0	57,2	41,9	37,2	32,4	0,3	0,3	0,3	13,2	2,4	15,9	117,9	120,1	55,8	65,6	73,8
Volgograd Oblast	19,1	73,4	79,2	70,3	63,3	38,4	40,6	34,5	1,1	1,1	0,9	11,7	16,9	18,0	83,6	104,1	47,9	52,4	80,7
Penza Oblast	19,6	67,3	46,8	45,4	43,9	37,4	34,3	31,2	0,4	0,4	0,3	14,9	10,2	22,1	76,8	90,6	52,8	46,6	47,8
Samara Oblast	27,1	119,2	138,3	166,8	143,5	46,7	51,9	38,2	3,2	4,3	3,0	32,0	8,1	16,6	118,2	76,6	70,0	62,7	61,4

Saratov Oblast	19,7	87,1	63,4	63,7	71,0	39,4	36,7	29,9	1,0	1,0	0,9	13,1	14,0	18,4	112,9	102,4	46,5	43,8	44,3
Ulyanov Oblast	19,6	71,7	92,6	82,5	95,6	38,1	35,6	32,9	0,5	0,5	0,5	19,7	24,5	25,9	78,1	102,5	39,2	31,5	30,2
Republic of Adygeya	23,0	67,0	32,1	44,6	38,3	37,6	32,8	26,6	0,1	0,1	0,1	8,2	-2,7	3,0	81,5	88,4	72,0	48,8	56,6
Republic of Dagestan	10,5	40,7	13,0	16,5	14,6	34,7	38,9	23,2	0,1	0,2	0,1	9,0	20,2	22,3	103,3	88,4	36,0	47,3	
Ingush Republic	26,2	115,1	40,8	21,5	20,5	91,2	80,8	50,4	0,2	0,1	0,1	1,9	4,8	1,6	67,4	110,5	100,0	73,0	83,3
Kabardino-Balkar Republic	16,6	67,0	42,2	34,4	36,1	31,2	24,0	19,3	0,1	0,1	0,1	24,2	31,2	70,5	55,4	81,6	46,0	33,5	30,1
Karachaevo-Cherkess Republic	18,6	67,7	36,7	39,4	36,3	39,6	31,2	26,0	0,1	0,1	0,1	9,8	20,1	25,9	81,1	94,1	70,4	58,8	
Republic of Northern Osetia	19,6	58,2	30,0	28,0	31,2	35,6	27,2	32,9	0,1	0,1	0,1	14,7	16,5	20,0	35,5	127,7	44,2	53,5	77,2
Krasnodar Territory	18,5	68,0	71,4	59,0	75,5	38,6	31,7	35,8	1,6	1,2	1,8	11,5	13,6	6,9	70,5	135,5	79,9	70,7	
Stavropol Territory	16,8	73,9	66,9	47,4	56,3	44,2	38,5	33,5	0,9	0,7	0,8	10,4	11,6	14,2	74,1	135,1	74,3	56,9	55,7
Rostov Oblast	19,6	64,6	60,7	53,2	65,7	40,3	34,1	31,2	1,2	1,0	1,2	25,9	17,9	14,5	68,5	129,7	67,1	56,2	38,1
Republic of Bashkortostan	19,8	83,9	109,2	103,6	104,1	27,0	27,8	17,8	1,4	1,5	1,0	19,6	33,7	41,6	49,4	52,1	63,5	47,0	
Udmurt Republic	23,3	85,3	81,5	79,0	85,1	38,9	39,9	39,7	0,8	0,9	0,9	6,1	8,1	6,3	114,2	120,2	47,3	37,8	36,0
Kurgan Oblast	17,9	52,5	54,3	46,0	52,0	36,4	25,3	20,7	0,3	0,2	0,2	10,2	13,8	18,0	54,8	81,5	45,2	29,9	25,6
Orenburg Oblast	20,4	79,6	90,6	90,8	91,5	38,9	34,8	29,9	1,0	0,9	0,9	16,4	4,4	17,3	74,7	89,8	43,7	43,8	42,4

Appendix A.2 (continued)

Individual Characteristics of the Territorial Structure of Tax Potential, in %

Region	Tax burden in 1997 as % of		Taxes/person, taking into account the subsistence level, % of average for the Russian Federation			Federal budget's share of taxes			Regions' share of federal budget taxes			Share of increment in arrears (total)			Fulfillment of plan for collection of federal budget taxes		Portion of "cash money" in regional budget taxes		
	GRP	Payroll fund	1996	1997	1998	1996	1997	1998	1996	1997	1998	1996	1997	1998	1997	1998	1996	1997	III quarter of 1998
Perm Oblast	24,8	94,4	117,2	124,4	114,0	44,6	43,1	28,8	2,1	2,3	1,5	16,1	2,9	18,9	100,8	88,8	57,7	47,3	
Komi-Permyat Autonomous Region		47,7		30,6	38,6	25,8	23,5	25,9	0,0	0,0	0,0	22,6	18,1	14,6	86,7	143,5	65,6	40,6	49,7
Sverdlovsk Oblast	24,0	81,9	110,1	89,8	99,3	39,9	34,0	31,6	3,4	2,5	2,8	9,0	18,0	10,3	58,6	113,2	47,4	40,9	
Chelyabinsk Oblast	22,4	77,0	102,0	95,1	100,3	31,9	29,9	20,1	1,7	1,4	1,1	10,0	17,8	9,4	61,8	85,8	37,4	43,0	43,0
Altai Republic	21,5	63,8	28,9	40,8	67,4	41,7	58,1	66,5	0,0	0,1	0,1	9,6	13,2	35,9	141,6	160,7	70,4	61,6	
Altai Territory	17,7	52,3	46,3	39,6	42,3	31,5	29,2	23,4	0,5	0,5	0,4	10,6	12,8	23,7	69,2	113,2	36,3	29,5	29,2
Kemerovo Oblast	21,7	67,4	100,5	82,9	87,8	33,8	25,7	26,7	1,7	1,1	1,3	26,4	31,1	8,2	56,4	100,7	32,6	35,8	
Novosibirsk Oblast	19,8	76,4	73,8	59,3	65,7	40,1	35,5	34,4	1,3	1,2	1,3	3,2	13,5	10,7	89,9	120,6	46,2	40,6	47,8
Omsk Oblast	20,8	79,4	111,7	94,3	83,3	49,5	36,9	33,2	1,6	1,1	0,9	14,5	13,1	4,3	97,9	84,2	43,6	31,8	31,3
Tomsk Oblast	27,6	112,5	120,4	128,1	105,6	42,2	36,7	25,9	0,9	0,9	0,5	4,6	11,2	10,8	142,4	74,0	57,4	60,4	40,1
Tyumen Oblast	34,8	97,0	101,6	97,3	94,3	36,8	31,9	27,5	1,1	1,0	0,8	0,3	7,3	9,3	112,4	81,7	50,8	44,8	53,7
Khanty-Mansi Autonomous Region		173,3		554,0	400,7	56,6	46,1	33,8	9,6	8,9	4,8	10,9	-7,9	10,2	117,7	64,7	42,4	37,6	

Yamal-Nenets Autonomous Region		143,1		526,3	495,5	39,4	36,1	26,8	2,4	2,9	2,1	19,1	2,7	13,7	98,7	83,0	22,4	18,3	
Republic of Buryatia	15,5	46,9	42,6	42,5	46,2	30,4	25,5	29,7	0,2	0,2	0,2	7,7	15,6	10,9	72,0	120,5	35,5	27,7	33,1
Republic of Tyva	13,5	28,8	14,4	14,1	13,9	26,9	22,3	15,0	0,0	0,0	0,0	9,9	10,1	13,4	105,7	76,0	64,9	60,4	53,6
Republic of Khakasia	17,8	57,4	59,5	54,8	60,4	19,6	21,5	19,4	0,1	0,1	0,1	23,1	7,2	25,9	63,8	120,8	33,4	25,2	35,5
Krasnoyarsk Territory	21,2	66,7	104,3	108,5	126,7	28,6	24,3	22,1	1,4	1,4	1,4	32,0	1,7	10,4	61,5	97,4	44,7	38,6	
Taimyr Autonomous Region		68,6		110,1	170,5	29,0	10,6	10,4	0,0	0,0	0,0	110,3	24,4	-42,6	15,4	83,8	78,9	90,4	66,4
Evenk Autonomous Region		41,5		45,5	81,5	18,5	24,3	21,9	0,0	0,0	0,0	38,5	30,5	6,5	55,5	145,5	27,2	20,5	7,3
Irkutsk Oblast	14,4	51,9	91,2	65,4	84,9	42,7	24,5	31,9	1,9	0,8	1,3	11,7	27,6	13,7	62,9	131,2	46,3	42,6	73,6
Ust-Orda Buryat Autonomous Region		34,7		18,1	17,7	25,8	22,0	16,8	0,0	0,0	0,0	17,9	2,2	7,6	75,1	77,1	60,1	39,2	42,2
Chita Oblast	17,1	42,0	36,8	31,8	37,0	30,0	19,4	26,4	0,3	0,2	0,3	3,4	10,7	4,0	54,0	126,7	40,6	36,3	36,4
Aga Buryat Autonomous Region		73,3		20,7	32,0	18,0	63,0	79,8	0,0	0,0	0,0	3,0	6,7	5,5	801,9	93,3	100,0	47,0	68,0
Republic of Sakha (Yakutia)	20,2	52,4	62,0	66,0	67,2	28,3	25,8	22,1	0,7	0,7	0,6	14,1	4,8	29,1	78,1	81,8	41,5	31,9	
Jewish Autonomous Oblast		37,7		26,4	29,5	27,5	22,4	18,8	0,0	0,0	0,0	25,9	21,0	9,1	85,8	96,3	50,4	39,3	40,4
Chukchi Autonomous Region	29,6	54,4		77,7	43,3	21,3	27,5	11,1	0,1	0,1	0,0	28,3	17,5	11,5	63,9	62,1	30,8	22,7	

Appendix A.2 (continued)

Individual Characteristics of the Territorial Structure of Tax Potential, in %

Region	Tax burden in 1997 as % of		Taxes/person, taking into account the subsistence level, % of average for the Russian Federation			Federal budget's share of taxes			Regions' share of federal budget taxes			Share of increment in arrears (total)			Fulfillment of plan for collection of federal budget taxes		Portion of "cash money" in regional budget taxes		
	GRP	Payroll fund	1996	1997	1998	1996	1997	1998	1996	1997	1998	1996	1997	1998	1997	1998	1996	1997	III quarter of 1998
Maritime Territory	20,7	58,0	62,6	57,9	53,3	34,5	34,9	28,5	0,9	0,9	0,7	8,5	10,3	27,3	96,4	101,3	51,5	50,6	57,7
Khabarovsk Territory	17,5	60,5	84,6	72,1	85,6	39,6	38,7	29,0	1,0	0,9	0,8	8,1	14,3	19,0	92,6	119,3	58,5	47,3	
Amur Oblast	11,9	39,6	61,5	39,1	42,1	39,6	22,0	21,8	0,5	0,2	0,2	1,9	34,7	20,5	48,5	102,4	46,3	35,7	
Kamchatka Oblast	18,4	35,9	51,2	42,4	51,5	27,2	28,5	21,2	0,2	0,2	0,1	14,5	20,0	23,4	53,9	94,3	59,0	50,0	36,0
Koryak Autonomous Region		36,4		44,8	32,7	24,9	22,5	10,2	0,0	0,0	0,0	44,9	29,3	51,8	66,3	44,4	100,0	66,6	75,2
Magadan Oblast	19,0	46,7	69,2	58,4	65,2	29,1	19,3	23,8	0,2	0,1	0,2	28,5	34,7	22,1	37,4	127,5	41,5	40,1	
Sakhalin Oblast	22,9	62,1	62,9	67,6	69,6	30,7	39,5	27,9	0,3	0,5	0,4	16,2	15,0	9,2	107,6	101,6	59,2	49,9	53,2
Kaliningrad Oblast	22,8	70,9	65,0	60,5	64,1	36,8	34,7	32,3	0,3	0,3	0,3	10,3	7,9	12,4	94,3	112,4	89,1	68,4	68,9
Russian Federation	25,7	96,2	100,0	100,0	100,0	43,6	41,0	37,1	100,0	100,0	100,0	11,7	8,5	14,5	90,7	116,6	58,2	53,9	52,3

Appendix to Chapter 4

Table A.3

Financial Aid to Subjects of the Federation from the Federal Budget

Region	Shares of subjects of the Federation									Evaluation of the aid's equalizing effect in 1998							
	in FFSSF* (approved)			in FFSSF* (actual)			in financial aid			Deficit			Per capita, adjusted for the subsistence level, % of national average				Portion of aid in revenues
													revenues			expen-ditures	
	1996	1997	1998	1996	1997	1998	1996	1997	1998	internal	with trans-fers	total	internal	trans.	total		
Republic of Karelia	1,0752	0,7991	0,7197	1,0208	0,9159	1,0226	0,7134	0,7957	0,6956	–22,6	–6,4	–4,4	68,9	76,3	73,7	73,7	14,6
Komi Republic	0,2017	0,3568	0,0000	0,3993	0,3962	0,0425	1,4139	0,8938	0,2733	–15,7	–15,4	–13,4	158,2	145,4	140,7	140,7	2,6
Arkhangelsk Oblast	0,6004	0,9689	1,1025	0,9241	0,7168	1,1184	1,1547	1,0643	0,8078	–14,5	–2,7	–1,8	63,6	66,3	63,2	63,2	12,7
Nenets Autonomous Region	0,2757	0,2049	0,1845	0,2484	0,2909	0,1799	0,1400	0,1866	0,1293	–21,9	–6,1	–5,2	180,5	198,7	189,5	189,5	14,3
Vologda Oblast	0,2271	0,2583	0,2327	0,6252	0,0336	0,5127	1,0231	1,0402	0,3611	–7,4	–2,8	–2,6	107,7	103,6	98,0	98,0	4,9
Murmansk Oblast	0,0000	0,8417	0,8629	0,0967	0,5678	0,9532	1,8168	2,3714	2,5233	–26,3	–19,4	0,5	95,8	95,9	113,1	113,1	26,3
St. Petersburg	0,9035	0,6714	0,0000	0,8724	0,6309	0,1570	0,5842	1,1054	0,1618	0,7	1,0	1,4	112,7	103,6	98,3	98,3	0,4
Leningrad Oblast	0,4862	0,5002	0,4504	0,3569	0,5700	0,4699	0,2755	0,6795	0,5828	–16,2	–12,3	–9,1	78,2	75,0	73,4	73,4	6,7
Novgorod Oblast	1,2270	1,0226	0,9210	1,1263	1,0747	1,0187	0,7815	0,8708	1,3812	–34,6	–16,6	1,4	75,1	87,8	100,8	100,8	35,5
Pskov Oblast	1,4845	1,1032	0,9938	1,7203	1,0418	1,1821	1,2106	1,0813	1,1327	–40,7	–13,1	–1,8	50,5	67,8	72,3	72,3	39,6
Bryansk Oblast	1,0618	0,7891	0,9828	1,3137	0,6652	1,1522	0,8957	0,6346	0,8854	–22,2	–1,3	1,5	54,4	63,2	61,4	61,4	23,3

Vladimir Oblast	1,3047	0,9696	0,9499	1,2271	1,1095	0,7537	1,1933	0,9226	1,5441	–27,6	–19,3	–2,8	68,6	70,0	79,7	79,7	25,5
Ivanovo Oblast	2,1760	1,6172	1,5075	1,7107	1,8307	1,4748	1,4620	1,4916	1,1179	–29,6	–3,8	–0,8	57,7	72,3	70,4	70,4	29,0
Kaluga Oblast	0,7205	1,1114	1,0428	0,8422	1,0672	0,9592	1,1641	0,9724	1,5470	–30,4	–16,2	3,4	70,2	77,4	90,2	90,2	32,6
Kostroma Oblast	1,0839	1,5588	1,4042	1,2990	1,3612	1,5711	2,1323	1,1326	1,3256	–31,0	–8,8	–3,4	104,8	127,0	127,1	127,1	28,5
Moscow	0,0000	0,0000	0,0000	0,0000	0,0000	0,0000	4,4210	3,2151	1,2929	–1,6	–1,6	–0,5	188,0	172,2	164,6	164,6	1,1
Moscow Oblast	0,0000	3,1018	0,0000	1,6329	2,1307	0,3917	2,2971	2,1370	1,4971	–4,5	–3,7	0,0	104,5	96,6	94,7	94,7	4,3
Orlov Oblast	1,2669	1,1143	1,3067	1,0639	1,6641	1,0630	0,9101	1,1921	0,8322	–25,9	–7,9	–5,1	82,4	93,9	91,4	91,4	21,8
Ryazan Oblast	0,5217	0,8728	0,7863	0,5820	0,6991	0,7931	0,7518	0,7927	0,7528	–12,8	–1,6	2,8	80,3	83,0	81,9	81,9	15,0
Smolensk Oblast	0,7547	0,5609	0,6998	0,6816	0,6676	0,7811	0,4169	0,5060	0,8716	–24,7	–11,9	–1,7	67,8	72,7	76,7	76,7	21,4
Tver Oblast	0,9438	0,8412	0,8343	0,9387	0,9424	0,9469	1,0886	1,2173	0,9174	–14,7	–4,4	0,1	78,6	80,7	79,8	79,8	14,7
Tula Oblast	0,8183	0,6082	0,9068	0,9514	0,6947	0,8215	1,3658	1,2846	0,8743	–17,4	–8,8	–3,9	76,2	77,1	76,8	76,8	14,0
Yaroslavl Oblast	0,1150	0,4516	0,4068	0,0683	0,5006	0,3590	1,3018	1,0986	0,6902	–17,8	–14,6	–2,6	100,8	95,9	103,3	103,3	8,0
Marii El Republic	1,1628	1,0444	0,9407	1,2891	1,1366	0,9055	0,6882	0,6593	0,6160	–23,7	4,5	4,5	49,0	61,5	58,2	58,2	24,8
Republic of Mordovia	1,5595	1,3076	1,3161	1,4909	1,5842	0,9359	1,3441	1,0919	1,0220	–34,2	–15,8	–4,7	59,0	69,2	74,0	74,0	28,2
Chuvash Republic	1,4209	1,0560	0,9512	1,4049	1,2848	0,8811	0,7742	0,8486	0,6250	–13,3	0,0	0,6	72,3	76,3	72,5	72,5	12,6
Kirov Oblast	2,1099	1,5680	1,4126	1,8407	1,7736	1,8211	0,8887	1,2797	1,6130	–21,2	–1,0	5,2	60,0	69,1	69,4	69,4	25,0
Nizhegorod Oblast	1,0846	0,8061	0,7260	1,1847	0,7583	0,8153	1,0698	0,7164	0,8402	–9,4	–6,6	–2,6	129,8	122,6	120,8	120,8	4,3

Table A.3 (continued)

Financial Aid to Subjects of the Federation from the Federal Budget

	Shares of subjects of the Federation									Evaluation of the aid's equalizing effect in 1998							
										Deficit			Per capita, adjusted for the subsistence level, % of national average				
	in FFSSF* (approved)			in FFSSF* (actual)			in financial aid						revenues				Portion of aid in revenues
Region	1996	1997	1998	1996	1997	1998	1996	1997	1998	internal	with transfers	total	internal	trans.	total	expenditures	
Belgorod Oblast	0,0761	0,2397	0,1878	0,1701	0,1927	0,1797	0,3798	0,2692	0,5896	–14,6	–12,7	–5,5	100,2	93,9	96,1	96,1	9,7
Voronezh Oblast	1,9870	1,4767	1,3301	1,8582	1,6648	1,3844	0,9625	0,8551	1,3662	–19,1	–8,3	–3,3	75,5	78,5	78,2	78,2	16,2
Kursk Oblast	0,8184	1,1004	0,9912	0,8237	1,0552	0,9048	0,3871	0,9019	0,7152	–20,9	–10,0	–7,8	90,2	94,0	91,0	91,0	11,8
Lipetsk Oblast	0,0000	0,0000	0,0000	0,0000	0,0000	0,0000	0,0539	0,1940	0,1205	–3,9	–3,9	–1,8	120,8	110,6	106,9	106,9	1,8
Tambov Oblast	1,2588	1,0462	0,9425	0,9297	1,1506	1,2287	0,6685	0,7556	1,0882	–23,2	0,3	7,4	61,7	73,8	74,7	74,7	27,7
Republic of Kalmykia	1,2428	0,9236	0,9213	1,0916	1,1063	0,6948	0,6470	0,6613	0,6472	–34,1	–7,0	2,9	88,0	113,8	119,1	119,1	36,0
Republic of Tatarstan	1,1244	0,8356	0,0000	0,0000	0,0000	0,0000	0,8745	0,6665	0,8787	–30,8	–30,8	–5,9	193,3	177,1	227,8	227,8	2,5
Astrakhan Oblast	1,9623	1,4584	1,3136	2,0000	1,5403	1,5219	1,1468	0,9364	1,1343	–22,8	4,2	6,9	61,1	75,5	73,2	73,2	27,5
Volgograd Oblast	0,9715	0,7220	0,6503	1,3893	0,6010	0,7416	0,9882	0,8404	0,9450	–9,8	–4,0	1,4	66,0	64,4	64,3	64,3	10,8
Penza Oblast	1,6433	1,2213	1,0999	2,0624	1,2917	1,1391	1,0643	0,7620	0,8628	–20,2	0,2	2,5	43,4	49,9	48,2	48,2	22,1
Samara Oblast	0,0000	0,0000	0,0000	0,0000	0,0000	0,0000	0,2152	0,2730	0,3708	–2,5	–2,5	–0,5	141,4	129,6	124,8	124,8	1,7

Saratov Oblast	2,5723	1,9117	1,8240	2,0435	1,9903	2,2917	1,4742	1,4652	1,8276	–14,1	0,4	2,9	80,2	85,8	83,1	83,1	16,5
Ulyanov Oblast	0,7307	0,9063	0,8162	0,8652	0,8079	0,9561	0,5708	0,5780	0,6619	–12,4	0,0	0,8	98,4	103,0	98,1	98,1	12,6
Republic of Adygeya	0,7710	0,6957	1,1671	0,8471	1,2407	1,2208	0,5607	0,6199	1,3171	–64,4	–24,7	–1,5	44,8	86,7	107,2	107,2	63,8
Republic of Dagestan	4,4083	3,4306	5,1659	3,1078	3,8093	4,9926	2,1399	3,1042	5,0779	–80,1	–23,3	4,8	16,2	57,0	73,6	73,6	80,9
Ingush Republic	0,5841	0,5958	0,7919	0,5541	0,5738	0,9809	0,9585	0,4241	1,1014	–82,3	–31,4	4,6	16,3	57,9	83,5	83,5	80,0
Kabardino-Balkar Republic	1,4551	1,0814	3,4155	1,5975	1,4931	2,8205	1,0725	1,4134	2,5825	–60,6	–16,1	–0,7	49,9	97,3	108,8	108,8	58,3
Karachaevo-Cherkess Republic	0,6926	0,5148	0,8465	0,5509	0,6798	0,8465	0,3613	0,4978	0,6091	–46,3	–2,5	0,0	42,6	70,8	68,6	68,6	46,1
Republic of Northern Osetia	1,4271	1,1160	1,4011	1,4472	1,1044	1,6139	1,1278	0,9844	1,3414	–57,1	–13,6	–2,1	35,6	65,8	70,5	70,5	54,3
Krasnodar Territory	4,2421	3,1527	2,8397	3,3839	3,6588	3,0188	2,1775	2,6504	2,2916	–13,3	–0,9	0,6	77,5	81,2	77,9	77,9	13,8
Stavropol Territory	2,4883	2,3654	2,3602	2,7317	2,3710	2,7930	1,7347	1,4613	2,4133	–27,2	–6,7	–0,4	59,7	70,2	70,8	70,8	26,1
Rostov Oblast	2,7457	2,3930	3,1110	2,3853	2,7877	2,5230	2,9331	1,8484	2,2874	–17,7	–5,4	–1,2	72,2	76,1	75,1	75,1	16,6
Republic of Bashkor-tostan	0,0000	0,0000	0,0000	0,0000	0,0000	0,0000	0,0065	0,0000	0,0000	–11,2	–11,2	–2,2	148,8	136,4	141,9	141,9	0,0
Udmurt Republic	1,3750	1,4932	1,5746	1,2930	1,5595	1,5415	1,4272	1,7324	1,9584	–29,9	–18,1	–6,9	82,2	88,0	94,6	94,6	22,4
Kurgan Oblast	1,3553	1,0073	0,9073	1,3820	1,1088	1,1794	0,9261	0,8063	0,9184	–23,5	–1,4	1,8	65,4	77,3	75,4	75,4	24,9

Table A.3 (continued)

Financial Aid to Subjects of the Federation from the Federal Budget

	Shares of subjects of the Federation									Evaluation of the aid's equalizing effect in 1998								
										Deficit			Per capita, adjusted for the subsistence level, % of national average					
	in FFSSF* (approved)			in FFSSF* (actual)			in financial aid				with transfers		revenues			expenditures	Portion of aid in revenues
Region	1996	1997	1998	1996	1997	1998	1996	1997	1998	internal	with transfers	total	internal	trans.	total	expenditures	Portion of aid in revenues
Orenburg Oblast	1,1173	0,8317	0,9790	1,4116	0,8474	0,7696	0,8250	0,7951	0,8564	–14,0	–9,1	–5,9	103,8	100,6	98,4	98,4	8,7
Perm Oblast	0,0000	0,6160	0,0000	0,1797	0,4079	0,3260	0,9861	0,8748	0,3323	–0,7	0,7	1,3	130,4	121,2	115,2	115,2	2,0
Komi-Permyat Autonomous Region	0,3557	0,2644	0,3147	0,4157	0,2698	0,3089	0,2924	0,2369	0,3528	–57,2	–22,4	1,1	45,1	74,9	92,2	92,2	57,6
Sverdlovsk Oblast	0,0000	0,0000	0,0000	0,0000	0,0000	0,0000	0,4260	1,1999	0,9567	–5,7	–5,7	–2,0	101,6	93,1	91,4	91,4	3,6
Chelyabinsk Oblast	0,3718	0,7666	0,6905	0,5369	0,6225	0,6887	1,5007	1,9571	0,4797	–6,5	–3,8	–3,7	105,3	99,3	93,9	93,9	2,8
Altai Republic	0,4750	0,3530	0,3177	0,6525	0,6085	0,2693	0,5127	0,5028	0,4136	–63,6	–43,2	–12,4	35,9	51,4	74,9	74,9	52,3
Altai Territory	5,3720	4,5412	5,5214	5,1677	5,0822	5,3462	3,7690	3,4058	4,5347	–41,2	–7,1	1,4	52,7	76,3	78,6	78,6	42,0
Kemerovo Oblast	1,9510	3,2129	3,9925	3,3932	2,6811	4,0539	4,3102	3,3424	3,9735	–22,9	–9,3	–2,8	104,2	112,3	113,8	113,8	19,9
Novosibirsk Oblast	1,3255	1,2680	1,1423	1,4089	1,7927	0,8929	1,0276	1,7439	0,7431	–4,7	0,5	1,7	67,3	65,1	62,2	62,2	6,3
Omsk Oblast	0,4759	1,6069	1,4475	1,4158	1,1820	1,5626	1,7370	0,9945	1,1028	–22,1	–13,0	–12,6	96,1	98,4	93,4	93,4	9,1
Tomsk Oblast	0,8320	0,9923	0,8965	0,8429	1,0334	1,0001	0,6458	0,8045	0,7362	–17,5	–6,3	–4,9	94,2	98,0	94,0	94,0	10,7
Tyumen Oblast	2,0459	1,5205	1,3694	1,4422	1,6307	2,0037	0,9382	1,0572	1,4482	–12,5	–0,8	0,0	115,4	120,0	114,2	114,2	12,5

Khanty-Mansi Autonomous Region	0,0000	0,0000	0,0000	0,0000	0,0000	0,0000	0,9941	0,0644	0,6153	–6,9	–6,9	–0,2	398,3	365,0	369,5	369,5	1,2
Yamal-Nenets Autonomous Region	0,0000	0,0000	0,0000	0,0000	0,0000	0,0000	0,2529	0,0155	0,0000	–7,2	–7,2	–7,1	548,3	502,4	475,3	475,3	0,0
Republic of Buryatia	2,2005	1,6354	2,5914	1,7254	2,3316	2,3728	1,4755	1,6740	2,0812	–42,3	–5,4	5,3	53,4	80,2	84,3	84,3	45,2
Republic of Tyva	0,9807	0,8768	1,4805	1,1292	1,0135	1,3930	1,0615	1,1229	1,2667	–76,1	–14,9	5,7	18,8	61,3	71,9	71,9	77,4
Republic of Khakasia	0,4616	0,3430	0,3091	0,5863	0,3444	0,3316	0,3884	0,4096	0,3041	–15,0	–7,7	–5,1	77,9	77,5	75,3	75,3	10,4
Krasnoyarsk Territory	0,0000	0,0000	0,0000	0,0000	0,0000	0,0000	0,6635	1,2200	0,2881	–6,3	–6,3	–5,0	144,5	132,4	126,9	126,9	1,4
Taimyr Autonomous Region	0,2234	0,2051	0,2003	0,2116	0,2536	0,2172	0,1472	0,1562	0,1592	–11,2	0,8	1,9	278,8	289,8	277,0	277,0	10,6
Evenk Autonomous Region	0,3329	0,2474	0,2483	0,2580	0,3788	0,2076	0,1826	0,3490	0,2056	–43,7	–19,3	–8,2	213,5	280,3	301,3	301,3	38,7
Irkutsk Oblast	0,0000	0,5865	0,9877	0,1158	0,4300	0,9403	1,2073	1,4417	0,9376	–12,4	–8,0	–5,5	93,7	90,2	87,5	87,5	6,8
Ust-Orda Buryat Autonomous Region	0,5454	0,4141	0,4624	0,4991	0,4592	0,5900	0,3285	0,2577	0,4778	–70,4	–4,6	9,6	28,4	83,9	91,1	91,1	70,4
Chita Oblast	1,0235	1,2017	1,7831	1,2559	1,2342	1,6914	0,8440	1,4523	1,2797	–24,7	1,2	4,1	44,4	54,7	53,2	53,2	27,7
Aga Buryat Autonomous Region	0,2320	0,2044	0,3114	0,2581	0,2246	0,2733	0,2351	0,1737	0,1997	–77,8	–2,8	2,7	11,0	44,0	43,9	43,9	78,4
Republic of Sakha (Yakutia)	5,4929	4,0823	3,6770	3,6621	2,7581	2,1803	3,5171	4,5414	1,4843	–49,1	–40,6	–40,3	84,0	89,8	85,3	85,3	13,1

Table A.3 (continued)

Financial Aid to Subjects of the Federation from the Federal Budget

	Shares of subjects of the Federation									Evaluation of the aid's equalizing effect in 1998							
										Deficit			Per capita, adjusted for the subsistence level, % of national average				
	in FFSSF* (approved)			in FFSSF* (actual)			in financial aid						revenues				
Region	1996	1997	1998	1996	1997	1998	1996	1997	1998	internal	with transfers	total	internal	trans.	total	expenditures	Portion of aid in revenues
Jewish Autonomous Oblast	0,6645	0,6705	0,8338	0,6377	0,7068	0,8921	0,3642	0,4562	0,6069	–53,0	9,5	9,5	41,0	87,5	82,7	82,7	57,1
Chukchi Autonomous Region	1,5713	1,1678	1,2051	1,3540	1,4902	1,1129	0,8497	1,0484	1,0606	–59,2	–21,6	–2,8	60,9	107,1	125,5	125,5	52,7
Maritime Territory	0,0000	4,7845	4,3097	0,3252	3,2441	4,1111	2,1673	3,1874	4,0651	–35,1	–13,1	–3,1	62,6	76,8	80,9	80,9	32,7
Khabarovsk Territory	1,3665	2,3629	2,1284	1,7599	2,3951	1,5611	2,4792	2,4034	1,9054	–17,9	–8,1	0,8	96,2	98,6	102,3	102,3	16,7
Amur Oblast	3,4739	2,5818	2,3257	2,3978	3,0011	2,6362	2,2088	2,0537	2,3778	–39,3	–5,6	7,8	53,3	76,0	82,0	82,0	41,0
Kamchatka Oblast	0,0000	1,2936	1,1653	0,6092	0,9636	0,9727	0,9316	1,3058	1,5085	–46,3	–31,1	–11,6	63,9	75,2	91,1	91,1	39,2
Koryak Autonomous Region	0,2992	0,4923	0,4436	0,4694	0,4656	0,4326	0,3925	0,3009	0,3543	–63,4	–20,0	–8,6	46,9	94,0	101,5	101,5	57,0
Magadan Oblast	2,1415	1,5915	1,4335	2,2240	1,7117	1,4828	1,4111	1,2845	1,1073	–30,4	0,2	3,2	82,4	108,7	105,8	105,8	29,4
Sakhalin Oblast	1,8409	1,5761	1,4197	2,0312	1,6749	1,5532	1,4775	1,5216	1,4210	–22,7	–3,2	3,6	80,1	91,9	93,0	93,0	25,2
Kaliningrad Oblast	0,4093	0,5026	0,4525	0,7052	0,6201	0,1689	0,5740	0,4516	0,3436	–14,5	–11,3	–4,9	73,0	69,4	70,4	70,4	9,0
Russian Federation										–15,6	–7,8	–2,5	100,0	100,0	100,0	100,0	11,1

* FFSSF — Fund for Financial Support of Subjects of the Federation.

Appendix to Chapter 5

Table A.4

Distribution of Direct Federal Expenditures among the Regions in 1998

	Direct expenditures per capita	Direct expenditures per capita, adjusted for the subsistence level	Government expenditures per capita	Government expenditures per government employee	Expenditures on industry in relation to gross industrial production	Expenditures on agriculture in relation to gross agricultural production	Expenditures on agriculture in relation to gross agricultural production at large enterprises	Expenditures on education per capita	Expenditures on education per student	Expenditures on public health per capita	Social expenditures per capita	Social expenditures per capita, adjusted for the subsistence level	Expenditures on culture per capita
Region	rub./per.	rub./per.	rub./per.	1000 rub./per.	1 : 1	1 : 1	1 : 1	rub./per.	rub./per.	rub./per.	rub./per.	rub./per.	rub./per.
Republic of Karelia	482	372	85	22,9	4,6	18	24	106	7 731	18,8	7,0	5,4	5,815
Komi Republic	997	771	82	25,9	92,7	12	17	109	9 402	13,5	8,5	6,6	0,068
Arkhangelsk Oblast	477	394	70	22,0	1,8	14	21	116	10 224	56,2	5,4	4,5	0,754
Nenets Autonomous Region	974	805	210			2	2	90		11,0	20,1	16,6	-
Vologda Oblast	241	244	51	16,1	1,0	15	23	46	3 111	9,3	5,5	5,6	0,030
Murmansk Oblast	470	348	98	29,0	2,5	36	38	94	11 180	27,9	8,5	6,3	-
St. Petersburg	629	734	35	15,2	14,1			177	3 933	109,6	5,8	6,8	61,036
Leningrad Oblast	324	376	34	19,1	11,5	10	14	38		17,8	15,3	17,8	0,131
Novgorod Oblast	288	328	51	13,8	3,5	15	25	63	4 094	15,8	23,5	26,6	0,568
Pskov Oblast	309	346	58	13,8	28,5	12	23	54	4 834	8,1	18,6	20,8	12,672

Bryansk Oblast	714	999	47	13,3	23,9	19	31	55	5 036	5,9	10,1	14,2	0,516
Vladimir Oblast	267	317	35	13,2	1,5	30	46	68	6 680	4,4	7,4	8,8	3,530
Ivanovo Oblast	315	383	46	13,4	8,1	10	15	98	4 754	38,1	8,6	10,5	0,866
Kaluga Oblast	462	580	49	13,6	2,4	11	18	54	5 225	53,9	14,2	17,9	2,500
Kostroma Oblast	364	441	60	13,9	13,3	9	15	84	5 329	18,9	10,9	13,3	3,833
Moscow	6 074	4 840	378	199,7	139,5			381	6 891	315,3	1 766,9	1 408,2	91,212
Moscow Oblast	339	368	33	22,1	12,7	23	29	29	2 513	32,3	10,1	11,0	7,649
Orlov Oblast	660	940	51	13,7	17,7	26	40	90	4 245	19,9	12,6	18,0	2,412
Ryazan Oblast	380	542	45	14,8	1,9	7	11	77	5 922	21,3	13,7	19,5	0,305
Smolensk Oblast	278	364	50	14,1	3,8	12	21	66	6 487	20,1	15,1	19,8	0,202
Tver Oblast	323	406	44	13,7	10,5	15	22	69	5 844	9,4	16,0	20,2	1,758
Tula Oblast	734	967	41	14,6	21,5	6	10	62	5 946	4,8	8,7	11,4	11,094
Yaroslavl Oblast	297	333	47	14,1	1,1	9	13	100	6 288	37,6	7,1	8,0	5,227
Marii El Republic	298	325	44	14,3	22,0	10	16	95	5 038	6,9	6,2	6,7	-
Republic of Mordovia	410	452	45	13,4	10,2	9	15	102	3 825	7,4	16,3	17,9	0,053
Chuvash Republic	262	347	39	14,7	8,8	20	34	72	4 057	12,0	2,4	3,2	0,262
Kirov Oblast	264	275	53	14,2	2,7	6	9	73	7 040	20,4	6,9	7,2	0,346

Table A.4 (continued)

Distribution of Direct Federal Expenditures among the Regions in 1998

	Direct expenditures per capita	Direct expenditures per capita, adjusted for the subsistence level	Government expenditures per capita	Government expenditures per government employee	Expenditures on industry in relation to gross industrial production	Expenditures on agriculture in relation to gross agricultural production	Expenditures on agriculture in relation to gross agricultural production at large enterprises	Expenditures on education per capita	Expenditures on education per student	Expenditures on public health per capita	Social expenditures per capita	Social expenditures per capita, adjusted for the subsistence level	Expenditures on culture per capita
Region	rub./per.	rub./per.	rub./per.	1000 rub./per.	1 : 1	1 : 1	1 : 1	rub./per.	rub./per.	rub./per.	rub./per.	rub./per.	rub./per.
Nizhegorod Oblast	256	335	37	13,5	3,4	8	13	58	3 505	31,6	7,6	9,9	0,539
Belgorod Oblast	337	470	40	13,8	8,4	11	15	62	3 571	5,7	21,9	30,5	1,618
Voronezh Oblast	302	411	41	14,8	3,0	7	10	89	4 335	18,5	16,1	21,8	0,693
Kursk Oblast	397	556	45	14,5	2,3	29	45	69	4 373	10,9	10,8	15,2	0,234
Lipetsk Oblast	274	378	39	14,0	0,2	7	11	54	4 868	11,7	11,6	16,1	
Tambov Oblast	272	418	44	12,7	6,1	12	19	93	6 306	5,6	18,0	27,7	
Republic of Kalmykia	579	698	86	15,5	14,7	87	163	69	3 753	9,5	51,4	62,0	
Republic of Tatarstan	107	158	18	9,2	0,1	2	3	44	2 445	4,7	8,4	12,4	0,019
Astrakhan Oblast	347	369	45	12,3	7,2	69	128	78	5 806	25,4	23,8	25,3	0,404
Volgograd Oblast	295	339	42	14,2	3,4	14	21	42	2 590	11,5	17,2	19,8	0,196

Penza Oblast	269	312	42	14,0	2,8	15	22	71	4 826	5,9	13,0	15,1	0,387
Samara Oblast	245	258	35	14,5	2,4	8	12	65	3 180	26,0	11,3	11,9	0,614
Saratov Oblast	421	445	41	13,5	22,6	34	55	89	4 369	34,7	19,5	20,6	1,892
Ulyanov Oblast	251	428	42	15,6	1,9	17	24	47	3 063	5,9	8,6	14,6	2,673
Republic of Adygeya	381	424	50	15,1	17,6	18	27	99	4 658	7,0	21,7	24,2	0,067
Republic of Dagestan	291	398	41	13,8	48,7	55	131	53	3 158	4,0	13,1	17,8	-
Ingush Republic	613	621	29	13,7	916,1	15	30	18	3 204	2,8	362,5	367,1	0,097
Kabardino-Balkar Republic	528	677	36	13,2	42,2	17	33	60	3 300	6,8	113,3	145,2	-
Karachaevo-Cherkess Republic	516	656	78	20,1	52,9	25	54	74	4 142	6,8	64,9	82,6	-
Republic of Northern Osetia	731	828	75	21,4	26,0	67	123	105	3 515	5,8	328,3	372,2	-
Chechen Republic													
Krasnodar Territory	285	386	33	14,5	4,4	24	31	53	4 910	24,8	21,0	28,3	0,115
Stavropol Territory	305	420	39	15,7	6,2	18	26	32	2 651	47,6	37,0	50,9	2,263
Rostov Oblast	567	775	35	13,0	97,5	25	35	101	4 901	38,8	13,0	17,8	0,833

Table A.4 (continued)

Distribution of Direct Federal Expenditures among the Regions in 1998

	Direct expenditures per capita	Direct expenditures per capita, adjusted for the subsistence level	Government expenditures per capita	Government expenditures per government employee	Expenditures on industry in relation to gross industrial production	Expenditures on agriculture in relation to gross agricultural production	Expenditures on agriculture in relation to gross agricultural production at large enterprises	Expenditures on education per capita	Expenditures on education per student	Expenditures on public health per capita	Social expenditures per capita	Social expenditures per capita, adjusted for the subsistence level	Expenditures on culture per capita
Region	rub./per.	rub./per.	rub./per.	1000 rub./per.	1 : 1	1 : 1	1 : 1	rub./per.	rub./per.	rub./per.	rub./per.	rub./per.	rub./per.
Republic of Bashkortostan	43	57	9	5,1	0,7	0	0	0	25	0,9	3,1	4,1	0,005
Udmurt Republic	299	300	45	15,6	1,4	6	10	79	4 320	8,3	12,9	13,0	0,144
Kurgan Oblast	349	414	52	14,8	6,5	11	17	105	8 576	36,1	19,1	22,7	-
Orenburg Oblast	302	362	46	15,9	1,0	9	13	143	10 075	7,5	15,4	18,5	0,121
Perm Oblast	327	357	43	15,4	11,4	7	11	94	6 579	14,1	14,3	15,6	0,124
Komi-Permyat Autonomous Region	440	481	73			3	6	46		12,1	11,7	12,7	12,853
Sverdlovsk Oblast	293	272	39	15,4	1,7	4	7	69	3 713	19,5	5,7	5,3	2,663
Chelyabinsk Oblast	335	370	41	15,4	10,1	16	25	70	4 285	24,6	7,7	8,5	1,109
Altai Republic	731	753	123	21,7	26,2	16	33	112	5 121	33,6	12,4	12,7	-

Altai Territory	323	361	52	16,6	9,5	9	13	84	5 307	10,4	31,0	34,7	0,030
Kemerovo Oblast	951	917	48	19,0	77,4	12	19	58	4 116	16,6	13,5	13,0	0,520
Novosibirsk Oblast	657	627	60	18,4	4,9	7	11	144	5 197	60,3	12,6	12,1	6,650
Omsk Oblast	344	395	46	16,1	4,7	5	7	114	5 832	17,2	14,1	16,2	0,104
Tomsk Oblast	592	587	76	23,8	8,3	7	12	210	5 678	78,0	19,4	19,2	0,028
Tyumen Oblast	356	248	68	8,9	0,3	10	15	102	7 268	9,3	17,6	12,2	0,089
Khanty-Mansi Autonomous Region	196	136	74			7	13	5		10,4	9,6	6,7	-
Yamal-Nenets Autonomous Region	300	209	84			42	70	4		22,1	14,1	9,8	-
Republic of Buryatia	481	449	67	21,1	6,6	17	31	134	7 059	8,7	7,8	7,3	0,029
Republic of Tyva	634	444	125	22,8	88,2	59	133	153	13 117	14,5	5,0	3,5	-
Republic of Khakasia	345	310	71	22,0	2,5	14	22	97	7 857	27,2	6,3	5,7	0,051
Krasnoyarsk Territory	500	505	68	20,5	1,0	14	20	164	7 980	28,8	6,5	6,5	0,842
Taimyr Autonomous Region	1 336	1 348	323			65	79	55		40,1	11,5	11,6	-
Evenk Autonomous Region	3 603	3 635	595			128	174	226		70,3	49,2	49,6	-

Table A.4 (continued)

Distribution of Direct Federal Expenditures among the Regions in 1998

	Direct expenditures per capita	Direct expenditures per capita, adjusted for the subsistence level	Government expenditures per capita	Government expenditures per government employee	Expenditures on industry in relation to gross industrial production	Expenditures on agriculture in relation to gross agricultural production	Expenditures on agriculture in relation to gross agricultural production at large enterprises	Expenditures on education per capita	Expenditures on education per student	Expenditures on public health per capita	Social expenditures per capita	Social expenditures per capita, adjusted for the subsistence level	Expenditures on culture per capita
Region	rub./per.	rub./per.	rub./per.	1000 rub./per.	1 : 1	1 : 1	1 : 1	rub./per.	rub./per.	rub./per.	rub./per.	rub./per.	rub./per.
Irkutsk Oblast	450	378	64	19,6	8,7	9	15	131	6 643	36,3	7,5	6,3	1,087
Ust-Orda Buryat Autonomous Region	180	151	74			1	2	29		9,4	6,8	5,7	-
Chita Oblast	446	305	75	19,2	20,5	14	28	109	11 252	52,0	4,5	3,1	2,863
Aga Buryat Autonomous Region	267	182	97			17	29	-		17,6	11,5	7,8	-
Republic of Sakha (Yakutia)	783	329	127	35,0	9,8	7	11	51	4 463	17,1	4,7	2,0	0,049
Jewish Autonomous Oblast	560	441	101	22,6	22,3	140	222	113	13 658	16,5	10,8	8,5	-

Chukchi Autonomous Region	2 939	1 357	418	51,3	49,2	45	54	77		93,1	7,7	3,5	0,234
Maritime Territory	565	446	69	21,1	33,3	26	42	152	8 256	23,7	6,0	4,7	0,485
Khabarovsk Territory	677	533	89	26,1	5,8	15	25	179	6 850	65,8	6,0	4,7	3,169
Amur Oblast	380	318	77	22,0	14,5	9	14	101	6 831	13,3	5,5	4,6	-
Kamchatka Oblast	1 214	542	203	32,9	4,5	19	25	132	10 717	47,2	12,2	5,5	-
Koryak Oblast	1 562	697	497			85	146	187		56,3	19,3	8,6	-
Magadan Oblast	1 305	610	292	38,9	40,3	404	472	151	12 924	51,3	7,1	3,3	0,119
Sakhalin Oblast	1 140	638	144	30,8	92,4	45	70	110	19 609	62,9	11,2	6,3	0,365
Kaliningrad Oblast	314	383	53	15,3	1,9	21	31	69	4 792	38,2	7,0	8,6	2,434

Appendix to Chapter 7

Table A.5

Individual Characteristics of Extrabudgetary Funds

Region	% of revenues collected in the regions going to the funds' territorial divisions						Per capita revenues, adjusted for the subsistence level, % of average			Portion of aid in revenues of the funds' territorial divisions, %			Exp./ per./ subs. level	Portion of income support in SEF*	Portion of benefit pay-ments in SIF**	Equalizing effect (revenues/per./subs. level, % of national average before and after aid) SEF,* 1998		MMIF,*** 1997	
	1996	1997	1998	1996	1997	1998	1998			1996	1997	1998	1998	1998	1998	before	after	before	after
Republic of Karelia	86,4	83,3	77,9	93,0	85,5	82,7	76,4	100,1	95,5	7,1	15,6	23,4	101,4	84,5	88,6	104,7	111,9	55,7	58,5
Komi Republic	92,4	92,6	84,1	71,4	85,4	69,6	145,7	136,3	138,2	0,4	0,9	6,7	130,0	70,0	82,5	140,6	138,2	127,5	125,5
Arkhangelsk Oblast	76,6	68,4	78,2	96,0	93,4	87,4	87,6	82,4	83,4	10,8	25,6	21,1	91,9	73,3	86,7	103,6	114,4	93,0	97,3
Nenets Autonomous Region				95,5	0,0	70,6	107,6	149,9	141,7				110,7	73,1	78,4	143,8	178,3	232,2	249,8
Vologda Oblast	91,4	84,4	93,9	98,0	84,0	73,2	94,6	122,8	117,3	4,1	12,1	11,4	120,2	71,5	79,0	121,0	116,8	99,7	101,8
Murmansk Oblast	99,1	99,5	99,8	94,8	84,6	80,8	80,5	110,0	104,2	0,3	1,6	6,1	102,3	74,5	75,3	134,8	139,0	142,1	142,1
St. Petersburg	77,3	88,2	94,2	42,7	61,1	66,7	106,4	27,5	42,9	0,2	1,4	2,3	26,6	54,4	64,2	109,7	105,9	96,1	94,6
Leningrad Oblast	78,0	70,1	85,7	61,7	70,4	56,6	74,5	366,1	309,4	8,5	25,5	14,1	337,0	77,3	72,8	69,8	83,8	83,1	87,5
Novgorod Oblast	72,1	76,8	66,9	91,8	77,9	70,6	75,2	99,3	94,6	13,8	15,5	34,5	134,2	67,9	71,6	90,0	90,9	103,4	111,6
Pskov Oblast	89,3	92,9	97,4	88,1	79,3	76,6	70,8	80,3	78,5	20,2	30,1	42,2	123,6	65,4	77,4	76,4	81,7	70,2	79,1
Bryansk Oblast	97,4	89,9	93,9	93,9	83,4	73,5	54,8	71,4	68,2	26,6	40,0	50,8	136,4	69,0	67,8	74,9	79,2	85,3	88,9

Vladimir Oblast	65,6	54,0	64,2	91,9	81,7	73,7	58,9	85,6	80,4	12,6	31,4	31,9	118,2	77,2	73,7	88,5	101,7	65,9	69,3
Ivanovo Oblast	56,0	44,2	52,6	91,2	83,9	85,3	64,6	65,5	65,3	21,8	39,6	46,5	120,8	56,9	73,9	75,5	86,7	47,2	50,2
Kaluga Oblast				89,3	77,2	68,9	60,5	93,5	87,0				126,0	64,3	74,1	93,3	90,3	143,8	146,7
Kostroma Oblast	58,5	57,2	64,7	97,1	92,2	87,0	116,0	83,7	90,0	24,3	30,2	49,5	116,7	74,6	72,6	85,6	103,5	69,7	70,5
Moscow				25,2	64,1	63,8	231,3	174,1	185,3				92,3			208,7	201,5	181,8	177,1
Moscow Oblast	69,5	78,7	81,3	93,4	69,1	51,6	54,8	112,7	101,5	5,2	14,0	11,4	115,8	58,9	62,1	104,6	102,1	100,2	97,1
Orlov Oblast				90,7	91,1	75,8	62,0	90,5	84,9				149,0	53,4	67,0	81,5	78,7	65,6	72,6
Ryazan Oblast				73,9	71,9	71,7	64,6	84,5	80,7				123,7	63,6	73,1	70,5	68,1	73,5	76,5
Smolensk Oblast	73,2	59,7	61,4	92,0	79,9	64,1	51,0	79,0	73,6	15,3	30,3	42,1	121,9	43,6	69,4	89,0	89,5	61,1	59,5
Tver Oblast				89,9	79,4	79,6	80,7	77,2	77,8				115,5	61,2	73,2	76,3	73,7	70,9	75,6
Tula Oblast	61,1	48,4	55,4	95,3	80,3	70,9	65,2	89,8	85,1	22,5	37,4	43,8	139,1	73,9	75,4	85,4	82,8	71,0	73,5
Yaroslavl Oblast	81,6	73,7	73,5	55,5	62,6	66,5	109,5	99,4	101,3	7,4	19,5	25,4	118,9	74,3	75,5	106,7	115,0	84,2	81,8
Marii El Republic	68,9	57,2	62,1	93,0	79,6	70,2	39,7	51,9	49,5	16,1	32,3	39,6	80,7	68,7	76,0	60,3	88,1	56,4	62,2
Republic of Mordovia				95,5	89,8	76,0	65,2	61,8	62,5				99,5	78,1	81,6	71,7	85,7	59,2	67,4
Chuvash Republic	71,2	57,2	61,3	87,4	81,9	70,2	41,6	63,4	59,2	16,1	32,0	34,9	94,3	74,8	84,9	73,2	74,8	58,1	62,1
Kirov Oblast	69,0	54,0	61,3	94,3	86,5	79,8	55,8	69,4	66,8	16,0	33,7	38,7	92,9	70,5	74,3	89,9	95,1	29,5	28,7
Nizhegorod Oblast				80,3	78,7	81,1	134,7	111,6	116,1				132,4	70,4	69,5	102,3	102,7	5,4	5,3

Table A.5 (continued)

Individual Characteristics of Extrabudgetary Funds

Region	% of revenues collected in the regions going to the funds' territorial divisions						Per capita revenues, adjusted for the subsistence level, % of average			Portion of aid in revenues of the funds' territorial divisions, %			Exp./ per./ subs. level	Portion of income support in SEF*	Portion of benefit pay-ments in SIF**	Equalizing effect (revenues/per./subs. level, % of national average before and after aid)			
																SEF,* 1998		MMIF,*** 1997	
	1996	1997	1998	1996	1997	1998	1998			1996	1997	1998	1998	1998	1998	before	after	before	after
Belgorod Oblast	69,1	66,3	66,6	95,7	83,8	86,1	145,4	107,2	114,6	8,6	24,3	27,9	140,6	46,5	75,5	118,0	114,0	92,2	95,7
Voronezh Oblast	64,1	49,4	56,9	94,6	88,2	81,0	76,2	76,4	76,4	18,4	36,2	43,0	117,3	62,9	76,9	71,9	69,6	62,4	62,8
Kursk Oblast	69,0	56,4	63,2	93,8	78,7	86,3	117,3	85,5	91,7	15,0	32,8	35,1	123,6	71,3	66,5	66,8	64,5	89,5	94,7
Lipetsk Oblast	86,0	75,0	72,1	96,5	86,4	74,5	143,3	116,8	121,9	5,6	19,4	28,0	139,2	46,5	78,8	110,1	106,3	89,3	89,4
Tambov Oblast	90,3	93,4	94,3	95,1	92,6	84,6	81,4	73,3	74,8	24,3	36,4	49,1	128,5	67,0	80,8	72,5	93,1	63,3	71,8
Republic of Kalmykia				73,5	52,5	20,9	60,6	77,0	73,8				91,1	69,7	77,3	76,3	81,6	58,0	66,9
Republic of Tatarstan				100,0	100,0	100,0	200,3	118,8	134,7				130,7			0,0	0,0	175,5	171,7
Astrakhan Oblast	95,1	90,2	98,9	73,4	59,2	61,6	45,0	90,4	81,5	7,1	17,3	7,4	93,8	72,7	63,1	95,1	99,4	86,9	93,2
Volgograd Oblast	74,6	75,8	72,4	85,0	81,3	72,6	71,6	76,4	75,5	5,1	15,0	19,7	93,1			77,5	74,8	103,1	104,5
Penza Oblast	63,7	56,0	58,0	91,8	93,2	85,3	66,0	56,8	58,6	17,3	31,8	41,6	92,5	65,2	74,6	55,5	67,1	61,7	62,9
Samara Oblast	99,8	99,8	99,9	82,3	73,3	75,8	151,1	144,6	145,8	0,3	2,1	2,5	144,1	78,5	68,3	129,5	125,1	269,4	263,7
Saratov Oblast	74,9	64,9	70,1	89,1	89,4	83,5	104,9	78,5	83,6	12,0	27,0	35,0	96,1	70,3	74,1	73,5	71,2	54,4	54,9

Ulyanov Oblast	98,3	98,5	95,8	92,0	79,7	82,2	104,0	92,1	94,4	10,0	25,0	31,8	118,1	65,9	80,8	98,6	95,7	65,8	69,3
Republic of Adygeya	98,5	95,4	99,5	93,7	74,6	67,6	41,4	71,4	65,6	20,9	33,3	48,0	126,5	66,9	68,4	62,1	60,0	70,9	71,8
Republic of Dagestan	42,0	29,9	37,2	94,9	95,7	90,1	17,8	35,4	32,0	33,8	45,6	58,1	81,5	71,6	88,5	32,6	53,3	32,3	35,9
Ingush Republic	71,6	76,9	75,0	87,7	23,9	20,7	4,3	38,5	31,8	12,1	12,4	41,1	66,1	78,6	70,0	39,0	89,3	39,8	40,5
Kabardino-Balkar Republic	45,8	29,0	29,0	0,0	92,4	80,4	31,2	32,8	32,5	32,2	40,1	58,5	92,7	77,6	75,4	42,3	59,3	91,2	93,1
Karachaevo-Cherkess Republic				83,8	69,9	60,6	13,2	52,5	44,8				98,8	58,2	77,0	51,0	53,5	38,5	39,1
Republic of Northern Osetia				95,7	90,7	78,2	19,3	44,5	39,6				87,0	70,4	78,4	48,5	59,7	32,2	34,0
Chechen Republic																			
Krasnodar Territory	96,9	95,6	98,7	89,3	82,6	80,9	72,2	99,8	94,4	15,1	18,2	32,9	125,1	73,1	72,7	92,6	89,5	63,5	61,6
Stavropol Territory	93,6	93,5	92,1	86,9	69,7	68,7	38,5	66,8	61,3	13,1	30,3	40,3	101,6	66,2	74,7	58,9	56,9	83,2	85,3
Rostov Oblast	66,4	63,0	62,3	93,5	80,3	71,6	52,4	72,8	68,8	2,4	10,6	7,8	120,5	47,6	75,1	79,9	77,2	159,6	159,0
Republic of Bashkor-tostan				100,0	100,0	100,0	213,8	103,5	125,0				113,7			0,0	0,0	122,1	119,9

Table A.5 (continued)

Individual Characteristics of Extrabudgetary Funds

Region	% of revenues collected in the regions going to the funds' territorial divisions						Per capita revenues, adjusted for the subsistence level, % of average			Portion of aid in revenues of the funds' territorial divisions, %			Exp./ per./ subs. level	Portion of income support in SEF*	Portion of benefit pay- ments in SIF**	Equalizing effect (revenues/per./subs. level, % of national average before and after aid)			
																SEF,* 1998		MMIF,*** 1997	
	1996	1997	1998	1996	1997	1998		1998		1996	1997	1998	1998	1998	1998	before	after	before	after
Udmurt Republic	86,3	79,0	82,6	74,7	85,0	80,9	86,1	88,6	88,2	6,5	18,3	19,1	97,4	55,9	78,3	100,3	119,3	68,2	69,0
Kurgan Oblast	94,9	92,9	96,8	93,2	85,4	81,5	75,9	75,7	75,8	15,5	31,7	37,6	106,5	65,3	72,0	97,9	108,9	56,5	59,6
Orenburg Oblast	77,8	71,5	73,9	71,9	67,8	65,0	90,7	96,0	95,0	6,0	18,6	21,5	105,6	31,9	80,3	87,2	84,3	93,8	92,6
Perm Oblast	100,0	100,0	100,0	76,3	64,1	69,9	147,6	130,0	133,5	2,0	7,6	4,8	124,6	69,5	78,0	136,4	131,9	139,9	137,6
Komi-Permyat Autonomous Region				87,6	59,0	66,4	29,1	66,6	59,3				115,5	56,1	82,9	67,9	87,8	49,4	48,5
Sverdlovsk Oblast	91,4	83,7	88,5	95,6	72,7	84,4	118,2	95,8	100,2	1,8	13,4	12,4	97,1	74,2	76,4	98,6	95,4	107,8	107,6
Chelyabinsk Oblast	93,7	80,9	80,1	96,0	82,1	85,5	109,9	101,8	103,4	2,2	15,8	18,2	112,1	46,1	75,3	114,6	110,7	117,2	115,7
Altai Republic	87,6	87,1	82,2	73,6	20,9	28,6	51,4	95,7	87,1	14,0	29,9	22,1	108,8	64,3	80,2	93,2	90,9	53,7	65,8
Altai Territory	65,3	53,7	55,7	85,2	81,7	83,0	60,3	55,7	56,6	19,3	34,3	45,5	92,1	60,1	80,3	77,3	75,2	50,0	51,9
Kemerovo Oblast	65,1	52,6	71,8	97,3	85,9	91,5	102,0	83,5	87,1	16,8	33,0	34,9	107,2	58,2	80,4	115,1	112,1	130,7	130,9

Novosibirsk Oblast	98,1	96,7	99,5	92,3	84,8	74,6	62,0	77,4	74,4	2,9	14,7	14,6	88,2	66,3	75,6	73,8	71,5	80,9	80,5
Omsk Oblast	63,4	77,4	99,6	24,6	44,8	44,2	136,3	75,1	87,0	8,4	22,1	31,0	96,6	48,9	78,6	88,7	85,6	58,9	58,0
Tomsk Oblast	100,0	100,0	100,0	88,3	55,8	77,6	118,6	113,0	114,1	1,1	5,2	11,5	112,0	69,6	78,0	89,5	93,9	152,8	152,6
Tyumen Oblast	94,9	94,3	87,6	93,2	85,5	73,3	80,2	92,8	90,4	0,6	3,4	7,0	88,1	56,2	56,0	97,0	93,7	73,0	72,4
Khanty-Mansi Autonomous Region				70,1	62,3	76,0	375,7	341,2	347,9				104,3	57,8	77,8	340,7	329,0	289,5	280,4
Yamal-Nenets Autonomous Region	99,6	81,2	99,7	94,4	90,2	87,4	325,0	334,8	332,9	0,0	0,1	0,1	118,5	47,8	77,8	258,6	249,8	203,6	199,5
Republic of Buryatia	76,0	63,2	71,4	84,2	79,2	75,0	51,1	78,5	73,2	8,9	26,0	25,0	89,0	67,0	82,7	74,1	71,6	128,4	131,9
Republic of Tyva				64,8	56,8	60,6	6,8	46,7	38,9				74,7	60,9	85,5	41,5	47,1	32,5	34,1
Republic of Khakasia	80,2	69,6	75,1	93,4	76,7	81,8	50,6	69,8	66,1	8,4	24,6	24,7	80,8	60,5	80,1	106,6	104,6	107,7	115,0
Krasnoyarsk Territory	94,8	95,2	98,0	74,1	77,7	81,9	131,1	149,4	145,8	0,3	0,9	0,9	124,1	64,0	77,6	166,9	161,2	140,0	139,1
Taimyr Autonomous Region				99,8	83,3	80,0	28,0	434,3	355,2				320,8	61,1	79,3	182,1	199,0	66,0	63,9
Evenk Autonomous Region				63,8	66,2	73,4	27,1	87,4	75,7				85,8	38,2	82,0	140,4	193,3	110,8	119,1

Table A.5 (continued)

Individual Characteristics of Extrabudgetary Funds

Region	% of revenues collected in the regions going to the funds' territorial divisions						Per capita revenues, adjusted for the subsistence level, % of average			Portion of aid in revenues of the funds' territorial divisions, %			Exp./per./subs. level	Portion of income support in SEF*	Portion of benefit payments in SIF**	Equalizing effect (revenues/per./subs. level, % of national average before and after aid) SEF,* 1998		MMIF,*** 1997	
	1996	1997	1998	1996	1997	1998	1998			1996	1997	1998	1998	1998	1998	before	after	before	after
Irkutsk Oblast	95,4	85,9	93,7	41,1	76,5	70,4	75,7	116,8	108,8	2,0	10,9	4,8	105,6	72,2	78,7	140,4	138,9	101,9	101,3
Ust-Orda Buryat Autonomous Region	100,0	100,0	100,0	98,2	88,1	87,4	14,3	44,9	38,9	26,1	31,4	60,8	89,6	42,5	82,9	50,3	48,6	63,6	71,1
Chita Oblast	72,0	82,6	98,2	78,5	79,4	75,8	29,8	70,9	62,9	8,1	9,9	1,6	60,1	70,1	75,1	63,9	61,7	47,6	50,9
Aga Buryat Autonomous Region	68,9	66,4	75,6	34,7	28,0	7,9	9,1	43,5	36,8	15,7	27,6	24,3	55,9	55,3	73,1	43,3	77,7		
Republic of Sakha (Yakutia)	98,5	95,4	95,4	88,9	93,2	86,2	51,5	77,7	72,6	0,4	2,1	0,7	66,7			125,0	124,3	97,4	95,7
Jewish Autonomous Oblast	59,5	70,9	65,2	84,5	84,5	82,8	39,6	72,0	65,7	16,4	13,1	27,7	93,2	67,6	73,3	77,0	92,6	153,9	171,0

Chukchi Autonomous Region				86,2	82,2	71,0	28,0	66,0	58,6				60,9	57,7	84,1	67,3	80,9	129,5	142,4
Maritime Territory	96,1	97,8	94,0	92,6	86,9	69,9	63,9	100,9	93,7	0,3	0,5	3,4	91,3	57,7	70,5	94,6	98,2	77,5	79,9
Khabarovsk Territory	95,4	98,1	97,8	65,1	74,9	63,5	70,3	118,9	109,5	2,2	1,8	6,0	103,7	64,1	77,9	111,5	118,2	144,8	146,7
Amur Oblast	95,7	95,6	95,9	92,9	87,5	86,1	71,3	87,0	83,9	2,0	12,1	13,4	74,1	58,1	83,4	82,1	81,5	84,6	87,3
Kamchatka Oblast	100,0	100,0	100,0	93,8	82,3	65,9	57,6	99,7	91,5	2,1	4,9	4,9	84,6	71,5	78,4	124,5	129,5	106,0	110,7
Koryak Autonomous Region				96,8	49,9	65,2	20,5	66,7	57,7				56,8	66,9	86,0	54,0	55,2	73,7	71,4
Magadan Oblast				81,6	74,4	69,7	53,9	225,8	192,4				70,0	55,6	78,3	89,9	92,8	69,8	71,7
Sakhalin Oblast				84,9	65,1	66,7	64,4	94,8	88,9				92,3	67,6	84,5	110,0	110,3	58,9	62,2
Kaliningrad Oblast	87,6	90,5	76,6	80,0	65,2	59,8	65,7	102,0	94,9	0,7	7,3	10,0	104,8	52,4	66,5	88,8	91,3	72,7	70,6
Russian Federation				70,6	74,3	73,0	100,0	100,0	100,0				100,0	57,9	74,6	100,0	100,0	100,0	100,0

* SEF — State Employment Fund.
** SIF — Social Insurance Fund.
*** MMIF — Mandatory Medical Insurance Fund.

Appendix to Chapter 8

Table A.6

Individual Characteristics of the Regions' Consolidated and "Expanded" Budgets in 1998

	Regions' consolidated budgets								Regions' "expanded budgets"					
						Subsidizing of			% of extrabudgetary component					
Region	Ratio of revenues to expenditures, %	Portion of federal expenditures, %	Expenditures/ subs. level, % of national average	Portion of production expenditures, %	Portion of social expenditures, %	the economy*	industry**	agriculture***	in revenues	in expenditures	Ratio of revenues to expenditures, %	Portion of production expenditures, %	Portion of social expenditures	Revenue/ GRP, % (1997)
Republic of Karelia	69,7	14,8	76,9	7,9	43,4	2,2	0,7	9,4	51,8	43,8	81,4	11,5	61,1	34,6
Komi Republic	80,1	17,9	150,4	13,8	34,2	4,9	3,9	16,0	40,7	35,5	87,1	16,0	50,4	37,9
Arkhangelsk Oblast	89,9	19,8	59,1	6,7	51,9	1,9	0,2	5,1	48,7	44,9	96,7	11,4	65,8	
Nenets Autonomous Region	84,5	10,5	190,3	10,2	45,9		0,0	39,8						
Vologda Oblast	103,8	8,9	81,3	9,6	51,3	1,3	0,1	5,5	44,6	44,7	103,7	13,9	64,5	33,9
Murmansk Oblast	86,6	10,5	93,0	6,3	44,9	1,6	0,3	14,2						
St. Petersburg	121,7	16,5	90,9	12,2	44,9	3,0	0,8		35,8	38,1	117,4	13,9	59,5	41,8
Leningrad Oblast	100,2	12,4	77,2	7,2	35,0	2,1	0,7	2,7	36,0	39,5	94,7	11,1	53,9	39,7
Novgorod Oblast	75,6	11,3	82,5	10,6	42,7	2,7	0,3	6,2	51,6	44,5	86,7	12,3	61,8	36,6
Pskov Oblast	69,9	16,8	65,1	10,3	51,1	2,8	1,2	5,3	46,8	48,8	67,3	11,4	68,9	30,0

Bryansk Oblast	73,7	39,4	73,4	9,5	39,0	2,9	1,2	4,5	40,8	46,9	66,1	9,6	63,0	30,8
Vladimir Oblast	97,4	13,9	70,0	7,7	42,1	1,8	0,2	3,4	46,7	46,0	98,7	10,0	62,9	41,6
Ivanovo Oblast	73,7	18,9	64,4	12,0	48,5	3,8	0,5	12,9	55,0	48,7	84,0	11,4	68,4	45,3
Kaluga Oblast	88,0	20,2	80,4	7,4	41,8	2,6	0,3	6,3						
Kostroma Oblast	78,6	12,2	110,3	10,1	40,3	3,2	1,1	4,4	46,7	40,6	87,6	19,4	51,1	40,5
Moscow	111,7	53,2	259,7	17,5	40,4	2,0	5,5							
Moscow Oblast	153,5	12,8	84,2	9,6	40,3	2,2	1,1	5,3	33,8	43,3	131,4	13,0	58,6	40,5
Orlov Oblast	71,7	25,5	95,5	12,2	44,6	6,6	0,9	13,4						
Ryazan Oblast	119,6	19,1	72,9	10,4	44,0	2,3	0,2	3,8						
Smolensk Oblast	88,7	15,2	67,7	12,2	48,0	2,1	0,2	5,4	49,3	46,9	92,9	12,1	66,8	34,0
Tver Oblast	99,0	16,3	70,1	10,3	47,1	2,9	0,7	6,0						
Tula Oblast	81,8	31,7	86,3	11,0	33,9	4,6	0,8	6,2						
Yaroslavl Oblast	101,6	9,9	99,2	12,1	41,4	2,7	0,3	6,0	38,8	39,2	100,9	14,3	57,4	36,0
Marii El Republic	79,3	18,1	54,4	8,5	52,7	2,4	1,1	3,9	50,0	43,8	89,1	10,2	68,0	35,2
Republic of Mordovia	66,1	19,1	77,3	9,6	40,3	2,7	0,6	5,5						
Chuvash Republic	87,4	14,2	67,3	14,1	49,1	3,1	1,1	3,9						

Table A.6 (continued)

Individual Characteristics of the Regions' Consolidated and "Expanded" Budgets in 1998

	Regions' consolidated budgets								Regions' "expanded budgets"					
						Subsidizing of			% of extrabudgetary component					
Region	Ratio of revenues to expenditures, %	Portion of federal expenditures, %	Expenditures/ subs. level, % of national average	Portion of production expenditures, %	Portion of social expenditures, %	the economy*	industry**	agriculture***	in revenues	in expenditures	Ratio of revenues to expenditures, %	Portion of production expenditures, %	Portion of social expenditures	Revenue/ GRP, % (1997)
Kirov Oblast	97,2	13,8	56,3	12,1	49,6	1,8	0,5	3,0						
Nizhegorod Oblast	121,9	9,8	101,2	12,2	42,1	2,2	0,3	6,7						
Belgorod Oblast	99,8	15,0	88,0	10,7	53,1	2,0	0,3	5,8	46,8	46,7	100,1	13,9	66,8	33,5
Voronezh Oblast	93,3	16,6	71,4	16,6	45,1	2,5	0,3	4,8	48,4	46,1	97,5	14,0	65,3	35,2
Kursk Oblast	78,6	15,8	99,2	15,9	32,5	4,2	0,5	9,3	46,0	39,9	87,4	16,8	52,1	32,8
Lipetsk Oblast	91,4	10,5	106,4	11,9	42,5	3,8	0,0	9,2	44,3	42,1	95,0	15,2	58,4	36,0
Tambov Oblast	89,4	18,1	64,4	9,8	52,0	2,6	0,8	3,4	40,9	50,7	74,6	11,5	69,7	31,7
Republic of Kalmykia	90,8	19,5	105,7	12,0	49,6	5,0	1,5	9,3						
Republic of Tatarstan	72,8	2,4	182,3	11,7	39,6	5,4	0,2	16,7						
Astrakhan Oblast	94,2	17,5	61,3	9,0	49,1	1,8	1,0	9,3	42,6	45,1	90,1	8,9	68,1	32,1
Volgograd Oblast	112,8	17,5	56,6	10,3	46,5	2,1	0,3	4,9	47,0	49,7	107,2	11,9	66,3	34,3

Penza Oblast	102,2	20,1	43,3	9,7	51,8	2,3	0,7	3,5	51,9	51,9	102,2	11,7	69,8	40,1
Samara Oblast	144,5	7,9	100,2	11,1	50,2	1,5	0,3	4,6	35,3	45,5	121,6	17,0	61,9	38,6
Saratov Oblast	96,9	19,6	73,9	18,6	47,7	4,7	1,3	12,8	44,9	44,1	98,4	21,4	59,8	35,2
Ulyanov Oblast	115,7	14,1	83,4	15,7	52,7	2,7	0,9	6,4	33,4	44,0	97,4	17,9	64,4	29,0
Republic of Adygeya	40,7	15,8	95,0	14,0	54,2	7,5	5,8	11,3	47,4	39,0	47,2	12,0	68,7	38,1
Republic of Dagestan	23,2	18,8	63,6	11,5	55,0	4,3	9,3	6,9	74,7	40,2	54,8	12,8	67,2	36,3
Ingush Republic	26,4	24,8	78,4	14,2	44,9	0,3	128,0	0,9	51,3	27,7	39,1	11,7	58,7	52,4
Kabardino-Balkar Republic	36,2	17,8	100,7	15,7	46,2	4,3	10,6	4,7	56,4	31,8	56,6	13,1	60,9	36,9
Karachaevo-Cherkess Republic	52,1	28,1	70,3	11,1	50,7	4,3	3,0	5,6						
Republic of Northern Osetia	41,2	30,7	76,3	11,7	50,9	6,3	5,2	13,0						
Chechen Republic														
Krasnodar Territory	111,4	16,7	68,4	9,3	57,6	2,4	0,6	4,5	38,1	49,0	91,8	13,2	69,9	30,8
Stavropol Territory	90,4	16,8	62,9	7,8	45,2	1,8	0,5	3,1						
Rostov Oblast	84,0	29,2	79,0	18,3	40,9	5,2	5,2	2,0						

Table A.6 (continued)

Individual Characteristics of the Regions' Consolidated and "Expanded" Budgets in 1998

Region	Regions' consolidated budgets								Regions' "expanded budgets"					
	Ratio of revenues to expenditures, %	Portion of federal expenditures, %	Expenditures/ subs. level, % of national average	Portion of production expenditures, %	Portion of social expenditures, %	Subsidizing of			% of extrabudgetary component		Ratio of revenues to expenditures, %	Portion of production expenditures, %	Portion of social expenditures	Revenue/ GRP, % (1997)
						the economy*	industry**	agriculture***	in revenues	in expenditures				
Republic of Bashkortostan	81,5	1,3	128,8	13,8	46,2	3,2	0,9	9,2						
Udmurt Republic	97,6	10,7	87,9	8,5	44,9	3,0	0,2	6,2	37,6	37,3	98,1	12,0	58,7	36,7
Kurgan Oblast	77,4	19,6	67,9	9,3	56,7	1,9	0,7	1,9						
Orenburg Oblast	104,7	12,8	88,2	11,4	49,8	2,6	0,2	5,2	40,1	41,2	102,8	13,7	63,5	34,7
Perm Oblast	121,6	11,6	94,7	12,4	51,1	2,2	0,6	9,6	36,5	42,8	109,6	16,1	62,9	
Komi-Permyat Autonomous Region	46,1	20,6	84,5	8,0	53,8		7,8	2,2						
Sverdlovsk Oblast	130,8	10,4	76,6	12,2	46,9	1,9	1,2	5,5	35,1	42,2	116,5	16,0	60,3	37,0
Chelyabinsk Oblast	120,7	13,7	83,9	11,6	45,5	1,8	0,6	2,7	39,5	43,6	112,4	15,4	60,4	37,5
Altai Republic	78,4	27,3	86,8	4,1	53,6	2,9	4,7	4,3	38,7	38,1	79,2	5,7	68,2	35,9
Altai Territory	63,1	15,7	67,6	11,5	45,4	3,5	1,4	5,6	52,6	41,7	77,6	13,4	61,5	38,3

Kemerovo Oblast	77,1	24,5	114,9	22,2	33,0	6,1	4,1	5,3	42,0	34,3	87,3	20,8	49,8	39,1
Novosibirsk Oblast	108,3	26,4	61,3	10,2	45,3	2,8	1,1	5,3	37,1	42,9	98,3	11,6	63,0	30,9
Omsk Oblast	87,9	12,2	95,7	10,5	44,0	2,8	0,8	6,5	42,6	37,1	96,4	10,9	60,5	33,1
Tomsk Oblast	103,4	17,0	103,1	10,2	42,3	2,3	0,5	12,0	33,0	38,1	95,6	14,1	56,5	38,2
Tyumen Oblast	103,5	8,7	92,0	14,6	45,2	6,0	1,9	13,3	35,6	35,7	103,3	16,8	57,4	
Khanty-Mansi Autonomous Region	119,4	1,1	338,9	6,6	33,1		0,5	31,8						
Yamal-Nenets Autonomous Region	108,2	1,1	462,3	21,9	25,7		6,9	185,7	25,7	15,8	122,6	24,6	31,3	
Republic of Buryatia	62,6	21,0	74,5	8,7	43,1	2,1	0,9	4,4						
Republic of Tyva	21,6	22,6	64,6	6,8	61,9	4,2	6,4	3,7						
Republic of Khakasia	90,7	13,1	67,2	10,4	48,7	1,9	0,3	4,6	43,5	40,4	95,7	11,4	64,1	32,8
Krasnoyarsk Territory	111,9	13,5	114,2	7,1	43,0	1,5	0,2	4,2						
Taimyr Autonomous Region	65,8	8,6	261,3	2,7	39,9		24,6	26,5						
Evenk Autonomous Region	26,5	22,1	309,9	12,0	29,9		82,9	39,0						

Table A.6 (continued)

Individual Characteristics of the Regions' Consolidated and "Expanded" Budgets in 1998

	Regions' consolidated budgets								Regions' "expanded budgets"					
						Subsidizing of			% of extrabudgetary component					
Region	Ratio of revenues to expenditures, %	Portion of federal expenditures, %	Expenditures/ subs. level, % of national average	Portion of production expenditures, %	Portion of social expenditures, %	the economy*	industry**	agriculture***	in revenues	in expenditures	Ratio of revenues to expenditures, %	Portion of production expenditures, %	Portion of social expenditures	Revenue/ GRP, % (1997)
Irkutsk Oblast	105,9	15,8	81,0	8,7	50,4	1,0	0,4	4,6	40,0	41,6	103,1	11,2	65,0	
Ust-Orda Buryat Autonomous Region	26,2	8,7	68,0	6,3	59,1		0,2	1,3	52,3	43,6	31,0	14,6	65,9	
Chita Oblast	77,7	21,8	48,1	9,9	53,6	2,1	2,3	3,7	45,2	37,5	88,6	9,9	67,3	
Aga Buryat Autonomous Region	86,1	16,2	37,5	5,2	69,4		1,0	1,8						
Republic of Sakha (Yakutia)	57,0	9,2	119,1	8,8	54,6	5,3	0,6	19,8	42,6	29,7	69,7	10,9	63,3	33,8
Jewish Autonomous Oblast	42,1	21,5	70,8	9,5	46,4		4,1	3,2	61,5	40,2	65,4	10,0	63,6	
Chukchi Autonomous Region	35,1	21,8	124,5	16,3	43,4	9,0	13,5	16,0						

Maritime Territory	71,1	18,5	75,7	14,6	38,1	3,9	3,4	7,1	47,0	38,7	82,3	14,1	56,9	35,0
Khabarovsk Territory	91,9	17,6	94,0	15,5	43,4	3,2	3,4	7,3	39,7	36,0	97,5	15,4	58,3	28,3
Amur Oblast	64,6	14,4	65,7	7,1	48,2	2,7	1,5	6,3	43,9	37,8	71,7	11,8	60,4	21,4
Kamchatka Oblast	55,3	19,2	93,9	10,5	35,3	4,2	2,8	5,4	46,1	34,1	67,6	10,8	53,6	
Koryak Autonomous Region	34,5	14,5	95,7	2,6	50,9		0,1	27,3						
Magadan Oblast	66,3	17,3	99,2	7,7	31,7	2,9	2,4	18,9						
Sakhalin Oblast	81,6	23,4	86,1	19,4	39,1	4,0	8,1	6,0						
Kaliningrad Oblast	90,4	14,6	71,5	5,5	42,5	2,0	0,3	7,0	46,8	43,1	96,7	8,5	62,0	38,4
Russian Federation	100,9	22,0	100,0	12,9	42,8	3,0	1,5	6,9						

* Ratio of production expenditures to GRP in 1997.

** Ratio of expenditures on industry, power generation, and construction to industrial output in 1998.

*** Ratio of expenditures on agriculture and fishing to agricultural output in 1997.

MAPS

MAP 1

Percentage of Funds Returned to the Regions According to the Balance of Financial Flows Taking into Account Financial Aid to the Regional Budgets in 1998

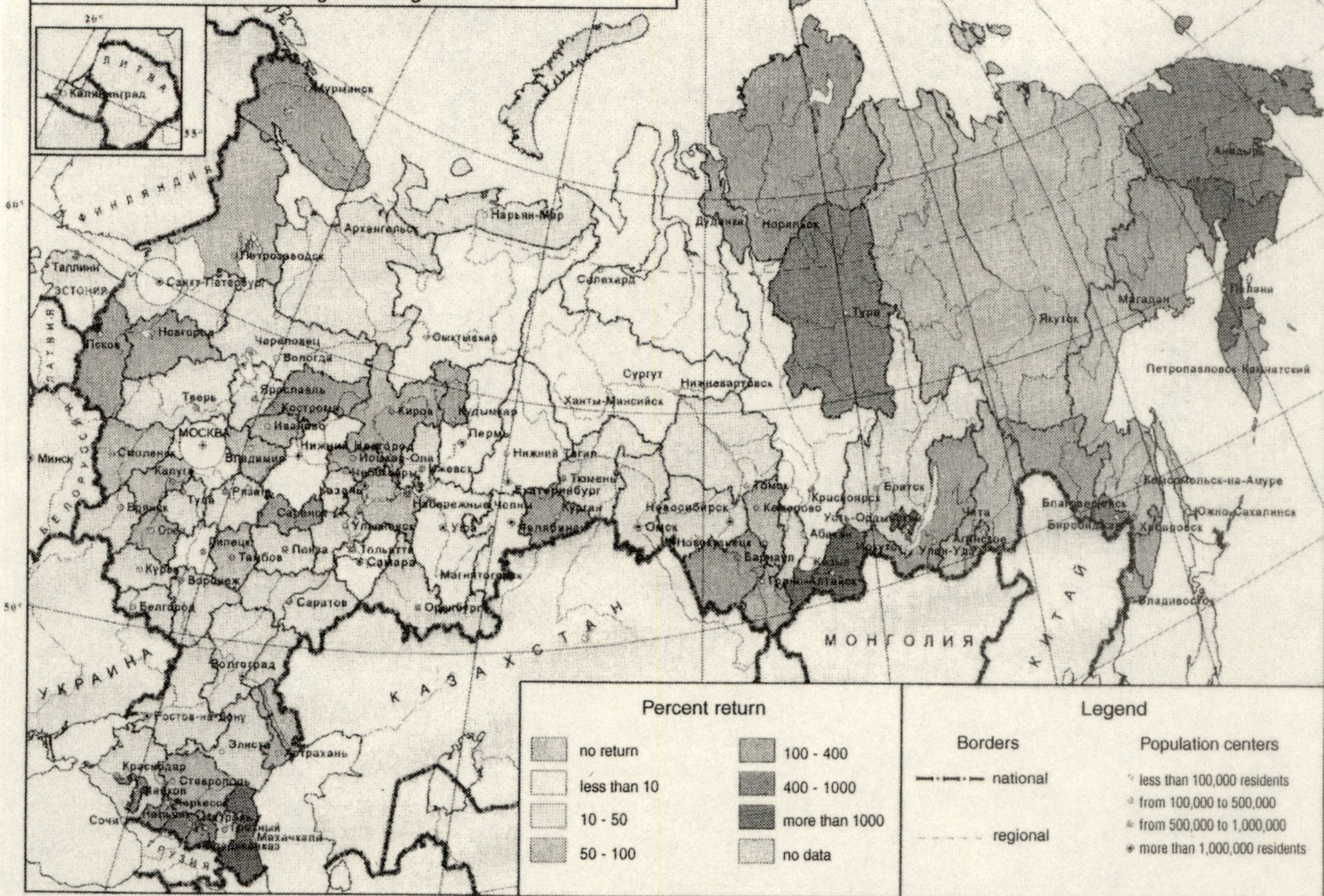

MAP 2

Per Capita Balance of Financial Flows Taking into Account Financial Aid to the Regions in 1998

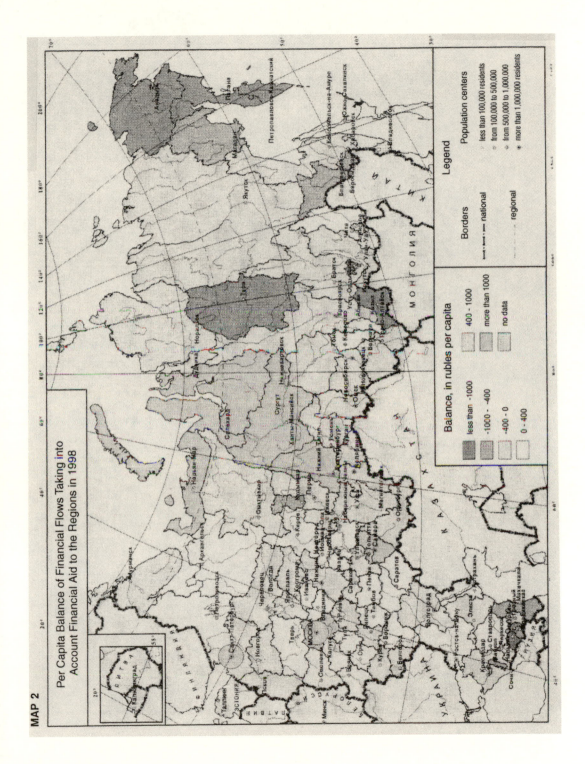

MAP 3

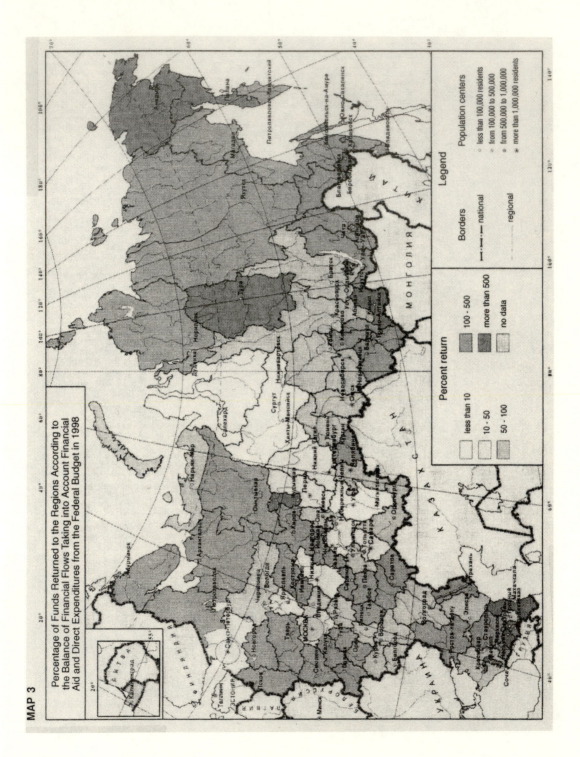

Percentage of Funds Returned to the Regions According to the Balance of Financial Flows Taking into Account Financial Aid and Direct Expenditures from the Federal Budget in 1998
Percent return
less than 10
10 - 50
50 - 100
100 - 500
more than 500
no data
Legend
Borders
national
regional
Population centers
less than 100,000 residents
from 100,000 to 500,000
from 500,000 to 1,000,000
more than 1,000,000 residents
МОНГОЛИЯ
КАЗАХСТАН
УКРАИНА
КИТАЙ

MAP 4

Per Capita Balance of Financial Flows Taking into Account Financial Aid and Direct Expenditures from the Federal Budget in 1998

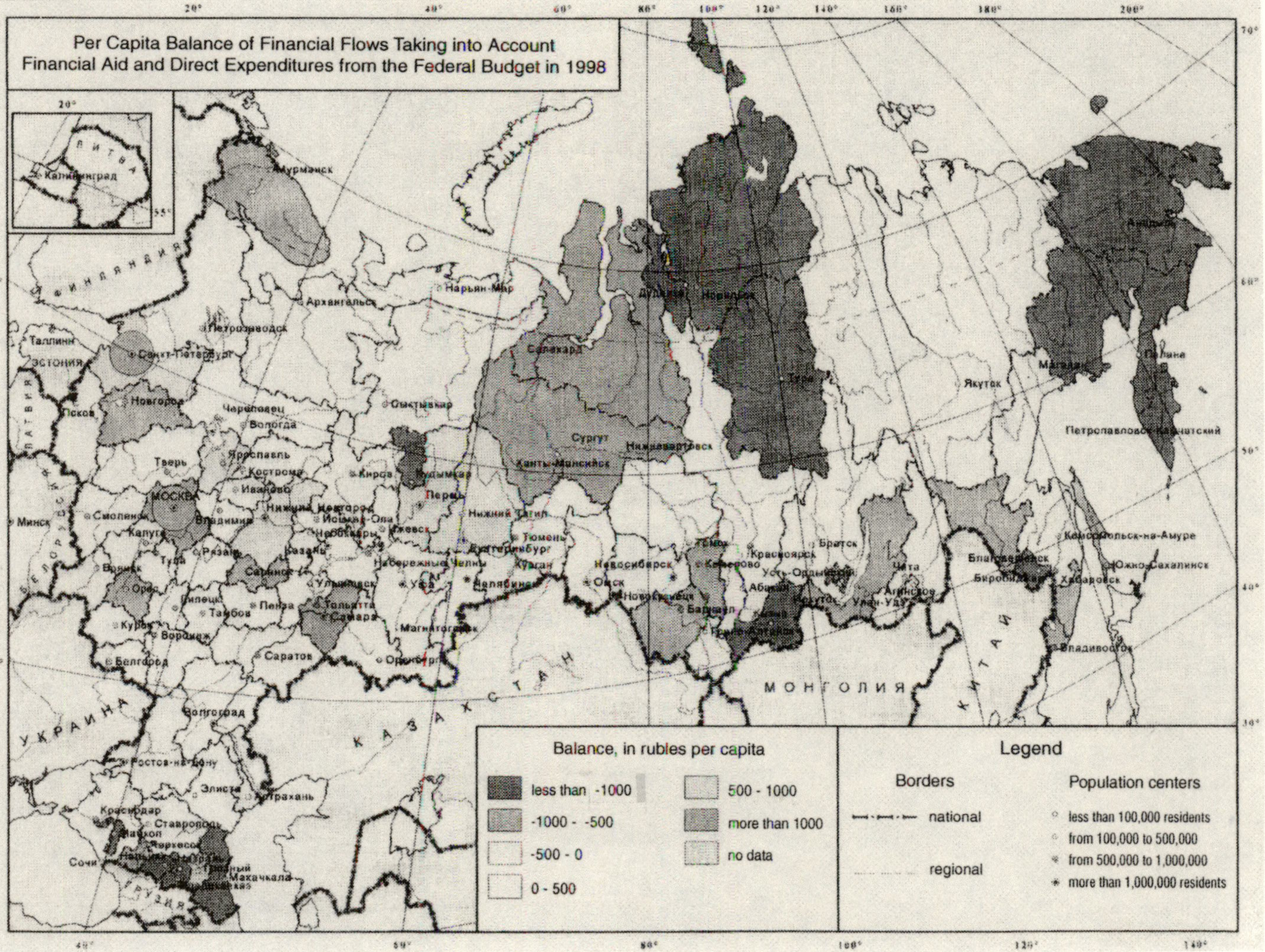

MAP 5

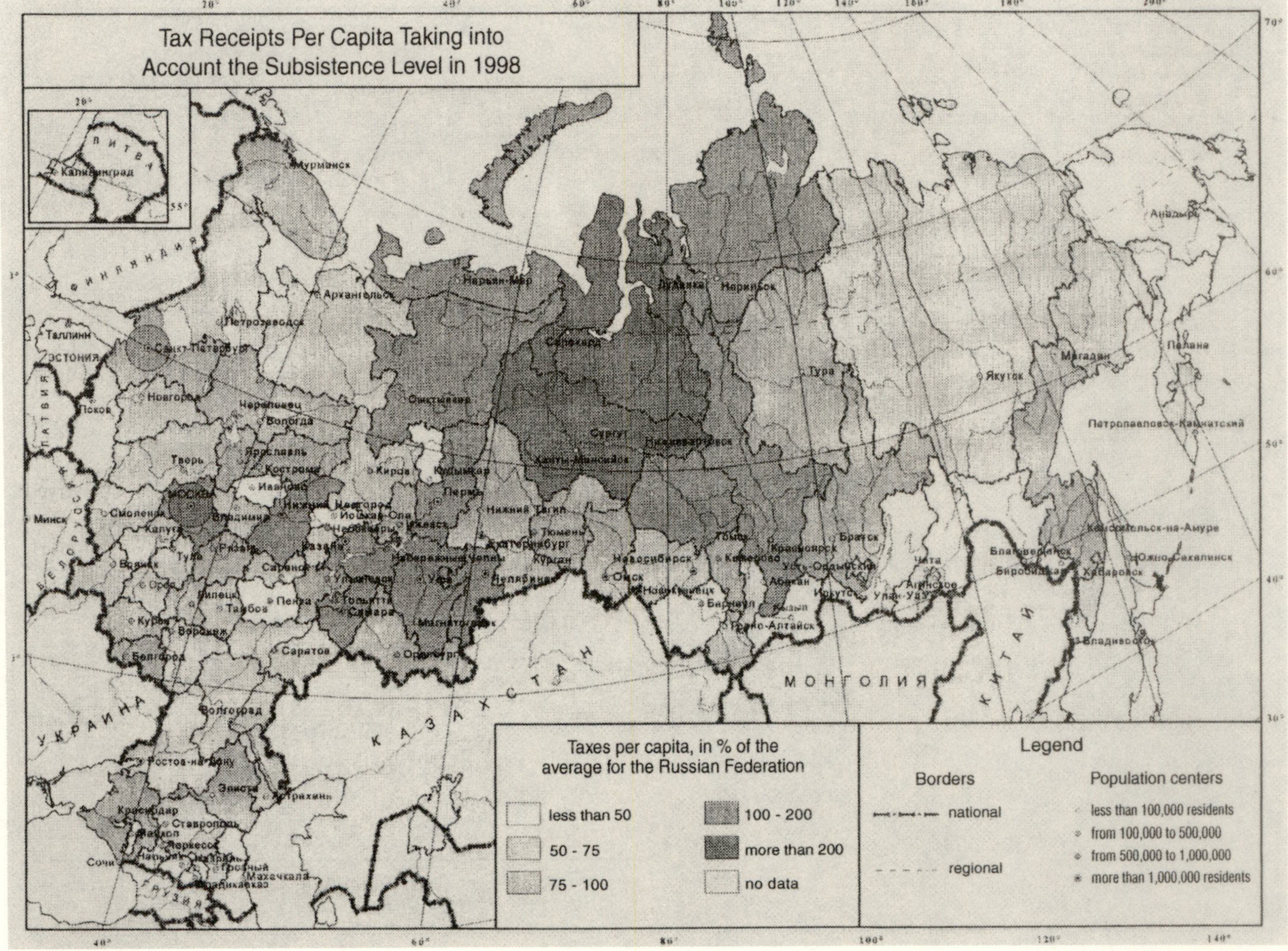
Tax Receipts Per Capita Taking into
Account the Subsistence Level in 1998
Taxes per capita, in % of the
average for the Russian Federation
less than 50
50 - 75
75 - 100
100 - 200
more than 200
no data
Legend
Borders
national
regional
Population centers
less than 100,000 residents
from 100,000 to 500,000
from 500,000 to 1,000,000
more than 1,000,000 residents
МОНГОЛИЯ
УКРАИНА
Москва
Архангельск
Петрозаводск
Новгород
Тверь
Смоленск
Минск
Псков
Таллинн
Кирде
Тамбов
Пенза
Саратов
Белгород
Волгоград
Ставрополь
Махачкала
Сочи
Сургут
Ханты-Мансийск
Нижний Тагил
Екатеринбург
Тюмень
Курган
Новосибирск
Омск
Кемерово
Красноярск
Братск
Абакан
Кызыл
Чита
Тура
Норильск
Якутск
Магадан
Палана
Петропавловск-Камчатский
Комсомольск-на-Амуре
Южно-Сахалинск
Благовещенск
Хабаровск
Владивосток

MAP 6

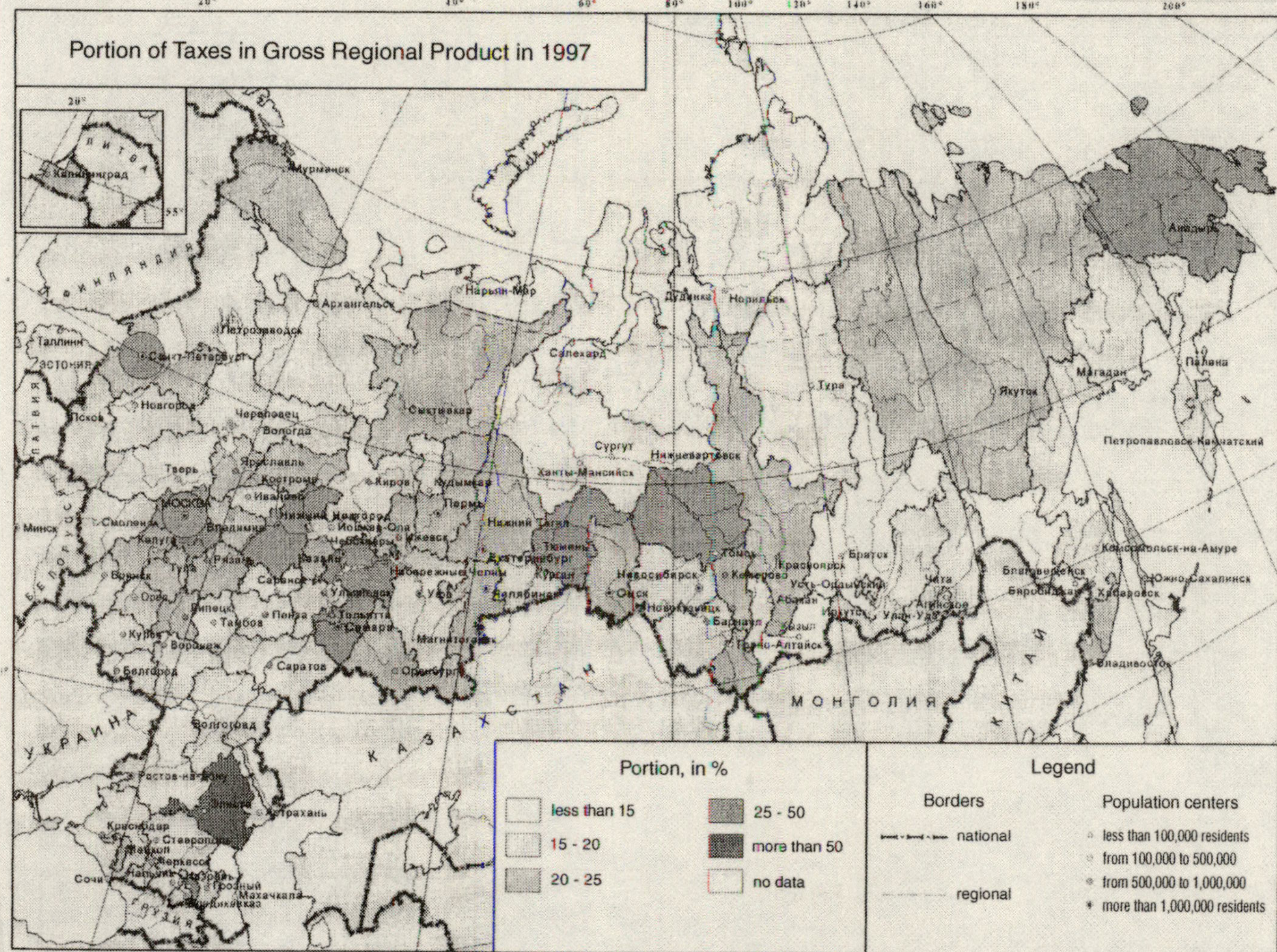

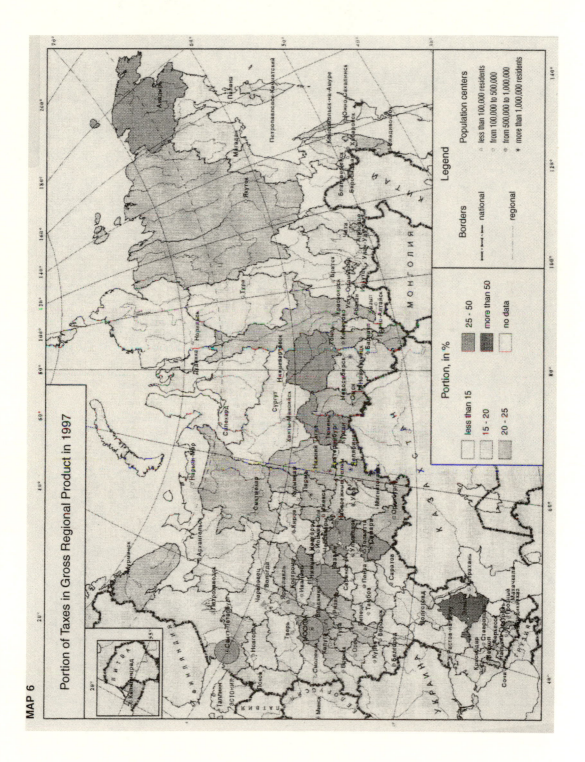

Portion of Taxes in Gross Regional Product in 1997
Portion, in %
less than 15
15 - 20
20 - 25
25 - 50
more than 50
no data
Legend
Borders
national
regional
Population centers
less than 100,000 residents
from 100,000 to 500,000
from 500,000 to 1,000,000
more than 1,000,000 residents
МОНГОЛИЯ
КАЗАХСТАН
КИТАЙ
УКРАИНА
ФИНЛЯНДИЯ

MAP 7

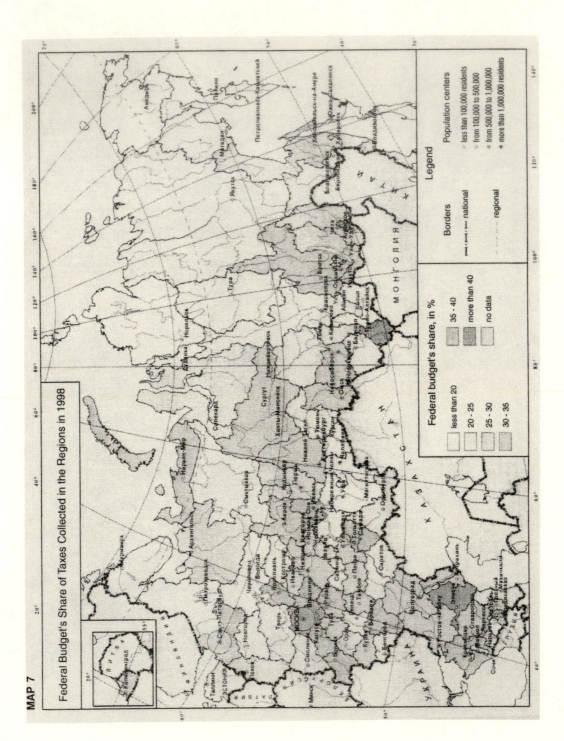

Federal Budget's Share of Taxes Collected in the Regions in 1998

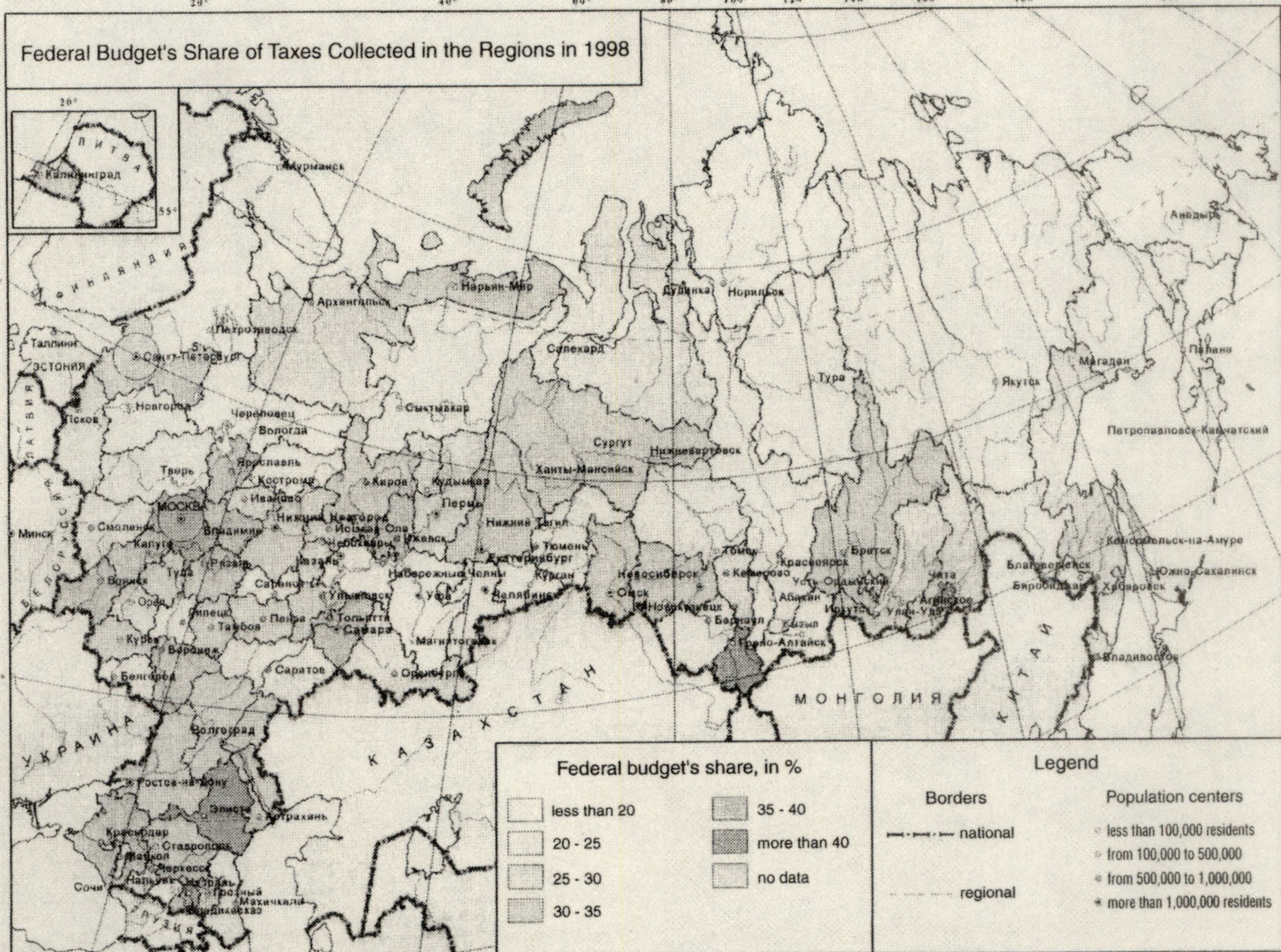

MAP 8

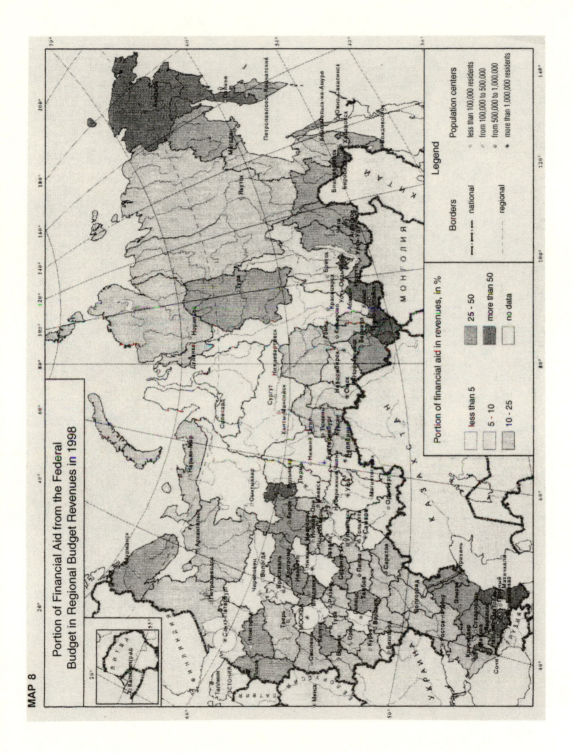

Portion of Financial Aid from the Federal Budget in Regional Budget Revenues in 1998

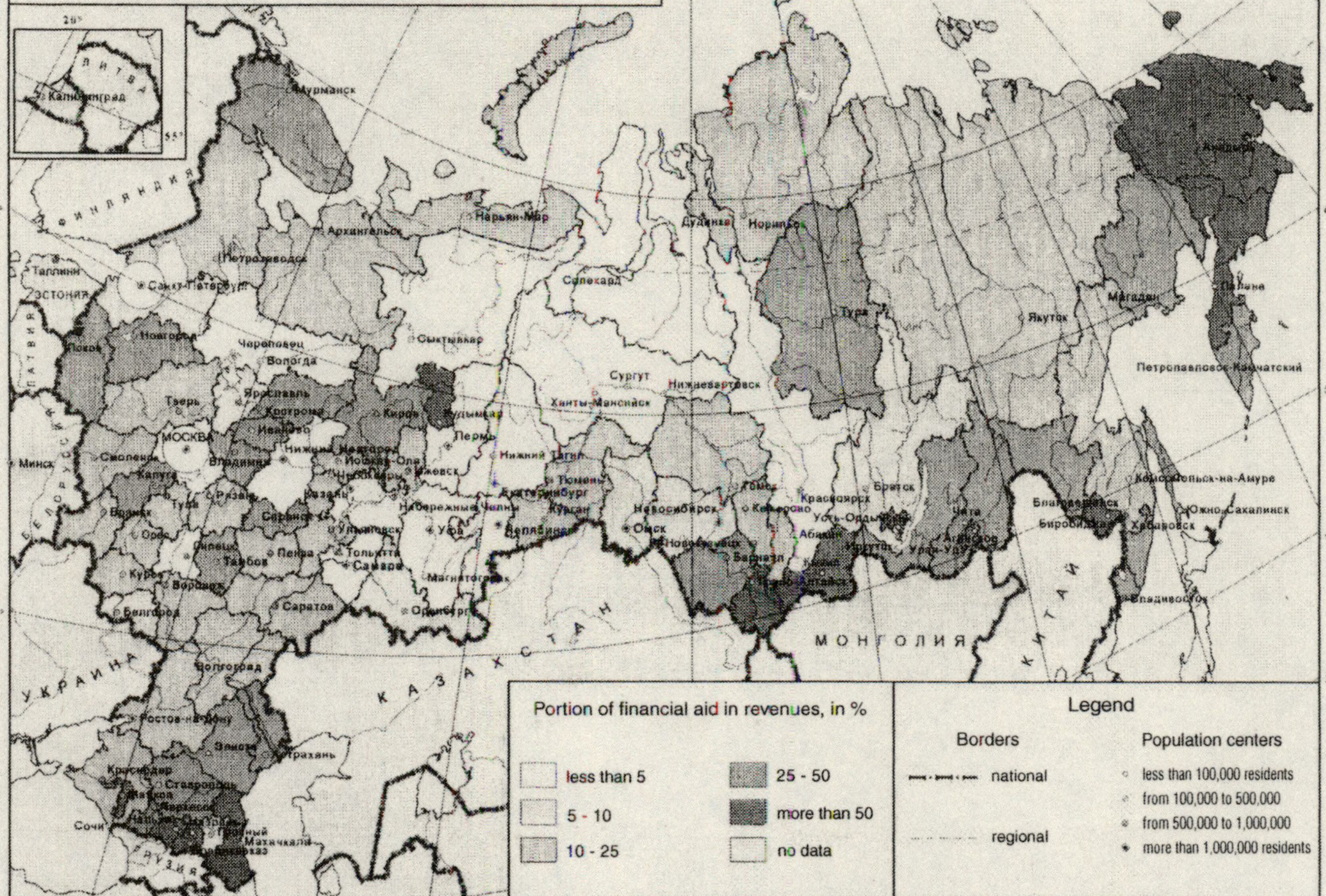

MAP 9

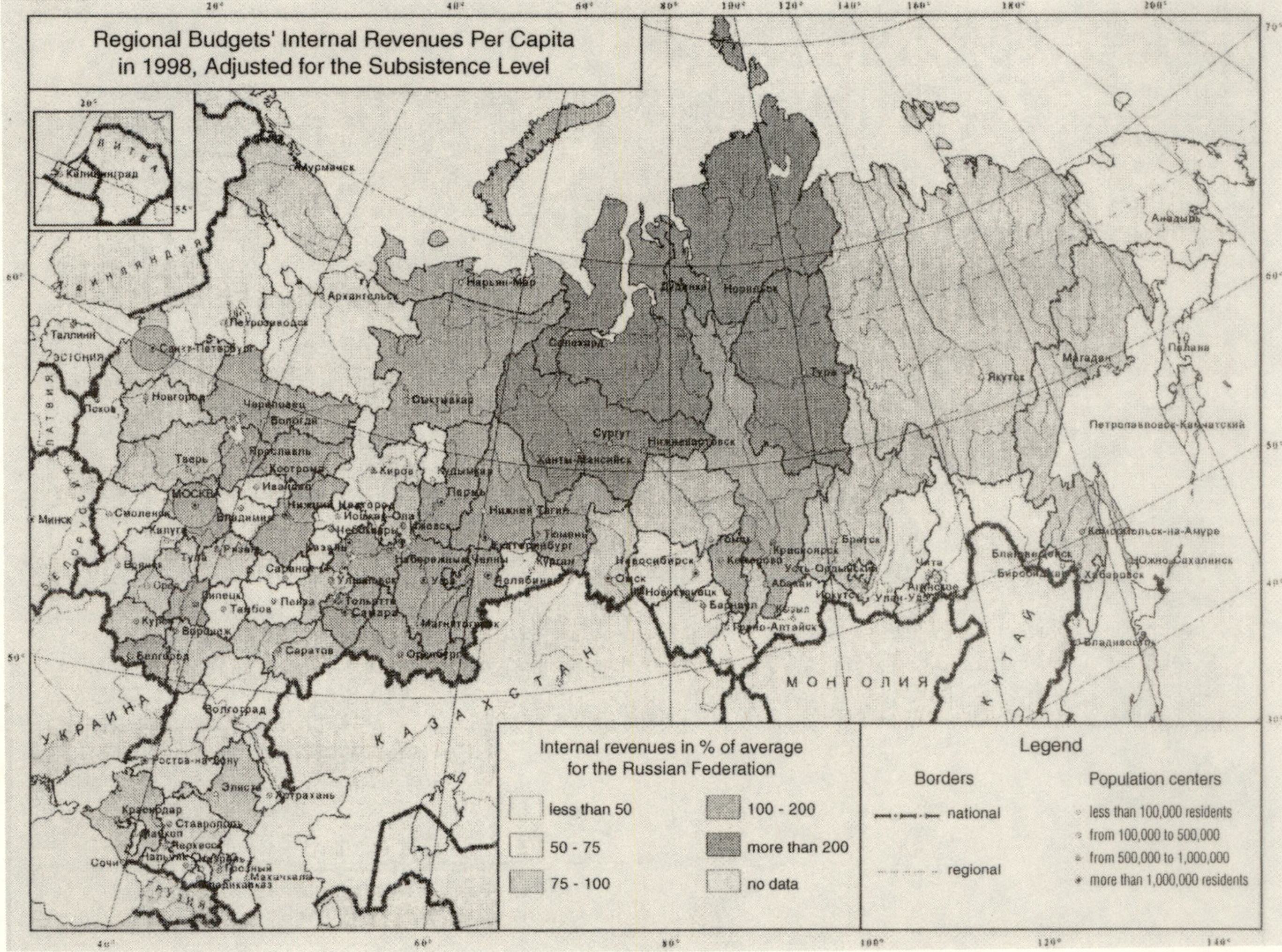
Regional Budgets' Internal Revenues Per Capita
in 1998, Adjusted for the Subsistence Level
Internal revenues in % of average
for the Russian Federation
less than 50
50 - 75
75 - 100
100 - 200
more than 200
no data
Legend
Borders
national
regional
Population centers
less than 100,000 residents
from 100,000 to 500,000
from 500,000 to 1,000,000
more than 1,000,000 residents
МОНГОЛИЯ
КАЗАХСТАН
УКРАИНА
КИТАЙ
ФИНЛЯНДИЯ
Мурманск
Архангельск
Петрозаводск
Нарьян-Мар
Сыктывкар
Салехард
Дудинка
Норильск
Тура
Якутск
Магадан
Анадырь
Палана
Петропавловск-Камчатский
Сургут
Нижневартовск
Ханты-Мансийск
Новосибирск
Омск
Красноярск
Кемерово
Благовещенск
Биробиджан
Хабаровск
Комсомольск-на-Амуре
Южно-Сахалинск
Владивосток
Таллинн
Псков
Новгород
Тверь
Смоленск
Минск
Киров
Пермь
Нижний Тагил
Тюмень
Саратов
Волгоград
Ростов-на-Дону
Элиста
Астрахань
Краснодар
Ставрополь
Сочи
Махачкала

MAP 10

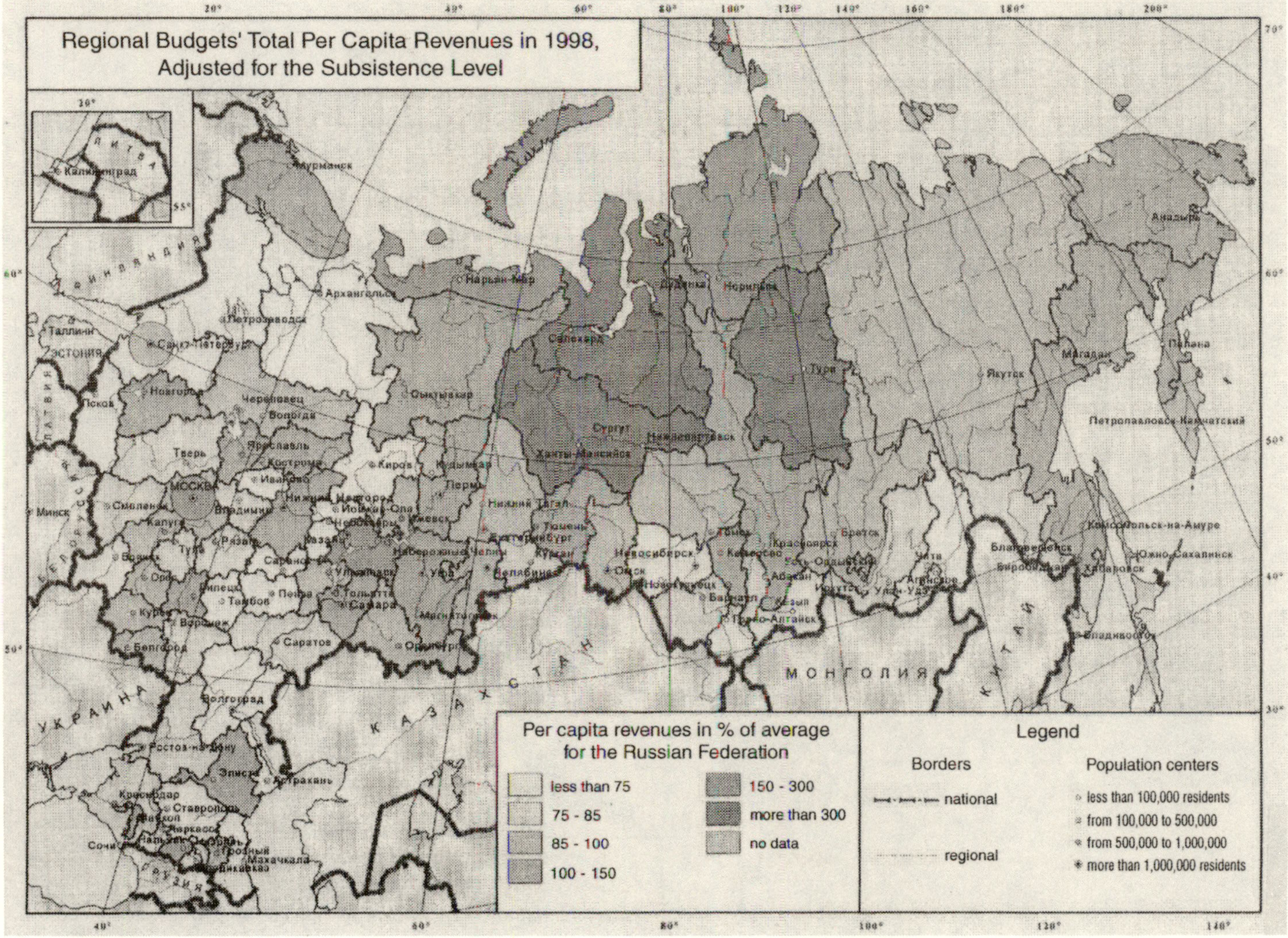
Regional Budgets' Total Per Capita Revenues in 1998,
Adjusted for the Subsistence Level
Per capita revenues in % of average
for the Russian Federation
less than 75
75 - 85
85 - 100
100 - 150
150 - 300
more than 300
no data
Legend
Borders
national
regional
Population centers
less than 100,000 residents
from 100,000 to 500,000
from 500,000 to 1,000,000
more than 1,000,000 residents
МОНГОЛИЯ
КАЗАХСТАН
УКРАИНА

MAP 11

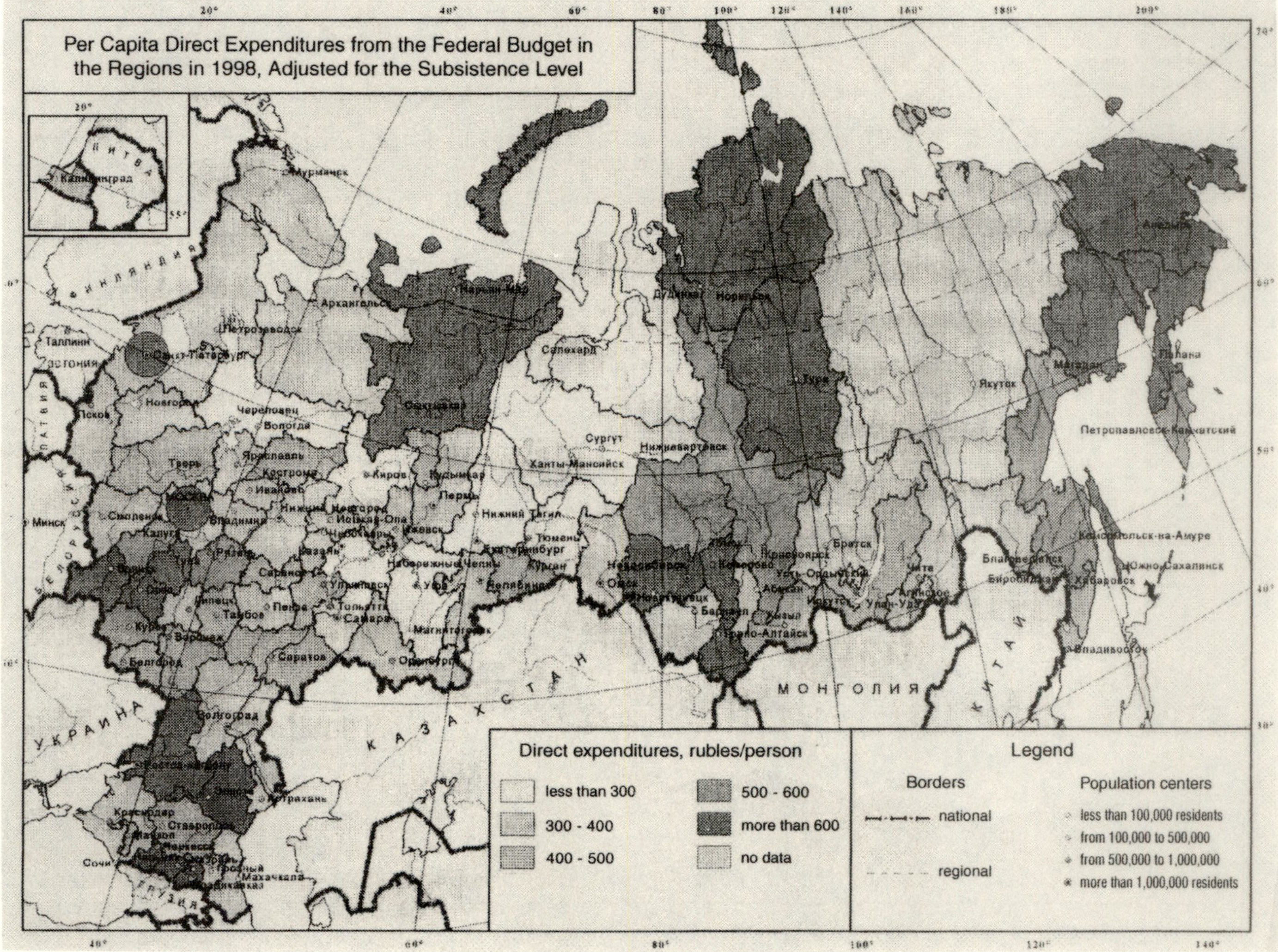
Per Capita Direct Expenditures from the Federal Budget in the Regions in 1998, Adjusted for the Subsistence Level
Direct expenditures, rubles/person
less than 300
300 - 400
400 - 500
500 - 600
more than 600
no data
Legend
Borders
national
regional
Population centers
less than 100,000 residents
from 100,000 to 500,000
from 500,000 to 1,000,000
more than 1,000,000 residents
ФИНЛЯНДИЯ
ЭСТОНИЯ
ЛАТВИЯ
ЛИТВА
БЕЛОРУССИЯ
УКРАИНА
ГРУЗИЯ
КАЗАХСТАН
МОНГОЛИЯ
КИТАЙ
Мурманск
Архангельск
Петрозаводск
Таллинн
Псков
Новгород
Череповец
Вологда
Ярославль
Кострома
Иваново
Тверь
Смоленск
Минск
Калуга
Владимир
Рязань
Липецк
Тамбов
Пенза
Воронеж
Белгород
Саратов
Волгоград
Астрахань
Краснодар
Ставрополь
Сочи
Махачкала
Грозный
Киров
Пермь
Казань
Ижевск
Ульяновск
Тольятти
Самара
Уфа
Набережные Челны
Нижний Тагил
Тюмень
Екатеринбург
Курган
Челябинск
Магнитогорск
Оренбург
Салехард
Сургут
Ханты-Мансийск
Нижневартовск
Дудинка
Норильск
Тура
Омск
Новосибирск
Барнаул
Кемерово
Красноярск
Абакан
Кызыл
Братск
Иркутск
Улан-Удэ
Чита
Якутск
Магадан
Палана
Петропавловск-Камчатский
Анадырь
Благовещенск
Биробиджан
Хабаровск
Комсомольск-на-Амуре
Южно-Сахалинск
Владивосток

MAP 12

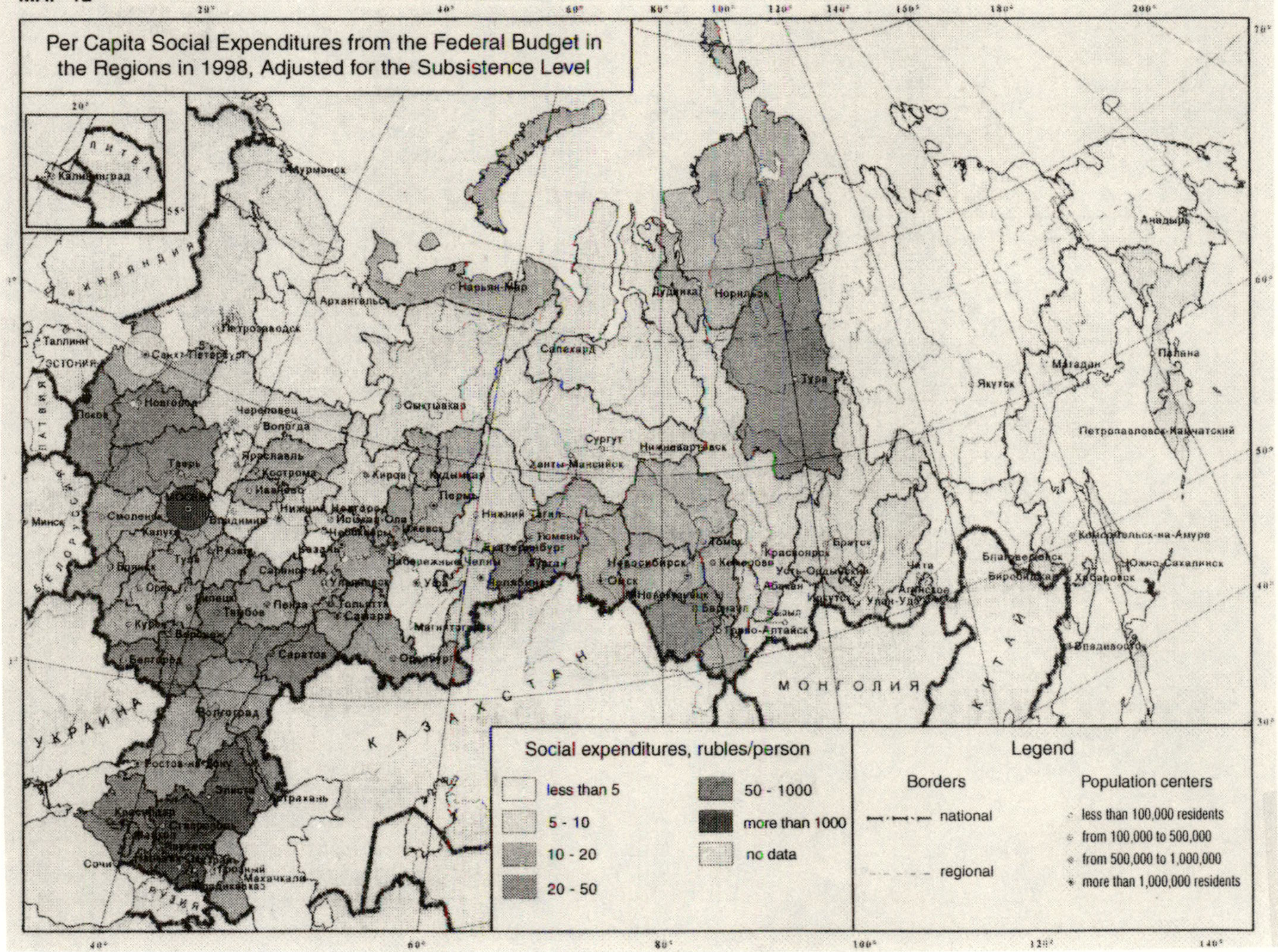

Per Capita Social Expenditures from the Federal Budget in the Regions in 1998, Adjusted for the Subsistence Level

MAP 13

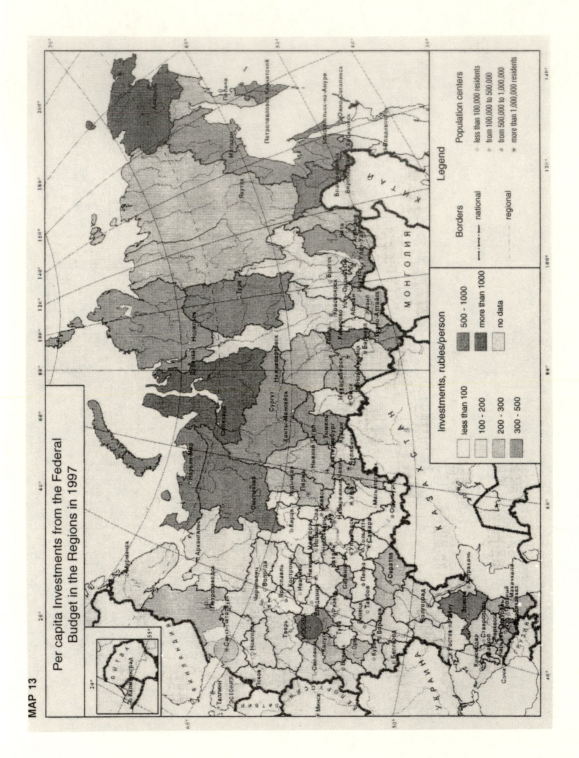

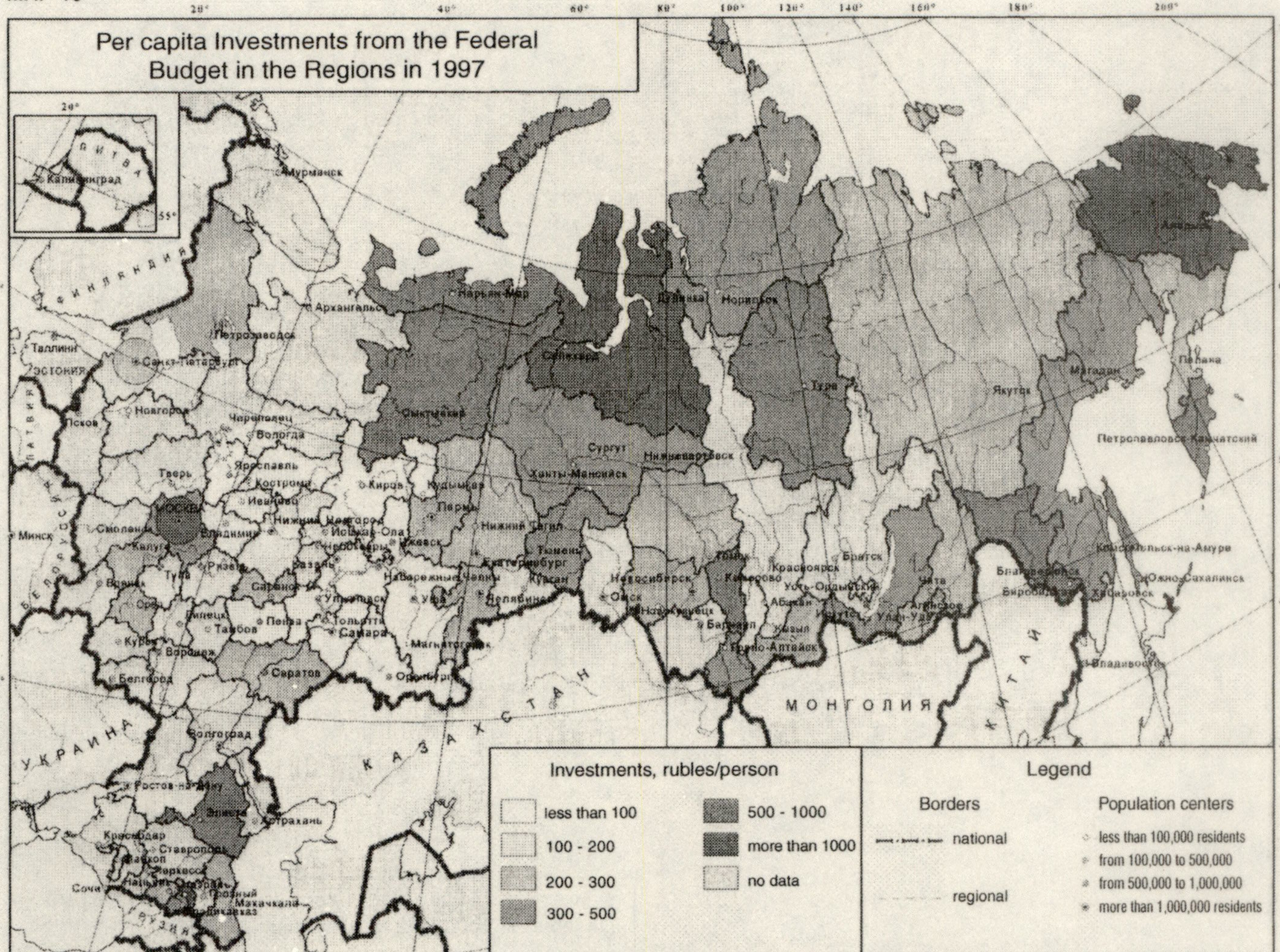
Per capita Investments from the Federal
Budget in the Regions in 1997
Investments, rubles/person
less than 100
100 - 200
200 - 300
300 - 500
500 - 1000
more than 1000
no data
Legend
Borders
national
regional
Population centers
less than 100,000 residents
from 100,000 to 500,000
from 500,000 to 1,000,000
more than 1,000,000 residents
ФИНЛЯНДИЯ
ЭСТОНИЯ
ЛАТВИЯ
БЕЛОРУССИЯ
УКРАИНА
КАЗАХСТАН
МОНГОЛИЯ
КИТАЙ
ГРУЗИЯ
ЛИТВА
Калининград
Мурманск
Архангельск
Петрозаводск
Санкт-Петербург
Таллинн
Псков
Новгород
Череповец
Вологда
Ярославль
Тверь
Кострома
Иваново
Москва
Смоленск
Минск
Калуга
Владимир
Тула
Рязань
Брянск
Орёл
Липецк
Тамбов
Курск
Воронеж
Белгород
Пенза
Саратов
Волгоград
Ростов-на-Дону
Элиста
Астрахань
Краснодар
Ставрополь
Черкесск
Грозный
Махачкала
Сочи
Киров
Пермь
Кудымкар
Ижевск
Чебоксары
Йошкар-Ола
Саранск
Ульяновск
Тольятти
Самара
Уфа
Набережные Челны
Магнитогорск
Оренбург
Челябинск
Курган
Екатеринбург
Нижний Тагил
Тюмень
Сыктывкар
Нарьян-Мар
Салехард
Ханты-Мансийск
Сургут
Нижневартовск
Дудинка
Норильск
Тура
Омск
Новосибирск
Новокузнецк
Барнаул
Кемерово
Томск
Красноярск
Абакан
Кызыл
Иркутск
Братск
Улан-Удэ
Чита
Якутск
Магадан
Анадырь
Палана
Петропавловск-Камчатский
Благовещенск
Биробиджан
Хабаровск
Комсомольск-на-Амуре
Южно-Сахалинск
Владивосток

MAP 14

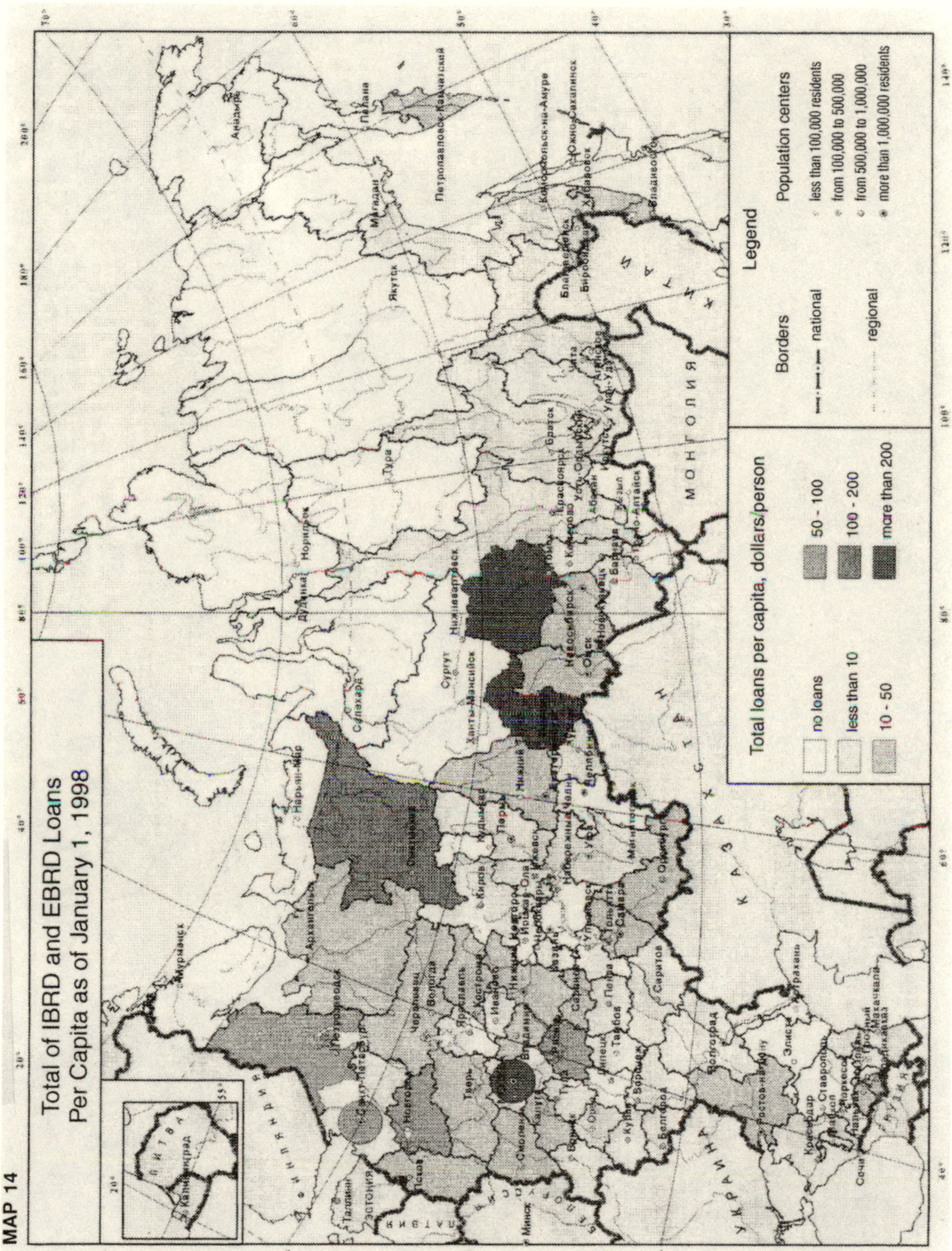
Total of IBRD and EBRD Loans
Per Capita as of January 1, 1998
Total loans per capita, dollars/person
no loans
less than 10
10 - 50
50 - 100
100 - 200
more than 200
Legend
Borders
national
regional
Population centers
less than 100,000 residents
from 100,000 to 500,000
from 500,000 to 1,000,000
more than 1,000,000 residents

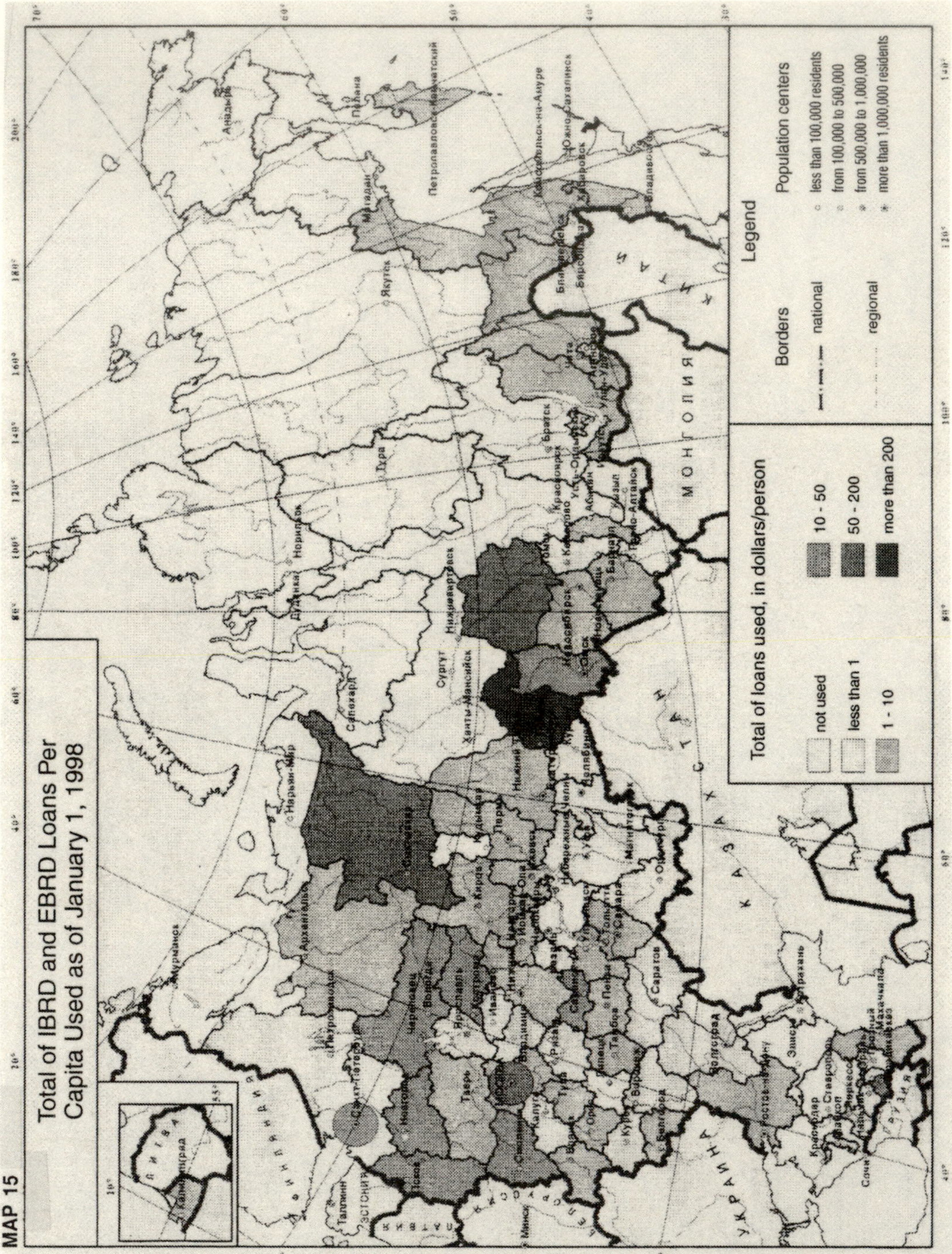
Total of IBRD and EBRD Loans Per Capita Used as of January 1, 1998
Total of loans used, in dollars/person
not used
less than 1
1 - 10
10 - 50
50 - 200
more than 200
Legend
Borders
national
regional
Population centers
less than 100,000 residents
from 100,000 to 500,000
from 500,000 to 1,000,000
more than 1,000,000 residents

MAP 15

MAP 16

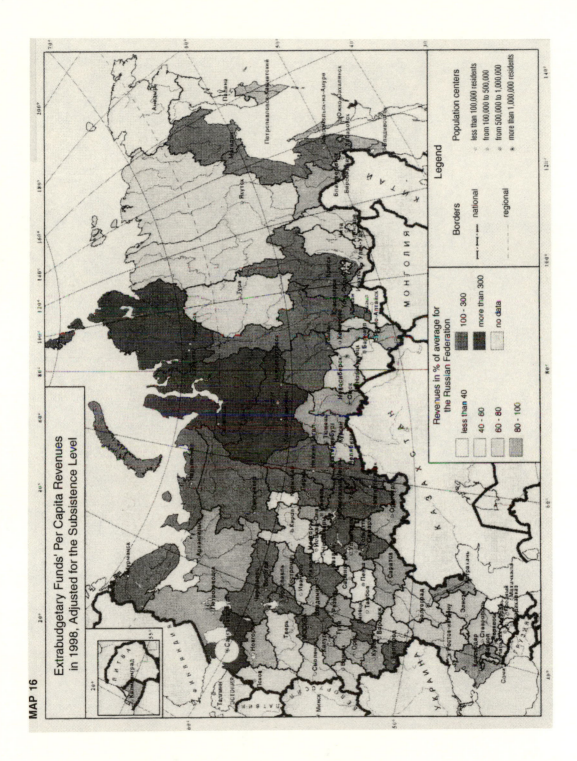

Extrabudgetary Funds' Per Capita Revenues in 1998, Adjusted for the Subsistence Level

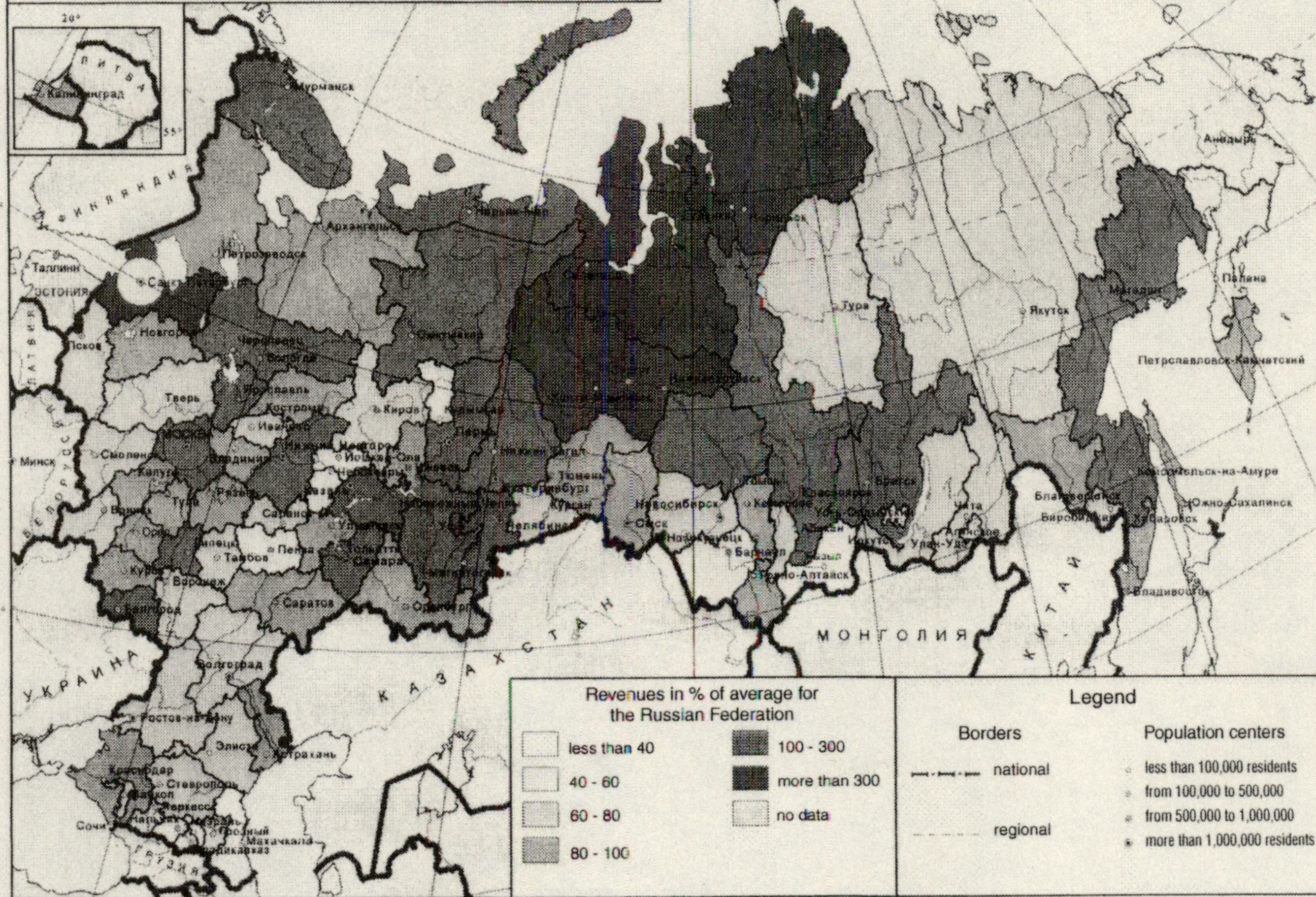

MAP 17

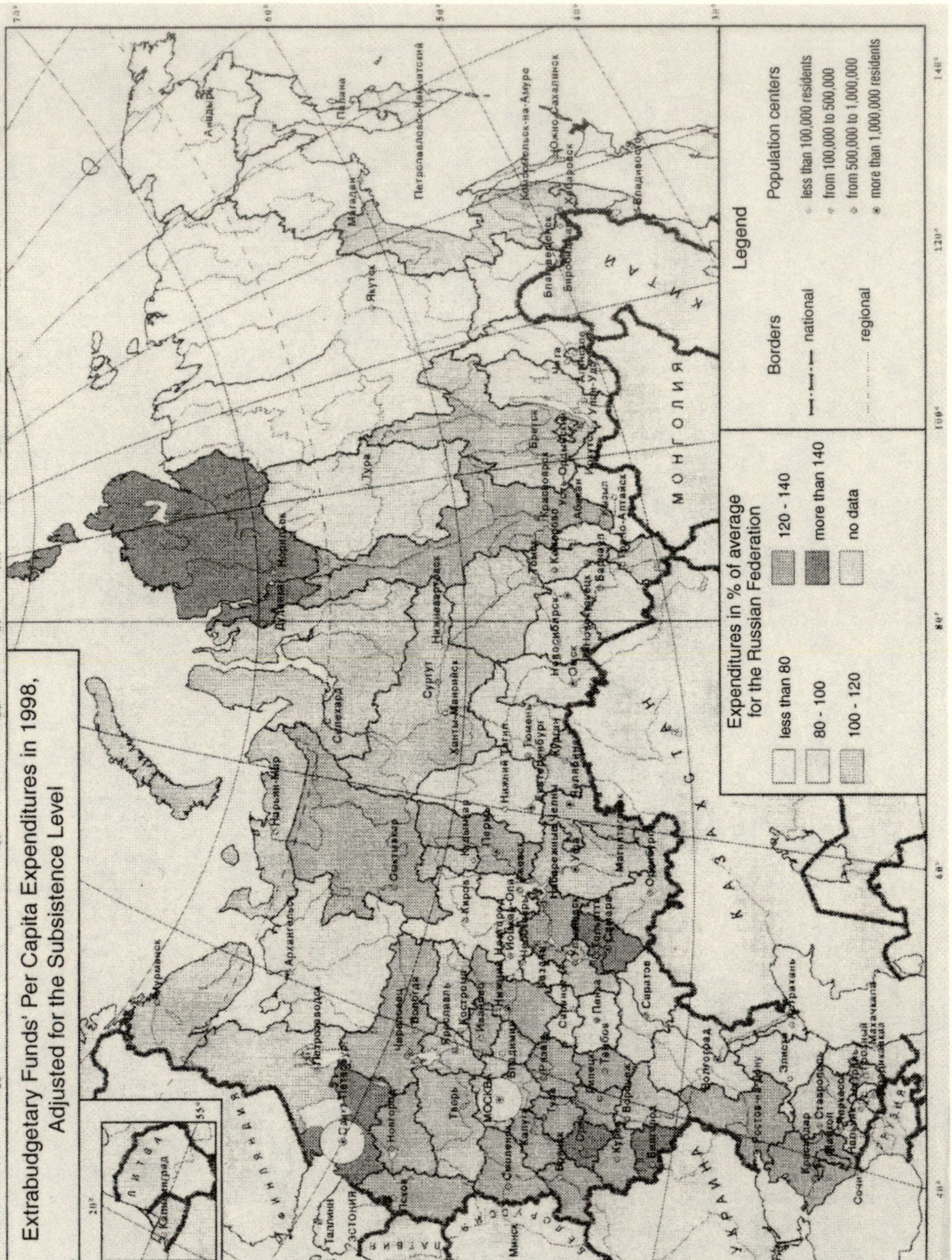

Extrabudgetary Funds' Per Capita Expenditures in 1998, Adjusted for the Subsistence Level

MAP 18

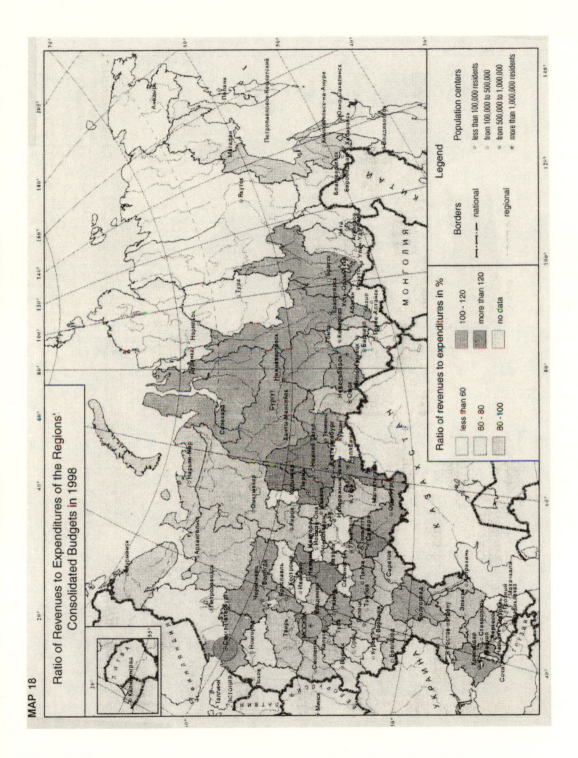

Ratio of Revenues to Expenditures of the Regions' Consolidated Budgets in 1998

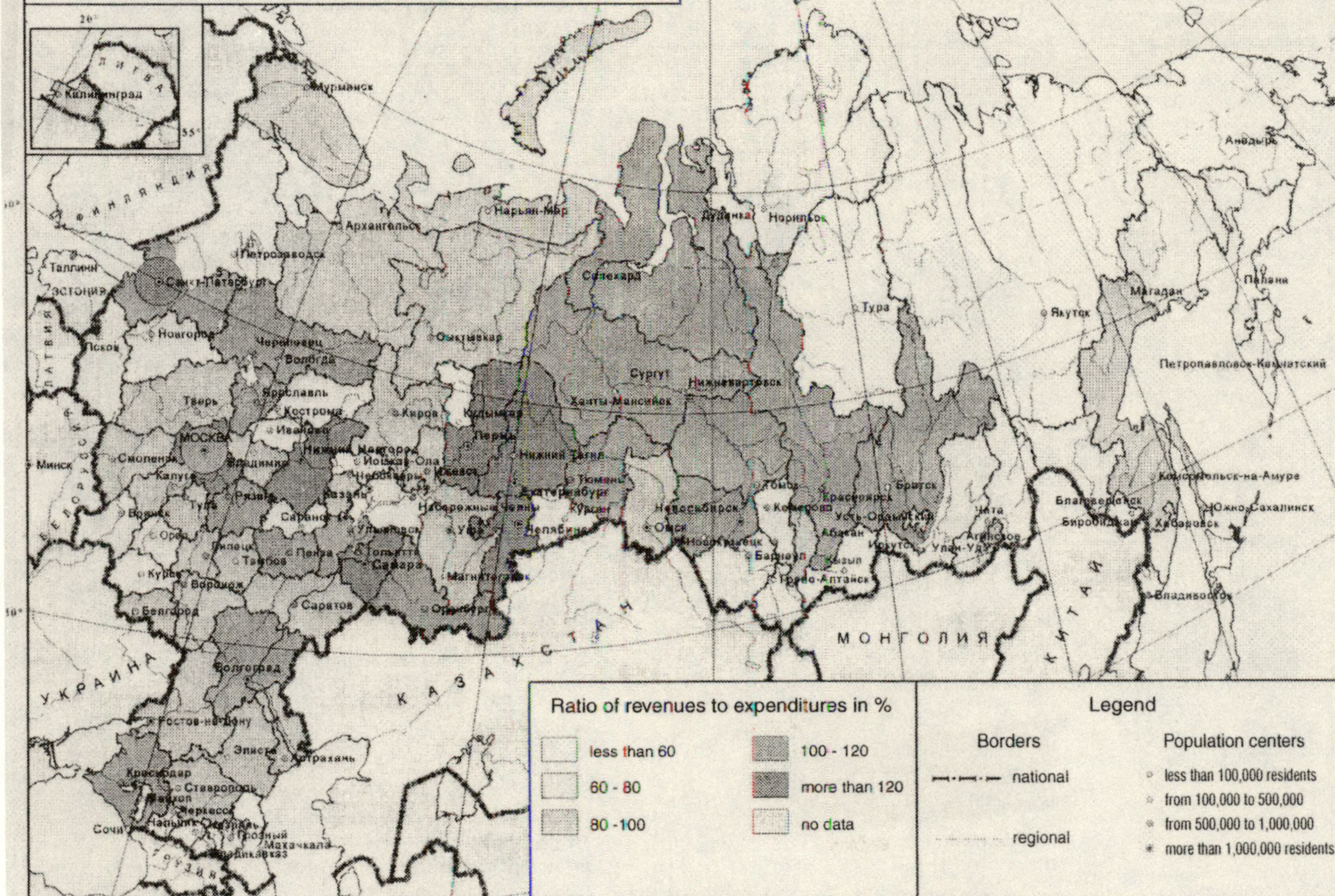

MAP 19

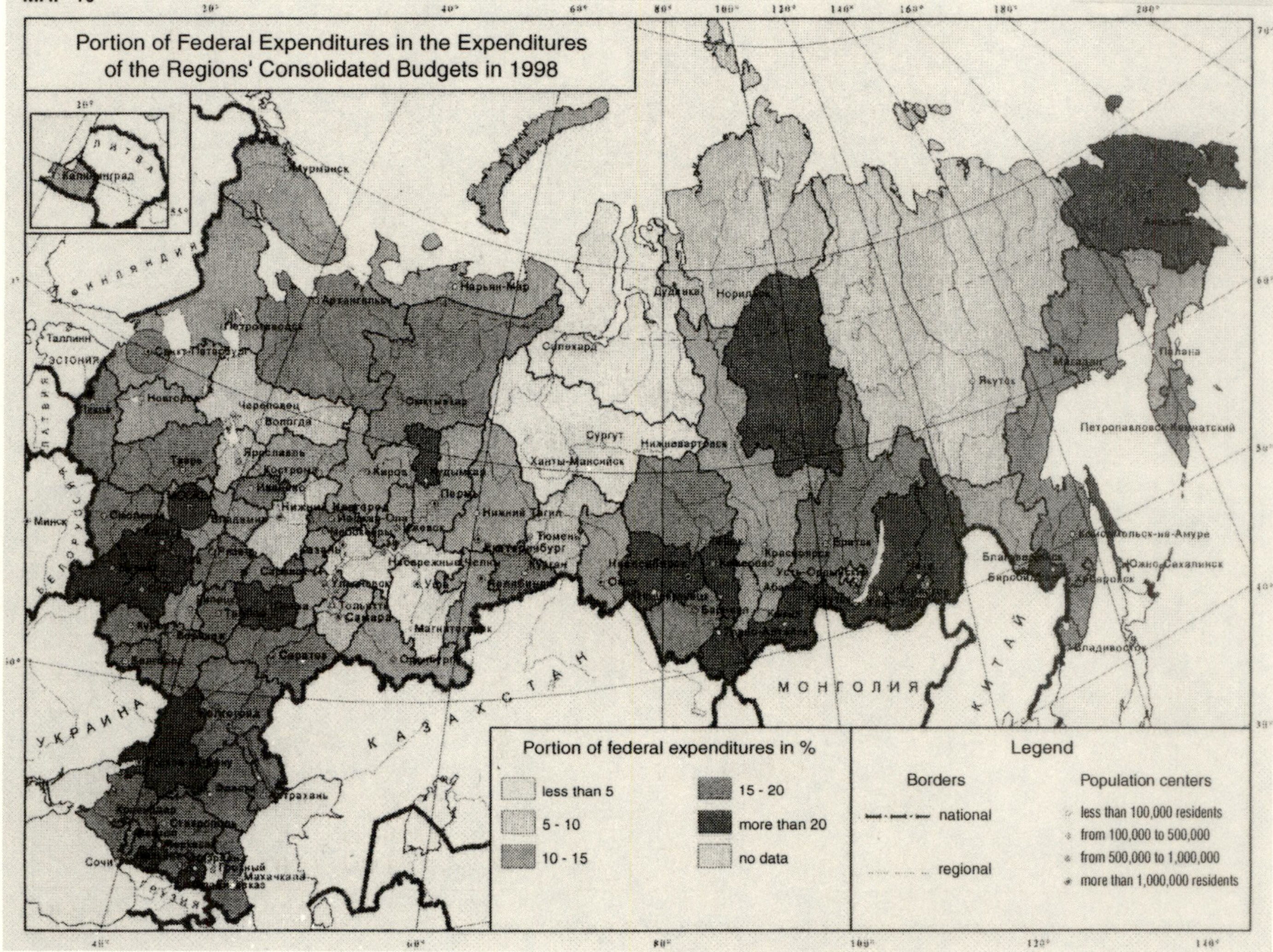
Portion of Federal Expenditures in the Expenditures
of the Regions' Consolidated Budgets in 1998
Portion of federal expenditures in %
less than 5
5 - 10
10 - 15
15 - 20
more than 20
no data
Legend
Borders
national
regional
Population centers
less than 100,000 residents
from 100,000 to 500,000
from 500,000 to 1,000,000
more than 1,000,000 residents
ЛИТВА
ФИНЛЯНДИЯ
ЭСТОНИЯ
ЛАТВИЯ
БЕЛОРУССИЯ
УКРАИНА
КАЗАХСТАН
МОНГОЛИЯ
КИТАЙ
ГРУЗИЯ
Мурманск
Таллинн
Минск
Нарьян-Мар
Салехард
Сургут
Ханты-Мансийск
Нижневартовск
Норильск
Якутск
Магадан
Палана
Петропавловск-Камчатский
Комсомольск-на-Амуре
Южно-Сахалинск
Владивосток
Братск
Тюмень
Нижний Тагил
Пермь
Самара
Саратов
Астрахань
Сочи
Махачкала
Ставрополь

MAP 20

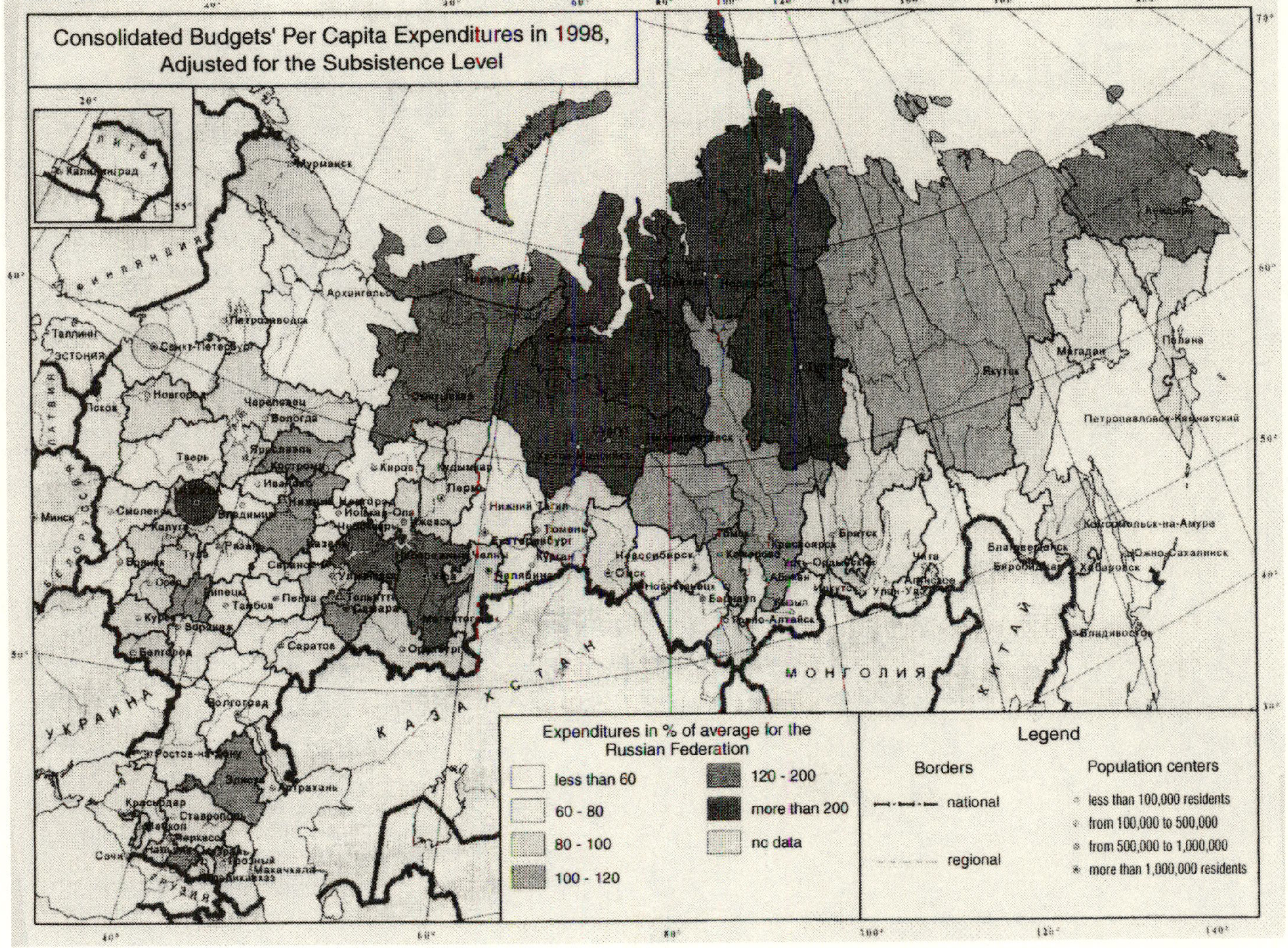
Consolidated Budgets' Per Capita Expenditures in 1998,
Adjusted for the Subsistence Level
Expenditures in % of average for the Russian Federation
less than 60
60 - 80
80 - 100
100 - 120
120 - 200
more than 200
nc data
Legend
Borders
national
regional
Population centers
less than 100,000 residents
from 100,000 to 500,000
from 500,000 to 1,000,000
more than 1,000,000 residents
Мурманск
Архангельск
Петрозаводск
Санкт-Петербург
Таллинн
ЭСТОНИЯ
ЛАТВИЯ
ЛИТВА
ФИНЛЯНДИЯ
Псков
Новгород
Череповец
Вологда
Тверь
Ярославль
Кострома
Иваново
Смоленск
Калуга
Владимир
Минск
БЕЛОРУССИЯ
Брянск
Тула
Рязань
Орел
Липецк
Тамбов
Пенза
Саранск
Курск
Воронеж
Белгород
Саратов
Волгоград
УКРАИНА
Ростов-на-Дону
Элиста
Астрахань
Краснодар
Ставрополь
Черкесск
Сочи
Грозный
Махачкала
Владикавказ
ГРУЗИЯ
Киров
Пермь
Ижевск
Нижний Тагил
Тюмень
Курган
Челябинск
Самара
Тольятти
Ульяновск
Оренбург
Новосибирск
Омск
Барнаул
Кемерово
Красноярск
Абакан
Кызыл
Горно-Алтайск
Братск
Иркутск
Улан-Удэ
Чита
Якутск
Магадан
Палана
Петропавловск-Камчатский
Благовещенск
Биробиджан
Хабаровск
Комсомольск-на-Амуре
Южно-Сахалинск
Владивосток
КАЗАХСТАН
МОНГОЛИЯ
КИТАЙ

MAP 21

Portion of Social Expenditures in the Expenditures of the Regions' Consolidated Budgets in 1998

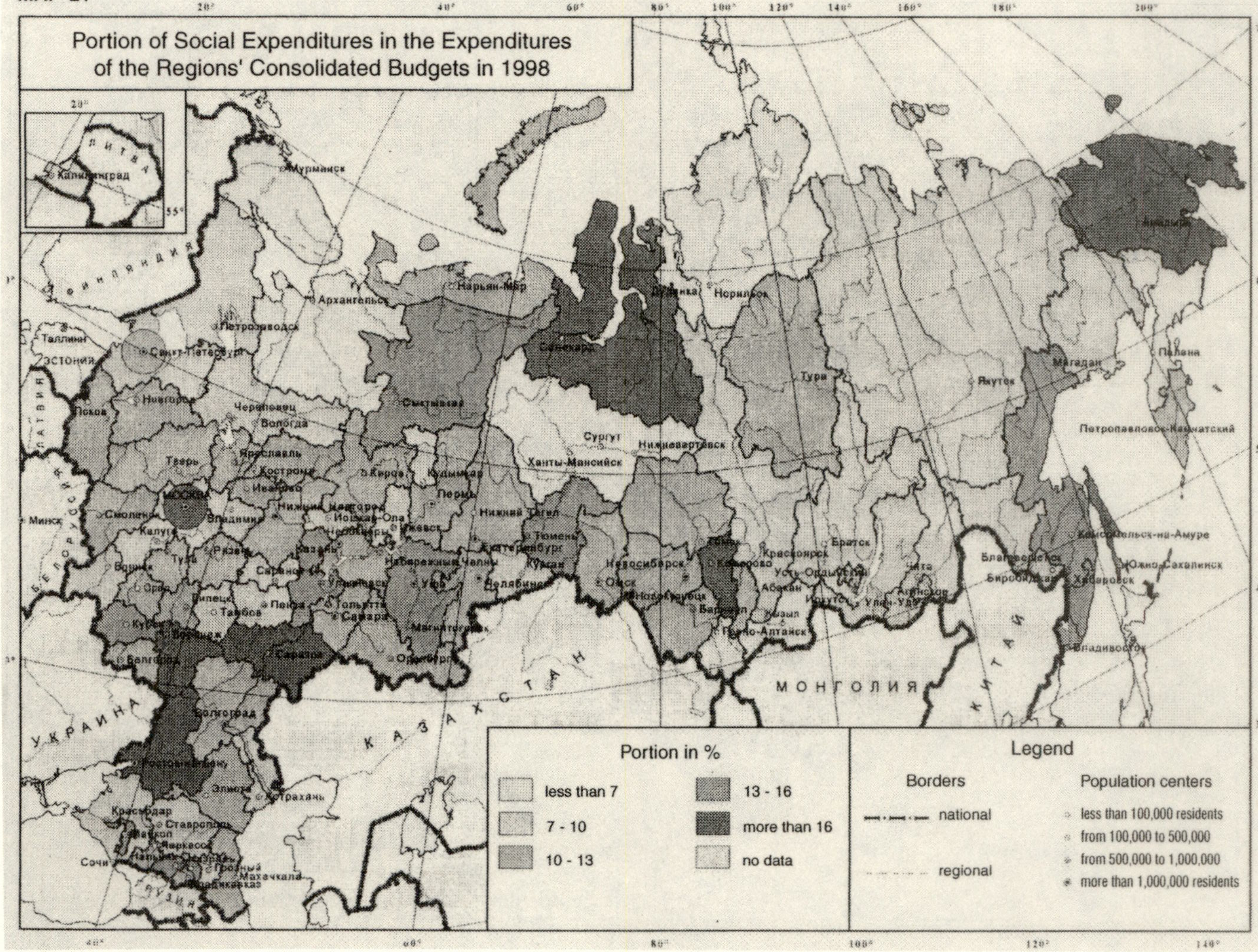

MAP 22

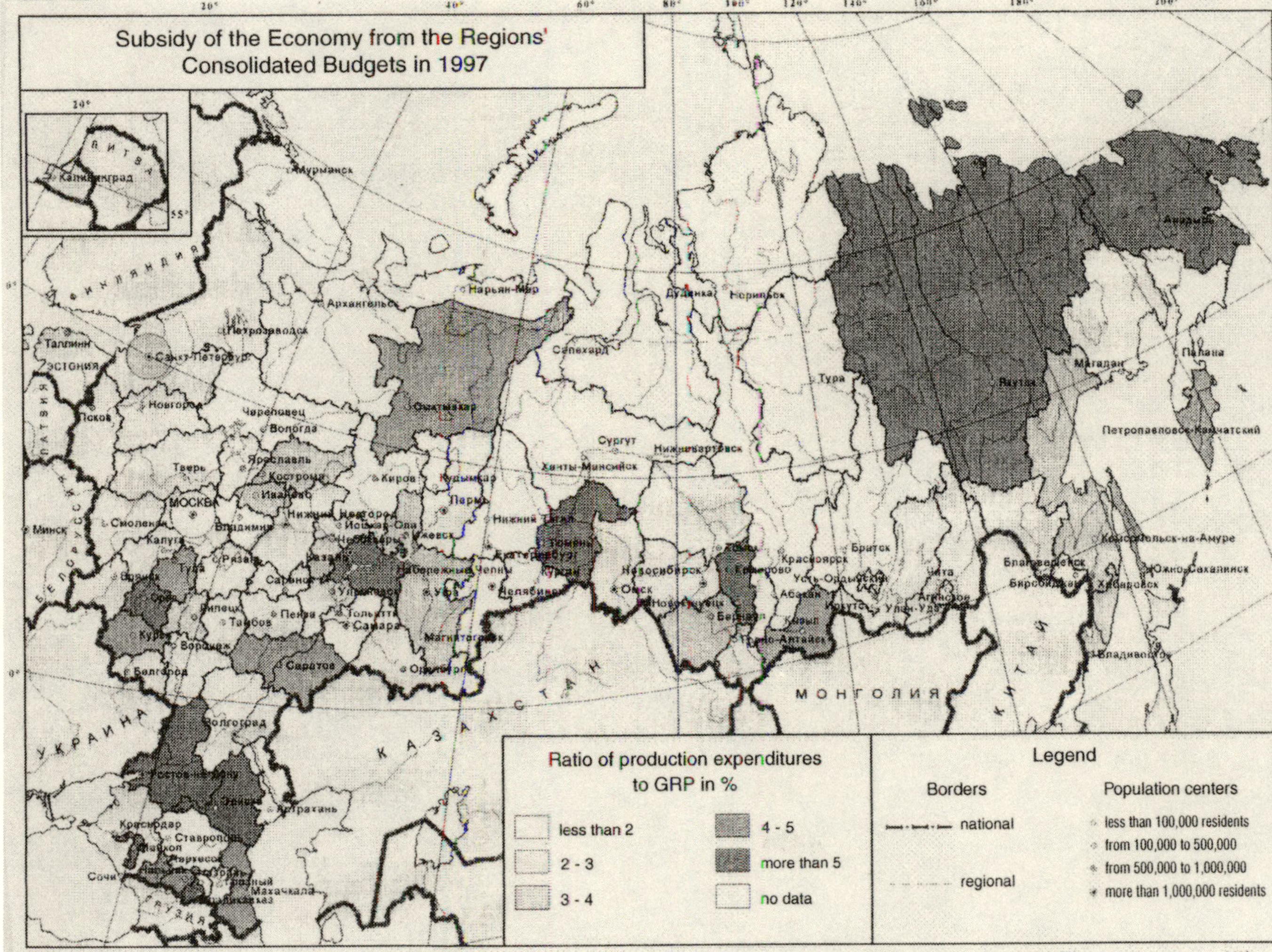
Subsidy of the Economy from the Regions'
Consolidated Budgets in 1997
Ratio of production expenditures
to GRP in %
less than 2
2 - 3
3 - 4
4 - 5
more than 5
no data
Legend
Borders
national
regional
Population centers
less than 100,000 residents
from 100,000 to 500,000
from 500,000 to 1,000,000
more than 1,000,000 residents
МОНГОЛИЯ
КАЗАХСТАН
КИТАЙ
УКРАИНА
ФИНЛЯНДИЯ
ЛАТВИЯ
ЭСТОНИЯ
ЛИТВА
ГРУЗИЯ
Мурманск
Архангельск
Нарьян-Мар
Петрозаводск
Таллинн
Новгород
Псков
Череповец
Вологда
Тверь
Ярославль
Кострома
Иваново
МОСКВА
Смоленск
Минск
Калуга
Владимир
Рязань
Тула
Орёл
Курск
Белгород
Воронеж
Липецк
Тамбов
Пенза
Саранск
Тольятти
Самара
Саратов
Волгоград
Астрахань
Краснодар
Ставрополь
Майкоп
Сочи
Махачкала
Киров
Пермь
Ижевск
Кудымкар
Нижний Тагил
Магнитогорск
Оренбург
Челябинск
Набережные Челны
Сургут
Салехард
Ханты-Мансийск
Нижневартовск
Дудинка
Норильск
Тура
Новосибирск
Омск
Красноярск
Братск
Абакан
Иркутск
Чита
Якутск
Магадан
Палана
Петропавловск-Камчатский
Комсомольск-на-Амуре
Южно-Сахалинск
Хабаровск
Благовещенск
Биробиджан
Владивосток

INDEX